# Observing Projects Using Starry Night Enthusiast™

Marcel W. Bergman

T. Alan Clark

William J.F. Wilson

W. H. Freeman and Company
New York
A Macmillan Higher Education Company

© 2014 by W. H. Freeman and Company
ISBN 10: 1-4641-2502-3
ISBN 13: 1-4641-2502-7

Printed in the United States of America

W. H. Freeman and Company
41 Madison Avenue
New York, NY 10010
Houndmills, Basingstoke RG21 6XS England

www.whfreeman.com

# CONTENTS

# PREFACE

This series of observing projects in astronomy uses the excellent planetarium program *Starry Night*™ to simulate situations in the Universe that are often difficult to observe directly in the sky or inconvenient to follow because of the protracted time-frame of events. The basics of astronomy can be outlined in textbooks and illustrated with diagrams and photographs, but astronomy is an observational science and the opportunity to make meaningful observations of the real sky is very important. Unfortunately, many students of introductory astronomy are denied the opportunity to study the sky because of light pollution or the lack of adequate equipment or resources. The projects described in this book provide an effective substitute for this observing experience by allowing these students to make significant and accurate observations of the virtual sky using the *Starry Night*™ program. It is hoped that these projects will also enhance the experience of students blessed with the resources to make real ground-based observations.

The "virtual" telescope provided by this package allows students to make observations that accurately convey current astronomical knowledge. Even with access to a dark sky, there are often situations where it may be very difficult or inconvenient for students to make meaningful observations in the real world and here, the use of simulation can be helpful. For example, observations that require months of real time can be made with a condensed time animation with this program. Observational hindrances such as daylight and the horizon can be removed to make measurements more easily understandable. Events and phenomena that can be difficult to understand when seen from the surface of a rotating and orbiting Earth can often be "viewed" from a simpler and more elegant frame of reference. This change of perspective can often make obvious an otherwise subtle or difficult concept.

The projects in this book allow students to examine the appearance and behavior of various astronomical objects interactively. Physical laws and astronomical concepts become more interesting when students can demonstrate them with their own "observations". As examples, the observation of Halley's comet as it follows its 76-year orbit demonstrates Kepler's Second Law, whereas the measurement of the motions of the moons around Jupiter explores the applicability of Kepler's Third Law to other orbital motions than simply the planets around the Sun. On a larger scale, examination of the Milky Way from various locations shows the place of the solar system in our home galaxy, while measurement of stellar parallax makes cosmic distances at once less daunting and more wondrous. The beauty of the cosmos unfolds throughout this sequence of projects, as students make observations of the planets and their satellites, the nearby stars, deep-sky objects and finally the three-dimensional soap-bubble structure of the Universe in the realm of galaxies, galaxy clusters and superclusters.

These observing projects present basic ideas at several levels. Most begin by providing an initial framework that introduces a basic concept to students in a simple way, using different viewing locations to illustrate this idea in the most effective manner. The simulations are then extended to include measurements and simple analysis in order to demonstrate specific physical principles. Many of the projects use measurements that cannot be carried out in real life. Some examine the Universe from locations that are inaccessible to us but which provide insight into the underlying science, whereas others compress time to allow observations that extend over very long time-scales. Interspersed questions help students to focus their observations upon particular concepts or theories. Several chapters in the book contain mathematical derivations, but these derivations always culminate in simple formulae to which the observations and measurements can be applied. Thus, the point of the observations can be demonstrated without necessarily requiring a full understanding of the mathematical derivations. Several exercises require graphing of the measurements in order to demonstrate a particular concept and include the elementary consideration of possible errors in the measurements. This approach—the application of mathematical formulae, graphing and error analysis to measured results—is designed to introduce students to the methodology of science. Data tables and graphs that are used to record and display measured results are conveniently placed on tear-out pages at the ends of each project. This allows the removal of completed tables and graphs for assessment by instructors if necessary, without destroying the integrity of the book.

Configuring *Starry Night*™ to illustrate the various concepts of astronomy can often be complex and time consuming, and can lead to annoying set-up problems. To avoid these difficulties, configuration files for these initial conditions have been prepared for all projects. These files have been included with *Starry Night*™ and are readily accessed from within the program. These files provide immediate access to the correct view on the screen, thereby allowing students to focus more clearly upon the astronomical concepts without the frustration of having to struggle with software interface techniques.

The first project is a comprehensive Tutorial outlining the main features of the program. This initial project allows students to become proficient in operating the whole system and introduces them to alternative techniques and shortcuts for accomplishing various tasks, including setting up their own scenarios to demonstrate other concepts. In addition, the User's Guide available with this software provides another avenue for exploring the operating steps and procedures of the program. Students should complete the whole Tutorial project as a prelude to carrying out the projects, referring to the User's Guide where necessary as they experiment with the many features of this program. An appendix to this tutorial provides a tear-out list of common instructions as a quick and convenient reference guide.

Several new projects have been incorporated into this edition to cover more general topics, such as a grand tour of the planets of our solar system and an outline of some of the relevant properties of light, while another project has introduced a more topical subject—the discovery of extrasolar planets orbiting other stars by outlining the planetary transit method used in recent years in the successful search for these fascinating objects.

Some of the projects in this book are relatively simple in concept and execution while others will appeal to more advanced students. In many projects, more advanced simulations have been added as Challenges or Bonus sections to provide extensions to the main project. Nevertheless, in all exercises, we have taken care to test and retest the set-up files and the instruction sequences so that they are very complete. They should permit all students to carry out the tasks efficiently and reproducibly.

It is a pleasure to thank the staff of W. H. Freeman and Company for the opportunity to develop this book and for their careful and professional approach to it. We thank particularly Amy Thorne for her guidance, constant encouragement and professionalism throughout this project and Jodi Isman and the editorial staff, particularly Anthony Calcara and Janet Bidwell, for shepherding the manuscript through the editing and production stages with skill and a constant concern for quality. We would also like to express gratitude to the reviewers of a previous version of this book for their careful assessments, especially James Dickinson, who provided comprehensive and relevant suggestions, many of which have been incorporated into the present edition. We also thank Pedro Braganca and the team of software designers of *Starry Night*™ at Simulation Curriculum Corp. for their help in streamlining the inclusion of the pre-configured set-up files in this project. The authors acknowledge the encouragement and support of the Department of Physics and Astronomy at the University of Calgary. Finally, the authors express their deep gratitude and thanks to their wives, Marcia, Jean and Dawn, respectively, for their patience and support during the development of this book.

# Tutorial

This tutorial will introduce you to *Starry Night*™ and demonstrate how to use this software to make valid and interesting astronomical observations. The observing projects in this book rely on files that are included with the W.H. Freeman and Company version of *Starry Night College*™ software. *Starry Night College*™ version 6.4.3 (or later) should be properly installed on your computer and you should know how to start the program.

As you work through this tutorial to gain familiarity with *Starry Night*™, you will also obtain advice on how to configure the program in order to use it most efficiently.

## A. Observing Projects and *Starry Night*™

The observing projects use *Starry Night*™ to simulate astronomical observations. Each project contains sequences of instruction steps that describe how to use the software to demonstrate a particular astronomical event, geometry or concept. Instruction steps look like this:

> 1. Launch *Starry Night*™.

Go ahead and follow this instruction to launch *Starry Night*™.

Menu commands, buttons that you must click in the *Starry Night*™ interface, and data that you need to enter or that is displayed in the *Starry Night*™ interface are shown in **this typeface**.

If this is the first time that *Starry Night*™ has run on your computer, you will need to register the software. Once you have registered and updated the software, you can set your Home location in the dialog box that appears.

> 2. In the Home Location dialog box, click the **List** tab. Use the scrollbar to the right of the list to search for the name of your city or town. [TIP: Type the name of your home location to jump to it in the list or, in North America, enter your Zip or Postal Code. If your location is not listed, you can enter your latitude and longitude by clicking the **Latitude/Longitude** tab and entering appropriate values for your location.]
>
> 3. With the name of your home city or town highlighted, click the **Save as Home Location** button. [TIP: If you ever need to change your home location, select **Set Home Location...** from the **File** (Windows) or **Starry Night** (Mac) menu.]

*Starry Night*™ opens with a view of a southern horizon and a depiction of the sky, as it would appear from your home location at the current time and date.

The screen has four main sections:

1) the main view window, which occupies the majority of the screen,

2) the main menu,

3) the toolbar between the menu and the main view window (in Windows, you can also show an optional buttonbar above the toolbar by selecting **View > Show Buttonbar**), and

4) side pane tabs, arranged vertically along the left border of the main view window.

4.  Click the **SkyGuide** tab to open the Skyguide side pane and then click the **Go to the Home page** icon to see a welcome screen that includes links to information about the features and basic use of *Starry Night*™. You are encouraged to use these resources, particularly the **Starry Night Features** and **Starry Night Basics** links and the **Tutorial** in the **Student Exercises** link, in addition to this Tutorial, to acquaint yourself with the *Starry Night*™ interface.

## B. Setting up a View

In this section you will begin to use the features of *Starry Night*™ to set up and save a particular view of the sky from your home location. This view will be the eastern sky at sunrise on September 23, 2015 AD.

5.  Click the **Home** button in the toolbar.

6.  *Set the Date* in the toolbar to **September 23, 2015 AD.** To do this, click the **month** display to highlight it and then type **9** (for September) or use the **up/down** cursor keys or the **+/–** keys on the keyboard to change the month. Similarly, click the **date** field and change the value to **23.** Then change the **year** to **2015.** [NOTE: In this tutorial, some phrases, such as the one that begins this instruction step, are italicized when first introduced. These phrases refer to procedures that you will use commonly as you work through the observing projects in this book. These procedures are also listed and described in the appendix at the end of this tutorial for easy reference. The perforated pages in this book allow you to tear out this appendix for ease of reference as you work through the observing projects.]

7.  *Set the Gaze* to the East by using the **E** keyboard shortcut or clicking the **E** button in the toolbar. [TIP: The default behaviour of *Starry Night*™ is to pan to found objects. You can bypass this feature. Select **Preferences...** from the **File** (Windows) or **Starry Night** (Mac) menu. Choose **Responsiveness** in the dropdown box near the top of the Preferences dialog window and uncheck the options for **Pan to found objects** and **Animate location changes.**]

8.  Look at the Time Flow Rate section of the toolbar. It contains a set of controls resembling those on a disc or music player and a panel showing the current setting for the Time Flow Rate, which displays **1x**, the equivalent of real time.

9.  Click the **Stop** button to stop the advance of time.

10. Click the **Sunrise** button on the left-hand side of the toolbar and then move the cursor into the main view window.

The default cursor is the adaptive cursor, which changes its behaviour and shape depending upon its position in the view. When over a blank region of sky it takes the shape of the Hand tool. The Hand tool is convenient for making quick adjustments to the gaze direction.

11. Move the Hand tool to a blank region of sky in the lower center part of the screen and click and hold the mouse button. The Hand tool "grabs" the view and allows you to drag it while a display appears in the upper-right corner of the view indicating coordinates of altitude and azimuth and the approximate compass direction corresponding to the center of the current view. Use the Hand tool to drag the view upward so that the horizon appears relatively flat while keeping the direction of the gaze toward the east.

The view shows the eastern horizon and sky just before sunrise on September 23, 2015.

> **Question 1.** When facing east in real life, is south to your right or left side? From the direction labels on the horizon in the view looking east, is south on the right or the left side of the screen?

*Starry Night*™ provides a convenient means of saving and accessing views using the Favourites side pane. Use the following procedure to save the view you have created.

12. Select **Favourites > Add Favourite Folder** from the menu. The Favourites side pane opens to the left of the view. It contains a folder directory and a new highlighted folder. Give this folder a name such as **My Views**.

13. With the new folder highlighted, select **Favourites > Add Favourite** from the menu and save the current view as a favourite named **Sunrise** in the My Views folder. Now you can easily retrieve this view in the future by navigating to it through the Favourites pane or menu.

Most of the observing projects in this book use views that you will find in the Observing Projects folder under the Favourites pane or in the submenu under the Favourites menu.

14. *Open* **Favourites > Observing Projects > Tutorial > Sunrise** to see a sample of the sunrise view as seen from Calgary, Canada on September 23, 2015. To do this, click the **Favourites** tab to open the Favourites side pane which allows you to navigate the folders to the desired view, or use the **Favourites** menu and navigate the submenus. The view that you saved with the name Sunrise should be similar to this view.

15. Open **Favourites > My Views > Sunrise** to return to the view of sunrise from your home location.

## C. Animate the View with the Time Controls

*Starry Night*™ allows you to control the flow of time in order to animate the view.

16. Click the **Play** button to *run time forward* at the rate of real time.

17. Click the number **1** in the Time Flow Rate control in the toolbar to highlight it. Now you can use the cursor **up/down** or **+/−** keys to increase or decrease the Time Flow Rate. You can also type a specific number in the highlighted field.

18. Click somewhere other than the numeral in the Time Flow Rate panel of the toolbar to see a menu of various pre-defined rates.

The Time Flow Rate options are divided into two groups: Time Flow and Discrete Time steps. When you select a Time Flow, this command takes effect immediately and the animation begins as though you had also clicked the Play button. If you select a Discrete Time step, time in the main view stops as though you had also clicked the Stop button.

19. Set the Time Flow Rate to **300x** and watch the Sun rise. [TIP: If you happen to click the wrong rate, select **Edit > Undo Time Step** from the menu and try again.]

20. Soon after the Sun has risen above the horizon, select a Time Flow Rate of **1 hour**. Since you have selected a discrete time step, the animation stops until you click one of the time control buttons.

21. Watch the view and the Time display in the toolbar and click the **Step time forward** button (at the far right of the time controls) to advance time by one hour.

22. Then click the **Step time backward** button (at the far left of the time controls).

23. Move the cursor over the Sun in the view.

When the adaptive cursor is over an object in the view, it changes to an arrow and a list of information appears on the screen. This information list is called the HUD (Head-Up Display). Many of the observing projects use data from the HUD and you may need to configure this HUD to display the data required for a specific project.

24. *Configure the HUD* for this tutorial. To do this, select **Preferences...** from the **File** (Windows) or **Starry Night** (Mac) menu. Click the dropdown box at the top-left of the Preferences dialog window and select **Cursor Tracking (HUD)** from the list of options. Scroll through the Show list and ensure that the options for **Constellation name, Name** and **Object type** are checked. It is also useful to check the option to **Show info in upper left corner of the screen** before closing the Preferences dialog window. [TIP: To hide the HUD temporarily, toggle its display off and on with the **Ctrl-I** (Windows) or **Cmd-I** (Mac) keyboard shortcut.]

Question 2. The Constellation name in the HUD indicates the constellation within which the cursor (and the object to which it points) is positioned. Within which constellation is the Sun on the morning of September 23, 2015?

The factory default setting in *Starry Night*™ includes the display of a halo and lens flares when the Sun is in the view. This feature will interfere with many of your observations in the projects ahead. Take this opportunity to turn off this feature.

25. *Open the contextual menu* for the Sun. To do this, position the cursor over the Sun in the view and right-click (Windows) or Ctrl-click (Mac) and select **Halo Effects > Never** from the contextual menu.
26. A normal left-click (Windows) or click (Mac) on the Sun displays a label for the Sun.

This is also an opportune time to deal with another housekeeping issue. The horizon panoramas that are shown by default, though realistic, interfere with some observations, such as the rising and setting times of objects. For this reason, most of the observing projects in the Favourites folder will use a flat grass horizon.

27. Select **Options > Other Options > Local Horizon...** from the menu. Click the **Default...** button to the right of the Horizon thumbnail in the Photorealistic section of the Local Horizon Options dialog window. A new window pops up showing thumbnails of various horizons. Scroll through these images and click the **Flat Grass** thumbnail and then the **Select** button. The horizon in the main view window changes to the flat grass image.
28. Before dismissing the Local Horizon Options dialog window, click the **Default...** button to the right of the **Clouds** thumbnail and highlight and **Select** the clouds thumbnail labeled **None**. Then close the dialog window.

You can now use the time controls and gaze controls to observe the Sun from sunrise to sunset.

29. **Centre** the Sun in the view. To do this, open the contextual menu for the Sun again and select **Centre**.
30. Set the Time Flow Rate to **300x**.
31. Now the view locks onto and tracks the Sun in the center of the view. [TIP: To break the lock on an object centered in the view, click the Hand tool on the view. To regain the lock onto the object, select **Edit > Undo Scroll**.]
32. Use the **+** and **−** buttons in the Zoom section of the toolbar to **Zoom in** or **Zoom out** on the view as necessary so that the horizon remains visible in the view. Click **Stop** when the Sun is about to set or click the **Sunrise** button to replay the animation.

**Question 3.** Describe the motion of the Sun across the sky from sunrise to sunset. Include in your description the shape of the Sun's path, the directions in which it rises and sets, its direction when it is highest in the sky (furthest from the horizon), and the steadiness of its motion across the sky.

33. With the Sun about to set in the view, click **Play** to resume the advance of time at 300 times its normal rate and observe the sky as darkness falls. Use the Hand tool and Gaze buttons to look all around the view. Click **Stop** and use the HUD to identify any interesting objects in this view. Open the contextual menu for some of these objects and select **Show Info** to obtain more information about them from the Info side pane.

34. Select **File > Revert** from the menu to return to the initial view of the pre-dawn sky on **September 23, 2015**.

**Question 4.** Describe the motion of the stars in the sky.

**Question 5.** Do the stars appear to move together or do they move at different rates and directions across the sky?

**Question 6.** Did you notice any objects in the view that move differently from the Moon and stars? What class of objects are these and what was it about their motion in the sky that caused you to notice them?

Man-made satellites streaking across the view of the night sky can be distracting and you will usually want to remove them from the display. You will have noticed that when you used the **File > Revert** command in the last step, the horizon also returned to the original horizon, rather than to the flat grass horizon you set up previously. It is simple to re-apply the horizon and cloudless sky options to the view you are creating in this tutorial while at the same time removing the man-made satellites from the view. A suitable set-up with these initial conditions has been prepared for this purpose.

35. Select **Options > Presets > Observing Projects Standard** from the menu to remove man-made satellites from the view and to show a flat grass horizon with a cloudless sky.

36. Select **Favourites > Save Favourite** and then click **Replace Favourite** to update your view so that these changes are now saved.

With the view showing the eastern sky above a flat horizon on September 23, 2015, note the two brightest objects in the pre-dawn sky.

37. Use the HUD to identify the two brightest objects in the pre-dawn sky.

**Question 7.** What type of objects are the two brightest objects in this view and what are their names? Which of these two objects is closest to the horizon?

38. *Magnify* the bright object that is furthest from the Sun in this view. To do this, go to the object's contextual menu by placing the cursor over the object, right-click the mouse and select **Magnify**.

The view shows a magnified image of the object. As you can see, this image is slightly washed out because of the twilight condition of the sky this close to sunrise. You could reverse time to obtain a better view of this object, but instead you can hide daylight altogether from the view.

39. *Hide **Daylight*** from the view to see this object more clearly. To do so, select **View > Hide Daylight** from the menu.

40. Open the contextual menu for this object and select **Surface Image/Model > Clouds** to see a more realistic image of this object as it would appear from Earth through a telescope.

**Question 8.** What is the shape of the bright section of this object?

41. *Show **Daylight*** again by selecting **View > Show Daylight** from the menu.

42. Click the object in the view to select and label it.

43. *Set the Zoom* to **10°**. To do this, click the Current zoom width and height panel on the right side of the toolbar and select **10°** from the Current Field of View popup menu.

In some of the observing projects you will need to use the time controls to *find the time of an event*. The next instruction step explains how to find the time, to the nearest minute, at which the object currently selected in the view rises above the horizon from your home location on September 23, 2015.

44. Use the **Shift-H** keyboard shortcut to reverse time in steps of one hour for each key press until the object disappears behind the eastern horizon. Now use the **T** keyboard shortcut to advance time in steps of 1 minute until the object reappears above the horizon.

**Question 9.** At what time does this object rise from your home location on September 23, 2015?

Now, explore the night time sky again, paying particular attention to the Moon.

45. **Select File > Revert** to return to the wide-angle sunrise view and click the **Sunset** button.

46. *Find* the Moon in the view. To do this, click the **Find** tab to open the Find side pane. Near the top of this pane is a search box with an icon of a magnifying glass in its left margin. If the label below this search box does not read Search All Databases, click the icon and select **Search All** from the popup menu. Then, clear any typing from the search box in order to obtain a list of Solar System items in the Find pane. Look through this list for The Moon. If the Moon is not listed, click the **+** icon next to the listing for the Earth. Then double-click the listing for the Moon in the list in the Find pane.

The view is now centered and locked upon the Moon and a label indicates its position. You may notice that the Moon appears quite large in the view, certainly much larger than the Sun did with the halo effects removed. This apparent size is artificial and is a feature of *Starry Night*™ that allows the Moon to be more easily seen in the view when the Zoom is set to a wide field of view.

47. Open the contextual menu for the Moon and click off the **Enlarge Moon Size** option to see the Moon at its actual size in the wide angle view. This enlarged Moon size is automatically cancelled when you zoom in on the Moon.

48. Hide **Daylight** from the view and then set the Time Flow Rate to **300x** and watch the Moon's motion across the sky.

49. Use the **+** zoom control (or the **+** key on the keyboard or the wheel of a wheel mouse) to zoom in on the Moon to a field of view about **2°** wide as indicated in the Zoom panel in the toolbar.

50. Use this close-up view to compare the apparent motion of the Moon with that of the stars, keeping in mind that the view is now centered and locked upon the Moon.

**Question 10.**   Describe the Moon's motion across the sky and compare its motion with that of the stars.

51. Click **Stop** and then the **Sunset** button.

52. Set the Zoom to **90°** and then tap the **K** key on the keyboard to display the patterns of stars in the sky known as the constellations.

53. Click the **Options** tab to open the Options pane. Expand the **Constellations** layer in the Options pane and select **Illustrations**. Look around this view of the sky. With some imagination, the star patterns can be seen to match the shape of the illustrations.

54. Deselect **Illustrations** and select **Boundaries** in the Constellations layer of the Options pane.

The view, which should still be centered upon the Moon with daylight hidden, shows the sky divided into the modern astronomical constellations.

**Question 11.**   In which constellation is the Moon on September 23, 2015?

55. *Set the Time* in the toolbar to **6:00:00 AM** (daylight saving time) on **September 24, 2015**. [TIP 1: To change Time and/or Date, click any component of the Time or Date and then use the **up/down** cursor keys or **+/−** keys on the keyboard to adjust that component to the required value. To move between the different components of the Time and Date use the left/right cursor keys or Tab and Shift-Tab.] [TIP 2: The small icon of a sun in the far left of the Time and Date panel in the toolbar indicates that daylight saving time is in effect. Click the icon to toggle daylight saving time off and on.]

56. Change the Gaze to the **East**.

57. Open the **Find** pane and click the checkboxes to the right of the entries in the Solar System items list for Venus, Jupiter and Mars in order to label these planets in the view.

58. Set the Time Flow Rate to **1 day**. Click the **Step time forward** button repeatedly to make successive daily observations of the sky. Use the Gaze and Zoom controls as required to help you to answer the following question.

**Question 12.**   From your daily observations, indicate whether each of the following is True or False:

    a.   The Moon, planets and the stars change their positions in the sky from one day to the next when observed from the same location at the same time of day.

    b.   The Moon and planets appear to move differently from the stars from day to day.

    c.   The Moon and planets both appear to move eastward from one day to the next with respect to the stars.

    d.   The stars appear to move slightly westward from day to day.

    e.   The constellations shift westward from day to day.

    f.   The stars appear to be fixed in the sense that they do not move relative to one another from one day to the next.

59. To test some of your conclusions, use the **Step time backward** button to bring the Date back to **September 24**, and alter the gaze as necessary so that Mars, Venus and Jupiter are visible in the view.

60. Change the Time Flow Rate to **1 sidereal d.** (one sidereal day). Each time you click the **Step time forward** button to advance time by 1 sidereal day, the stars will return to the same position in the sky. [NOTE: One sidereal day is defined as the time taken for the Earth to rotate once with respect to the distant stars.]

**Question 13.**  Is a sidereal day of longer or shorter duration than a regular 24-hour (mean solar) day? [HINT: Look at the Time display in the toolbar.]

## D. Changing Locations

You have learned about the time controls in *Starry Night*™ and used these controls to animate and observe the apparent motions of objects in the sky. This section will introduce you to the location controls in *Starry Night*™. You will find that observing events in the sky from different locations can give you important insights into the geometry of celestial events and this in turn can help you to understand other observations.

61.  Select **File > Revert** to return to your initial view of the pre-dawn sky on **September 23, 2015**. Change the Time Flow Rate to **300x** and observe sunrise from your home location.

62.  Select **Edit > Undo Time Step** to return to sunrise.

63.  *Change the viewing location.* To do this, select **Options > Viewing Location** to open the Viewing Location dialog window. Click the **Latitude/Longitude** tab in the dialog window and edit the Latitude value to the same value as your home location but in the opposite hemisphere. If your home location is in the northern hemisphere, replace the N following the value in the latitude box with an **S**. Conversely, if your home location is in the southern hemisphere, replace the S in the latitude box with an **N**. Do not change the Longitude value. Then click the **Go To Location** button and the view shifts to the new observing location. [TIP: Tap the spacebar after clicking the Go To Location button to jump immediately to the new view.]

64.  Change the Gaze to the **E**ast horizon.

65.  Select a Time Flow Rate of **300x** and watch sunrise from this location.

**Question 14.**  Describe sunrise as seen from this location. What is the significant difference between sunrise at this location and sunrise in your home location?

**Question 15.**  From your observations of this sunrise from locations of equal latitude but opposite hemispheres of the Earth, speculate upon what you might expect to see if you watched this sunrise from the equator (latitude 0°) and, using instruction steps 63–65 as a guide, configure Starry Night to test your hypothesis.

66.  Select **File > Revert** to return to the sunrise view at your home location.

An interesting tool in *Starry Night*™ known as the Location Scroller can be activated by holding down the Shift key while the adaptive cursor is in effect or by selecting it specifically with the Tool Selection control at the left side of the toolbar. Moving this cursor over the screen with the mouse button held down will change the view as if you are flying over the Earth at a constant altitude. If you are on the surface of Earth, you will move as if you are driving across the landscape.

67.  *Use the Location Scroller* to see its effect on the view. Select **Location Scroller** from the Tool Selection control at the left side of the toolbar. The cursor changes into the Location Scroller, shown as four arrowheads. With the east horizon near the bottom-center of the view, move the cursor to the center of the view window and click and drag the view upward on the screen as you watch the Viewing Location panel. Repeat this action several times and you will see the names of towns to the west of your home location appear in this panel. Repeat the action while dragging the mouse downward to shift your location back towards the east. Moving the mouse sideways will move your location north or south. The direction that your location moves will depend upon the direction in which you are facing. Experiment with the Location Scroller so that you understand its behavior.

68.  Select **File > Revert** to return to the view from your home location, facing east just before sunrise. Use the Time controls to find the time at which the Sun first rises. Now, move the Location Scroller upwards to shift your viewing location to the west of your home location.

69.  Use the Time controls to find the time at which the Sun first appears above the horizon from this more westerly location.

**Question 16.**     As the observing location moves toward the west, does the Sun rise earlier or later?

As you see, the Location Scroller changes your viewing location as if you were driving across the landscape. If you were above the Earth's surface, using the Location Scroller would be equivalent to flying over the Earth at a constant altitude.

70. Select **File > Revert** to return to your home location.

71. In the Viewing Location section of the toolbar, click and hold the ***Increase current elevation*** button, which is to the left of the Home button, and watch as the viewing location rises above the surface of the Earth. Release the mouse button when the Viewing Location panel indicates that the current elevation is between about **400 km** and **500 km** above your home location.

72. Use the Location Scroller to "fly" over the surface of the Earth.

73. Click and hold the **Increase current elevation** button until the viewing location is between **7000 km** and **8000 km** above the Earth's surface. **Centre** the Earth in the view. [TIP: The image of the Earth as seen from space can be depicted without an atmosphere, the **Default,** or with an atmosphere, **Clouds,** in the **Surface Image/Model** command of the contextual menu for Earth.]

From this elevation you should be able to recognize the geography surrounding your home location. Note that the line between dark and light on the Earth (the terminator) passes through your home location as expected at the time of sunrise.

74. Change the Time Flow Rate to **300x.** You will notice that the Earth remains stationary in the view while the background stars appear to move.

**Question 17.**     Toward which direction on the Earth does the terminator move as time advances?

75. Click the Viewing Location panel in the toolbar to open a drop down menu. Near the bottom of the menu, you will see a section called Tracking and a checkmark beside the option Rotate with Earth. This option indicates that the view is as if you are at the top of a long flagpole that is based at your home location.

76. Select **Hover as Earth Rotates**. Click **Play,** if necessary, to recommence time flow and observe the Earth rotating in space.

77. Use the Location Scroller to observe the Earth from this elevation.

**Question 18.**     In the view, toward which direction is the Earth rotating? [HINT: Toward which direction is any location upon Earth moving?]

## E. Measuring Angles and Distances

Many times in the observing projects that follow, you will need to measure angles and distances between objects.

78. Select **File > Revert** to return to the view of sunrise from your home location.

79. Change the Gaze to the zenith, the point in the sky straight overhead of the observing location, by clicking on the **Z** button in the Gaze section of the toolbar. Select **View > Alt/Az Guides > Zenith/ Nadir** from the menu to show this point on the sky.

80. **Zoom out** to the maximum field of view of **191° x 191°.**

The view shows the complete sky in each direction, with the horizon depicted as a band around its circular perimeter. The circle of the horizon divides the sky into the hemisphere above the horizon, and the hemisphere below the horizon. Each of these hemispheres comprises 180 degrees of the 360 degrees of the complete sphere of the sky, the celestial sphere.

81. Select the **Angular Separation** tool from the **Tool Selection** control at the left side of the toolbar.

82. *Use the Angular Separation tool* to measure the angular distance between the Zenith and the horizon. To do this, move the cursor over the point marked as the Zenith, and click and drag the cursor toward the horizon. Notice that this tool tends to "snap" to objects on the celestial sphere.

The Angular Separation tool draws a line from the origin point to the current cursor position in the view and shows two items of information: the Angular separation and the Position angle. The Angular separation is a measure of the angular distance between the origin of the line and the current cursor position. This angular distance is measured in units of degrees, arcminutes, and arcseconds. Any two points on the celestial sphere, such as the zenith and the current cursor position define a circle with the observing location at its center. Since the complete circle is 360 degrees, the distance between the two points defining this circle is some proportion of 360 degrees. To refine the measurement, each degree is subdivided into 60 arcminutes and each arcminute is subdivided into 60 arcseconds.

**Question 19.**    How many arcseconds are there in one degree?

The position angle of the line drawn by the Angular Separation tool is the angle the line makes at its origin with a line directed toward the north having a position angle of 0°.

**Question 20.**    What is the angular separation between the zenith and the east point of the horizon? Consider the accuracy of your measurement and round the result to the nearest whole degree. [HINT: Use the Angular Separation tool to draw a line from the Zenith to the East point on the horizon.]

**Question 21.**    (a) What is the angular separation between the zenith and the west point of the horizon? (b) What is the angular separation between the west and east points of the horizon?

**Question 22.**    What is the position angle of the east point on the horizon?

**Question 23.**    What is the position angle of the west point of the horizon?

**Question 24.**    What is the position angle of the northeast point of the horizon?

The measurement of the positions of celestial objects in the sky over time was the foundation of astronomy. Indeed, it is by carefully observing and measuring the positions of celestial objects in the sky over time that their distances from Earth can be determined.

83. Open the **Find** pane and click the checkboxes to label the Sun and the planets Venus, Mars, and Jupiter.

84. Use the Angular Separation tool to measure the angular distance between the position of the Sun and the planet Venus in the view. You will notice that when this tool measures the angular separation between two celestial objects, it also displays the actual physical distance between the two bodies. [TIP: When measuring the angular separation between two celestial bodies, allow the tool to snap the celestial body and make sure that the HUD confirms the identities of the two objects.]

**Question 25.**    What is the angular separation in the sky between the Sun and Venus as seen from Earth on this date? [HINT: Use the "snap" feature of the Angular Separation tool to measure this separation to the nearest arcsecond.]

**Question 26.**    What is the physical distance separating the Sun and Venus on this date?

**Question 27.**    What is the position angle between the Sun and (a) Venus, (b) Mars, (c) Jupiter?

## F. Challenge: Fly Solo!

Now that you have been introduced to *Starry Night*™, it is time to try using the controls of the interface to set up views on your own. To do so, you will need to start a new instance of *Starry Night*™ and close the current view.

85. Select **File > New File** from the menu to open a new instance of *Starry Night*™.

86. Now you can close the previous instance of *Starry Night*™ by selecting **Window > Sunrise** from the menu to return to the Sunrise view and then **File > Close** from the menu to close this view. When *Starry Night*™ asks if you want to save the changes to this file, click **Don't Save** to leave the file in its original state. Then *Starry Night*™ will switch to the new instance view with the default name Untitled. Use this view to set up the scenes outlined below.

Scene 1: Set up a view showing the sky as seen from Alice Springs, Australia, at midnight on April 4, 1986 AD, looking southeast.

**Question 28.**  What is the name of the unusual object in the sky?

Scene 2: On July 20, 1969 AD, at 3:17:40 PM Central Daylight Time, Neil Armstrong and Buzz Aldrin landed the lunar module, *Eagle*, at Tranquility Base on the Moon. Configure *Starry Night*™ to show a view of the Moon as it appeared at that time from Mission Control in Houston, Texas (Central Time Zone).

**Question 29.**  (a) Describe the position of the Moon in the sky as seen from Houston on the afternoon of July 20, 1969. Include in your description the Constellation the Moon was in, its general direction in the sky and its Azimuth and Altitude. [HINT: Use the Info pane for some of these data.] (b) At what phase was the Moon at this time?

Scene 3: Simulate the view of the Earth that the astronauts had when they looked through the window of their lunar module toward the Earth after landing at 20:17:40 UT (Universal Time) on July 20, 1969, and again as Neil Armstrong would have seen the Earth as he stepped onto the lunar surface at 02:56:15 UT on July 21, 1969. [TIP 1: The Viewing Location dialog box contains a listing of the locations of each of the Apollo landing sites. TIP 2: The down arrow icon in the Time and Date panel has an option to display the time in Universal Time.]

**Question 30.**  Describe the view of Earth that Neil Armstrong and Buzz Aldrin had of the Earth at the time of their historic landing on the Moon. Include which continents they would have seen and comment on their orientation. Why do you suppose NASA planned the landing for this particular time? [HINT: Select **Markers and Outlines...** from the contextual menu for the Earth. In the popup list, click the checkbox for **Houston, Texas** and close the dialog window in order to mark the position of this city on the Earth.]

**Question 31.**  At the historic moment that Neil Armstrong stepped onto the lunar surface and announced: "That's one small step for [a] man, one giant leap for mankind," which continent of Earth was coming into view for him? [HINT: Use the time flow controls to determine which continent is rotating into view.]

Scene 4: On August 20, 1977, *Voyager 2* was launched from Florida and carried out a magnificent tour of several of the outer planets of our solar system. Open **Favourites > Observing Projects > Tutorial > Voyager 2** to see the route taken between these planets. This initial view is from a location over 3.5 AU, or 500 million kilometers, from the Earth. The view is centered and locked on the *Voyager 2* probe on the date that it was launched. An overview of the mission path of this amazing spacecraft is shown in yellow. The planets are labeled and their orbits are shown. Because the viewing location is centered upon the *Voyager 2* probe, when you click Play you will be able to fly along with this remarkable spacecraft as it makes its Grand Tour of the solar system. Use the controls to slow time flow as *Voyager* encounters the planets Jupiter, Saturn, Uranus and Neptune. With the time flow reduced, decrease your distance from the *Voyager* probe (use the decrease current elevation button) or zoom in and use the Location Scroller to observe each encounter. Use **File > Revert** as often as you like and experiment with setting up other interesting points of view. For example, before clicking **Play,** you might enjoy decreasing the current elevation from *Voyager 2* and using the time flow controls to fly alongside this spacecraft for its entire journey. As the mission progresses, center the view on the next planet that *Voyager* will encounter and reduce the time flow rate as the planetary encounter nears so that you can use the Location Scroller to enjoy the flyby.

**Question 32.**    What was the month and year in which *Voyager 2* encountered each of the planets along its Grand Tour of the solar system?

87.    When you have finished your explorations and wish to exit *Starry Night*™, click **Don't Save** when asked if you wish to save the changes to the view.

## G. Conclusion

While this tutorial has introduced you to some of the many features of *Starry Night*™, it is by no means exhaustive. You should certainly read the User's Guide that is available under the **Help** menu to acquaint yourself with *all* of the features of this software and explore the **Starry Night features** and **Starry Night basics** options in the **Sky Guide** side pane.

The observing projects in this book will familiarize you with many more of the features of *Starry Night*™. Still, the best way to become proficient with the software is to use it. Take every opportunity to use *Starry Night*™ to model astronomical concepts.

# Appendix: Observing Projects Instruction Reference

This appendix contains a list that you can refer to if you forget how to perform one of the commonly used procedures in the instruction steps of the Observing Projects. There are often several ways to accomplish these procedures. While the procedural steps in the observing projects reflect the authors' preferences and experience, you will soon develop your own preferences and shortcuts. You can use the perforations in this book to tear out the pages of this appendix to make it more convenient to refer to as you work through the observing projects.

## Centre/Magnify an object in the view

The **Centre** command locks the gaze onto an object or point in the sky, keeping it centered in the view even as time changes. **Magnify** does the same but with the object centered in a smaller field of view. There are two methods for achieving these commands:

Method 1: If the object is visible on the screen, position the cursor over the object in the view and then right-click (Windows) or Ctrl-click (Mac) and select **Centre** or **Magnify** from the contextual menu.

Method 2: If the object is not identifiable in the view, use the **Find** pane to retrieve the object from the appropriate database and press the Enter key, or select **Centre** or **Magnify** from the drop down menu icon beside the object's name in the found objects list.

## Configure the HUD

Choose **Preferences** from the **File** (Windows) or **Starry Night** (Mac) menu to open the Preferences dialog window. Select **Cursor Tracking (HUD)** from the dropdown box at the top of the window. Beside the Show label is a scrollable list of data items with checkboxes to show or hide those data in the HUD. It is usually also helpful to activate the option to **Show info in upper left corner of the screen**. Then close the Preferences dialog window.

## Find an Object

Click the **Find** tab and click the magnifying glass icon in the search box near the top of the Find side pane to choose the database you wish to search. Then type the name of the object into the search box. If the object is in the database, it will appear in the found items list. Notice that when the search box is empty and the Search All Databases option is in effect, the found items list defaults to Solar System items.

## Find the Time of an Event

When timing an astronomical event, you will frequently need to do so to the nearest second. Since there is no dedicated keyboard shortcut for steps of one second, set the Time Flow Rate in the toolbar to **1 second**. Then use the keyboard shortcuts in the table below to change the Date and Time. Alternatively, if you click the value for the **hour, minute,** or **second** in the Time panel, that value will be highlighted. Then you can use the + and − keys to increase or decrease, respectively, the selected value.

### Keyboard Shortcuts for Date and Time

| To move in steps of one: | Step Forward in time | Step Backward in Time |
| --- | --- | --- |
| Year | Y | Shift-Y |
| Month | M | Shift-M |
| Day | D | Shift-D |
| Hour | H | Shift-H |
| Minute | T | Shift-T |
| Time Flow Rate interval | U | Shift-U |

### Hide/Show Daylight

Method 1: Select **View > Hide Daylight** or **View > Show Daylight** from the menu.

Method 2: Use the keyboard shortcut **Ctrl-D** (Windows) or **Cmd-D** (Mac) to toggle daylight on and off.

Method 3: Open the **Options** pane and click **Daylight** under the **Local View** layer.

Method 4 (Windows Only): Click the **Daylight** button in the buttonbar.

### Hide/Show Horizon

Method 1: Select **View > Show Horizon** or **View > Hide Horizon** from the menu.

Method 2: Use the keyboard shortcut **Ctrl-H** (Windows) or **B** (Mac) to toggle the horizon on and off.

Method 3: Open the **Options** pane and click **Local Horizon** under the **Local View** layer.

Method 4 (Windows Only): Click the **Horizon** button in the buttonbar.

### Increase/Decrease Current Elevation

Click the **Increase** and **Decrease current elevation** buttons aligned with the left side and below the Viewing Location panel in the toolbar. You can adjust the size of the elevation step produced by each click of these buttons in the **Responsiveness** category of the **Preferences** dialog accessible from the **File** (Windows) or **Starry Night** (Macintosh) menu.

### Measure the Angular Separation/Distance/Size

Select the **Angular Separation** tool from the **Tool Selection** control at the left side of the toolbar. Place the cursor over the first object (or position) and click and drag the cursor to the second object (or position). In addition to tracing a line from the point where the mouse was first clicked, the Angular Separation tool displays the angular separation between the first point and the current cursor position and the position angle of the current position with respect to the first point (position angle is 0° for north and goes through 90° for east, 180° for south and 270° for west). If the line traced out by the Angular Separation tool starts and ends on specific objects, the physical distance separating the two objects will also be displayed. The Angular Separation cursor will snap to an object when it is close to that object. When measuring the angular size of a particular object, it is usually most efficient to measure the object's angular radius, beginning from the center of the object, to which the cursor will snap, out to the object's edge or boundary.

### Open/Select a Favourite

You can retrieve a Favourite view from either the menu or Favourites pane. Generally, the steps in the projects will simply instruct you to open a Favourite view, allowing you to choose whether to do so from the menu or the Favourites pane. Usually it is easiest to open views from the Favourites pane.

## Open the Contextual Menu

Right-click (Windows) or Ctrl-click (Mac) on the object in the view to open its contextual menu. If the object is not easily identifiable in the main view window, use the **Find** pane to list the object and click the icon to the left of its name in the found item list to open its contextual menu.

## Remove Halo Effects

If the Sun is in the view, open the contextual menu for the Sun and select **Halo Effects > Never**. If the Sun is not in the view, open the **Find** pane. Empty the search box near the top of the Find pane and ensure Search All Databases is shown below the search box. (If this is not the case, click the magnifying glass icon in the search box and select **Search All** from the drop down menu.) Click the icon to the left of the Sun in the Solar System Items list and select **Halo Effects > Never** from the drop down menu.

## Run time forward

Click the **Play** button.

## Set/Change the Date/Time

To set the Date or Time of the view, click the appropriate Date field in the toolbar to highlight it. Then either type the value required (use a number 1–12 for the month) or use the +/– or cursor Up/Down keys to increment or decrement the highlighted value, respectively. You can use the Tab key or cursor keys to move between fields in the Date and Time panel of the toolbar. Click the icon of the Sun in the Time display panel to switch between standard time and daylight saving time. [TIP: It is often more convenient to change the Date or Time in the toolbar with the keyboard shortcuts described under Find the Time of an Event.]

## Set/Change the Gaze

Method 1: Use the direction buttons, **N, S, E, W**, and **Z** in the toolbar to orient the gaze toward the north, south, east, west, or zenith, respectively.

Method 2: Use the keyboard shortcuts **N, S, E, W**, and **Z** to orient the gaze toward the north, south, east, west, or zenith, respectively.

Method 3: Use the Hand tool to drag the screen and change the gaze direction.

Method 4: Use the cursor keys to change the gaze direction.

Method 5: Use the scrollbars to change the gaze direction. Select **View > Show Scrollbars** from the menu to display the scrollbars on the screen.

## Set/Change the Viewing Location

Select **Options > Viewing Location...** from the menu. In the Viewing Location dialog window that opens, make the appropriate selections in the View from: dropdown boxes at the top of the Viewing Location dialog window. If the view is from the surface of a planet or moon, use the tabs to select the appropriate location on that surface. If a specific city or town on Earth is the desired viewing location, use the keyboard to type the first letters of the name of the city or town to jump to it in the list. When the appropriate location is chosen or set, click the **Go To Location** button. To avoid the panning animation of a change in location, tap the spacebar.

## Set/Change the Zoom and Zoom in/Zoom out

If a particular zoom is specified, click the Zoom panel in the toolbar to select the indicated zoom from the zoom menu. To zoom in or out generally, use any of the following methods:

Method 1: Click the **+** and **−** zoom buttons in the toolbar to zoom in or out, respectively.

Method 2: If no fields are highlighted in the toolbar you can use the **+** and **−** keys on the keyboard to zoom in or out, respectively.

Method 3: If no fields are highlighted in the toolbar you can use the wheel on a wheelmouse to zoom in or out.

### Use the Angular Separation tool

See Measure the Angular Separation/Distance/Size above.

### Use the Location Scroller

Select **Location Scroller** from the **Tool Selection** control at the left side of the toolbar and then click on and drag the view to change the observing location. If the adaptive cursor is in effect, pressing and holding the **Shift** key on the keyboard also activates the Location Scroller.

# Stars and Constellations    2

This project will familiarize you with the patterns of bright stars that make up several of the major constellations that can be seen from mid-northern latitudes on the Earth. Once you know these patterns and can find them in the night sky, you can use them to locate other stars and constellations. With practice, you can become expert at finding your way around the sky.

Historically, a constellation is a group of stars that outlines a familiar object or pattern, or represents this object or pattern in some way. For example, the bright stars in the constellation of Orion roughly outline the body of Orion, the hunter, while the long line of stars making up the constellation Draco resemble the curved shape of a dragon. Many of these names have their origins in the myths and stories of antiquity.

In modern astronomy, constellations are defined differently. Each constellation is an area of the sky with precisely defined boundaries, rather than a group of stars. Together, the 88 officially designated constellations cover the entire celestial sphere. In this way, the constellations provide us with an atlas of the celestial sphere. Thus, when we say that the star Regulus is in the constellation Leo, this tells us the location of Regulus in the sky in the same way that saying that Grenoble is in France tells us where Grenoble is on the Earth. However, most people—including most astronomers—picture a constellation more often in terms of the historical star pattern than as a set of invisible boundary lines dividing the sky into sections.

## A. Constellations

In this section, you will use the *Starry Night*™ program to understand the difference between the historical and modern definitions of constellations.

1. Launch *Starry Night* ™ and configure the HUD to include **Constellation name** and **Name**.
2. Click **Stop** and then change the Time in the toolbar to midnight, **12:00:00 AM standard time**, at your home location.
3. Select **View > Constellations > Astronomical** and **Labels > Constellations** from the menu.

The view shows the familiar historical definition of the constellations. Stars within a constellation are grouped to form a recognizable pattern.

4. Use the Hand tool to survey the various constellations visible from your home location.
5. Hide the **Horizon** and use the Hand tool to see all of the constellations on the celestial sphere.
6. Click the **Options** tab and expand the Constellations layer in the Options pane. Click the **Boundaries** option on and click the **Stick Figures** option off.

Now, the sky is divided by boundaries like countries on a map. Each "country" shows the modern astronomical definition of a constellation. A constellation contains all of the stars within its boundaries, regardless of whether these stars are also included in the more familiar historical pattern of the constellation.

> **Question 1.**     Name three of the smallest constellations on the celestial sphere.
>
> **Question 2.**     Name three of the largest constellations on the celestial sphere.
>
> **Question 3.**     Approximately what is the length in degrees of the largest constellation on the celestial sphere? [HINT: The standard field of view is 100° wide.]

The division of the sky into constellations originates in ancient mythology and varies from culture to culture.

> **7.**     Click the **Illustrations** option in the Options pane. Use the Hand tool to look around the sky.

These striking representations may help you to remember the form of the constellations when you come to explore the real sky with none of these guides available.

## B. Asterisms

Some prominent patterns of stars that have common historical names are not constellations. These are called **asterisms**. Some asterisms are part of a constellation. For example, the Big Dipper asterism forms a part of the constellation Ursa Major. Other asterisms, such as the Summer Triangle, extend over two or more constellations.

> **8.**     Open **Favourites > Observing Projects > Stars and Constellations > Big Dipper.**

The view shows the night sky looking west at midnight on June 4, 2014, from Calgary, Canada, which is at latitude 51° North. Constellation labels, patterns, and modern boundaries are visible. You can see Ursa Major, commonly known as the Big Bear, to the right of center in the view.

> **9.**     Select **View > Constellations > Asterisms.**

The view now shows the asterisms that are found in this part of the sky. You will see that the Big Dipper asterism, so named because its shape resembles that of a scoop or dipper, is within the boundaries of Ursa Major but forms only a part of the constellation's more extensive pattern. Notice also the large asterism named the Diamond of Virgo. Each of the four stars comprising this asterism is within a different constellation.

> **10.**     Toggle back and forth between the view of the asterisms and the view of the traditional constellations and their modern boundaries by selecting **View > Constellations > Astronomical** and then **View > Constellations > Asterisms** to answer the following questions.

> **Question 4.**     Which constellations contribute stars to the Diamond of Virgo asterism?
>
> **Question 5.**     Which constellation is almost completely encompassed by the Diamond of Virgo asterism but does not contribute a star to the asterism's pattern?
>
> **Question 6.**     What are the names of the four stars that form the Diamond of Virgo asterism?

As the Earth rotates, the orientation of constellations and asterisms varies with respect to compass directions on Earth. Their visibility will depend on your location on the Earth and the season. Nevertheless, their easily recognizable patterns make asterisms and constellations invaluable guides for finding your way in the night sky. The table below shows the optimum times for observing major constellations or well-known asterisms from mid-latitude northern hemisphere sites.

| Constellation or Asterism | Time of Best Visibility |
|---|---|
| Big Dipper | February to August |
| Cassiopeia | August to March |
| Auriga | November to April |
| Bootes | April to August |
| Virgo | April to July |
| Leo | March to June |
| Orion | December to April |

## C. Finding the Big Dipper

The Big Dipper asterism within the constellation Ursa Major, the Great Bear, is a very useful guide to the sky for Northern Hemisphere observers. This asterism is in the shape of a spoon or scoop that might be used to serve soup or scoop water from a barrel. It is made up of seven bright stars. Three of them in the tail of the bear make up the handle of the dipper, while the other four make up the scoop and are in the body of the bear. If you live between latitudes of about 40° N and 60° N and want to find the Big Dipper asterism in the actual sky, face approximately north and look at a point about halfway up from the horizon. Imagine that this point is the center of a circle. This circle starts at a point on the northern horizon and curves up to the left to a point near the zenith, then curves down to the right and back to the starting point on the northern horizon. The easily recognized pattern of the Big Dipper should be somewhere along or slightly inside this circle. If you live south of 40° N latitude, the Big Dipper may be below the horizon during certain times of the year or at certain times of the night. Consult the previous table for the best times to view the Big Dipper. If you live north of 60° N latitude, the imaginary circle described above will include points to the south of the zenith.

The Big Dipper can have any orientation, including upside down or hanging downward from its handle, depending on the time of night and the time of year. The important thing is to be able to recognize its pattern.

> 11. Open **Favourites > Observing Projects > Stars and Constellations > Constellations**.

The view is of the northern sky from Newark, New Jersey, USA, at 10:00 PM EDT on September 1. Using the technique described above, you should find the Big Dipper quickly.

> 12. To confirm that you have correctly identified the Big Dipper in the view, select **View > Constellations > Asterisms** and **Labels > Constellations** from the menu.

**Question 7.** In addition to the Big Dipper, which other asterisms are visible in the view?

> 13. Select **Labels > Constellations** to turn the labels off again.

## D. Star Names

Many of the stars visible to the naked eye have names that originate in antiquity.

> 14. Use the HUD to find the Name of each of the seven stars that form the Big Dipper.

The names shown in the HUD are the stars' common or proper names that are derived from their original Arabic or Greek names.

> **Question 8.** What are the proper names of the seven stars that form the Big Dipper asterism?

As astronomy advanced, various star catalogs were developed, each with its own naming convention. In 1603, the German astronomer Johann Bayer published a catalog of 1564 stars. In the Bayer system, stars within a constellation are generally ranked according to their apparent brightness with Greek letter prefixes. For example, the brightest star in the constellation Leo, the Lion, is called *alpha Leonis*; the next brightest star is called *beta Leonis*, and so on.

In 1725, a catalog of 2935 stars compiled by the English astronomer John Flamsteed was published. Flamsteed numbered the stars within a constellation according to their position from west to east. Thus, the westernmost star in the constellation Leo is given the Flamsteed designation 1 Leonis.

In 1989, the European space agency launched the Hipparcos satellite, which operated until 1993 and succeeded in determining precise positions for millions of stars. In the Hipparcos and Tycho star catalogs produced from the data obtained during this mission, stars are named with the prefix HIP or TYC and a number.

15. Select **Options > Stars > Stars…** from the menu. Drag the Stars Options dialog window to a convenient location on the screen so that the complete asterism of the Big Dipper is visible.

16. Leaving the dialog window open, click the **Labels** checkbox. Adjust the slide control in the lower section of the dialog window toward the right until all seven of the stars that form the Big Dipper in the view are indicated with labels. Next, choose each of the options **Catalogue Number, Bayer Letter,** and **Flamsteed Number** in turn from the Show drop down menu and note the names given to the stars in the view. Then click the **Cancel** button to dismiss the dialog window and remove the labels in the view.

> **Question 9.** What is the designation of the star Alkaid, at the end of the handle of the Big Dipper, in each of the three catalogs?

## E. Describing Directions from the Big Dipper

The Big Dipper is an important asterism because its member stars can be used as guides to locate many other stars and constellations. In order to use the Big Dipper as a guide to other constellations, asterisms and stars, we first need to define the directions "northward" and "southward" relative to the Big Dipper.

17. Use the **H** keyboard shortcut to advance time by two hours to **12:00:00 AM** so that the dipper shape is oriented horizontally and close to the horizon.

Imagine the bottom of the bowl resting on a flat table and the handle extending toward your left. In this orientation, the bowl opens upward, and it is in this sense that we shall use the term "northward." Conversely, downward is the direction in which water would drip if the bowl of the dipper leaked, and we refer to this direction as "southward." Remember, the bowl of the Big Dipper always opens "northward" (toward the North Celestial Pole) no matter which orientation the Big Dipper has in the sky.

18. Click **Play** and watch the changing orientation of the Big Dipper in the night sky as time advances and click **Stop** at approximately **5:00 AM EDT** on **September 2,** as daylight begins to interfere with the view.

The orientation of the Big Dipper changes with respect to the horizon as time progresses and the sky rotates around the North Star due to Earth's rotation. By 5:00 AM, the Big Dipper is standing on its handle on the right side of the view.

> **Question 10.** (a) In this orientation, which corner of the screen is "northward" from the bowl, as defined above? (b) Which corner of the screen is "southward" from the bowl?

As you will see in the next section, this nomenclature is perfectly logical since two of the stars of the bowl of the Big Dipper point almost directly to the North Celestial Pole, the extension of the Earth's rotation axis, at this time in history. We are fortunate that the North Star, Polaris, is very close to this celestial pole at this time.

## F. Finding the North Star

To find the North Star, Polaris, using the Big Dipper as a guide, first locate the handle of the Big Dipper and then find the two stars that are on the end of the bowl farthest from the handle. These two stars are often called the "pointer stars" because they point to the North Star.

19. Select **File > Revert** and use the Angular Separation tool to draw a line from the bottom pointer star (the star at the bottom of the bowl farthest from the handle) and directly through the top pointer star (the star at the top of the bowl) and extend it a distance equal to about seven times the distance between the two pointer stars, or about 35°, where the cursor will snap to a star and display its name, Polaris, the North Star.

The pointing is not perfect but it is fairly close. While the North Star is not a really bright star, it is the brightest star in that little patch of the sky.

**Question 11.** What are the names of the two "pointer" stars in the Big Dipper?

**Question 12.** What is the actual angular distance between the bottom star of the pointers and the Pole Star?

## G. Finding the Little Dipper

Polaris is the end star in the handle of the Little Dipper, an asterism in the constellation Ursa Minor. Starting from Polaris, you should be able to discern a line of four stars curving in an arc toward the handle of the Big Dipper. The first three of these stars are fainter than Polaris and the fourth is about equal in brightness to Polaris. The latter two stars in this arc form a rectangle with two other stars in the direction away from the arc of the Little Dipper's handle. These four stars form the bowl of the Little Dipper.

20. Search for and identify the Little Dipper.
21. Use the **K** keyboard shortcut to toggle the display of asterisms and their labels on to verify that you have found the Little Dipper and then press the **K** key again to turn these displays off.

The four stars forming the bowl of the Little Dipper have apparent magnitudes of very close to 2, 3, 4, and 5. [NOTE: The magnitude scale of star brightness is inverted, with larger magnitude values indicating fainter stars.] Thus, they represent a useful sample of calibrated star brightness. You can use them to estimate the transparency and degree of light pollution at your observing site by looking for the faintest of this sequence of stars that is visible on a given night. The two stars at the end of the bowl of the Little Dipper nearest to the handle of the Big Dipper are often referred to as the Guardians. As the sky turns, the Guardians always remain between the Big Dipper and Polaris and "guard" Polaris from the Great Bear.

**Question 13.** What are the proper names of the two Guardians?

## H. Finding Cassiopeia, or the "W"

At the time depicted in the view, with the Big Dipper to the west of north in the view, the constellation Cassiopeia is found by imagining a straight line from the handle of the Big Dipper to the North Star and extended by almost an equal distance past the North Star. The brightest stars in the constellation Cassiopeia (the Queen of Ethiopia) form an asterism shaped like a W. The end of this line should place you within this group of stars. In the orientation on your screen, the W is tipped up on one end.

22. Use the **K** keyboard shortcut to toggle the display of labels and asterisms on to confirm your identification of the W asterism and then turn these options off again.

Question 14.    What are the names of the stars that make up the W asterism?

## I. Finding the Star Capella and the Constellation Auriga

Capella is the brightest star in the constellation Auriga, the Charioteer. To find this star, first locate the two stars on the top of the bowl of the Big Dipper. One of these two stars, Megrez, marks the point where the handle joins the bowl, and the other is the upper of the two pointer stars, Dubhe.

23. Use the Angular Separation tool to draw a line from Megrez through Dubhe and extend it across the sky (toward the right on your screen) a distance of about six times the spacing between Megrez and Dubhe (about 60°). The brightest star near the end of this line is Capella. Use the HUD to verify your identification of this star.

Capella is actually slightly above the imaginary line you have drawn in the previous step, but it is the only really bright star that stands out in that part of the sky. When you look at Capella in the actual sky you may notice that it has a yellowish color. This is because Capella has a surface temperature similar to that of the Sun. However, while our Sun is a dwarf star, Capella is a supergiant star with a radius approximately 14 times larger than that of the Sun and is therefore intrinsically much brighter than the Sun.

The brightest stars of the constellation Auriga consist of five stars, including Capella, in the form of a stretched pentagon.

24. **Centre** the view on Capella and select **View > Constellations > Astronomical** and **Labels > Constellations** from the menu. Use the **H** keyboard shortcut to advance the Time to **1:00:00 AM** to see the pattern of the constellation Auriga.
25. Select **View > Constellations > Boundaries**.

Question 15.    (a) What is the name of the star that is on the boundary between Auriga and Taurus?
(b) To which constellation does this star belong? [HINT: Check the Constellation Name for this star in the HUD.]

## J. Finding the Star Arcturus and the Constellation Bootes

26. Select **File > Revert**.
27. Adjust the view so that the gaze direction is between W and NW, with the horizon low on the screen.

In this view, the Big Dipper is to the right in the view. To find the star Arcturus, start by looking at the handle of the Big Dipper. Notice that the handle is curved and forms an arc in the sky. Imagine continuing this arc through the sky in a direction away from the bowl of the Big Dipper for a distance roughly equal to the total length of the Big Dipper asterism. You should discover that this arc passes more-or-less through a bright star just below and to the left of the center of the view. This star is Arcturus. A good way to remember how to find this star is to "follow the arc to Arcturus."

Arcturus is the brightest star in the constellation Bootes, the hunter. [NOTE: The two "o's" in Bootes are pronounced separately: Bo-otes. Writing the name of the constellation as Boötes indicates this. The "e" is also pronounced. To hear this pronunciation, open the **Find** pane and click the magnifying glass icon in the search box and select **Constellation** from the drop down menu. Click the menu button next to the listing for Bootes and select **Pronounce**. Before leaving the Find pane, click the magnifying glass icon again and select **Search All** from the drop down menu.]

If you look up and to the right from Arcturus in the view, you should see a pentagon of five stars. Arcturus plus the other five form a kite or ice cream cone shape in the sky.

> 28. Select **View > Constellations > Astronomical** and then **Labels > Constellations** from the menu to turn on the stick figures and labels of the constellations in the view and check that you have found Bootes correctly.

Question 16.  Which stars (apart from Arcturus) make up the "kite" or "ice cream cone" shape of Bootes?

In the real sky, Arcturus has a yellowish or even slightly orange tint because it is slightly cooler than the Sun. It is also a giant star—much smaller than the supergiant Capella but still much larger than our Sun.

With the constellation lines and labels on in the view, you can see another constellation, Canes Venatici, below the handle of the Big Dipper. Canes Venatici (Latin for "dogs of the hunter") consists of two relatively faint stars joined by a single straight line.

Question 17.  What are the names of the two stars in Canes Venatici?

In mythology, Bootes is hunting the Great Bear. As the sky turns counter-clockwise around the North Star, Bootes follows the Great Bear around the sky. The two stars in Canes Venatici are the two hunting dogs belonging to Bootes, nipping at the heels of the Great Bear as it circles the North Star, trying to get away from Bootes.

> 29. Click the **Illustrations** checkbox under Constellations in the Options pane to display these mythological figures. Then turn this feature off again.

## K. Finding the Star Spica and the Constellation Virgo

> 30. Press the **K** key to turn off the stick figures and labels of the constellations.
> 31. Change the Time to **8:30:00 PM**.
> 32. Set the gaze to due **W**est.

In this view of the twilight sky, locate the arc of the Big Dipper in the upper right of the view (the complete Big Dipper asterism may not be visible in this view but the arc of its handle should be obvious). To find Spica, start at the handle of the Big Dipper and "follow the arc to Arcturus!" Continue this arc for roughly the same distance again past Arcturus to "speed on to Spica." Spica is the relatively bright star near the horizon, between the west and southwest compass points.

> 33. Use the HUD to identify Spica.

Spica is the brightest star in the constellation Virgo, the Virgin. Spica is much hotter than our Sun and when viewed in the actual sky, it appears to have a slightly bluish tint.

> 34. Press **K** to see the pattern of stars in the constellation Virgo.

Question 18.  What are the names of the two constellations that lie between Virgo and Ursa Major?

## L. Finding the Star Regulus and the Constellation Leo

To find Regulus in the constellation Leo, the Lion, you will need to change the date to December.

> 35. Select **File > Revert**.
> 36. Use the **M** keyboard shortcut to change the Date to **December 1**.
> 37. Turn **Daylight Saving Time** off (click the "Sun" icon in the Time display in the toolbar).
> 38. Change the Time to **1:00:00 AM standard time**.
> 39. Change the gaze to NE, with the horizon near to the bottom of the screen.

In this view, locate the Big Dipper, standing on its handle in the center of the screen. To find the star Regulus, locate the two stars in the Big Dipper on the opposite side of the bowl from the pointer stars (i.e., the star where the bowl of the dipper meets the handle, Megrez, and the star Phecda to the right of Megrez in this view).

> 40. Starting at Megrez, use the Angular Separation tool to draw a line in the direction of Phecda and extend it a distance about 10 times the distance between Megrez and Phecda (about 50°). The bright star at the right hand end of a small grouping of stars is Regulus. Use the HUD to verify your identification of Regulus.

Regulus, like Spica, is hotter than our Sun and has a bluish tint when viewed in the real sky. Regulus is the brightest star in the constellation Leo. The most easily recognized part of this constellation is a line of stars running toward the upper left from Regulus, forming the shape of a sickle or backward question mark.

> 41. To see the Sickle asterism, select **View > Constellations > Asterisms** and **Labels > Constellations** from the menu.

The Sickle asterism represents the head of the lion in the constellation Leo. The hind end of the lion is formed by a triangle of stars below and to the left of the Sickle.

> 42. To see the pattern of the constellation Leo, select **View > Constellations > Astronomical** from the menu.
> 43. Click the **Illustrations** checkbox under the Constellations layer of the Options pane to see an illustration of the mythical lion, Leo.

Question 19.    What is the constellation that lies between Leo and Ursa Major?

## M. Conclusion and Suggested Extensions

This project has shown you how to find your way around the sky by using an easily located constellation, the Big Dipper, as a guide. You can use the techniques discussed in this project to locate these stars and constellations in the real sky. One further practical hint, as you navigate the sky, is the fact that when held at arm's length, the thumb and finger of your outstretched hand subtends an angle of about 20° and the width of your fist covers about 10°. You can then use a star atlas or printouts from your *Starry Night*™ software and maybe a pair of binoculars to explore other constellations to extend your knowledge of the night sky.

# Astronomical Coordinate Systems

# 3

The concept of the **celestial sphere** is a simple and useful model of the sky. In this model, the sky is considered to be a vast spherical shell centered upon the Earth. All of the objects that appear in the sky are assumed to be infinitely distant from the Earth on the celestial sphere, rendering the sky as a two-dimensional spherical surface.

The spherical geometry of astronomical coordinate systems is less familiar than the Cartesian coordinate systems used for flat surfaces, but the basic concepts are equivalent. One difference between the coordinate system of a flat surface (often referred to as an "X – Y coordinate system") and that of a spherical surface is that distances on a flat surface are measured linearly in units of length, while distances on a spherical surface are arcs that are measured in angular units, the angles referring to those subtended by the arcs at the center of the celestial sphere.

In this project, you will explore methods for specifying the positions of objects in the sky based upon the model of the celestial sphere.

## A. Spherical Geometry

In Figure 1, the sky is modeled as a spherical shell with its center at **O**. Any plane containing **O** will intersect the sphere on a circle defined as a **great circle**. One specific great circle is chosen as a reference plane for a spherical coordinate system and is known as the **equator** since it divides the sphere into two equal hemispheres.

A line passing through the center of the sphere perpendicular to the reference plane intersects the sphere at two points called **poles**. Each pole is at the center of its respective hemisphere. Any plane perpendicular to the equator passing through the center of the sphere will include both poles and intersect the sphere in specific great circles known as **meridians**.

We can select a reference point on the equator, point **A** in the figure, such that the meridian through **A** becomes the reference meridian. The position of any object on the sphere, such as the star at **S**, can now be specified by two coordinates. The first is the angle $\theta$ describing the angular distance along the equator from the reference point **A** to point **B**, where the meridian passing through the object intersects the equator. The second is the angle $\Phi$ describing the angular distance from **B** to **S** from the equator to the object.

A familiar example of a spherical coordinate system is that of latitude and longitude upon the surface of the Earth.

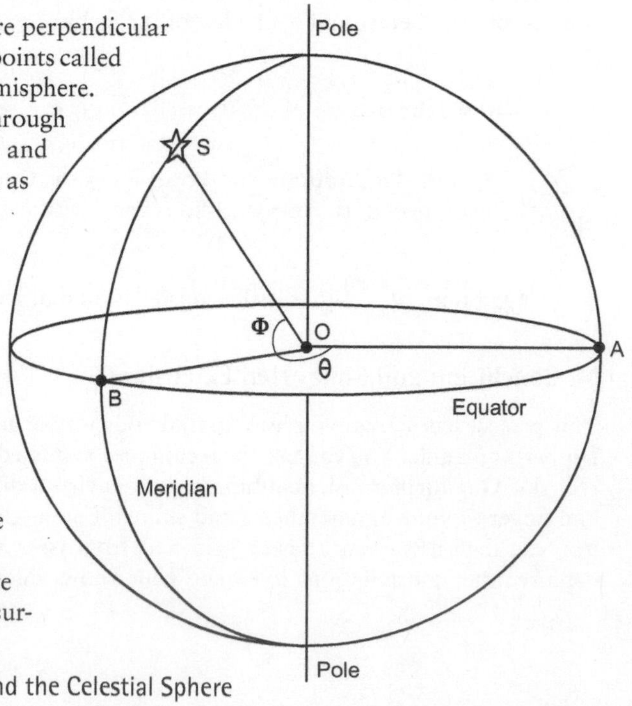

Figure 1. Spherical Coordinates and the Celestial Sphere

1. Launch *Starry Night™* and configure the HUD to include **Altitude** and **Azimuth**.
2. Open **Favourites > Observing Projects > Coordinate Systems > Latitude and Longitude**.

The view shows Earth as seen from a viewing location 12,000 kilometers above its surface along a line connecting the center of the Earth and the center of the Sun. The image of the Earth is overlaid with a grid representing the terrestrial spherical coordinate system of **latitude** and **longitude**. The equator is displayed as the red line running horizontally across the center of the Earth. The reference plane of the equator is chosen to be perpendicular to the rotation axis of the Earth. In this way, the north and south poles of the coordinate system, indicated by the short blue and yellow lines extending from the top and bottom of the Earth's surface in the view, coincide with this rotation axis.

Latitude is the angular distance north or south of the equator. The view shows several parallels of latitude, so-called because they are parallel to the equator. Notice that they are labeled in units of degrees, positive to the north of the equator and negative to the south of the equator.

The vertical red line across the surface of the Earth is the reference meridian for longitude. (By standard usage, a **meridian of longitude**, or a **terrestrial meridian**, is half of a great circle, and extends from one pole through the equator to the other pole.) This reference meridian, also called the **prime meridian**, was chosen earlier in history to pass through the site of the Old Royal Observatory at Greenwich, England. Longitude is measured east or west of this prime meridian. The two coordinates of latitude and longitude uniquely specify any location upon the surface of the Earth.

**Question 1.**   Are the meridians of longitude great circles? Why or why not?

**Question 2.**   Are the parallels of latitude great circles? Why or why not?

**Question 3.**   Which of the two coordinate angles depicted in Figure 1, ($\theta$ or $\Phi$), corresponds to (a) latitude, and (b) longitude?

3. Use the Location Scroller to look nearly straight down onto the North Pole (indicated by the blue pole stick). Note that the meridians of longitude converge at the pole. Now use the Location Scroller to move your location so that the view is nearly straight down onto the South Pole (yellow pole stick). Notice again that the meridians of longitude all intersect at the pole.

Perhaps you noticed that *Starry Night™* labels the meridians of longitude in units of time (hours), rather than units of angle (degrees). The reason for this is that the Earth rotates once on its axis in 24 hours with reference to the direction to the Sun. Consequently, any location on the Earth moves 360° around a circle parallel to the equator in one day of 24 hours. Thus, longitude can also be expressed in units of time, one hour of longitude being equal to the angle through which the Earth rotates in that time, 360° ÷ 24 = 15°.

4. Select **File > Revert** from the menu. From this perspective, you can see that the prime meridian lines up with the poles.
5. Set the Time Flow Rate to **3000x**.

As time passes, note that the meridians of longitude move with the Earth as it rotates toward the east. The coordinate system is fixed on the Earth.

**Question 4.**   Does the passage of time affect the latitude and longitude of a location on the surface of the Earth? Why or why not?

6. Select **File > Revert**.
7. Change the Time Flow Rate to **2 hours** and **Step time forward**. Note that, with each step forward in time, the meridians of longitude shift along with the Earth toward the east so that a different meridian lines up with the center of the Earth as seen from this vantage point in space.
8. Continue to **Step time forward** until the prime meridian once again lines up with the poles.

**Question 5.** How long did it take for the prime meridian to return to its original alignment with the poles?

**Question 6.** What is the angular distance in degrees between the meridians of longitude shown in the view?

**Question 7.** What is the approximate longitude of the location marked **Messina** in southern Africa, expressed in degrees?

## B. Horizontal Coordinates

A natural coordinate system describing positions in the sky for an observer on the surface of the Earth is one that is centered on the observer's location with a reference plane tangent to Earth's surface at this point. This reference plane intersects the celestial sphere in a great circle at the observer's **horizon**, the equator of the horizontal coordinate system. The sky occupies the hemisphere above the horizon and the point directly overhead, 90° from the horizon, is one of the poles of the coordinate system and is called the **zenith**. The **nadir** is the opposite pole, hidden by the Earth at the center of the hemisphere beneath the horizon.

Figure 2 shows the horizontal coordinate system for an observer on the Earth at the point marked **O**. In this figure, the Earth's polar axis is vertical. The point marked **A** indicates the north point on the observer's horizon, the chosen reference point on the equator of the horizontal coordinate system.

In the horizontal coordinate system, the position of an object's meridian along the horizon measured in degrees eastward from the north point is its **azimuth**. The great circle that passes through the zenith and the north point of the horizon is called the **local** or **celestial meridian**.

The position of an object above (or below) the horizon along its meridian is its **altitude**, also measured in degrees. Altitude is positive for objects above the horizon and negative for objects below the horizon. With these two coordinates, azimuth and altitude, you can specify any location on the celestial sphere.

You can use *Starry Night*™ to view the sky from the center of this coordinate system and use the coordinates of azimuth and altitude to specify the positions of several objects.

> 9. Click the **Home** button.

*Starry Night*™ will show a view of the horizon and sky looking south from your home location at the current time and date. Compass points are indicated along the horizon. The Gaze panel in the toolbar displays the horizontal coordinates of the center point in the view.

> 10. Click on the Gaze buttons in the toolbar (**N, E, S, W,** and **Z**) to look around the view and use the Gaze display panel to help you to answer the following questions.

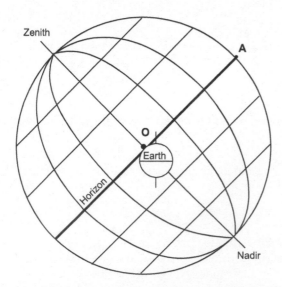

Figure 2. Horizontal Coordinate System for Observer at **O**

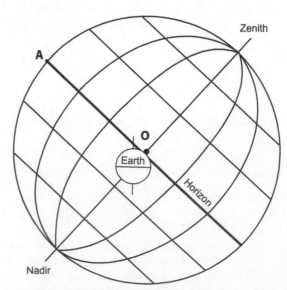

Figure 3. Horizontal Coordinate System for Observer at **O** Twelve Hours Later

Question 8.    What is the azimuth of each of the compass points (a) North, (b) East, (c) South, and (d) West?

Question 9.    What is the altitude of the zenith?

Question 10.    Can a value of azimuth be assigned to the zenith? [NOTE: When *Starry Night*™ moves to the zenith, it incorrectly assigns an azimuth value that depends upon the previous view direction.]

11.  Open the **Options** pane and expand the **Guides** and **Alt-Az Guides** layers. Select all of the options: **Local Equator (Horizon)**, **Grid**, **Meridian**, and **Poles**.

12.  Use the Gaze and Zoom buttons to look around the view.

The view shows a grid of the horizontal coordinate system. Parallel to the horizon line are circles of altitude. Meridians of azimuth run perpendicular to the horizon and converge on one pole of the coordinate system, the zenith, which is visible overhead. One particular meridian of azimuth, which contains the zenith and the north point on the horizon, is chosen as the reference meridian. It is called the Local Meridian, or simply the meridian, and it is marked in degrees of altitude in this view.

Question 11.    Are the circles of altitude great circles? Why or why not?

Question 12.    Are the meridians of azimuth great circles? Why or why not?

Question 13.    Which of the two coordinate angles depicted in Figure 1 ($\theta$ and $\Phi$) corresponds to (a) altitude, and (b) azimuth?

13.  Hide the **Horizon** and then use the Gaze and Zoom controls to look around the view again, particularly directly down at the nadir and directly up at the zenith.

Question 14.    In addition to the zenith and the north point on the compass, what other specific points are included on the great circle described by the local meridian?

Question 15.    What is the altitude of the nadir?

The horizontal coordinate system is convenient for describing the sky from one location at a particular time, to point out a particular position in the sky to a companion for example. However, these coordinates are specific to the observer's position on the surface of the Earth because different locations will have different horizon planes and zenith positions. Furthermore, these coordinates change with time.

The following observations demonstrate these characteristics.

14.  Open **Favourites > Observing Projects > Coordinate Systems > Altitude-Azimuth**.

The view shows the horizon and sky looking south from Munich, Germany, at noon on January 22, 2014. The horizontal coordinate system is displayed and the Sun and Venus are indicated with labels.

Question 16.    Using the local grid as a guide, what is your estimate of the altitude and azimuth of (a) the Sun, and (b) Venus from this location at this time and date?

15.  Use the HUD to find the Altitude and Azimuth of the Sun and of Venus.

Question 17.    As seen from Munich, Germany at noon on January 22, 2014, what are the altitude and azimuth of (a) the Sun, and (b) Venus?

You can now change your location upon Earth and again obtain the horizontal coordinates of these objects from this new position.

16. Change the viewing location to **Algiers, Algeria.**

17. Set the Gaze to the **S**outh, and use the HUD to determine the horizontal coordinates of the Sun and Venus from Algiers at noon on January 22, 2014.

**Question 18.** As seen from Algiers at noon on January 22, 2014, what are altitude and azimuth of (a) the Sun, and (b) Venus?

Comparison of these two sets of values for the horizontal coordinates of the Sun and Venus demonstrate that these values depend on the observer's location.

The horizontal coordinates of objects in the sky also change with time as the observer's location is carried eastward by the Earth's rotation. As an example, Figure 3 shows how the coordinate system for the observer at the location marked **O** in Figure 2 appears 12 hours later, when the Earth's rotation has carried the location through 180°. You can change the observing time at Algiers to show this effect.

18. Set the Time in the toolbar to **2:00:00 PM standard time**. (Warning: Ensure that the Time does not switch to Daylight Saving Time during this step.) Use the HUD to determine the horizontal coordinates of the Sun and of Venus.

**Question 19.** As seen from Algiers at 2:00:00 PM Standard time on January 22, 2014, what are the altitude and azimuth of (a) the Sun, and (b) Venus?

**Question 20.** What are the advantages and disadvantages of the horizontal coordinate system?

## C. Equatorial Coordinates

The horizontal coordinates of objects in the sky are specific to the observer's location and local time and thus are inconvenient when attempting to communicate an object's position to someone at another location. It is desirable to define a coordinate system in which the coordinates of objects in the sky do not vary with changes in the observer's location or the passage of time. One such coordinate system is the **equatorial coordinate system,** depicted in Figure 4.

In the equatorial coordinate system, the center of the celestial sphere coincides with the center of the Earth. The reference plane is an extension of the plane of the Earth's equator, hence the name for this coordinate system. This reference plane intersects the celestial sphere in a great circle called the **celestial equator.** The line perpendicular to this plane that passes through the center of the Earth thus coincides with the rotation axis of the Earth and points to the **North** and **South Celestial Poles** of the coordinate system.

In the equatorial coordinate system, the perpendicular angular distance of an object from the celestial equator is called **declination.** Declination is similar to altitude in the horizontal system and to latitude in the terrestrial coordinate system: It is measured in degrees and is positive north of the celestial equator and negative south of the celestial equator.

The coordinate denoting position around the celestial equator is called **right ascension.** The reference point from which an object's right ascension is measured is a specific point known as the **vernal equinox** (marked **A** in Figure 4). The vernal equinox is the point

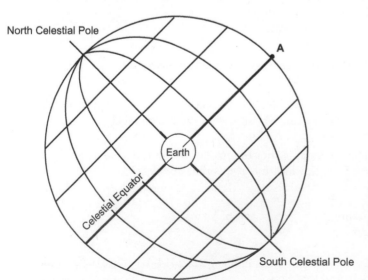

**Figure 4.** Equatorial Coordinate System

in the sky at which the Sun passes northward across the celestial equator in its apparent annual motion across our sky. Thus, the Sun is at this position on the first day of spring in the northern hemisphere of the Earth every year. Right ascension is usually measured in units of time. The reason for this is that, because of the Earth's rotation, the vernal equinox moves through 360° in 24 sidereal hours as seen by any individual observer. Right ascension increases in an **eastward** direction from the vernal equinox.

> **Question 21.**      Which of the two coordinate angles depicted in Figure 1 (θ and Φ) corresponds to (a) declination, and (b) right ascension?
>
> **Question 22.**      What will be the equivalent angle in degrees to 1 hour of Right Ascension?

> 19.   Open **Favourites > Observing Projects > Coordinate Systems > Coordinates From North Pole.**

The view shows the sky from the North Pole of Earth. The two coordinate systems are superimposed on the view, with the horizontal coordinate system for this location shown in grey and the equatorial coordinate system in red. The location of the North Pole provides a special perspective from which to compare the two coordinate systems. Note that the horizon and the celestial equator are coincident from this observing location.

Recall that in the horizontal coordinate system, the celestial sphere is centered on the observer's location on the surface of the Earth. The center of the celestial sphere in the equatorial coordinate system is at the center of the Earth. At the North Pole, the plane of the horizon (the reference plane in the horizontal coordinate system) is parallel to the plane of the Earth's equator (the reference plane in the equatorial coordinate system) and the zenith coincides with the north celestial pole. (In fact, the center of the celestial sphere shifts by a distance equal to the radius of the Earth between the two coordinate systems, but this distance is negligible compared to the infinite distance to the surface of the celestial sphere. Thus, in the view from the North Pole, the coordinate systems are equivalent and parallels of altitude and parallels of declination are coincident.)

This view also shows the position in the sky of the vernal equinox, the reference point for the equatorial coordinate system. The right ascension line (half of a great circle) that passes from the north celestial pole through the vernal equinox to the south celestial pole in this coordinate system is the zero line of right ascension, 0 hours. Right ascension in hours increases eastward. These values are shown by the grey labels along the celestial equator (which is equivalent to the horizon at this location) and indicate the right ascensions of other great circles shown in the equatorial coordinate grid.

> 20.   Use the Gaze buttons to look around the view. As you look towards the zenith, open the **Options** pane and turn off the **Poles** option under the Celestial Guides layer to remove the label for the North Celestial Pole (NCP) and turn on the **Poles** option under the Local Guides layer to display the label for the Zenith. Note that, from the North Pole of Earth, the Zenith and the North Celestial Pole are coincident.

> Question 23.      (a) What is the altitude of the North Celestial Pole for an observer at the North Pole of the Earth? (b) What is the declination of the North Celestial Pole? (c) Does your answer to part (b) depend on your observing location on the Earth? Why or why not?

> 21.   Select **File > Revert** from the menu.
> 22.   Click **Play** and observe the relative motion of the two coordinate grids.
> 23.   Select **Edit > Undo Time Flow** to return to the initial view.
> 24.   Change the Gaze to the **Zenith**.
> 25.   Click **Play** to observe the relative motion of the two coordinate grids again in this view.

Note that the stars all appear to follow circles around the zenith when observed from the North Pole of Earth.

**Question 24.** How do you explain the relative motion between the equatorial coordinate system and the horizontal coordinate system as time passes for an observer on the Earth? [HINT: Consider what effect the rotation of the Earth will have upon each of these coordinate systems.]

**Question 25.** How do the stars and other objects in the sky move relative to the two coordinate system grids as time progresses?

26. Open **Favourites > Observing Projects > Coordinate Systems > Coordinates From Mid-Northern Latitude.**

At the left of the view, you will notice a label indicating the star **Hamal**. Observe and compare the altitude and azimuth coordinates of this star with its right ascension and declination coordinates as seen from this mid-northern latitude of Earth.

27. Configure the HUD to include **Dec (JNow)** and **RA (JNow)**.

28. Use the HUD to find the Altitude and Azimuth, as well as the equatorial coordinates of RA (JNow) and Dec (JNow) for the star Hamal.

29. Open the **Info** pane for the star Hamal and expand the **Position in Sky** layer where the Altitude and Azimuth and the RA and Dec of Hamal are also displayed.

30. Click **Play** and observe how the passage of time affects the values of the coordinates of this star in the two different systems.

31. Open **Favourites > Observing Projects > Coordinate Systems > Coordinates from North Pole.** Note the local and equatorial coordinates of the star Hamal from this location as given in the HUD. Select **Edit > Undo "Favourite" Item** and **Edit > Redo "Favourite" Item** to see the coordinates of this star at each location again.

**Question 26.** Is either coordinate system independent of the observer's position; in other words, does either coordinate system designate coordinates that remain constant from location to location?

**Question 27.** Is either coordinate system independent of the passage of time; in other words, does either coordinate system designate coordinates that remain constant over time?

**Question 28.** If you wanted to produce an enduring map of the sky with coordinates for the objects that appear on the celestial sphere, which coordinate system would you choose: horizontal or equatorial?

**Question 29.** If you and a friend were observing the sky together from the same location and you wanted to indicate the position of a particular star to your friend, which coordinate system would be most useful?

**Question 30.** If you wanted a fellow astronomer in a distant city to observe a specific object in the sky, what coordinates would you provide to your colleague?

In fact, the equatorial coordinate system is locked to the Earth and is not a fixed system since the precession of the spinning Earth results in a slow drift of the polar axis and therefore a slow drift in the Right Ascension and Declination values of any object. Thus, these coordinate values will change slowly with time and when specified, must be assigned an epoch for which they apply. Astronomers (or their computers!) routinely "precess" the coordinates for objects that they want to observe before pointing their telescopes. Precession of the Earth is discussed in more detail in a later project in this book.

## D. Bonus: Other Coordinate Systems

*Starry Night*™ includes overlays of two other coordinate systems on the celestial sphere. The first of these, the ecliptic coordinate system, is used mainly for observations of objects in the solar system.

32. Click **Home.** Open the **Options** pane, expand the **Ecliptic Guides** and click on all the checkboxes except the **Axes** option. Then use the Gaze and Zoom controls and hide the **Horizon** and **Daylight** as necessary to examine the components of the ecliptic coordinate system.

**Question 31.**    (a) Where is the center of the ecliptic coordinate system? (b) What is the reference plane in this system?

**Question 32.**    Do the positions of the stars move relative to the ecliptic coordinate system as time progresses?

The second coordinate system is the galactic coordinate system, which is used in studies of our own galaxy.

33. Click **Home.** Open the **Options** pane and click all of the checkboxes under **Galactic Guides** except the **Axes** option. Then use the Gaze and Zoom controls and hide the **Horizon** and **Daylight** as necessary to examine the components of the galactic coordinate system.

**Question 33.**    (a) Where is the center of the galactic coordinate system? (b) What is the reference plane in this system?

**Question 34.**    Do the positions of the stars move relative to the galactic coordinate system as time progresses?

## E. Conclusion

In this project, you have learned about spherical geometry and how we apply this geometry to generate various coordinate systems that are used by astronomers to map the sky.

# Changing Latitude 4

The ancient Greeks knew that if they traveled south, they would see stars above the southern horizon that could not be seen from Greece. Conversely, when they traveled north, stars that they could see in Greece no longer rose above the southern horizon.

The Greeks realized that this is exactly what would happen if the Earth were round. On a flat Earth, the same stars should be above the horizon for all observers, regardless of where they were located. On a round Earth, on the other hand, our view of the sky changes when we move to different latitudes.

In this observing project you will learn how our view of the stars and constellations changes as we move to different latitudes on the Earth.

## A. The Southern Sky Observed From Northern Latitudes

1. Launch *Starry Night*™ and configure the HUD to include **Altitude**.
2. Open **Favourites > Observing Projects > Changing Latitude > Mexico City**.

The view shows the sky looking south from Mexico City, Mexico, at 1:29:30 AM Standard Time on April 24, 2015. The stick figure outline of the constellation Scorpius is shown. The top of this figure is shaped like a letter "T" tilted over on its right side, and the bottom is shaped like a fishhook. The star at the center of the "T" labeled Dschubba will serve as a reference star in the next series of observations.

3. If you wish to remove the outline of Scorpius, choose **Deselect Scorpius** from the contextual menu. Use **File > Revert** to retrieve the outline of Scorpius.

Note that the reference star, Dschubba, is due south in this view, transiting the meridian at this time. Therefore, you are seeing it at its highest position in the sky from this observing location. This occurs because the stars and constellations rise in the eastern part of the sky and set in the western part, just as the Sun does. They are highest in the sky when they are half way between rising and setting (i.e., when they are due south as seen from the northern hemisphere).

4. Open the **Status** pane and expand the **Location** layer. Note the Latitude of Mexico City in Data Table 1 at the end of this project. [TIP: To record data more easily, you can use the perforations in this book to tear out the Data Table page.]
5. Use the HUD to find the Altitude of Dschubba and record this value in Data Table 1.

In order to see how our view of the sky changes with latitude, we will move progressively northward and note the altitude of Dschubba when it transits the meridian at each new location.

6. Select **Favourites > Observing Projects > Changing Latitude > Chicago**.

7. Obtain the Latitude of Chicago from the Location layer in the **Status** pane, as before, and record this in Data Table 1. Use the HUD to find the Altitude of Dschubba as seen from Chicago and record this value in Data Table 1.

8. To answer the following questions you may want to switch back and forth between the views from Mexico City and Chicago. To do so, open the **Favourites** pane, expand the **Observing Projects > Changing Latitudes** folder and select **Mexico City** and **Chicago** alternately from the list.

**Question 1.**  In which direction does the constellation Scorpius move with respect to the south horizon as the viewing location moves north from Mexico City to Chicago?

**Question 2.**  Why is the time at which Dschubba transits the meridian different for the two locations?

9. Select **Favourites > Observing Projects > Changing Latitude > Regina**. You can see that the Time is different again in order to place Dschubba on the meridian at this new location.

10. Use the **Status** pane and the HUD to find the Latitude of Regina and the Altitude of Dschubba and record these values in Data Table 1.

**Question 3.**  Where is Scorpius with respect to the horizon on the screen, as seen from Regina? Is any part of Scorpius missing?

11. Select **Favourites > Observing Projects > Changing Latitude > Fairbanks** and note the Latitude of Fairbanks and the Altitude of Dschubba in Data Table 1.

12. To help answer the following questions, open the **Favourites** pane, expand the **Observing Projects > Changing Latitude** folder and select **Mexico City, Chicago, Regina,** and **Fairbanks** in turn.

**Question 4.**  Where is Scorpius with respect to the horizon on the screen as seen from Fairbanks? What part of Scorpius is visible? Where is the rest of Scorpius, relative to the horizon?

**Question 5.**  For which of the cities in Data Table 1 is the outline of the stick figure of Scorpius completely above the horizon?

13. With the data from the observations that you obtained and recorded in Data Table 1, use Graph Template 1 at the end of this project to plot the Altitude of Dschubba (A) on the Y-axis against the Latitude of the Observing Location ($\lambda$) on the X-axis.

**Question 6.**  For an observer traveling north, at about what latitude would the reference star Dschubba NEVER rise above the horizon?

**Question 7.**  Which of the following describes the relationship between the latitude of the observing location and the altitude of a reference star?

(a) As latitude increases, the reference star's altitude increases.

(b) There is no relationship between the reference star's altitude and the observer's latitude.

(c) As latitude increases, the reference star's altitude decreases.

**Question 8.**  Suppose that a scientist in Fairbanks has applied for a research grant to study a globular cluster of stars near the middle of Scorpius, using an observatory just outside Fairbanks. If you were on the grant-assessment committee, what would be your response to this proposal? Would your response change if the research proposal included a request for funds to travel to an observatory in Texas?

**Question 9.** What is the mathematical relationship between λ, the latitude of the observing location on the Earth, and A, the Altitude of the reference star Dschubba?

    (a) $λ – A$ = Constant.

    (b) $A = 90° – λ$.

    (c) $λ + A$ = Constant.

    (d) $A$ = Constant $× λ$

## B. Altitude of the Pole Star from Different Latitudes

14. Select **Favourites > Observing Projects > Changing Latitude > Minneapolis**.

The view is now northwards from Minneapolis, Minnesota, at 8:23:00 PM standard time on October 1, 2015, with daylight hidden. Polaris, the Pole Star, is labeled. Identify the Big Dipper in the constellation Ursa Major on the left of the view.

15. **Run time forward** and watch what happens in the sky.

**Question 10.** What happens to stars on the left side of the view as time progresses? That is, do they move upwards or downwards?

**Question 11.** What happens to stars on the right side of the view as time progresses? That is, do they move upwards or downwards?

**Question 12.** Is there one star that appears to remain at rest, while all other stars move in circles around it? Which star is this?

As the sky rotates, watch what happens to the Big Dipper, especially between about 10 PM and 1 AM. In the lower left side of the view, stars are setting below the horizon, and on the lower right side of the view, stars are rising above the horizon. From Minneapolis, however, the Big Dipper never sets. It approaches the northern horizon, but passes above this horizon without setting, and then gets higher in the sky again.

As the Big Dipper is starting to rise again, you will notice the star labeled **Vega** on the left side of the view. Vega, a bright, blue main-sequence star in the constellation Lyra the Lyre, is the second brightest star in the northern hemisphere.

**Question 13.** What happens to Vega at about 3:45 AM?

Stars or constellations that never set as they move in circles around the Pole are called **circumpolar**.

**Question 14.** As seen from Minneapolis, which of the following statements is correct?

    (a) Vega is circumpolar while the stars of the Big Dipper are not.

    (b) The stars of the Big Dipper are circumpolar while Vega is not.

    (c) Neither Vega nor the stars of the Big Dipper are circumpolar.

    (d) The stars of the Big Dipper and Vega are circumpolar.

16. Select **File > Revert** from the menu to return to the initial view.

17. From the **Status** pane, note the Latitude of Minneapolis in Data Table 2 at the end of this project.

18. Use the HUD to find the Altitude of Polaris and record this value in Data Table 2.

**Question 15.** How does the altitude of Polaris compare to the latitude of Minneapolis?

19. Select **Favourites > Observing Projects > Changing Latitude > Houston**.

This view, with daylight removed, is to the north from Houston, Texas, at the same time and date as the previous view from Minneapolis.

20. Use the **Status** pane and HUD to find the Latitude of Houston and the Altitude of Polaris from Houston and record these values in Data Table 2.

   Question 16.   How does the altitude of the Pole Star, Polaris, compare with the latitude of Houston?

21. **Run time forward** and watch what happens in the sky.

Note that all of the stars of the Big Dipper except the one at the top right corner of the bowl (the one closest to the Pole Star) set below the horizon and then rise again later.

   Question 17.   How does the number of stars that are circumpolar as seen from Houston compare with the number that are circumpolar as seen from Minneapolis (i.e., Are more, less or the same number of stars circumpolar, as seen from Houston)?

   Question 18.   Based on your observations, which one of the following statements do you think is correct?

   (a) The altitude of the Pole Star is equal to the latitude of the observing location.

   (b) The altitude of the Pole Star equals 90° minus the latitude of the observing location.

   (c) The altitude of the Pole Star is not affected by the latitude of the observing location.

22. Select **Favourites > Observing Projects > Changing Latitude > Equator**.

The view is north toward Polaris at the same time and date as the previous observations.

23. **Run time forward**.

   Question 19.   Looking north from the Equator, are any stars circumpolar?

24. Select **Magnify** from the contextual menu for Polaris and then change the Time Flow Rate to **3000x**.

   Question 20.   Is Polaris circumpolar as seen from the equator?

25. Select **Favourites > Observing Projects > Changing Latitude > North Pole**.
26. **Run time forward**. As time flows, use the Gaze controls to scroll the view through a full 360°.
27. Click the **Z** button in the Gaze section of the toolbar to see Polaris near the zenith.
28. Select **View > Alt/Az Guides > Zenith/Nadir** from the menu and change the Time Flow Rate to **3000x**.

From this simulation, you can see that the Pole Star moves around the zenith in a small circle because it is not quite at the position of the North Celestial Pole, which occupies the zenith from the North Pole.

> **Question 21.** From the North Pole, are there any stars that are **not** circumpolar?
>
> **Question 22.** If you were south of the equator, say in Australia, would you expect to see circumpolar constellations anywhere in the sky? If so, in what part of the sky would they be?
>
> **Question 23.** At which latitude on Earth is it possible over the course of a full year to see all of the stars of the entire celestial sphere?

29. Set the Zoom to **5°**.

30. Select **View > Celestial Guides > Celestial Poles** from the menu and then select **View >Alt/Az Guides > Zenith/Nadir** from the menu to remove this marker.

31. Click **Stop** and use the Angular Separation tool to measure the angular distance between Polaris and the North Celestial Pole.

32. Select **Favourites > Observing Projects > Changing Latitude > Minneapolis**. Change the **Time** in the toolbar to **2:23:00 AM** and use the HUD to find the Altitude of Polaris. Compare this value with the value you recorded in Data Table 2.

> **Question 24.** What is the angular separation of the Pole Star from the North Celestial Pole at this time in history?
>
> **Question 25.** How do your observations in the previous two steps affect your answer to Question 18?

## C. Simple Celestial Navigation

Imagine that you have decided to lead an expedition recreating Columbus's historic 1492 voyage to the New World. Your only navigational aids will be a compass and a quadrant, a device used to measure the elevation angle (altitude) of stars and planets.

Like Columbus, you leave Palos de la Frontera, Spain, on August 3 and use dead reckoning and coastal navigation to reach La Gomera, in the Spanish Canary Islands. There you take on supplies and effect any necessary repairs to your ships.

On September 6, you set sail from La Gomera to cross the Atlantic Ocean, intending to arrive in Nassau, Bahamas, (latitude 25° 3' N) some time in October.

33. Select **Favourites > Observing Projects > Changing Latitude > La Gomera**.

34. **Run time forward** and observe the night sky, looking particularly for stars and constellations that will aid you in your navigation. Locate the Pole Star and note its Altitude.

Unfortunately, four days into the voyage, a storm that lasts for five days hits your ship and blows you off course. Adding to the difficulty, a careless sailor dropped the compass overboard during the second day of the storm. You are lost. Nine days after leaving La Gomera, the night sky is finally clear. You need to determine whether to correct your subsequent heading toward the north or south in order to reach Nassau.

35. Select **Favourites > Observing Projects > Changing Latitude > Lost**.

36. **Run time forward** and observe the sky through the night.

> **Question 26.** To get back on course, do you need to adjust your heading to the south or north of west after surviving the storm?

## D. Effect of Observer's Latitude on the Sun's Rising Angle

It is interesting to explore the path of the Sun as it rises above the eastern horizon and to measure the angle that this path makes with the horizon from various latitudes. There is a great difference between sunrises (and in an equivalent manner, sunsets) when they are observed from different latitudes. For example, at the equator, the Sun appears rather suddenly and rises rapidly into the sky after only a short period of twilight. In contrast, at high latitudes the Sun moves more slowly across the horizon after a prolonged period of twilight. At very high latitudes during the summer, the Sun is always above the horizon.

In this section of the project, you will measure the angle between the Sun's track and the horizon, which we can call the "rising angle," and investigate the effect of changing the latitude of the observing location on this angle.

> 37. Select **Favourites > Observing Projects > Changing Latitude > Seattle Sunrise**.

The view shows the Sun just rising in the East as seen from Seattle on March 20, 2014. This date, the first day of spring in the northern hemisphere, (and the first day of fall or autumn in the southern hemisphere!) has been selected to place the Sun very close to the East point on the horizon at sunrise as a convenient reference point. The time step is set to one hour.

> 38. **Step time forward** one hour and note the direction in which the Sun has moved.

The Sun will have moved upwards and to the side during this first hour after sunrise.

**Question 27.** In which sideward direction has the Sun moved (e.g., W, E,...)?

The geometry of the Sun's position one hour after sunrise is shown in Figure 1. In the hour since rising, the Sun has moved some distance upwards from the horizon and some distance sideways from the East point on the horizon. The distance that the Sun has moved above the horizon in the interval of one hour is the shortest distance between the Sun and the horizon. This is the distance SH in Figure 1, measured along the line that intersects the horizon at a right angle. As you can see from the figure, the line SE from the Sun to the East point of the horizon is the hypotenuse of a right triangle. (In practice, the track of the Sun across the sky will be slightly curved and the use of its position one hour after sunrise will underestimate the true rising angle, but this method is sufficiently accurate for our purposes.)

You can measure two angular separations, SH and SE, on the sky and these can be assumed for this purpose to be distances. The ratio of these two "distances," SH / SE, is the sine of the rising angle, θ, and is a trigonometric function written as sin θ. The inverse sine of this value gives the rising angle, θ.

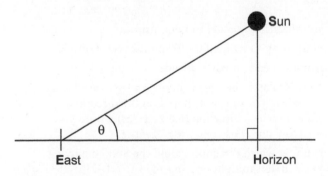

**Figure 1.** Rising Angle, θ, of the Sun

**Sequence 1**

39. Open the **Status** pane and expand the **Location** layer. Note the Latitude of the current viewing location and record it in the appropriate column of Data Table 3 at the end of this project.

40. Use the Angular Separation cursor to measure the angular distance from the Sun to the point on the horizon directly below the Sun. Note the measurement in degrees and arcminutes, to the nearest arcminute, in Data Table 3 under the heading Measured SH. Convert this measurement to decimal degrees by dividing the number of arcminutes by 60 and adding this quotient to the number of degrees in the measurement. Write this value in the column labeled SH in Data Table 3.

41. Next, measure the angular distance from the Sun to the East point of the horizon. Note this measurement in degrees and minutes of arc to the nearest arcminute in Data Table 3 under the column labeled Measured SE. Then convert this measurement to decimal degrees and write the result in the column labeled SE in Data Table 3.

42. Calculate the ratio SH/SE and enter the value in Data Table 3 under the column Sin θ.

43. Use the inverse sine function on a calculator or spreadsheet to determine the angle, θ, in degrees that corresponds to the calculated value of Sin θ.

In order to explore the effect of the observer's latitude on this "rising angle" of the Sun, you will need to repeat your observations for the other locations on the Earth that are listed in Data Table 3.

44. For each location listed in Data Table 3, select the appropriately named **Sunrise** view from the **Favourites > Observing Projects > Changing Latitude** folder.

45. **Step time forward** by 1 hour and repeat the procedure outlined in Sequence 1 above.

The position and time of sunrise will vary somewhat between sites because of time zone differences. The situation at the North Pole is interesting. You will have to consider what is the "rising angle" if the Sun just skims across the horizon!

**Question 28.** At what angle from the horizon does the Sun rise for someone at 0° latitude?

**Question 29.** At what angle from the horizon does the Sun rise for someone at 90° latitude?

**Question 30.** How does the rising angle of the Sun change as you move from Quito, Ecuador, (0° latitude) to Honolulu, then to Seattle, to Murmansk, and finally to the North Pole (90° latitude)?

**Question 31.** Based on your answers to the questions above, which ONE of the following statements is correct?

(a) The rising angle of the Sun at your location is equal to your latitude.

(b) The rising angle of the Sun at your location is equal to 90° minus your latitude.

(c) The rising angle of the Sun does not depend on your latitude.

**Question 32.** Suppose that you are in Dunedin, New Zealand, the time is noon, and you are facing east, toward the point on the horizon where the Sun rises. Based on the direction toward which the Sun rises in Dunedin, in which direction (left or right) would you need to turn to face the Sun at noon? How does this compare to Seattle?

**Question 33.** Based on how the Sun rises in Dunedin, in which direction would the Sun be moving if you were facing toward it at noon (from left to right or from right to left)? How does this compare to what you saw in Seattle at noon?

46. Check your answer to the previous question directly by opening **Favourites > Observing Projects > Changing Latitude > Dunedin Sunrise** and adjusting the Time in the toolbar to **12:00:00 PM** (noon).
47. Change the Gaze to the **N**orth.
48. Set the Time Flow Rate to **1 minute**, and **Run time forward**.

Question 34.    Toward which compass direction would the Sun be moving at noon in Dunedin (from east to west or from west to east)? Check the compass directions near the bottom of the view. How does this compare to what you would see in Seattle?

Question 35.    Describe the differences between the sunrise in Dunedin, New Zealand, and the sunrise in Seattle?

## E. Challenge: The Rising and Setting of Objects at Night

We have observed the rising of the Sun in both hemispheres. It is interesting to verify that other objects, when observed at night, also show the same motion and geometry as they pass over the horizon.

49. Click the **Home** button and set up a view that allows you to observe the rising and setting angles of the Sun and the stars from your home location.

Question 36.    How does the rising angle of the stars compare with that of the Sun?

Question 37.    How do the rising and setting angles of the stars compare?

Question 38.    Use your observations to calculate the latitude of your home location. How does your result compare with the Latitude for your home location as given in the Status pane?

Question 39.    What are the features of the Earth that produce these rising and setting angles of the celestial objects?

## F. Conclusions

In this project, you have seen that the view of the sky becomes more and more restricted as you move from lower to higher latitudes until only about one-half of the sky is visible at the pole. Related to this, you have seen that more and more of the stars on this celestial sphere become circumpolar as you move to higher latitudes.

The other major fact that you have verified is that the angle between the horizon and the North Celestial Pole, approximated at this time in history by the Pole Star, is equal to the latitude of the observing site. You have had the opportunity to discover how early navigators made use of this fact.

You evaluated the relationship between the observer's latitude and the angle at which objects rise and set relative to the horizon and observed the difference in sunrises between the two hemispheres and the unusual sunrises at the North Pole.

**Data Table 1.** Altitude of Dschubba Transit from Cities at Various Northern Latitudes

| Location | Latitude (λ) | Altitude of Dschubba (A) |
|---|---|---|
| Mexico City, Mexico | | |
| Chicago, USA | | |
| Regina, Canada | | |
| Fairbanks, USA | | |

**Data Table 2.** Latitude and Pole Star Altitude from Minneapolis and Houston

| Location | Latitude (λ) | Pole Star Altitude (A) |
|---|---|---|
| Minneapolis | | |
| Houston | | |

**Data Table 3.** Rising Angle of the Sun from Locations at Different Latitudes

| Location | Latitude | Measured SH | | SH | Measured SE | | SE | Sin θ | θ |
|---|---|---|---|---|---|---|---|---|---|
| | ° | ° | ' | ° | ° | ' | ° | = SH / SE | ° |
| Seattle | | | | | | | | | |
| Honolulu | | | | | | | | | |
| Quito | | | | | | | | | |
| Dunedin | | | | | | | | | |
| Murmansk | | | | | | | | | |
| North Pole | | | | | | | | | |

**Graph Template 1.** Altitude of Dschubba vs. Latitude

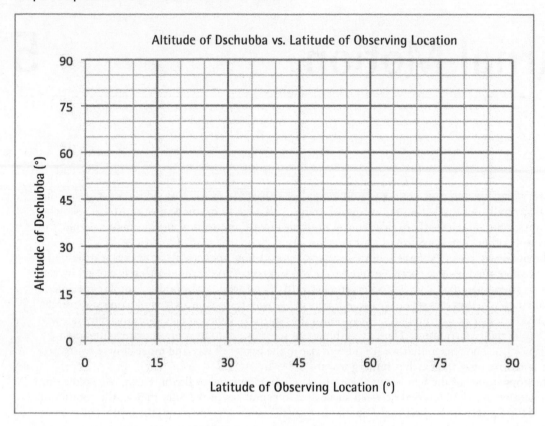

# Diurnal Motion 5

Every day, the Sun rises in the east and moves (or appears to move) toward the west across the sky, finally setting below the western horizon. All objects in our sky—the Moon, planets, stars, and galaxies—share this **diurnal motion**, but we notice this motion only at night for most objects other than the Sun.

The ancient Greeks explained diurnal motion by assuming that the Earth was stationary and that the rest of the universe rotated around it. We now know that diurnal motion is caused by the Earth's rotation on its axis, carrying observers eastward. If you are unsure of this, a simple experiment may convince you that it is true. Try turning yourself slowly toward the left while looking straight ahead and watch your surroundings. Every object that starts on your left will appear to move slowly toward your right as you turn. Thus, everything you see appears to move in the opposite direction to your motion. The reason that we see the Sun rise in the east each day and move slowly westward until it sets is because the Earth is turning toward the east.

The appearance of the Sun in our sky every day is fundamental to life on Earth. We define our time system by the time interval between successive appearances of the Sun; that is, the rotational period of the Earth with respect to the Sun, known as the **solar day**. However, the Earth's motion in its orbit around the Sun means that the Sun, as seen from Earth, appears to move slowly against the background stars. Thus, the solar day is not the intrinsic rotation period of the Earth, since it uses the Sun, a moving object, as a marker. The more fundamental rotation period of the Earth with respect to the background stars is known as the **sidereal day**.

In this project you will observe the diurnal motion of the Sun and other celestial objects. You will also measure the sidereal day and compare it to the solar day.

## A. Characteristics of the Diurnal Motion of Objects in the Sky

Observations of the diurnal motion of objects in the sky can be used to evaluate some of the characteristics of the Earth's rotation.

1. Launch *Starry Night*™ and configure the HUD to include **RA (JNow)**.
2. Select **View > Solar System > Satellites** to remove artificial Earth-orbiting satellites from the view.
3. Set the Date to **September 21** and the Gaze to the **East**.
4. Select **Labels > Planets-Moons**.
5. Click the **Sunrise** button in the toolbar and set the Time Flow Rate to **300x**.
6. Observe the sunrise and then increase the Time Flow Rate to **3000x** to watch the Sun's motion across the whole sky. Use the Gaze controls to keep the Sun in the view.
7. **Stop** time flow once the sun sets below the horizon.

**Question 1.**    In which direction (north, south, east, or west) does the Sun appear to move?

**Question 2.**    If the diurnal motion of the Sun is caused by the rotation of the Earth, in which direction is an observer on the Earth moving?

**Question 3.**    Does the Sun appear to move at a steady rate or does it appear to speed up, slow down, or move irregularly?

**Question 4.**    Is there any way to tell from your observations whether this motion is the result of the Sun moving across the sky or the Earth rotating beneath the sky?

The Moon and several of the planets may appear as sunset approaches and stars become visible after sunset. It is instructive to examine the motion of these objects briefly to show how they share a common motion produced by the Earth's rotation.

8. Set the Gaze to the **E**ast.

9. **Run time forward** at 300×. Observe the motion of the objects in the sky. Use the Gaze controls to look all around the sky.

10. Hide **Daylight** when the Sun rises again.

11. Set the Gaze to the **S**outh and observe the motion of objects in this region of the sky.

**Question 5.**    In which direction do the stars appear to move?

**Question 6.**    In which direction do the Moon and planets appear to move?

To the Earthbound observer, it is apparent that the natural heavenly bodies appear to share a common motion. This common apparent motion results from the Earth's rotation, at least over this limited time frame. However, many of these objects move with respect to the background. In the next sequence, you will observe the paths of these different natural celestial bodies across the sky. Your observations will help you to determine which of the celestial objects, or class of objects, most clearly reflects the rotation of the Earth on its axis by their diurnal motion. You can first examine the motion of the Sun in more detail by using *Starry Night*™ to trace its motion across the sky.

12. Select **Favourites > Observing Projects > Diurnal Motion > Sun's Diurnal Path**.

The view shows the Sun in the sky, looking south from Reliance in northern Canada, at a latitude of 62° N, on September 27, 2008, at 12:00:00 PM local standard time.

13. **Run time forward** at 15,000× until the Sun returns almost to its original position and stop time flow. *Starry Night*™ traces the path of the Sun through time with a green line.

14. **Centre** the view on the Sun and set the Zoom to **5°**.

15. Find the time at which the Sun returns to its original position and has traced a complete path around the sky.

16. Hide the **Horizon** and use the Hand tool to explore the path that the Sun has made across the sky.

**Question 7.**    What is the general shape of the path that the Sun traces in the sky?

**Question 8.**    Does the Sun take exactly 24 hours to return to the same position in the sky?

17. Select **Favourites > Observing Projects > Diurnal Motion > Diurnal Paths of Moon and Planets**.

The view is the same as that in the previous sequence except that the Moon, Mercury, Venus, Mars, and Saturn are labeled in addition to the Sun. Note that the time is midday, 12:00:00 PM.

18. **Run time forward** at 20,000× and **Stop** time flow when the Sun is close to its original position. Adjust the Time to place the Sun as close as possible to its original position. You may want to hide **Daylight** to make this observation easier. You might also **Zoom in** on the Sun to adjust the **Time** more precisely. Then **Zoom out** to the full view again.

19. Use the Hand tool to explore the paths that these objects have traced out in the sky. Hide the **Horizon** to see the complete paths.

20. Select **File > Revert** and press the **D** key on the keyboard to step forward in time by 1 day to display the positions of these objects after this interval of time.

Question 9.  How long does it take for the Sun to return to its starting point, in solar time?

Question 10.  What is the overall shape of the path that the planets trace in the sky?

Question 11.  Do the planets and the Moon all return to approximately their original positions at the same time as the Sun? Why do you think that this is so?

Question 12.  Which of the labeled objects seems to be furthest from its starting position after this time interval? [HINT: Step 20 will help to answer this question.]

Question 13.  Based on their observed deviation from their original positions after one day, which of these objects most accurately reflects the rotation of the Earth?

In the following sequence, you will observe the diurnal motion of the background stars and explore the definition of sidereal time and the length of the sidereal day.

21. Open **Favourites > Observing Projects > Diurnal Motion > Diurnal Paths of Stars**.

The view is the same as that of the previous sequences, but now the time has been set to 5:00:00 PM. Also, *Starry Night*™ has been set to hide the Moon, Sun and planets and to show *only* the brightest stars in the sky.

22. Hide **Daylight** and then click **Play**. Observe the stars as they move across the sky. The stars should leave a track of their motion. [NOTE: It is possible that the graphics equipment of your computer will not support the display of these trails. If this is the case on your computer, jump to the alternate instructions beginning at step 29.]

23. Select **File > Revert** from the menu to return to the initial configuration and erase the star trails from the screen.

24. Select **View > Alt-Az Guides > Zenith/Nadir** from the menu.

25. Set the Gaze first to the **N**orth and then to the **Z**enith so that the Gaze panel shows Alt: 90° Az: 0°.

26. Hide **Daylight** from the view.

27. **Run time forward** at 1000× and observe the paths traced out by the diurnal motion of the stars in this region of the sky. **Stop** time flow once the stars have traced out a complete path.

28. If your graphics equipment successfully showed star trails, skip the next sequence of instructions, steps 29–31.

29. Select **Favourites > Observing Projects > Diurnal Motion > Diurnal Paths of Stars – No Trails**.

30. Hide **Daylight** in the view. The star Sabik just above the S point of the horizon is labeled in the view.

31. **Run time forward** until the stars have completed a full path around the sky and the star Sabik is again above the S point of the horizon. Adjust the minutes and seconds of the time to return Sabik to its original position above the south point of the horizon.

Question 14.  Is the motion of the stars smooth and regular, or do they appear to speed up and slow down as they move across the sky?

Question 15.  What is the shape of the path that the stars trace out in the sky?

**Question 16.**  Do the stars move in a clockwise or counter-clockwise direction in the view?

**Question 17.**  Is the path of the stars in this region of the sky a closed curve? In other words, do the stars return to exactly the same position in the sky after a period of time?

**Question 18.**  Do all of the stars visible in the view return to their starting points simultaneously?

**Question 19.**  From your observations of the diurnal motions of the Sun, the Moon, several planets, and the stars, which of these objects do you think most clearly reflects the actual rotation of the Earth on its axis?

**Question 20.**  Does the Earth rotate smoothly on its axis or does it speed up and slow down over the course of a day and a night?

## B. Orientation in Space of the Rotation Axis of the Earth

The paths that the stars trace across the sky as a consequence of the rotation of the Earth are called **diurnal circles**. The center of these diurnal circles indicates the orientation of the Earth's axis in space. This axis passes through the North and South Poles of the Earth and its extension intersects the celestial sphere at the **North** and **South Celestial Poles**.

The plane that passes through the center of the Earth and is oriented perpendicular to its rotational axis intersects the surface of the Earth at the equator. The extension of this plane intersects the celestial sphere at the **celestial equator**.

32. Open **Favourites > Observing Projects > Diurnal Motion > Rotating Earth.**

The view is from a point in space hovering 11,000 kilometers above the surface of the Earth. The red line on the image of the Earth indicates the Earth's equator, while the red line crossing the sky behind the Earth is the celestial equator. Blue and yellow poles indicate the North and South Poles of the Earth, respectively, and indicate the axis around which the Earth rotates. The boundaries and labels of the constellations are displayed on the stellar background. From the perspective of a point on the equatorial plane of the Earth, you can see that the Celestial Equator and the Earth's equator are aligned.

33. Use the Location Scroller to look all around the view. You will notice that the North and South Celestial Poles are marked on the sky.

**Question 21.**  In which constellation in the sky is the North Celestial Pole?

**Question 22.**  In which constellation in the sky is the South Celestial Pole?

**Question 23.**  Toward which constellations is the rotation axis of the Earth pointed?

34. Select **File > Revert** and then click **Play** to observe the Earth's rotation against the background stars. The stars remain stationary in the view because the observing location is fixed with respect to the stars as time advances.

35. Now use the Location Scroller to observe the view of the Earth rotating in space from different perspectives, particularly from positions looking down on the Earth from above each of its poles.

**Question 24.**  When looking nearly along the rotational axis of the Earth toward the North Celestial Pole from a position over the South Pole, (a) in which sense does the Earth rotate, clockwise or counter-clockwise? (b) toward which compass direction does an observer on the Earth move?

**Question 25.**  When looking nearly along the rotational axis of the Earth toward the South Celestial Pole from a position over the North Pole in a direction approximately opposite to the view described in the previous question, (a) in which sense does the Earth rotate, clockwise or counter-clockwise? (b) toward which compass direction does an observer on the Earth move?

36. **Open Favourites > Observing Projects > Diurnal Motion > Diurnal Circles.**

37. Set the viewing location to a position on the Earth where you expect the diurnal circles traced out by the stars to be centered on the zenith. [HINT: Where on the Earth would the zenith coincide with a celestial pole?]

38. Select **View > Alt-Az Guides > Zenith/Nadir** to label these locations in your sky.

39. Set the Gaze to the **Z**enith.

40. Hide **Daylight** and then click **Play** to confirm that the diurnal circles traced out by the stars are centered on the zenith at the location you have chosen.

**Question 26.**   (a) Where on the surface of the Earth are the diurnal circles traced out by the stars centered on the zenith? (b) In which sense do the stars appear to rotate from this location, or these locations, clockwise or counter-clockwise?

The orientation of the rotation axis of the Earth is important in the mounting of an astronomical telescope. In an **equatorial mount,** the **polar axis** of the telescope is aligned accurately with the Earth's axis, as shown schematically in Figure 1. An observer in the northern hemisphere would point this axis of the telescope to the North Celestial Pole, and a southern hemisphere observer would point this axis to the South Celestial Pole.

A clock drive mounted on this polar axis can rotate the telescope at the appropriate rate for it to follow the diurnal path of objects in the sky by counteracting the rotation of the Earth. Without such tracking, the rotation of the Earth quickly carries objects out of the small field of view of a telescope. The second axis of rotation on the telescope mount, the **declination axis,** is aligned perpendicular to the polar axis, and is used to point the telescope at any declination in order to follow any object in the sky.

**Question 27.**   An observer in the northern hemisphere uses a telescope with a clock drive on its polar axis to observe the sky. Could this observer use the same telescope as easily in the southern hemisphere? Why or why not?

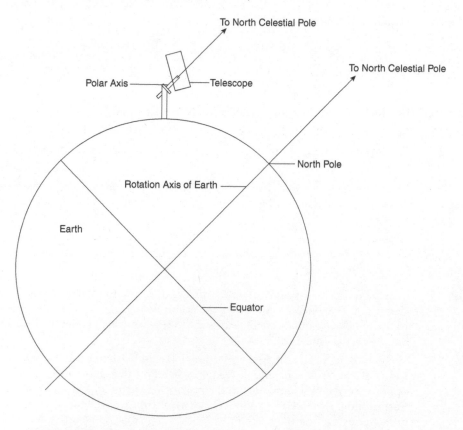

**Figure 1.** Polar axis of a telescope

## C. Diurnal Motion and the Duration of the Day

In this section, you will determine how long it takes for the Earth to make one complete rotation on its axis. This period is defined as the **day**. Each day is divided into 24 equal hours. Each hour, in turn, is divided into 60 equal minutes and each minute is divided into 60 equal seconds.

To measure the duration of the rotation period of the Earth, use an imaginary line on the sky called the **meridian** that passes through the north and south points of an observer's horizon and also through the observer's zenith.

41. Open **Favourites > Observing Projects > Diurnal Motion > Solar and Sidereal Day**.
42. Use the Hand tool to look around the view and note particularly the line representing the meridian for this viewing location, superimposed on a sky in which daylight has been removed.

As the Earth rotates, the meridian sweeps across the sky. The meridian is fixed to the observer's location on the Earth and to this observer the meridian appears fixed and it is the sky that appears to rotate past the meridian.

43. Select **File > Revert** and then click **Play**.

When an object in the sky crosses an observer's meridian, it is said to **transit**. Thus, we can use the duration between transits of a celestial object to provide a measure of the rotational period of the Earth and, therefore, of the length of the day. As you will see, the duration that we call one day depends on the reference object chosen.

44. Select **File > Revert**.

The observing location is on the prime meridian of Earth, longitude 0°. At this time, 12:00:00 PM local standard time on September 1, 2013, for an observer at this location, the center of the Sun and the star TYC5492-842-1 are both transiting the meridian.

45. Set the Zoom to **60°** and use the **D** keyboard shortcut to advance time by 24 hours to local noon on September 2, 2013, and note the positions of the Sun and the star TYC5492-842-1 relative to the meridian.

An **apparent solar day** is the time between successive transits of the Sun.

46. **Magnify** the Sun in the view.
47. Find and note the time at which the center of the Sun transits the meridian on September 2.

Question 28.  (a) At what time on September 2 does the center of the Sun transit the meridian?
(b) What is the duration of the apparent solar day, the rotational period of the Earth with respect to the actual Sun, from September 1, 2013, to September 2, 2013, as measured by the duration between the transits of the center of the Sun on these two dates?

A **sidereal day** is defined as the time between successive transits of a star.

48. **Zoom out** so that the star TYC5492-842-1 is visible in the view.
49. **Centre** the view on the star TYC5492-842-1 and set the Zoom to **3°**.
50. Find the time at which the star TYC5492-842-1 transits the meridian on September 2, 2013.

Question 29.  (a) At what time on September 2 does the star TYC5492-842-1 transit the meridian?
(b) What is the duration of the sidereal day, the rotational period of the Earth with respect to the stars, from September 1, 2013, to September 2, 2013, as measured by

the duration between the two transits of the star TYC5492-842-1 on these two dates?

**Question 30.** Does the common day of 24 hours used in our standard clocks precisely equal the rotation period of the Earth with respect to the Sun or the stars?

The motion of the Earth around the Sun in an elliptical orbit inclined to the celestial equator causes the Sun to appear to move non-uniformly through the year when viewed from Earth. For accurate timekeeping, a mean rate of rotation of the Earth with respect to the Sun is defined by international agreement and the accepted average time period of 24 standard hours for the length of the day is called the **mean solar day** based on a hypothetical mean Sun that moves at a constant rate throughout the year.

**Question 31.** Which of the following statements are correct?
   (a) The apparent solar day varies through the year.
   (b) The mean solar day is equal to 24 hours.
   (c) A sidereal day is shorter than a mean solar day by 3 minutes and 56 seconds.
   (d) The length of the normal day of 24 hours is always equal to the duration between transits of the Sun.
   (e) The length of the normal day of 24 hours is equal to the duration between transits of a star.
   (f) A sidereal day is equal to a mean solar day.
   (g) An apparent solar day is equal to a mean solar day.

You can demonstrate that the apparent motion of the hypothetical mean Sun against the background stars over the course of a year is what would be expected as the Earth moves once around the Sun in its orbit. The mean Sun is a hypothetical point in the sky but is not displayed by *Starry Night*™. However, in its place you can use the fact that, by definition, the mean Sun is always on the observer's meridian at local noon, mean solar time. If a star can be found that lies on the meridian at noon on one date and a second star can be found that lies on the meridian at noon on a second date, then the Right Ascensions (RA) of their positions can be used to determine the difference in RA of the meridian, and hence the difference in position of the mean Sun, over that time period.

51. Select **File > Revert** and change the Time Flow Rate to **15 days**.

The star TYC5492-842-1 is transiting the meridian at local noon on September 1, 2013, as seen from this observing location and represents the hypothetical mean Sun on this date.

52. **Step time forward** by one interval of 15 standard mean solar days.

Fifteen days later, the star TYC6652-439-1 is transiting the meridian at local noon, marking the position in the sky of the hypothetical mean Sun on this date. In other words, the right ascension of the hypothetical mean Sun on these two dates fifteen mean solar days apart in time would be the same as the right ascensions of these two stars.

53. Use the HUD to find the right ascension, RA (JNow), of the two labeled stars representing the position of the hypothetical mean Sun on these two dates.

54. Subtract these values to obtain the advancement of the hypothetical mean sun against the background stars in units of minutes of RA over a time interval of 15 mean solar days.

55. Divide this change of RA by 15 to determine this change in minutes of time per day and divide this value by 60 to translate this value into units of hours per day.

56. RA is measured in units of time, reflecting the rotation of the Earth by 360° in 24 hours. 1 hour of time is thus equivalent to 15° of angle. You can thus multiply the calculated RA change in hours of time by 15 to determine the change in angle in degrees of the Mean Sun against the background stars in 1 day.

**Question 32.** What is the motion of the hypothetical mean Sun in degrees per day?

57. Multiply this daily motion by 365.25 to determine the expected motion in 1 year.

**Question 33.** What would be the apparent motion of the mean Sun over a full year?

**Question 34.** Through what angle, in degrees, does the Earth move in its orbit over a full year?

**Question 35.** Does your calculated motion of the mean Sun against the background stars represent the annual motion of the Earth in its orbit over a full year?

You have seen that the position of the actual Sun in our sky is not a very reliable indicator of the rotational period of the Earth because the Earth moves in an inclined and elliptical orbit around the Sun. In contrast, you have seen that the position of the stars in our sky is more reliable for timekeeping.

58. Select **File > Revert** and set the Zoom to **60°**.

59. Change the Time Flow Rate to **1 sidereal day** and then **Step time forward** repeatedly.

**Question 36.** If a solar astronomer wishes to track the Sun with an appropriately filtered telescope, at what approximate rate would the clock drive of the polar axis need to turn in degrees per hour of time? [HINT: Consider the Sun to be the same as the hypothetical mean Sun for this calculation.]

**Question 37.** If an astronomer is interested in tracking a star with a telescope, at what rate would the telescope drive need to turn in degrees per hour?

## D. Conclusion

In this project, you have explored the diurnal motion of celestial objects. From your observations, you have been able to deduce the orientation of the rotation axis of the Earth in space. You have seen how this rotation of the Earth affects the design of mounts and tracking mechanisms of telescopes. Finally, you compared the rate of the diurnal motion of the Sun with that of the stars and used these data to determine the intrinsic rotation period of the Earth.

# Earth's Orbital Motion 6

Our view of the night sky is constantly changing. The most obvious change is the apparent motion of the stars and constellations towards the west over the course of a single night, caused by the Earth's rotation around its axis. This makes the sky appear to rotate around the Earth's polar axis once in almost 1 day and makes the Sun, Moon, and stars rise in the east and set in the west each day.

A much slower change is the shift of the stars toward the west over the course of a year when viewed at the same time each night, caused by the Earth's motion around the Sun. The Earth makes a full orbit of 360° in about 365 days, and so our view of the universe at any given time of the night changes by about 1° per day. One result of the combination of these two changes is that, in terms of our Sun-based time, each star rises nearly four minutes earlier each night.

## A. The Shifting Constellations

If you go out at the same time each night and observe the sky, you will see that the positions of the constellations change as the months pass.

1. Launch *Starry Night™*.
2. With the viewing location set to your **Home** location, set the Time Flow Rate to **1 day**.
3. Set the Time to **12:00:00 AM standard time**.
4. Set the Gaze direction to the **S**outh if your home location is in the northern hemisphere and to the **N**orth if you live in the southern hemisphere.
5. Select **View > Constellations > Astronomical** and **View > Constellations > Labels**.
6. **Step time forward**, one day at a time.

Question 1.     Toward which direction do the constellations appear to move, night by night?

7. Select **View > Alt-Az Guides > Meridian**.
8. Note the Date from the display in the toolbar and select a constellation on or near the meridian.
9. **Run time forward** and when the selected constellation returns to the meridian, click **Stop**. Compare the Date shown in the toolbar with that of the previous step.

Question 2.     Approximately how long does it take for a particular constellation to return to the meridian?

This daily shift of the background stars is the result of Earth's orbital motion around the Sun. The interval between frames in the previous animation was one solar day, the time required for the Earth to make one complete rotation on its axis with respect to the Sun. Consequently, since the time is midnight, each frame of the animation shows the sky along a line of sight directly away from the Sun. As the Earth orbits the Sun, the line of sight sweeps out a complete circle around the celestial sphere. The next sequence shows this from a position in space directly between the Earth and the Sun, looking out toward the midnight sky of Earth.

10. Open **Favourites > Observing Projects > Earth's Orbital Motion > Earth's Motion.**

This view is from a position 15,000 kilometers above the prime meridian of Earth (illustrated by the vertical red line on the image of the Earth). The date is December 20, 2014, at noon over this location on Earth. The Sun is directly behind the observing location. From this point of view, the star Betelgeuse in the constellation Orion is on the meridian, just above the North Pole of Earth. You are looking down on the sunlit half of the Earth at midday, but you can see the sky beyond the Earth. For a person on the opposite side of the Earth, it is midnight and Betelgeuse is transiting the meridian.

11. **Step time forward** by 1 day.

In the time required for the Earth to rotate once on its axis with respect to the Sun, it has also moved a short distance along its orbit. Because the view is centered on the Earth and you are traveling through space along with it, this motion shows up as a movement of the background in the opposite direction.

12. **Run time forward** and, when the Earth returns to a position where its meridian aligns once again with Betelgeuse, click **Stop** and note the Date displayed in the toolbar.

Question 3.     How long does it take for Betelgeuse to return to alignment with the meridian?

Of course, the distant stars are a fixed background and it is the Earth that is moving.

13. Select **File > Revert.**
14. **Centre** the view on Betelgeuse and **Step time forward** several days.

The view is now locked onto the background stars. The viewing location remains fixed at a point 15,000 kilometers from the surface of the Earth on a line connecting the Sun and the Earth. Now however, the Earth will appear to move while the background stars remain fixed in the view. Your viewpoint is still moving with the Earth but your field of view is always centered on Betelgeuse.

15. Click **Play** and let time advance until the local meridian and the Sun (indicated with a label) appear to align with Betelgeuse. **Step time backward** or **forward** in intervals of 1 day to find the Date on which the Sun and the local meridian are most closely aligned with Betelgeuse.

Question 4.     On what date does the Sun align with Betelgeuse on the local meridian?

16. Click **Play** and let time advance until Earth reappears in the view and aligns once more with Betelgeuse. Note the Date of this alignment.

Question 5.     How long did it take for the Earth to move completely round its orbit to return to alignment with Betelgeuse?

## B. The Solar and Sidereal Day

In the previous animations the observing location remained fixed over a point on the Earth and the background sky appears to move.

17. Select **Favourites > Observing Projects > Earth's Orbital Motion > Sidereal and Solar.**

The view appears unchanged, but now the observing location is a point in a fixed direction from the center of the Earth with respect to the background stars.

18. Change the Time Flow Rate to **3000 x** to see how this observing location affects the view. Then select **Edit > Undo Time Step** or **File > Revert** to return to the initial view.

The Time Flow Rate in the view is 1 sidereal day, the time required for the Earth to make one complete rotation with respect to the background stars.

19. **Step time forward** by 1 sidereal day.

> Question 6.    What time is displayed in the toolbar?
>
> Question 7.    By how many minutes is the display time different from the initial time of 12:00:00 PM (i.e., by what interval of time is 1 sidereal day less than 1 solar day)?
>
> Question 8.    The Earth rotates in the same direction as its orbital motion, that is, counterclockwise when looking down on the North Pole. If the Earth rotated in the opposite direction to its orbital motion, would 1 sidereal day be shorter or longer than 1 solar day? [HINT: Draw a diagram to help you to answer this question.]

20. Click **Play** and observe the sunlit hemisphere of the Earth, which indicates the Sun's direction. **Zoom out** to a very wide field of view in order to see the Sun.

From this observing location at a fixed direction from the center of the Earth, as time advances in steps of one sidereal day, the Earth's position with respect to the background stars remains fixed and it is the Sun that appears to move.

21. Select **File > Revert** to return to the initial set-up.
22. Change the Time Flow Rate to **1 day**.
23. **Step time forward** by one day.

Time now advances by one solar day. In this interval, the Earth will have moved along its orbit a short distance. The orientation of the line joining the Earth and the Sun has shifted in space with respect to the background stars. For the Earth's prime meridian to return to a position where it points directly at the Sun, as it does in one solar day, the Earth must compensate for its orbital motion by rotating a small extra amount relative to the stars.

> Question 9.    Toward which compass direction on the Earth has the prime meridian of the Earth shifted over the course of one solar day as seen from this location?

24. Select **File > Revert** to return to the initial view at noon on December 20.
25. Open the **Status** pane, expand the **Location** layer and note the value given for the Longitude. This is the longitude that is directly beneath the hovering viewing location.
26. Use the **D** keyboard shortcut to advance the Date by one solar day to **December 21**, and, from the Status pane, note the Longitude of the point that is directly beneath the observing location after one solar day. The difference in longitude of the location indicates the amount of extra rotation that the Earth will complete in order to compensate for its orbital motion and return the Sun to the meridian at noon.

**Question 10.** By what extra angle relative to the stars did the Earth rotate in order compensate for its orbital motion? [HINT: Look at the longitude change.]

As a check of this calculation, you can now measure the angular distance moved by the Earth in 1 day by using a background star as a reference point against which to measure this motion.

27. Open **Favourites > Observing Projects > Earth's Orbital Motion > Earth's Motion**.
28. **Magnify** Betelgeuse in the view.
29. **Step time forward** by one solar day.
30. **Zoom out** as necessary and use the Angular Separation tool to measure the angular distance from Betelgeuse to the meridian. Use the shortest measurement, which will be where the line drawn by the angular separation tool meets the meridian at a right angle. Since the meridian is fixed with respect to the Earth, you can calculate the angular distance that the Earth has moved in its orbit in the duration of one day from the angular distance that Betelgeuse has moved from the meridian, thereby determining the orbital motion of the Earth in 1 day.

**Question 11.** By what angular distance along its orbit did the Earth move in one solar day? How does your answer compare to that of the previous question? [HINT: Ignore the measurement limitations and focus on the relative size of the values.]

**Question 12.** Since the Earth rotates on its axis a full 360° with respect to the Sun in 24 hours of solar time, how long does it take to rotate the extra angular distance noted in question 10?

**Question 13.** How does your answer to the previous question compare to the difference between the lengths of the sidereal and the solar day?

**Question 14.** What is the ratio of 1 solar day to 1 sidereal day? [HINT: Divide the total minutes in 1 solar day by the total minutes in 1 sidereal day.]

**Question 15.** Multiply the ratio in Question 14 by 365.25 (the number of days in one solar year) to calculate the number of sidereal days in one year. How do you account for this number?

From this position close to the Earth, you can now watch the change in the apparent position of the Sun with respect to the stars as time advances and the Earth moves in its orbit.

31. Select **File > Revert**.
32. Open the **Find** pane and select **Magnify** from the drop down menu for the **Sun**.

Now you are looking toward the Sun. A label indicates a reference star, TYC 6841-175-1. In one year, the Earth will move completely around the Sun in its orbit so that the Sun will be in the same position against the background stars as it was a year earlier. You can step time forward by 1 solar year, which is 365.25 solar days, to verify that the Sun returns to the same position with respect to the reference star.

33. Set the Time Flow Rate to **365 days** and **Step time forward**. Then change the Time Flow Rate to **6 hours** (i.e., 0.25 day) and **Step time forward**.

You can now advance time by 1 sidereal year, that is the number of sidereal days calculated in Question 15, and check that the Sun returns to the same position in our sky after this time.

34. Change the Time in the toolbar to **12:00:00 PM** and the Date to **December 20, 2014**.
35. **Step time forward** by **6 hours** to account for the quarter day part of the year and then change the Time Flow Rate to **sidereal days** and enter the number of sidereal days in one year that you calculated in question 15 into the numerical field of the Time Flow Rate panel. **Step time forward** to check your answer. The Sun should once again be in the same direction in the sky as the star TYC6841-175-1.

## C. Motion of the Sky in Solar Time and the Zodiac

It is interesting to examine the change in appearance of the sky as seen from the surface of the Earth as time changes in units of solar days. In the following simulation, the stars will move across your sky while the Sun remains at approximately the same azimuth, in the present case almost due south. The Sun will move through a range of elevation angles because of the tilt of the Earth's spin axis to its orbital plane. This change of elevation angle through the year is important in defining the seasons on the Earth and is covered in more detail in the project on the analemma.

36. Click the **Home** button in the toolbar to go to your home location on Earth and then hide **Daylight** in the view.
37. Set the Time Flow Rate to **1 day**.
38. Set the Time in the toolbar to **12:00:00 PM standard time**.
39. Open the **Find** pane and double-click on the **Sun** to center the view on the Sun and label it and then click **Play**.

Day-by-day, the Earth advances along its orbit and as this happens, the Sun will appear to move against the background stars, accompanied by the planets. With time flowing in intervals of one solar day and the gaze locked on the Sun, the Earth's orbital motion around the Sun causes the background stars to appear to move in the opposite direction. This is like standing on a merry-go-round looking inward with your gaze fixed on its center. As you move round in one direction, the stationary background scenery appears to move in the opposite direction.

You can watch the Sun as it moves along the ecliptic, the projection of the Earth's orbit onto the sky. Note that this line is labeled with time in months.

40. Click **Stop** and then select **View > Ecliptic Guides > The Ecliptic**. A green line showing the ecliptic appears in the view.
41. **Step time forward** at one-day intervals and compare the Date shown in the toolbar with the position of the Sun with respect to the demarcations on the ecliptic.

**Question 16.** To which part of the month does the demarcation labeled with the name of the month correspond?

The ecliptic passes through a limited set of constellations known as the Zodiac.

42. Select **View > Constellations > Zodiac, View > Constellations > Boundaries,** and **View > Constellations > Labels**.

The view displays the boundaries, labels, and astronomical illustrations of the constellations of the traditional zodiac. The zodiac is a band of constellations through which most of the brightest planets and the Moon appear to move as they orbit close to the ecliptic plane. This region of our sky played an important role in early astrology because the positions of the Sun and the planets were used to predict the future. These zodiacal constellations or "signs" are still used in modern astrology.

43. Use the **Play, Stop,** and **Step Time** controls in the toolbar to move through time at one-day intervals, noting particularly the dates when the Sun enters and leaves each zodiacal constellation in Data Table 1 at the end of this project, and use this information to answer the following questions.

**Question 17.** What are the names of the constellations in the traditional zodiac?
**Question 18.** Which constellation(s), if any, are absent from the traditional list? [HINT: To see the names of all of the constellations, select **View > Constellations > Astronomical**.]

44. Look up the Zodiac dates in a newspaper or online horoscope and enter these into your Data Table 1 for comparison with the actual Sun timings.

**Question 19.** Is the Sun in the constellation of your astrological sign on your birthday?

**Question 20.** How well do the actual dates for entry and exit of the Sun into constellations in the zodiac agree with those used in astrology?

**Question 21.** How does this influence your confidence in the validity of your horoscope for today?

## D. Challenge: Verify Kepler's Second Law

If we could see the stars during the day, the effect of the Earth's orbital motion around the Sun would be an apparent motion of the Sun against the stars. In real life, the blue sky of daylight, the result of scattering of sunlight by the Earth's atmosphere, hides the background stars. *Starry Night™* allows you to remove the effect of this obscuring atmosphere.

> 45. Open **Favourites > Observing Projects > Earth's Orbital Motion > Sun's Apparent Motion.**

The view shows the sky looking south from Chicago at noon on December 20, 2014. Daylight has been removed to reveal the background stars. The Sun is near the center of the view. The Time Flow Rate is set to one sidereal day. Thus, the background sky will return to exactly the same position in the view and the stars will appear to remain stationary as time advances. The motion of the Sun against these background stars is then much easier to see.

> 46. **Step time forward** one sidereal day at a time.

**Question 22.** In 1 sidereal day, in which direction does the Sun appear to move in our sky?

You can measure the apparent speed of the Sun across the sky. Since you are measuring this solar motion from a moving Earth, this motion simply reflects the speed of the Earth in its orbital path. This motion will carry the Earth around a full orbit in a time of 1 year. However, because the Earth's orbit is elliptical, this speed will vary through the year, following Kepler's Second Law of Planetary Motion. You can make a series of simple measurements of the Sun's apparent motion through the year to verify this law.

The consequence of this law is that the speed of a planet in its orbit around the Sun (v in Figure 1) is inversely proportional to its distance from the Sun (R in Figure 1). Mathematically, this can be expressed by

$$v = k/R,$$

where $k$ is a constant.

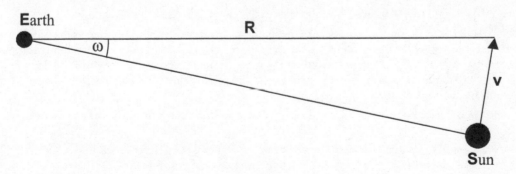

**Figure 1.** Angular Speed of the Sun Across the Sky in 1 Sidereal Day

In Figure 1, $\omega$ is the Sun's angular speed across the sky. If $\omega$ were measured in radians per sidereal day then, using the small-angle relation, $\omega$ would be given by

$$\omega = v/R.$$

Rearranging this equation gives

$$v = \omega \times R.$$

Since you will actually measure angular speed, $\alpha$, in arcseconds per sidereal day and 1 radian $= 2.06 \times 10^5$,

$$\omega = \alpha/2.06 \times 10^5 \text{ and } v = \alpha \times R/2.06 \times 10^5,$$

where $\alpha$ is in arcseconds per sidereal day.

From Kepler's Second Law, $v = k/R$. Substituting this expression for $v$ into the above equation gives

$$k/R = \alpha \times R/2.06 \times 10^5.$$

Rearranging this equation and assuming that constant $k$ multiplied by the constant conversion factor $2.06 \times 10^5$ is equal to a new constant A, this then becomes

$$\alpha \times R^2 = A.$$

Thus, you can verify Kepler's second law by demonstrating that $\alpha \times R^2$ remains constant as the Earth moves along its elliptical orbit at a varying speed by measuring the Sun's apparent motion across the sky when viewed from Earth throughout the year. The following procedure will accomplish this.

47. Open **Favourites > Observing Projects > Earth's Orbital Motion > Kepler's Second Law**.
48. Configure the HUD to include **Distance from Observer**.

The view is a close-up of the Sun surrounded by a reference circle that is 1° in diameter. The colored line crossing the view is the ecliptic.

49. Select a star that is on or near to the ecliptic and within or near the 1° reference circle. If necessary, use the **D** or **Shift-D** keyboard shortcuts to move forward or backward in steps of one day to find an appropriate star. Open the contextual menu for this star and click the **Select** option to label the star. Open the object contextual menu over the star again and select **Centre** to move the reference star to the center of the field of view.
50. Note the Date from the toolbar and record this in Data Table 2 at the end of this project.
51. Use the HUD to find the Distance from observer to the Sun and record this in Data Table 2.
52. Use the Angular Separation tool to measure the angular separation from the center of the Sun to the selected star, and enter this distance, in arcseconds, into Data Table 1 under the column Star-Sun Angular Separation Measurement #1. Convert the measurement to arcseconds by multiplying the number of arcminutes in the measurement by 60 and adding this product to the number of arcseconds in the measurement.
53. **Step time** by 1 sidereal day either forward or backward to move the Sun to the other side of the centered reference star.
54. Measure the angular distance between the center of the Sun and the reference star again, convert it to arcseconds and enter it into Data Table 2 under the column Star-Sun Angular Separation Measurement #2.
55. **Centre** the view once more on the Sun.
56. Press the **M** key on the keyboard twice to advance the Date in the toolbar two calendar months and reset the Time to **12:00:00 PM**. Then go back to step 49 and repeat the measurements until you have data for a full year.

The following calculations will allow you to verify Kepler's Second Law from your observational data.

57. To determine the angular distance the Sun moves in 1 sidereal day, add the two angular measurements together and record the sum in arcseconds in Data Table 2 under the column Angular Motion of the Sun, $\alpha$ in arcseconds per sidereal day.

58. Calculate the square of the Earth-Sun distance and multiply it by $\alpha$, the Angular Motion of the Sun. Enter this value of $A = \alpha \times R^2$ in Data Table 2.

59. Calculate the average, $A_v$, of all your values of $\alpha \times R^2$.

60. As a measure of the spread of these values from the average value, calculate the percentage difference between each value and the average value by taking the difference between each value and this average value, $A_v$, divide this difference by $A_v$ and multiply by 100. You can examine these values of $100(A - A_v)/A_v$ to see by what percentage they vary from the mean value.

If these values of the calculation of $\alpha \times R^2$ are constant over this 1-year series of measurements, then you have shown that the Earth obeys Kepler's second law.

Question 23.    Using the data from your Data Table, what is the speed of the Sun across your sky in December, in arcseconds per sidereal day?

Question 24.    Using the data from your Data Table, what is the speed of the Sun across your sky in June, in arcseconds per sidereal day?

Question 25.    Are your values of $A = \alpha \times R^2$ sufficiently constant to verify Kepler's second law? Do these values vary over the full year by 1%, 0.5%, or 0.1% from each other?

## E. Conclusions

This project has shown you the apparent motion of the Sun through our sky against the background stars. It is impossible to see this in the real world because of the presence of scattered sunlight in the daytime. Furthermore, you have been able to measure the variation in speed of the Sun across the sky caused by the variation of the speed of our observing platform, the Earth, as it moves in its elliptical orbit and thereby verify Kepler's Second Law of planetary motion with these measurements.

**Data Table 1.** Dates of Entry and Exit of the Sun from the Zodiacal Constellations

| Zodiac Constellation | Date of Sun Entry Into Constellation | Date of Sun Exit From Constellation | Horoscope Sign Start Date | Horoscope Sign End Date |
|---|---|---|---|---|
|  |  |  |  |  |
|  |  |  |  |  |
|  |  |  |  |  |
|  |  |  |  |  |
|  |  |  |  |  |
|  |  |  |  |  |
|  |  |  |  |  |
|  |  |  |  |  |
|  |  |  |  |  |
|  |  |  |  |  |
|  |  |  |  |  |
|  |  |  |  |  |

**Data Table 2.** Sun's Apparent Motion in One Sidereal Day Throughout the Year

| Date | Earth-Sun Distance, R (AU) | Star-Sun Angular Separation Measurement #1 (") | Star-Sun Angular Separation Measurement #2 (") | Angular Motion of the Sun, $\alpha$ ("/Sidereal day) | $A = \alpha \times R^2$ | Variation in A (%) |
|---|---|---|---|---|---|---|
|  |  |  |  |  |  |  |
|  |  |  |  |  |  |  |
|  |  |  |  |  |  |  |
|  |  |  |  |  |  |  |
|  |  |  |  |  |  |  |
|  |  |  |  |  |  |  |
|  |  |  |  |  |  |  |
|  |  |  |  | Average, $A_v$ |  |  |

# Seasons 7

Life on Earth at temperate latitudes is strongly influenced by seasonal variations. The year is conveniently divided into the seasons of spring, summer, autumn, and winter to describe these variations. Summers are warm and winters are cool while spring and autumn, or fall, are seasons of change. The cause of these variations is the tilt of the Earth's axis of rotation with respect to the plane of the Earth's orbit. Since the direction of this axis is maintained in space as the Earth moves around in its orbit, the Sun illuminates different parts of the Earth throughout the year.

In June, the North Pole is tilted toward the Sun, giving more direct sunlight and warmer temperatures to northern latitudes and less direct sunlight and cooler temperatures to southern latitudes. Thus, it is summer in the northern hemisphere and winter in the southern hemisphere.

In December, the Earth has moved to the opposite side of the Sun. Now, the North Pole is tilted away from the Sun and the northern hemisphere receives less direct sunlight, resulting in cooler winter temperatures while the South Pole is tilted toward the Sun and the southern hemisphere receives more direct sunlight leading to warmer summer temperatures.

The overall heating of the Earth's surface changes as the direction of sunlight and the length of daylight changes from winter to summer. The delay between the time of maximum heating, when the Sun is highest in the sky at a particular location, and the time of highest temperatures, is caused by the fact that it takes time to heat up the Earth's surface and oceans. This delay varies somewhat depending on location but amounts to about a month on average at mid-latitudes.

In this observing project, you will explore the orientation of the Earth's axis relative to its orbital plane and see how this orientation produces the seasons. You will also investigate the effect of the changing seasons on the length of daylight, and how this varies with latitude on the Earth.

## A. Earth's Tilted Axis of Rotation

1. Launch *Starry Night*™ and open **Favourites > Observing Projects > Seasons > Axial Tilt.**

The view, from a location in space 3.5 AU from the Sun, shows the Earth greatly exaggerated in size. Superimposed on the image of the Earth is the equator shown in red, and pole sticks indicating the orientation of the Earth's axis of rotation. The green oval shows the Earth's orbit and the green grid depicts the plane defined by this orbit, the ecliptic plane. The date is March 20, 2015.

2. Use the Location Scroller to adjust the view so that the ecliptic plane is edge-on and the Sun is directly between the Earth and the observing location.
3. Select **View > Celestial Guides > Equator** to see the celestial equator, the projection of the plane of Earth's equator onto the sky.

As you can see, the ecliptic and equatorial planes are tilted with respect to one another. To measure the extent of this tilt, you can measure the angular distance between the celestial and ecliptic poles because these poles are perpendicular to their respective planes.

4. Use the Location Scroller to adjust the view so that the observing position is nearly directly over one of the Earth's poles and the red crosses indicating the positions of the celestial and ecliptic poles are visible. Then use the Angular Separation tool to measure the angular separation between the ecliptic and celestial poles in the view.

**Question 1.**    To the nearest ½°, how far is the Earth's axis tilted away from the perpendicular to the ecliptic plane?

5. Select **File > Revert** and click **Play** to observe the Earth for at least one year of simulated time as it spins along its orbit. Use the Location Scroller to see the view from different perspectives. Stop the animation occasionally and use the zoom controls to observe details.

**Question 2.**    During which month is the North Pole tilted closest toward the Sun?

**Question 3.**    During which month is the South Pole tilted closest toward the Sun?

**Question 4.**    During which months is neither pole tilted toward the Sun?

## B. Equinoxes and Solstices

A direct consequence of the tilt of Earth's rotational axis is that the Sun, as seen from Earth, moves north and south in the sky through the year. If you observe the Sun at midday throughout the year, this north-south motion becomes obvious.

6. Open **Favourites > Observing Projects > Seasons > Minneapolis** and configure the HUD to include **Altitude**.

The view shows the Sun in the southern sky as seen from Minneapolis on March 20, 2015, the first day of spring in the northern hemisphere.

7. Notice that the Time Flow Rate is set at **1 day**. Click the **Play** button to observe the change in the position of the Sun in the sky at midday throughout the year.

**Question 5.**    During which months is the Sun moving northward in the sky?

**Question 6.**    During which months is the Sun moving southward in the sky?

The Sun's apparent motion over the course of a year, as seen from the Earth, arises from the Earth's orbital motion around the Sun. The apparent path of the Sun around the celestial sphere, as seen from the Earth, is called the ecliptic. The ecliptic can also be thought of as the projection of the Earth's orbit onto the celestial sphere. As you observed in the previous section, the tilt of the Earth's axis causes the ecliptic to be tilted with respect to the Earth's equatorial plane.

Now you can make some more precise observations of this motion of the Sun in the sky.

8. Select **File > Revert** to return to **March 20, 2015**.

9. Select **View > Ecliptic Guides > The Ecliptic** and **View > Celestial Guides > Equator** from the menu.

The ecliptic is superimposed on the sky in green and the celestial equator in red.

> 10. Use the HUD to find the Altitude of the Sun in the Minneapolis sky on this date.

> **Question 7.** On March 20, 2015, which is the date of the March equinox, where is the Sun with respect to the ecliptic and the celestial equator?
>
> **Question 8.** What is the Altitude of the Sun as seen from Minneapolis on this date?

> 11. Use the time flow controls to advance time and find the date on which the Sun reaches the northernmost point of its motion. [HINT: The Sun will be at its most northerly point as seen from Minneapolis when its Altitude, as shown in the HUD, is greatest.]

> **Question 9.** On which date does the Sun reach its northernmost point in the sky?
>
> **Question 10.** What is the Altitude of the Sun on this date?
>
> **Question 11.** What is the difference, to the nearest ½ degree, between the altitude of the Sun on this date and its altitude on the March equinox? What is the significance of your answer? [HINT: Recall your answer to Question 1 above.]

The northernmost point in the Sun's motion is called the June solstice, the word "solstice" meaning that the Sun stands still in its north-south annual motion. More traditionally, it was called the summer solstice because it marked the beginning of summer in the northern hemisphere.

> 12. Open the **Options** side pane and expand the **Guides** and then the **Celestial Guides** layers. Then click the checkboxes for **Summer/Winter Solstice** and **Vernal/Autumnal Equinox** to display indicators to these points in the sky.
>
> 13. Use the time flow controls to advance time to **September 23, 2015**.

As you can see, on September 23, 2015, the Sun is at the September equinox, traditionally called the Autumnal, or Fall, equinox, when the Sun crosses the celestial equator.

> **Question 12.** During which equinox is the Sun moving southward in the sky?

> 14. Advance time to **December 22, 2015**.

Now the Sun has reached the southernmost point of its motion in the sky, the December solstice, before moving northward again.

> 15. Finally, advance time to **March 20, 2016**.

After one year, a complete cycle of seasons has elapsed and the Sun is once more at the March equinox.

> **Question 13.** Where in the sky would an observer on the equator of the Earth see the Sun near midday on this date? [HINT: Where is the celestial equator in the sky for an observer at the equator of Earth?]

16. Open the contextual menu for the Sun and click **Deselect Sun** to remove the label. Then click Off the **Vernal/Autumnal Equinox** and **Summer/Winter Solstice** options in the **Guides** layer of the Options pane. Then select **Options > Viewing Location...** from the menu. Click the **Latitude/ Longitude** tab in the Viewing Location dialog window and enter **0** in the Latitude box. Click the **Go To Location** button. Select **View > Alt/Az Guides > Zenith/Nadir** from the menu. Finally, use the Hand tool or gaze buttons in the toolbar to find the Sun in the view and check your answer to the previous question.

## C. Solar Illumination of the Earth Through the Year

You have seen how the tilt of the Earth's axis of rotation with respect to its orbit results in the Sun appearing to move north and south in the sky as seen from Earth. But of course, it is the Earth that is revolving around the Sun. It is interesting to observe how this tilted axis affects the way in which the Sun illuminates the Earth throughout the year.

17. Open **Favourites > Observing Projects > Seasons > March Equinox.**

The view looks back on the Earth from a location about 12,000 km in space, directly toward the Sun at the time of the March equinox. Superimposed on the image of the Earth is a grid of latitude and longitude, with the equator shown in red and pole sticks indicating the Earth's axis of rotation.

18. Use the Location Scroller to observe the pattern of solar illumination on the Earth on this date. Note the position of the terminator, the boundary between the illuminated and dark hemispheres of the Earth, particularly with respect to the poles. Click the **Play** button and use the Location Scroller to observe the pattern of solar illumination on the Earth as the planet rotates on its axis.

On this date, observers at both of Earth's poles would see the Sun on the horizon. Any observer at locations other than the poles will be in sunlight for one-half of the rotation period and daylight will last for 12 hours; hence the name equinox, meaning equal day and night.

**Question 14.**   On this date, where is the terminator with respect to the Earth's North and South poles?

19. Click the **Stop** button and change the Date in the toolbar to **June 21, 2015,** the June solstice. Again, use the Location Scroller to observe the Earth. Examine particularly the regions of the North and South Poles and note the position of the terminator relative to these poles.

Note that the most direct sunlight now falls on a region north of the equator. The terminator is now beyond the North Pole of the Earth and illumination from the Sun fails to reach the South Pole. For an observer at the latitude of the Tropic of Cancer, 23.5° north, the Sun would pass through the zenith at midday.

20. Click the **Play** button and use the Location Scroller to observe the pattern of solar illumination on the Earth as the planet rotates. Note the parallels of latitude that the terminator reaches in the north and south hemispheres.

Question 15.    Which Pole of the Earth is tilted toward the Sun on this date?

Question 16.    To which approximate parallel of latitude does the Sun's illumination extend beyond the North Pole? What is the difference between this latitude and the 90° latitude of the pole?  [NOTE: The lines of latitude are 30° apart.]

Question 17.    From the illumination pattern on the Earth, what season is beginning in the southern hemisphere?

Question 18.    What amount of daylight does an observer at the South Pole of Earth experience on this date?

Question 19.    What amount of daylight does an observer at the North Pole of Earth experience on this date?

21.   Click **Stop** and change the Date to the September equinox, **September 23, 2015**. Use the Location Scroller to observe the pattern of solar illumination on the Earth. [HINT: You can move around to the dark side of the Earth to a point where the Sun appears in your view. Note where it appears with respect to the Earth's equator.]

Question 20.    Where would an observer at either of the Poles of Earth find the Sun on this date?

Question 21.    Where would an observer at the equator find the Sun at midday on this date?

22.   Change the Date to the December solstice, **December 22, 2015**. Use the Location Scroller to observe the pattern of solar illumination on the Earth. Then click **Play** and use the Location Scroller again to see the pattern of sunlight on the Earth as the planet rotates.

Question 22.    Which hemisphere of the Earth receives the most direct sunlight on this date?

Question 23.    To which parallel of latitude does the Sun's illumination extend beyond the South Pole?

Question 24.    What season is beginning in the southern hemisphere of Earth on this date?

## D. The Tropical, Temperate and Arctic Latitudes of Earth

The Earth's latitudes are divided into tropical, temperate and arctic regions. While the names suggest that the division into these regions is based on their climate, in fact the defining feature of these regions is astronomically specific.

   You have already seen that the Sun, as seen from Earth, crosses the celestial equator on two dates in a year, the March and September equinoxes. For observers at the equator of Earth, the Sun will pass directly overhead on these dates. At roughly the midpoint between these equinoxes, the Sun reaches its most northerly and southerly points in the sky, the solstices.

23.   Open **Favourites > Observing Projects > Seasons > Tropic of Cancer.**

This wide-angle view of the sky on the date of the March equinox shows the Sun above the southern horizon on the celestial equator at midday, as seen from the latitude of 23.5° north of the equator, which is called the Tropic of Cancer. A label indicates the zenith, the point in the sky directly overhead as seen from this location.

24.   Click **Play** and observe the motion of the Sun in the sky as time advances in steps of one day.

> **Question 25.** At the Tropic of Cancer, on which date does the Sun pass through the zenith at midday?
>
> **Question 26.** On which date of the year would you expect the Sun to pass through the zenith at midday if you were an observer at the Tropic of Capricorn, 23.5° south?
>
> **Question 27.** What is the defining feature of the tropical latitudes, those between the Tropic of Cancer in the north and the Tropic of Capricorn in the south?

> 25. Open **Favourites > Observing Projects > Seasons > North Pole.**

The view is centered on the position of the Sun, which is below the horizon at midday on March 15, 2015, but a label indicates its position. The viewing location is the North Pole of the Earth and the Time Flow Rate is 6 hours.

> 26. **Step time forward** and observe the position of the Sun until it has risen completely above the horizon.

> **Question 28.** On which date in 2015 does the Sun rise above the horizon as seen from the North Pole of the Earth in 2015?

> 27. Use the **H** keyboard shortcut to advance time in 1-hour steps to see how the Sun skims the horizon on this first day of summer at the North Pole.
>
> 28. Click **Play** to advance time in 6-hour steps and observe the Sun rise in the sky as time proceeds. Click **Stop** when the Sun returns near to the horizon and then **Step time forward** and note the date on which the Sun sets [NOTE: Use the date on which the Sun's lower edge first touches the horizon.]
>
> 29. Set the Time in the toolbar to midday, **12:00:00 PM**, the time of day when the Sun is expected to be highest in the sky, and then change the Time Flow Rate to **1 day**. Click **Play** and observe the position of the Sun at midday as seen from the North Pole until it rises again.

> **Question 29.** On which date in 2015 does the Sun set as seen from the North Pole of Earth?
>
> **Question 30.** What would you see if you were observing the Sun from the South Pole of the Earth on this date?

> 30. Open **Favourites > Observing Projects > Seasons > Antarctic Circle** and configure the HUD to include **Rises** and **Sets**.

The view is centered on the Sun at midnight on December 21, 2015. The viewing location is at the latitude of the Antarctic Circle, approximately 66.5° south. Note that the Sun is below the horizon.

> 31. Position the cursor over the Sun and note that the HUD displays a Rises time but not a Sets time.
>
> 32. Use the **D** shortcut key to advance the Date to **December 22, 2015,** the date of the December solstice and use the HUD to find the time of sunrise and sunset on this date. Advance the Date again to **December 23** and note that the HUD now displays a Sets time but not a Rises time for this date.

> **Question 31.** For how many days of the year is an observer at the Antarctic Circle in the land of midnight Sun; that is, how many days in the year will this observer have 24 hours of daylight?
>
> **Question 32.** What would an observer at the Arctic Circle at approximately 66.5° north experience on the December solstice?

**Question 33.** The Arctic and Antarctic circles, at 66.5° north and south latitudes, are the boundaries between arctic regions of Earth, which have latitudes greater than 66.5° and temperate latitudes, which extend from the Tropics of Cancer and Capricorn to the Arctic and Antarctic Circles, respectively. What is a defining feature of arctic latitudes?

## E. Seasonal Variation of Temperature

A common misconception is that summer is warmer than winter because the Earth's elliptical orbit brings the planet closer to the Sun during the summer and further from the Sun in the winter. Of course, if this were the case, then both the north and south hemispheres of the Earth would experience summer at the same time of year. The fact that the southern hemisphere of Earth experiences summer while the northern hemisphere is in winter disproves this theory. However, you can also test this theory directly.

33. Open **Favourites > Observing Projects > Seasons > Minneapolis** and configure the HUD to include **Distance from Observer**.

34. Use the **M** shortcut key to advance time in steps of one calendar month at a time and for each month, position the cursor over the Sun and use the Distance from observer value shown in the HUD to find the distance from Earth to the Sun on that date.

**Question 34.** What season is it in the northern hemisphere when the Sun-Earth distance is the greatest?

In fact, summer is warmer than winter because the **insolation**, the intensity of solar radiation falling on the surface of the Earth, is higher in the summer. As you can see from Figure 1, insolation depends on the angle at which the radiation strikes the surface (the dependence is proportional to the sine of the angle of incidence on the surface). A beam of radiation that falls obliquely on a surface (Beam A) is spread over a greater area than if the same beam were to strike the surface perpendicularly (Beam B).

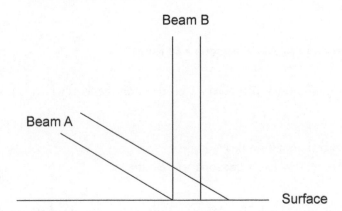

**Figure 1.** Insolation

Because of the tilt of Earth's axis, the Sun is higher in the sky in summer and its rays strike the Earth more directly. In winter, the Sun's altitude in the sky is lower and its rays strike the surface more obliquely.

The heating of the Earth depends not only on the direction of the incident solar radiation, but also on the duration of the exposure to the Sun's illumination. Depending on the latitude, the length of daylight throughout the year can vary significantly over the cycle of seasons. You have already seen that high latitudes on the Earth can experience long stretches of uninterrupted daylight with the extreme being at the poles, where each "day" is six months long, followed by six months of night. At the other extreme, the equator, things are quite different.

35. Open **Favourites > Observing Projects > Seasons > Equator**.

The view is centered on the Sun, which is about to rise as seen from this viewing location on the equator of Earth on the date of the March equinox. The Time Flow Rate is 6 minutes, which is equal to 0.1 hours.

### Sequence 1

36. Use the keyboard shortcut, **H** to advance time in steps of one hour. Count each step until the Sun nears the horizon and is about to set. If you overshoot, use **Shift-H** to reverse time by one hour and subtract one from your count. Note the number of whole hours and then use the **U** keyboard shortcut to advance time in steps of 6 minutes and count the number of tenths of an hour that elapse until the Sun touches the horizon and add this count to the number of whole hours. If you overshoot and the Sun disappears below the horizon, use **Shift-U** to move back in time 6 minutes and reduce your count of tenths of an hour by one. Record the final total duration of daylight for this date in Data Table 1 at the end of this project.

37. Change the Date in the toolbar to **June 21, 2015,** the solstice.

38. Click the **Sunrise** button in the toolbar to set the time to just before sunrise on this date.

39. Repeat the instructions in step 36 to find the duration of daylight on this date at this latitude.

40. Change the Date in the toolbar to **September 23, 2015,** and find the duration of daylight on this date.

41. Finally, change the Date in the toolbar to **December 22, 2015,** and find the duration of daylight on this date.

42. Plot your results for the duration of daylight through the year from this latitude on Graph Template 1 at the end of this project.

43. Connect the data points on your graph with straight-line segments using a color specific for the data points for this latitude. [NOTE: You will need to use a different color for each of the other latitudes for which you make observations.]

> **Question 35.**    To the nearest hour, what is the duration of daylight through the year at the latitude of the equator?

44. Open **Favourites > Observing Projects > Seasons > 50 North.**

The view, from a location on Earth at latitude 50° north, is centered on the Sun, which is just about to rise on March 20, 2015.

45. Repeat the steps of Sequence 1 above, for this latitude.

46. Open **Favourites > Observing Projects > Seasons > 50 South.**

This view shows the Sun about to rise on March 20, 2015, as seen from the latitude of 50° south.

47. Repeat the steps of Sequence 1 above, for this latitude.

48. Finally, plot the hours of daylight throughout the year at the North Pole on your graph. (Remember that, as seen from the pole, the Sun remains above the horizon for six months after rising and remains below the horizon for the other six months of the year.)

> **Question 36.**    From your graph, on which dates do the various latitudes across the Earth experience the same duration of daylight? What duration is the daylight at these latitudes on these dates?

Question 37. How do the hours of daylight for latitude 50° south compare with the duration of daylight at latitude 50° north?

## F. Challenge: Seasons on Other Planets

It is interesting to see if other planets in the solar system might experience seasons.

49. Open **Favourites > Observing Projects > Seasons > Solar System Seasons.**
50. Click **Play** to observe how the tilted rotation axis of Earth that causes the seasons on our planet appears as seen from the Sun.

The Earth appears to wobble on its axis because the view is tracking the Earth as it revolves around the Sun. As time advances, different regions of the Earth tilt more directly toward the Sun.

51. Open the **Find** pane and click the icon in the search box and select **Seach All** and then clear the search box of any text. The found objects list will show the planets of the solar system.
52. For each planet in the solar system, click the icon to the left of its name and select **Magnify** from the drop down menu. Click **Play** to observe the rotational axis of the planet as indicated by the pole sticks. If necessary, increase the Time Flow Rate.

Question 38. Which of the major planets of the solar system would experience seasons most similar to those of Earth?

Question 39. Which of the major planets of the solar system would experience the least seasonal variation?

Question 40. Which of the major planets of the solar system would experience the greatest seasonal variation?

## G. Conclusions

You have explored the cause of the seasons and observed the relative lengths of day and night in winter and summer at various latitudes. The tilt of the Earth's axis is the main contributor to the seasonal effects at mid-latitudes, where the changing inclination of sunlight to the Earth's surface and the varying duration of daylight changes the heating efficiency of this sunlight. These seasonal effects are also present on other planets.

Data Table 1. Duration of Daylight Through the Year at Different Latitudes on Earth

| Date | Duration of Daylight Hours at Latitude | | |
| --- | --- | --- | --- |
| | Latitude 0° (Equator) | Latitude 50° North | Latitude 50° South |
| March 20, 2015 | | | |
| June 21, 2015 | | | |
| September 23, 2015 | | | |
| December 22, 2015 | | | |

Graph Template 1. Hours of Daylight Through the Year at Different Latitudes on Earth

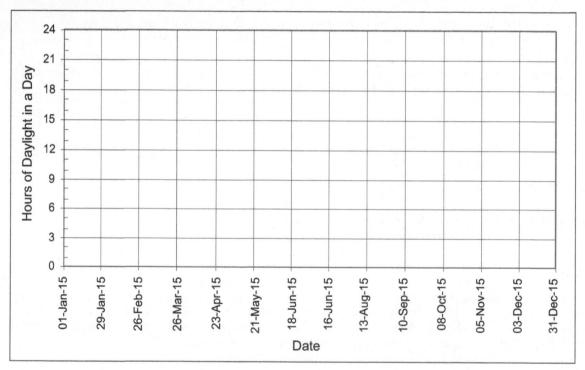

# The Analemma  8

The Sun reaches its highest point in the sky when it crosses an observer's celestial meridian, which occurs close to midday every day. The **celestial meridian,** often called simply the meridian, is an imaginary line passing through the observer's zenith and the North and South Celestial Poles and is shared by all observers on the same line of longitude on Earth. From the northern hemisphere, this meridian passes vertically through the south point of the observer's horizon. In fact, all objects in the background sky reach their highest point on the observer's sky as they pass through the meridian.

However, if we observe the Sun's position at twelve o'clock each day throughout the year we will rarely find it on the meridian. There are several reasons for the Sun being offset from the meridian at noon.

The first reason is that the observer's location may not be at the center of the time zone. This produces a constant offset of the Sun from the observer's celestial meridian at noon. If time zone boundaries were ideal, this offset might be as large as half an hour. For political reasons, time zone boundaries sometimes differ from the ideal positions, resulting in larger offsets in some locations.

The second reason is that the Earth's orbit is elliptical. This means that both the Earth's orbital speed and its distance from the Sun vary through the year, as described by Kepler's second law. These variations cause the apparent speed of the Sun against the background stars to change day by day, as seen from Earth.

The third reason is that the Earth's orbital plane, the ecliptic plane, is tilted with respect to the Earth's equatorial plane. This tilt causes an additional variation in the effective speed of motion of the Sun in a direction parallel to the Earth's equator.

The combination of the Earth's elliptical orbit and its axial tilt causes a variable east-west offset of the Sun from the meridian at midday, the offset following a cyclic pattern over the course of a year. At the same time, the tilt of the Earth's axis causes the Sun to drift north and south of the equator through the progression of the seasons. The result is a figure-8 pattern for the Sun's midday position in our sky over the course of a year. This figure-8 pattern is called the **analemma**, and is often found on globes representing the Earth.

The shape of the analemma was important when sundials were used to tell the time. The analemma provided corrections to sundial times, amounting to as much as 16 minutes at certain times of the year. The graph of the difference between the time of the Sun's passage through the meridian and actual midday, the time error of a simple sundial, is sometimes known as the **Equation of Time.** This observing project demonstrates the analemma and shows how Earth's axial tilt and elliptical orbit produce its overall shape.

## A. The Shape and Size of the Analemma

In the first simulation you will view the analemma from Calgary, Alberta, Canada, a city that lies at a longitude of about 114° W, within the Mountain Time zone. The standard meridian for this zone is 105° west of the Greenwich Meridian. The Greenwich Meridian, also known as the prime meridian, passes through London, England, and defines the zero point of longitude. Universal Time, a common standard time used throughout the world, is maintained at the Greenwich Meridian, 0 hours UT being midnight on this meridian.

The average time between two successive passages of the Sun through the meridian is 24 hours, Mean Solar Time. If we assume that the Earth has rotated through 360° in this time, then the rotation rate is 360/24 = 15° per hour. Thus, the standard time in the Mountain Standard Time zone (MST) is 105/15 = 7 hours behind Universal Time. (In practice, the Earth rotates slightly more than 360° in 1 solar day since the Earth has moved about 1° in its orbit. The time taken to rotate through 360° with respect to the distant stars is 23 hours, 56 minutes 4 seconds, a time known as 1 sidereal day.)

In fact, Calgary is 9° west of the standard meridian for the Mountain Standard Time zone, which means that, when a person on the standard meridian sees the Sun on the celestial meridian, a person in Calgary sees the Sun 9° east of the celestial meridian. We must therefore adjust the time to allow for this 9° offset in order to place the Sun on the meridian in Calgary on average throughout the year. At 15° per hour, this offset amounts to 36 minutes of time. Because Calgary is west of the standard meridian, the Sun crosses the meridian later, at 12:36 pm, MST.

**Question 1.** Boston, Massachusetts, is at longitude 71° W in the Eastern Time Zone. The standard meridian for this zone is 75° W. On the basis of Boston's position in the time zone, where would you expect to find the Sun relative to the meridian at noon Eastern Standard Time, if a person at 75° W sees the Sun on the meridian?

**Question 2.** If a person at 75° W sees the Sun on the meridian at noon, at what time would a person in Boston see the Sun on the meridian?

1. Launch *Starry Night*™ and open **Favourites > Observing Projects > Analemma > Solar Time**.

The view shows the southern horizon from Calgary on December 21. The local meridian is displayed as a line from the south point on the horizon to the zenith beyond the top of the screen. Time is set to 12:34:02 MST to place the Sun on the meridian for Calgary's specific position within the Mountain Standard Time zone on this date.

At this time of the year in the northern hemisphere, the Sun is at a low angle above the southern horizon. A vertical pole acting as a sundial at this location would cast a long shadow away from the south point on the horizon, toward the north.

It is interesting to see a track across the sky of the position of the Sun at midday as the year progresses.

2. Click **Play** and observe the change in position of the midday Sun at 1-day intervals through the year. Allow time to run for a year or two and then click **Stop**.

You can see that the position of the midday sun traces out a figure-8 pattern in a full year, climbing high in the sky in summer and returning to low elevation angles in winter. For a sundial to agree with our clocks, the Sun would have to be on the meridian at the same time every day.

**Question 3.** From your observation of the midday position of the Sun through the year, as represented by the analemma, how reliable is the Sun as a timekeeper?

## B. The Tilt of the Earth's Spin Axis

The reason for the north-south motion of the Sun in the sky during the year is the tilt of the Earth's axis to the ecliptic plane. It is this tilt that produces seasonal changes on the Earth. You can use the analemma to measure the maximum north-south excursion of the Sun, in degrees. This maximum excursion will be twice the tilt-angle of the Earth's spin axis to its orbital plane.

3. Hide **Daylight** and use the time controls to move the Sun's position to the bottom of the analemma.
4. Use the Angular Separation tool to measure the angle between the Sun and the top of the analemma.

**Question 4.** By what angle is the Earth's spin axis tilted from the perpendicular to its orbital plane?

## C. Errors in Sundial Times

The analemma represents the Sun's midday position with respect to an observer's meridian throughout the year. If you needed to use a simple sundial to tell the time (on a desert island as part of a television "reality" *Survivor* program, maybe!), the point at the end of the shadow of a vertical pole at midday each day would trace out the analemma on the ground. However, as you can see, your improvised clock would be in error on any given day by the time taken for the Sun to move through the angle represented by the difference between the analemma and the meridian. Your "clock" would be slow or fast, depending on whether the point on the analemma was east or west of the meridian, respectively. We can measure these errors, using the traced analemma pattern.

5. **Run time forward** until the Sun is at the widest point of the analemma on the east (left) side of the meridian. Record the Date of this greatest deviation of the Sun from the meridian in Data Table 1 at the end of this project.

6. Measure the angular distance, $\theta$, between the Sun and the meridian and convert this angle into degrees and fractions of a degree. To do so, divide the number of minutes of angle in the measurement by 60 and add the result to the number of degrees in the measurement. Note this angle in Data Table 1. [TIP: Use the Zoom and Gaze controls to increase the accuracy of your measurements.]

7. Repeat this measurement by moving the Sun to the equivalent position on the west side of the analemma and measure and record the error angle and the Date in Data Table 1.

The Earth rotates through 360° in almost 24 hours. For this measurement, we can assume that this time is exactly 24 hours, with the meridian moving across the background sky at a rate of 15° an hour. Thus, it takes 4 minutes of time for the meridian of the Earth to cover 1° of angle. You need to multiply the measured angle $\theta$ in degrees by 4 to calculate the sundial error in minutes of time.

**Question 5.** By how many minutes of time is the sundial in error on these two dates of maximum error?

**Question 6.** At what times of the year will the sundial be most inaccurate? (In practice, determination of the date of maximum error is not very precise.)

You will notice from the analemma that a sundial is accurate when compared to our clocks on some days of the year.

8. Use the time flow controls in the toolbar to find the dates of the year when the sundial error is zero and note these dates. [TIP: Use the Gaze and Zoom controls to increase your accuracy.]

**Question 7.** On what dates in the year will a sundial be most accurate?

## D. The Analemma from Other Latitudes

The shape of the analemma will be the same from any position on Earth. You can test this hypothesis by moving to another location.

9. **Stop** time flow, **zoom out** until the full analemma is visible and change the Date to **June 21.** The specific year is not important.

10. Select **Options > Viewing Location...** and change the observing location to **Sao Paolo, Brazil.**

11. Change the Time in the toolbar to **12:00:00 PM standard time.**

12. Set the Gaze direction to due **North.**

13. Adjust the view so that the Sun is near the bottom of the screen and the meridian is vertical.

14. You can erase the green path line of the Sun that appeared when the location was changed by clicking the **Decrease current elevation** button once in the toolbar after "changed".

15. **Run time forward** to trace out the analemma from Brazil and **Stop** when the Sun has traced out the full pattern.

You will note that the shape of the analemma is the same as it was from Calgary. Measurements equivalent to those carried out above will confirm that it has exactly the same dimensions when observed from Sao Paulo. There is, however, one difference.

Question 8.    In what way is the analemma different when viewed from Brazil? Why is this?

## E. Analemma Details

In this section, we will explore in more detail how the tilt of the Earth's axis and its motion in an elliptical orbit around the Sun produce the sundial errors measured in the previous section. As the previous simulations have shown, the Sun sometimes runs slow and at other times fast compared to the time on clocks. This is because clocks are built to run at a steady rate, calibrated to what is called the **mean solar day**. A hypothetical mean Sun is assumed to move eastward across the sky at a steady rate throughout the year. The duration of a mean solar day is the time between successive crossings of the position of this hypothetical Sun through the meridian at any site. Sundials, on the other hand, measure the **apparent solar day**. The length of the apparent solar day is the time required for the actual Sun to return to the same position in the sky as seen from a particular location on Earth. Sundial errors, as demonstrated by the analemma, represent the degree to which the actual Sun lags behind or runs ahead of the hypothetical mean Sun through the year. These errors, as mentioned above, are known as the Equation of Time.

The two effects that combine to produce this offset of the Sun from its mean position day by day are the eccentricity of the Earth's orbit and the tilt of the Earth's spin axis to its orbital plane. We can demonstrate the effect on the analemma of each of these orbital parameters in turn by introducing a fictitious planet, which we will call Vulcan, into *Starry Night™*. Initially, we will create an orbit for Vulcan with the same properties as those of Earth's orbit. We can then edit these orbital properties to remove the effects individually and observe the resulting shape and size of the analemma.

16. Select **File > Revert**.

17. Select **File > New Asteroid Orbiting Sun...** from the menu. This will open a dialog window in which you will create the fictitious planet Vulcan.

18. At the top of the dialog window, type **Vulcan** in the edit box to replace the name Untitled.

19. Select the **Orbital Elements** tab in the lower section of the window and set the values of the parameters on this page as follows:

    | | |
    |---|---|
    | **Style:** | Near-circular |
    | **Ref Plane:** | Ecliptic 2000 |
    | **Mean distance (a):** | 1.0  AU |
    | **Eccentricity (e):** | 0.0167058 |

    [HINT: Type these precise values into the relevant boxes, rather than using the slide controls.]

20. Click the **Other Settings** tab in the dialog window and set the following values:

    | | | |
    |---|---|---|
    | **Rotation rate:** | 1.002738 | rotations per day |
    | **Pole declination:** | 90.0 | degrees |

21. Minimize, and do not close, the Asteroid: Vulcan dialog window.

22. Open the **Find** pane and type **Vulcan** in the search box. The list in the Find pane should now display an entry for Vulcan.

23. Click the drop down menu button for Vulcan and select **Go There**.

The view is looking down on Vulcan.

24. Select **Options > Orientation > Equatorial** from the menu.

25. In the Find pane, clear the text from the search box and when the list defaults to solar system objects, **Centre** the gaze on the Sun. Adjust the Time in the toolbar to bring the Sun close to the meridian.

26. Click **Play** and adjust the view as required to see the complete path of the analemma.

The parameters that you used to create Vulcan are virtually the same as the orbital elements for the Earth. The rotation rate of Vulcan, its orbital eccentricity and distance from the Sun and the tilt of its axis relative to its orbital plane are the same as those of Earth. Hence, the analemma looks virtually identical to that of Earth with the same general shape consisting of asymmetrical lobes and an axis that is tilted slightly with respect to the meridian.

You can now adjust the parameters of the orbit of this fictitious planet to see the effect of each of them on the shape of the analemma. First, you can remove the eccentricity to make the planet's orbit circular.

27. With time continuing to flow, restore the Asteroid: Vulcan dialog window.
28. Click the **Orbital Elements** tab and set the Eccentricity (e) to **0**. Minimize the Planet: Vulcan window.

This step has reduced Vulcan's orbit to a circle. The resulting analemma is the result ONLY of the effect of the tilt of the planet's axis to its orbital plane, in this case, the Ecliptic Plane.

> **Question 9.** What effect does eliminating the eccentricity from Vulcan's orbit have on the appearance of the analemma?

You can now adjust the orbital parameters of Vulcan to demonstrate the effect of eccentricity only, without the tilt of its spin axis to the perpendicular to its orbital plane. You will also need to restore the eccentricity of Vulcan's orbit.

29. Restore the Asteroid: Vulcan window and under the **Orbital Elements** tab, change the Eccentricity (e) back to **0.0167058**. Then change the Ref Plane to **Earth Equatorial 2000**. This tilts the planet's orbital plane to correspond to its equatorial plane.
30. Minimize the Asteroid: Vulcan window and observe the analemma.

Vulcan now has an elliptical orbit again but its spin axis is perpendicular to its orbital plane.

> **Question 10.** Describe the analemma for Vulcan when its orbit is elliptical but its spin axis is perpendicular to its orbital plane. How do you account for the shape of the analemma under these orbital conditions?

31. Restore the Asteroid: Vulcan window and change the Eccentricity (e) to **0** once again. Then minimize the Asteroid: Vulcan window and observe the Sun in the view.

Vulcan is now moving in a circular orbit and rotating once per day on an axis perpendicular to the plane of its orbit.

> **Question 11.** Describe the "analemma" as it appears on Vulcan under these orbital conditions. Explain your observations.
>
> **Question 12.** How accurate would a sundial be on the planet Vulcan as it is currently configured?
>
> **Question 13.** How would the two types of solar day, mean and apparent, compare on Vulcan as it is configured in this view?

32. Close the Asteroid: Vulcan window and click the **Don't Save** button in the message box that appears.

## F. Sunrise Time at the Winter Solstice

The shape of Earth's analemma can help to answer the following question often asked about sunrise time: "If the Sun is at its furthest South on the shortest day of the year, at the time of the December solstice, why is this NOT the date of latest sunrise?" In fact, the date of latest sunrise is nearer to the end of the year! We will define sunrise as the moment when the upper limb or edge of the Sun just touches the horizon. Since this time will depend to some extent on the local horizon, the official definition assumes that the observer is at sea level. In order to simulate this situation, some of the following sequences use a line to represent a flat horizon.

> 33. Open **Favourites > Observing Projects > Analemma > Morning Analemma.**

The view is from Calgary looking southeast just after sunrise on December 21, the date of the winter solstice.

> 34. **Run time forward** to show the path traced out by the Sun at this time every day of the year, the analemma for this time of the day.

In contrast to the view of the analemma at midday, this pattern is now tilted at a distinct angle to the horizon and is not perpendicular to it. Furthermore, the lowest point of the analemma pattern is no longer the position of the Sun at the winter solstice. Sunrise will occur at its latest time on the date when the Sun is at its lowest point on this tilted analemma. You can determine the time of sunrise for a few days around the winter solstice.

> 35. Open **Favourites > Observing Projects > Analemma > Latest Sunrise.**

The view is from Calgary on December 21 just before sunrise. The gaze is centered on the Sun and the full horizon has been removed from the display and replaced by a line.

> 36. Adjust the Time in the toolbar to the moment of sunrise, when the upper edge of the Sun just touches the horizon line. Record the time of sunrise in Data Table 2 at the end of this project.
> 37. Change the Date to **December 23**. Note that the Sun is below the horizon on this morning. Once again, adjust the Time in the toolbar to the precise moment of sunrise, and record this time in Data Table 2. Repeat this step for the rest of the dates in Data Table 2.

> **Question 14.** What is the date of the latest sunrise during the winter?

You can readily see that the date of latest sunrise is many days later than the date of the winter solstice. The motion of the Sun because of Earth's orbital parameters, as represented by the shape of the analemma, affects the sunrise time. You can demonstrate this by running the analemma on the date of the latest sunrise.

> 38. **Favourites > Observing Projects > Analemma > Morning Analemma.**
> 39. Set the Date and Time in the toolbar to the latest sunrise of the year.
> 40. Use the time controls to trace out the lower region of the analemma at this time.

> **Question 15.** By about how many days after the winter solstice does the latest sunrise occur?
> **Question 16.** By how many minutes and seconds is this sunrise later than that at the solstice?

## G. Challenge: Sunset Time at the Winter Solstice

It would be a useful exercise for you to use the techniques of the previous section to demonstrate this equivalent effect on sunset times.

> 41. Use the views named **Evening Analemma** and **Earliest Sunset** in the **Observing Projects > Analemma** folder in the **Favourites** pane and follow the ideas presented in the sequences of the previous section to explore sunset near the winter solstice.

**Question 17.**   What is the date of earliest sunset around the time of the winter solstice?

There will be similar time shifts of the earliest sunrise and latest sunset around the time of longest day in the summer.

**Question 18.**   Do you think that these shifts of earliest sunrise and latest sunset around the June solstice would be equal to, less than, or greater than the shifts of latest sunrise and earliest sunset around the time of the December solstice? Use the shape of the analemma to support your answer.

## H. Conclusions

In this project, you have demonstrated the combined effects on the position of the Sun at midday through the course of the year of both the Earth's elliptical orbit and the tilt of the Earth's spin axis to the perpendicular to this orbit. You have seen this effect displayed as the analemma on the sky and you have measured the possible errors in a simple sundial because of these effects. These errors, when plotted for the whole year, are known as the Equation of Time. This "equation" is often displayed on modern sundials. You have also used the analemma to demonstrate that the date of latest sunrise in the winter is not the date of the shortest day of the year at the winter solstice.

Data Table 1. Maximum Sundial Errors

| Date | Angular Distance of Sun from Meridian, θ (°) | Sundial Error, θ x 4 (minutes of time) |
|---|---|---|
|  |  |  |
|  |  |  |

Data Table 2. Time of Sunrise near the Winter Solstice

| Date | Dec 21 | Dec 23 | Dec 25 | Dec 27 | Dec 29 | Dec 31 | Jan 2 | Jan 4 |
|---|---|---|---|---|---|---|---|---|
| Time of Sunrise |  |  |  |  |  |  |  |  |

# Precession and Nutation of the Earth

# 9

As the Earth orbits the Sun in the ecliptic plane, it also rotates in space with a period of one sidereal day around an axis that is inclined to this orbital plane. This angle of inclination varies over very long periods but is about 23½° at the present time.

If the Earth's shape were a perfect sphere, its rotation would be undisturbed and the direction of the axis would remain fixed in space. However, the Earth's rapid rotation, particularly during its formative stages, has distorted it into a flattened shape known as an oblate spheroid in which its equatorial diameter is now 43 km longer than its polar diameter. In addition to the direct gravitational forces that act between the centers of the Earth, the Moon, and the Sun to maintain their respective orbital motions, this slightly distorted Earth now becomes subject to the influence of differential gravitational forces from both the Moon and the Sun.

The differential force from the Moon, for example, arises where the gravitational force from the Moon pulls more strongly on the portion of the Earth's equatorial bulge facing the Moon than on the portion of the bulge on the opposite side of the Earth from the Moon. If the Earth were not rotating, the combined differential forces from the Moon and the Sun acting at an angle on Earth's equatorial bulge would tip the Earth's equator toward the plane of its orbit, the ecliptic plane. Since the Earth is spinning, these forces cause the spin axis to move in a conical motion called **precession**.

This slow coning precessional motion of the axis is similar to the motion of a child's spinning top. When a spinning top is placed on the ground with its axis inclined to the vertical, there are out-of-balance forces acting on the top that are attempting to cause it to fall over. Indeed, if it were not spinning, the top would fall over under gravity. In both cases, the spinning top and the rotating Earth, out-of-balance forces cause classical precession of the spin axis. The actual dynamics are relatively simple but a full explanation requires knowledge of the physics of rotational motion that is beyond the scope of this book.

The consequences of this precessional motion on life on Earth are very small and affect almost no one. However, they do affect the orientations of the equatorial plane and the spin axis of Earth with respect to the background stars. Since the equatorial plane is used to define the equatorial coordinates of **right ascension** and **declination** that are used by astronomers to define positions of objects in our sky, this precession causes the right ascension and declination of each star to change slowly and continuously over time as the direction of the Earth's rotation axis changes. Star atlases have to be specifically labeled with the epoch for which they are applicable. Those in use today have been drawn for the epoch 2000.0. In order to point a telescope accurately at any object in the sky whose right ascension and declination are known from this atlas, corrections have to be made night-by-night to allow for this slow drift. This adjustment is known as **precessing the coordinates** of an object and is always done before pointing a telescope toward the object. In modern telescope systems, this adjustment is carried out automatically by the telescope control system.

In this project, you will display and measure the precessional motion of the northern extension of the spin axis of the Earth, the North Celestial Pole or NCP, by compressing time so that you can "observe" the sky over very long periods. You will also examine and measure the motion of the **vernal equinox** across the sky because of precession. The vernal equinox is one of the two points at which the Earth's orbital plane intersects its equatorial plane and is used as the zero point of right ascension. The Sun passes through the vernal equinox on the first day of spring in the northern hemisphere every year, hence its name. In the final section of the project, you will observe and measure a tiny additional wobble of the spin axis of Earth known as **nutation** that is superimposed on the smooth and long-term precession. This effect is caused by shorter-term variations of the differential forces.

## A. Observation of Precessional Motion

You will use *Starry Night*™ to view the northern polar region of the sky and follow the motion of the North Celestial Pole (NCP) against the background stars as time is advanced rapidly. The NCP is easily found at the present epoch because it is close to a bright "marker star", Polaris, the so-called Pole Star of the northern hemisphere.

1. Launch *Starry Night*™.
2. Open **Favourites > Observing Projects > Precession and Nutation > Precession.**

The view shows the northern sky as seen from Toronto, Canada, on March 21, 2007, at local midnight. This wide-angle view is centered on the North Celestial Pole, NCP, marked by a red cross. Polaris is visible just below the North Celestial Pole. Since the NCP is the position in space to which the Earth's spin axis points, this gaze direction is parallel to the rotation axis of Earth. The stars will appear to move as time changes because the view is locked on to the NCP. In reality the stars represent a fixed background against which the NCP moves.

3. With the Time Flow Rate set to **50 years**, click the **Play** and **Reverse** buttons to follow the track of the North Celestial Pole across the sky over relatively long time periods.

You will see that, as a result of precession, the North Celestial Pole appears to move in a circle around a fixed position among the stars. This fixed position is known as the **North Ecliptic Pole.**

4. Open **Favourites > Observing Projects > Precession and Nutation > View Along Axis.**

This view is from a location about 173,000 km, or approximately 0.001 AU above the South Pole of the Earth, with the view centered on the Earth. Thus, you are looking along the spin axis toward the North Celestial Pole, hidden behind the center of the Earth in this view. The line from the Earth's center to the North Ecliptic Pole is perpendicular to the ecliptic plane and is the axis of the cone through which the rotation axis of Earth moves under precession. The cone angle is about 23½°.

5. Set the Zoom to **90°** and then measure the angular separation between the center of the Earth and the North Ecliptic Pole. Since you are looking along the spin axis of Earth, this is equivalent to measuring the angular separation between the NCP and the North Ecliptic Pole.

**Question 1.**   What is the angular separation between the North Celestial Pole (directly behind the center of the Earth in the view) and the North Ecliptic Pole?

6. Select **File > Revert** and with the Time Flow Rate set to **50 years**, click the **Play** and **Reverse** buttons to follow the track of the North Celestial Pole over time.

Note that the North Ecliptic Pole marks the fixed position around which the stars appear to rotate. Also note how fortunate we are in the Northern Hemisphere to have a star as bright as Polaris, our "Pole Star", so close to the North Celestial Pole at the present time in history.

It is interesting to use this time compression to investigate the position of the North Celestial Pole in history and in the future.

7. Open **Favourites > Observing Projects > Precession and Nutation > Earth Center.**

This view is nearly identical to that of the previous sequence except that the observing location is at the center of a transparent Earth. The gaze remains along the rotation axis of Earth toward the North Celestial Pole.

8. Manipulate the Zoom and Time controls in the toolbar (including adjusting the Time Flow Rate) and use the Angular Separation tool to help you to answer the following questions. [HINT: You might want to **Centre** and lock onto the star in question to make some of these measurements.]

Question 2.  Currently, is the North Celestial Pole getting closer to or moving away from Polaris, our Pole Star?

Question 3.  In what year will the North Celestial Pole be closest to Polaris? What will be the angular separation between Polaris and the North Celestial Pole on this date?

Question 4.  In the past, the star Thuban was the Pole Star. On what date was the most recent close approach of the North Celestial Pole to this star? How close did the North Celestial Pole get to Thuban at this time?

Question 5.  Does the North Celestial Pole get closer to Polaris or Thuban during this precessional motion?

9. Select **File > Revert**.
10. Select **View > Constellations > Boundaries**, and **View > Constellations > Labels** from the menu.
11. Manipulate the Gaze and Time controls to answer the following questions.

Question 6.  In which constellation is the North Celestial Pole at this time? Into which constellation will the North Celestial Pole move next? In which year will this occur?

Question 7.  In which constellation is the North Ecliptic Pole?

Question 8.  Does the plane of the Earth's orbit around the Sun shift with respect to the stars over time? How can you tell?

Question 9.  In what year will the North Celestial Pole be closest to the star Vega in the constellation Lyra?

Question 10.  In the future, how close will the North Celestial Pole move to Vega?

## B. Measurement of Precessional Motion of the North Celestial Pole

You can measure the precessional motion of the rotation axis of Earth easily by finding a time, in history or in the future, when this axis is pointing toward a star in our sky. You can then use this star as a reference point and measure the angle moved by the end of the axis, the North Celestial Pole, after a specified period of time. An example of this type of close approach occurred in 1417 AD when the North Celestial Pole was close to the star designated TYC4641-683-1.

12. Open **Favourites > Observing Projects > Precession and Nutation > TYC4641-683-1.**
13. Set the Zoom to **15'** and use the Hand tool to drag the view so that the North Celestial Pole is at the center of the view and the red line labeled Celestial Meridian is exactly horizontal on the screen.

This view shows the North Celestial Pole next to the labeled reference star, TYC4641-683-1. You can now advance time by a certain interval and measure the movement of the North Celestial Pole from its position adjacent to the reference star. The selected measurement interval is 19 years, for reasons which will become apparent in Section D, below. From this observation, you can then determine the change in the orientation of the Earth's spin axis per year and determine how long it takes for this axis to complete a full circle in the sky.

14. **Step time forward** by one 19-year step and measure the angular separation between the North Celestial Pole position and its previous position next to the reference star. Note this value in arc minutes and arcseconds.

15. Convert the measured value to arcseconds by multiplying the number of arcminutes by 60 and then adding the number of arcseconds to give the total measured separation in arcseconds and divide this value by 19 to obtain the rate of motion of the NCP across the sky in arcseconds per year.

16. Divide your result from the previous step by 3600 (the number of arcseconds in one degree) to obtain the angular rate of motion of the North Celestial Pole, $\Omega$, in degrees per year.

17. Follow the calculations outlined below to determine the revolutionary period of the precessional axis around a full circle.

Calculations

The circle followed by the NCP in the sky will have a circumference of $2\pi R$, where $R = 23.42°$ in angular units. Thus, since speed of motion of the NCP, $\Omega$, is equal to the distance divided by the time,

$$\Omega = 2\pi R/t,$$

where t, in years, is the time taken for the axis to precess through one full cycle.

Thus

$$t = (2\pi R/\Omega) = 147.34/\Omega$$

**Question 11.** How fast does the North Celestial Pole move across our sky, in arcseconds per year?

**Question 12.** How long will it take the spin axis of Earth to move once around the precessional cone?

18. Open **Favourites > Observing Projects > Precession and Nutation > Earth Center** and adjust the Date to place the NCP next to Polaris and then run time forward by your calculated time interval in order to verify your result.

## C. Motion of the Vernal Equinox

Another manifestation of the precessional motion of the sky is the year-by-year movement of the vernal equinox, one of the points of intersection of the **ecliptic** and the **celestial equator**. The vernal equinox defines the zero point of right ascension in the equatorial coordinate system. This position is also involved in the questionable practice of astrology, though practitioners of astrology do not follow the modern sky and its positions. Nevertheless, there are two references to the position of the vernal equinox that have achieved a certain significance, the first one historic and the second one modern.

The vernal equinox is sometimes referred to by its historical name of the First Point of Aries since, at a certain point in history, it was found to be within this constellation. We can determine the date when this label ceased to be relevant by tracing the era in which the equinox actually left the constellation of Aries.

A more modern reference to the motion of the vernal equinox has entered the lexicon of modern English, namely the "Age of Aquarius", referring to the future. You can use *Starry Night*™ to predict the dawning of this age of infinite promise, which is presumed to start when the vernal equinox enters the constellation of Aquarius.

19. Open **Favourites > Observing Projects > Precession and Nutation > Vernal Equinox.**

You will note that, on the first day of spring in 2010 AD, the Sun is at the vernal equinox as expected. During the year, the Sun moves along the ecliptic at about 1° per year, to return to the vernal equinox each year. The time required for the Sun to return to the vernal equinox is called a **tropical year** and is 365.2422 mean solar days in duration. *Starry Night*™ defines the year as 365 days. Thus, the Sun will not return precisely to the vernal equinox in the view and the Date in the toolbar will slowly regress as time passes. Nevertheless, the rapid passage of time in the simulation will allow you to observe and measure the drift of the vernal equinox against the background stars that results from precession.

20. With the Time Flow Rate set at **20 years**, click **Play** and observe the motion of the vernal equinox against the background stars. In this rapid advancement of time, you will note that planets move very rapidly across the sky and that the Sun drifts along the ecliptic because of the time discrepancy discussed above.

You can now use a similar view to determine the two interesting dates referred to above, the date when the vernal equinox left Aries and the date when it will enter Aquarius to begin the "Age of Aquarius".

21. Open **Favourites > Observing Projects > Precession and Nutation > Age of Aquarius**. To reduce confusion, the view does not show the Sun or the planets.

22. Manipulate the Time controls, Time Flow Rate and Zoom controls in the toolbar to answer the following questions.

> **Question 13.** In what constellation is the vernal equinox located at the present time?
>
> **Question 14.** When did the vernal equinox, also called the First Point of Aries, actually leave the constellation of Aries?
>
> **Question 15.** When will we reach the "Age of Aquarius", defined by the vernal equinox moving into the constellation of Aquarius?

You will note that we are going to have to wait a significant time before we reach this age of great promise!

Since the vernal equinox is also the zero point of the celestial coordinate system, this motion changes the right ascension and declination coordinates of stars and other objects on a day-by-day basis. We can follow and measure this motion.

23. Open **Favourites > Observing Projects > Precession and Nutation > HIP112813**.

The view shows the star HIP112813 centered in the view. Note that this star lies almost on the ecliptic, the plane of the Earth's orbit around the Sun, represented by a green line.

24. Open the **Info** pane and expand the **Position in Sky** layer and note the RA (JNow) and Dec (JNow) values, the equatorial coordinates of the star HIP112813 on this date in May 3319 AD.

25. Measure the angular separation between the labeled star HIP112813 and the vernal equinox.

26. With the Time Flow Rate set at **19 years, Step time forward** by one step. Note now that the vernal equinox is very close to the reference star. You can also see from the **Info** pane that the RA and Dec of this star have changed.

27. Watch the RA and Dec of the star in the Info pane and **Step time forward** by one more step of 19 years. It is this kind of change in RA and Dec that needs to be taken into account before pointing a telescope at a particular star, in a procedure known as *precessing the coordinates,* as discussed above.

28. Repeat the measurement of the angular separation between the reference star and the vernal equinox.

29. Calculate the average of the two measurements you made of the distance between the vernal equinox and HIP112813 and divide this average by 19 to obtain the rate of motion of the vernal equinox across our sky in arcseconds per year.

**Question 16.** How fast does the vernal equinox travel across our sky in arcseconds per year?

## D. Nutation

In addition to the slow but significant motion of the spin axis of Earth and the vernal equinox because of precession, the varying effects of the gravitational forces from the Moon and the Sun cause a much smaller wobble in the Earth's axis, with a period reflecting the motions of the Moon. This wobble is known as **nutation** and can be observed and measured.

30. Open **Favourites > Observing Projects > Precession and Nutation > Nutation.**

In this 1° field of view, a reference star, TYC4662-45-1, lies close to the North Celestial Pole. In this view, the North Celestial Pole will remain fixed as time advances. Thus, although the North Celestial Pole, which is defined by the rotation axis of the Earth, is in reality moving across the sky because of precession, it will appear to remain stationary while the stars will appear to move. Running time forward, you will see the precessional motion of the pole reflected in horizontal motion of the stars.

31. With the Time Flow Rate set at **1 year**, click **Play** and observe the motion of the stars.

You may have noticed that there is a small but perceptible wobble in the vertical positions of these stars as they execute their horizontal precessional motion. Since the view is locked on to the NCP, this apparent wobble is indicating a short-term nutational wobble of the Earth's spin axis. In the next sequence of observations, you can measure this nutational motion and quantify it.

32. Select **File > Revert.**
33. Change the Date in the toolbar to **June 1, 2074 AD.**
34. Change the Time Flow Rate to **2 years**.
35. **Zoom in** to a field of view about **18'** wide.
36. If necessary, use the Hand tool to adjust the view so that the North Celestial Pole is near the center of the screen and that the red line across the view that represents the celestial meridian is horizontal. The reference star TYC4662-45-1 should be visible near the left edge of the view.
37. Use the Angular Separation tool to measure the perpendicular distance from the star to the reference meridian (the horizontal red line). Note the year and your measurement in Data Table 1 at the end of this project.
38. **Step time forward** in 2-year steps and repeat this angular measurement after each step.

The data points in Data Table 1 can be plotted on a sheet of graph paper, or entered into a spreadsheet program and plotted as a graph, to reveal the pattern of the nutational motion of the North Celestial Pole. Plot the angular distance of the star TYC4662-45-1 from the reference meridian along the vertical axis of the graph and the date along the horizontal axis. From the graph, you can determine the relevant parameters of this motion: its period and its amplitude.

39. Open **Favourites > Observing Projects > Precession and Nutation > Nutation Trails.**

The view is a close-up of a region of the sky near the celestial meridian at a time when several bright stars are near this reference line.

40. **Step time forward** in 1-year intervals. Each star leaves a trail of dots—one dot per year—as time steps forward. The result should resemble the graph you drew from the data in Data Table 1.
    [TIP: Show **Daylight** to erase trails.]

Question 17.  Which of the following options best describes the line connecting the data points?

a) A straight horizontal line

b) A straight line sloping up over time

c) A straight line sloping down

d) A sinusoidal line (i.e., a wavy line that goes alternately up and down over time)

Question 18.  If the star shows a periodic variation, what is the period of this variation (i.e., how many years does it take for the graph to move from a maximum value through a minimum value and back to a maximum value)?

Question 19.  What is the amplitude of this variation, if any? (Amplitude is the difference between the maximum value and the minimum value divided by two, that is, one-half of the full variation of the angular separation of the star from the reference line.)

## E. Conclusions

The relatively smooth precessional motion of the Earth's spin axis, measured in Sections A, B, and C, is caused by the average effect of the differential gravitational forces from the Moon and the Sun acting on the Earth's equatorial bulge. These forces do not always act in the same direction, however, because of the motion of the Moon along an orbital path that is inclined to the ecliptic plane. The points where the Moon's orbital path crosses the ecliptic, the nodes of the Moon's orbit, slide around the ecliptic plane with a period of about 18.6 years. As seen in Section D, this produces small differences in the gravitational influence of the Moon on the Earth's bulge, resulting in the small nutational wobble superimposed on the smooth precessional coning of the Earth's spin axis.

**Data Table 1.** Angular Distance of TYC4662-45-1 from Reference Meridian

| Year | Angular Distance in Arcseconds (") |
|------|-----------------------------------|
|      |                                   |
|      |                                   |
|      |                                   |
|      |                                   |
|      |                                   |
|      |                                   |
|      |                                   |
|      |                                   |
|      |                                   |
|      |                                   |
|      |                                   |
|      |                                   |
|      |                                   |
|      |                                   |
|      |                                   |
|      |                                   |
|      |                                   |
|      |                                   |
|      |                                   |
|      |                                   |

# The Moon's Motions and Phases

# 10

The Moon orbits the Earth in 27.3 days with respect to the background stars. This period is known as a **sidereal month**. The time required for the Moon to return to the same position with respect to the Sun and thus complete a full cycle of phases, is 29.5 days. This period is known as a **synodic month**. The changing appearance of the Moon during its cycle of phases arises from the fact that the Moon is a spherical body that orbits the Earth and is illuminated by the Sun. One half of the Moon's surface is in light and the other half is in shadow at all times. The proportion of the illuminated hemisphere visible from Earth depends on the position of the Moon with respect to the orientation of the Earth and the Sun.

In the monthly cycle of phases, the Moon appears first as a very thin crescent in the western sky, quite close to the Sun. It then proceeds to show more of its illuminated side to Earth as it moves farther from the Sun in the sky. In this **waxing**, or growing, half of the cycle it will pass through **crescent, first quarter,** and **gibbous** phases before reaching **full Moon**. At its full phase, the Moon is opposite to the Sun in our sky and the entire sunlit hemisphere of the Moon faces the Earth. The Moon's angular separation from the Sun then begins to decrease as it moves into its **waning**, or diminishing, half of the cycle. It proceeds through **gibbous, last quarter,** and **crescent** phases until it again appears in the same direction in the sky as the Sun and its dark hemisphere faces the Earth at **new Moon**.

In this project, you will observe the motion and phases of the Moon and investigate this relationship between the Moon's phases and its position with respect to the Sun in the sky.

## A. The Moon's Motion Across the Sky and its Angular Speed

1. Launch *Starry Night*™ and open **Favourites > Observing Projects > Moon > Motion**.

The view shows the sky over Chicago near the time of sunset on July 19, 2016. The gaze is centered on the full Moon, which is rising in the eastern sky.

2. Open the contextual menu for the Moon and click the **Enlarge Moon Size** option if it is not checked.
3. Click **Play** and observe the motion of the Moon and stars through the night.

The westward drift of the Moon and stars in the sky results from our own eastward motion on the rotating platform of the Earth. However, careful observation shows that the Moon appears to drift against the background stars.

4. Select **File > Revert** and set the Zoom to **5°**. Click **Play** and observe the motion of the Moon compared to that of the stars.

Question 1.    In which direction does the Moon move against the background stars over this time? (E, W, N, S?)

Observing the Moon at successive intervals of one sidereal day will allow you to explore this independent motion of the Moon more easily.

5. Select **File > Revert**.

6. Click the **S** button in the toolbar to change the gaze to the south. Use the **H** keyboard shortcut to advance the Time to **4:05:00 AM daylight time** on **July 20**.

7. Change the Time Flow Rate to **1 sidereal day** and **Step time forward**.

In the interval of one sidereal day, the stars have returned to the same position in the sky but the Moon, having proceeded some distance along its orbit around the Earth, has moved against the background stars. You can measure how far the Moon moves in our sky in one day.

8. Open the contextual menu for the Moon and select **Local Path**.

9. Use the **D** keyboard shortcut to advance time by one solar day.

10. Measure the angular distance from the current position of the center of the Moon to the endpoint of the green line representing the position of the center of the Moon on the previous day.

Question 2.    To the nearest degree, what is the angular speed of the Moon's motion in degrees per day? How long would it take the Moon to move through a complete circle of 360°?

11. Select **File > Revert** to return to moonrise on **July 19, 2016**.

12. Use the **D** keyboard shortcut to advance the time one day.

Question 3.    How does the eastward motion of the Moon affect the time of moonrise from one day to the next?

## B. The Waxing Phases of the Moon

To observe the phases of the Moon from Earth, we must observe the sky at different times of the night on different days. The best time to observe the early waxing phases is just after sunset when the Moon appears in the western sky. The phases around full Moon are best observed near midnight, while the waning phases can be most effectively seen in the dawn sky.

13. Select **File > Revert** and then change the Date to **July 4, 2016**.

14. Configure the HUD to include **Age of Moon** and **Disk Illumination**.

In this view of the sky looking west from Chicago at 9:05:00 PM, Central Daylight Time, the Sun is about to set. The Moon appears as a faint silver disk in the twilight with a very thin crescent of brightness on the edge of the Moon closest to the Sun in the sky. The portion of the Moon not lit by the Sun is sometimes visible from Earth at this time because of **earthshine**—sunlight that has been reflected from the surface and clouds of the Earth to illuminate the Moon. This appearance was referred to in earlier times as "the old moon in the new moon's arms." Recall that the image of the Moon is artificially enlarged in the view and so looks larger than the Sun.

15. Use the HUD to find the phase and age of the Moon.

Question 4.    What is the phase and age of the Moon on July 4, 2016?

Question 5.    In which direction in the sky is the Moon relative to the Sun?

16. Use the **D** shortcut key to advance time 3 solar days to **July 7, 2016**. Each time step is one solar day and the local time remains the same, close to sunset.

17. Hide **Daylight** and set the Zoom to **Sample 10 x 50 Binoculars (7°)** to observe a magnified image of the Moon.

Question 6.    In which way do the "horns," the sharp endpoints of the crescent shape of the illuminated portion of the Moon, point with respect to the direction of the Sun?

18. Show **Daylight** and set the Zoom to **120°**.

Question 7.    Toward which compass direction in your sky do the "horns" of the waxing crescent moon point, as seen from the Earth? [HINT: This direction is opposite in the sky to the direction of the illuminated portion of the Moon.]

19. Use the **D** shortcut key to advance time in steps of one solar day to **July 11, 2016**.

By July 11, the Moon's orbital motion has carried it some distance away from the Sun in the sky. You can measure the angular distance between the Sun and the Moon as seen from Earth and thereby gain some insight into how the relative positions of the Sun, Moon, and Earth produce the various phases of the Moon.

20. Adjust the gaze so that the Sun is visible on the right side of the view. Then measure the angular distance between the Sun and the Moon.

21. Use the HUD to find the phase and age of the Moon as well as the Disk Illumination, the percentage of the hemisphere of the Moon facing the Earth that is illuminated by the Sun.

Question 8.    (a) What is the angular distance between the Sun and the Moon on July 11, 2016? (b) What is the phase of the Moon? (c) How many days have elapsed since the Moon was new (i.e., what is the age of the Moon)? (d) What percentage of the hemisphere of the Moon facing the Earth is illuminated by the Sun?

Question 9.    As seen from Earth, which side of the Moon's disk, east or west, is illuminated by the Sun?

22. **Centre** the view on the Moon and then use the **D** shortcut key to advance time in one-day intervals to **July 19, 2016** and observe the successive phases of the Moon.

Question 10.    What is the name given to the phase of the Moon between July 12 and 18, 2016?

Question 11.    What is the phase of the Moon on July 19, 2016?

Question 12.    In which direction in the sky is the Moon in the view on July 19, 2016?

Question 13.    Is the Moon rising or setting in the view?

23. **Zoom out** as necessary and adjust the view so that both the Sun and the Moon are visible in the view.

Question 14.    What is the approximate angular separation between the Moon and the Sun on July 19, 2016? [HINT: The Sun and the Moon are nearly at opposite sides of the field of view.]

## C. The Waning Phases of the Moon

24. **Centre** the view on the Moon and set the Zoom to **90°**.
25. Press the **D** keyboard shortcut to advance the time to **July 20, 2016**.

The Moon is just below the horizon at sunset on July 20, 2016. To observe the waning phases of the Moon, you need to change the time.

26. Use the **H** keyboard shortcut to change the Time in the toolbar to **02:05:00 AM** on **July 21, 2016**.
27. Use the **D** keyboard shortcut to advance time in one day intervals to **July 27, 2016**.

Question 15.   As seen from Earth, which side of the Moon's disk, east or west, is illuminated by the Sun?

Question 16.   What is the phase of the Moon on July 27, 2016?

28. To continue to follow the waning phases of the Moon, click the **Sunrise** button.
29. Use the **D** keyboard shortcut to advance time in one-day intervals to **July 30, 2016** and watch the phase of the Moon.
30. Hide **Daylight** and set the Zoom to **Sample 10 x 50 Binoculars (7°)** to observe a magnified image of the Moon.

Question 17.   In which way do the "horns" of the waning crescent moon point with respect to the direction of the Sun?

Question 18.   Toward which compass direction do the "horns" of the waning crescent moon point as seen from the Earth?

31. Show **Daylight** and set the Zoom to **90°**. Use the **D** shortcut key to advance time to **August 1, 2016**.
32. Use the HUD to find the age of the Moon (i.e., the elapsed time since the Moon was in its new phase).
33. Measure the angular distance between the Moon and the Sun.

Question 19.   Based on your calculation in Question 2, has the Moon moved through a complete circle in the sky? Has the Moon completed a full cycle of phases? What is the angular distance still separating the Moon and the Sun?

34. Advance time one day to **August 2**.

On August 2, the Moon is rising just before sunrise. Since July 4, it has nearly completed the entire cycle of phases. By August 3, 2016, the Moon will once again be a thin crescent in the western sky at sunset.

35. Change the Gaze to the **West**. Use the **D** shortcut key to advance time by one solar day and then click the **Sunset** button.

You can zoom in on the Moon and re-run this entire lunar cycle of phases again to watch the line between dark and light regions of the Moon (known as the terminator) sweep across the lunar features.

36. **Magnify** the Moon in the view.
37. Hide **Daylight** and the **Horizon** from the view.
38. Step through the full cycle of phases in 1-day steps to see how the Moon's motion in its orbit around Earth allows us to see more or less of the illuminated hemisphere.

Note in particular how you see almost the same hemisphere of the Moon throughout this cycle. This "locked-in" situation is evidence of synchronous rotation of the Moon, where the Moon rotates once on its axis in the same time that it takes to orbit the Earth. This has been caused by the gravitational force of the Earth on non-uniform mass distribution within the Moon that is related to the dark maria on its Earth-facing hemisphere. You will also observe that the Moon appears to wobble slightly about this locked-in alignment, in a motion known as **libration**. This libration allows us to see more than one-half of the Moon's surface over several lunar cycles.

## D. The Synodic Month

The synodic month is the time taken for the Moon to return to the same position with respect to the Sun in its orbital motion as seen from Earth. Since the phases of the Moon depend on its relative position with respect to the Sun as seen from Earth, the synodic month is also the time required for the Moon to complete a full cycle of phases from one new Moon to the next.

39. Select **Favourites > Observing Projects > Moon > Synodic Month**.

The view is from Chicago on July 4, 2016. The horizon and daylight have been removed from the view to give an unobstructed view of the Moon in the sky. Notice the relative positions of the Sun, Moon, and the star Mekbuda.

40. **Step time forward** in intervals of one day. Stop after 27 such daily steps and note the relative positions of the Sun, Moon, and Mekbuda. Since this interval of 27 days is close to one sidereal month, the Moon is back to the same region of the sky with respect to the background stars, as expected.

Question 20.　Is the Sun in the same position in the view relative to the background stars as it was on July 4, 2016? If not, in which direction has it moved?

41. Continue to **Step time forward** in intervals of one day and determine the duration of the synodic month, the number of days required to bring the Moon back to the same direction in the sky as the Sun and return to its new phase.

Question 21.　How long, in days, is a synodic month?

Question 22.　Why is the synodic month longer than the sidereal month?

### E. The Phases of the Earth

You can explore the phases displayed by the Earth to an observer on the Moon over the same time period as the previous sequences.

> 42. Select **Favourites > Observing Projects > Moon > Phases of Earth.**

The view is of the Earth from the surface of the Moon on July 4, 2016, when the Moon will be at its new phase as seen from Earth.

> **Question 23.** At this time, when the Moon is in its new phase as seen from Earth, what is the phase of the Earth as seen from the Moon? [HINT: Draw a diagram of the Sun-Earth-Moon system for new Moon as seen from Earth.]

> 43. **Step time forward** in intervals of one day to the date of full Moon as seen from Earth, namely **July 19, 2016,** and observe the changing phase of the Earth as seen from the Moon.

> Question 24. Is the Earth waxing or waning?
>
> Question 25. What is the phase of the Earth as seen from the Moon on the date when the Moon is full as seen from Earth (July 19, 2016)?

> 44. **Step time forward** in single day steps to the date of the next new Moon (**August 2, 2016**).

> **Question 26.** In this period of time, while the Moon wanes as seen from Earth, what phases does the Earth go through as seen from the Moon?

It is interesting to observe the Earth as seen by astronauts on the Moon.

> 45. Select **File > Revert** from the menu.
> 46. Change the Time Flow Rate to **30,000x.**
> 47. Click **Play** and observe the lunar horizon and the Earth as time progresses through at least one full cycle of phases of the Earth.

This provides a fascinating view of our Earth rotating on its axis while remaining in approximately the same position in the lunar sky as it shows phases equivalent to those of the Moon seen from Earth. Another glimpse of life for an astronaut on the Moon can be seen as you watch the abrupt arrival of sunrise on the Moon. Since there is no atmosphere, there will be no twilight, so the Sun suddenly floods the landscape with light.

> **Question 27.** Note that the horizon does not get in the way of the Earth at any time during this sequence. Why?

### F. Bonus: Lunar Occultations

One striking consequence of the lunar motion is that, as the Moon moves against the background stars, it occasionally covers and uncovers stars in its path. Such an event is called an **occultation**. An occultation of a star by the Moon is an exciting event to observe through a telescope. When the Moon covers a star, the event is called a **disappearance,** and when it uncovers a star, this event is known as a **reappearance**. These events are particularly exciting to watch when they occur against the unlit limb (edge) of the Moon. Because the stars are (almost) true points of light in the sky, and because the Moon has no atmosphere, the star vanishes nearly instantaneously from view in a disappearance event against the dark limb of the Moon. In fact, a star's angular size can sometimes be determined by a precise measurement of the diminution of the star's intensity during an occultation.

48. Open **Favourites > Observing Projects > Moon > Occultation**.
49. Click **Play** and observe the motion of the Moon against the background stars. You will note that several faint stars become occulted by the dark advancing limb of the Moon.

An occultation event is particularly interesting when circumstances are such that only the mountains and crater walls of the Moon's southern or northern polar regions pass in front of the star. When such a **grazing occultation** is observed from the correct location on Earth, the star is seen to wink out several times as it moves behind these higher regions at the Moon's poles. This allows astronomers to make important observations of the topography of regions of the Moon that are otherwise difficult to measure. If several observers watch the occultation through telescopes from sites spaced at right angles to the shadow path of the Moon across the Earth and carefully time the disappearances and reappearances of the star, a detailed profile of the topography along the Moon's limb can be constructed. Unfortunately, it is very difficult to simulate this kind of event.

**Question 28.** An occultation event can be a disappearance or a reappearance and can occur against the bright or the dark limb (edge) of the Moon. For each combination below, identify whether the Moon is waxing or waning.

(a) Disappearance at the dark limb

(b) Reappearance at the bright limb

(c) Reappearance at the dark limb

(d) Disappearance at the bright limb

## G. Conclusions

In this project, you have observed the phases of the Moon from different viewpoints as the Moon moves around the Earth in its orbit, while noting the relative positions of the Moon with respect to the Sun in the sky for each phase. You have measured the Moon's angular speed across our sky and you have compared the sidereal and synodic periods of the Moon as measured from the Earth. You have also examined the phases of the Earth as they would appear to an explorer on the Moon and have seen that these phases are complementary to those of the Moon as seen from Earth.

# Solar Eclipses

# 11

A solar eclipse occurs on Earth when the Moon passes in front of the Sun and casts its shadow upon the Earth's surface. Most observers within this shadow on the Earth will see the Moon obscure or occult a portion of the solar disc in a partial solar eclipse. By a fortunate coincidence, the angular sizes of the Sun and the Moon as seen from Earth are similar and under certain conditions some observers on Earth will see a total solar eclipse, in which the Moon completely covers the bright disk of the Sun.

The total eclipse of the Sun is one of nature's finest spectacles. Only at this time can you see the tenuous but hot outer atmosphere of the Sun directly, without the need for protection for the eyes or special instrumentation. (Of course, it is vital that eye protection be used in the time before and after totality, since even the partially eclipsed Sun is bright enough to cause permanent eye damage.) Scientifically, eclipses are important because many phenomena can be seen and measured ONLY during the brief period known as totality. A thin layer of the Sun's outer atmosphere directly above the Sun's visible surface that is seen primarily in the red light emitted by hydrogen gas is known as the chromosphere. Extending out into space is a very tenuous but extremely hot outer gas called the corona. Eclipse observations of these layers of the solar atmosphere have contributed materially to our understanding of the Sun over the past century. In this project, you will explore the conditions that produce the different types of solar eclipses observable from Earth.

---

**IMPORTANT! Never look directly at the real Sun, even when it is partially eclipsed, without proper eye protection (Welder's glass #14 or specially designed aluminized glass or plastic filters). In the absence of proper eye protection, observe a projected image of the Sun. Looking at the Sun without proper protection can produce serious and permanent eye damage!**

---

## A. Conditions Required for Solar Eclipses

For the Moon to move in front of the Sun as seen from Earth, obviously it must be in the same direction in the sky as the Sun and therefore in its new phase. Thus, a solar eclipse can occur only when the Moon is new. If the Moon's orbit was in the same plane as the Earth's orbit around the Sun then a solar eclipse would occur at every new Moon. However, the orbital plane of the Moon is inclined to the Earth's orbital plane, the ecliptic plane, by about 5°.

1. Launch *Starry Night*™ and configure the HUD to include **Age of Moon** and **Angular Size**.
2. Select **Options > Solar System > Planets-Moons...** Clear the checkboxes for the options to **Enlarge Moon size at large FOVs** and **Show solar lens flare when looking at Sun** and set the Sun Halo option to **Never**. Then click **OK** to dismiss the dialog window.
3. Open **Favourites > Observing Projects > Solar Eclipses > Moon's Orbit**.

The green line stretching horizontally across the view shows the Earth's orbit, which defines the ecliptic plane. The Moon's orbit is also shown (the shorter green slanted line). Clearly, the Moon's orbit is in a different plane than the ecliptic, but it does cross the ecliptic at two points, one on the side of its orbit closest to the viewing location and one on the opposite side of the Earth from the viewing location. These two points at which the Moon's orbit intersects the ecliptic plane are called **nodes**.

4. Use the Location Scroller to move the viewing location a small amount vertically so that the Moon's orbit opens into a thin ellipse with two wedge-shaped symbols visible on this orbit, above and below the image of the Earth.

The wedge-shaped icons represent the two nodes of the Moon's orbit. These nodes are distinguished as the **ascending node** (indicated by the solid wedge) when the Moon crosses the ecliptic moving northward, and the **descending node** (indicated by the hollow wedge) when the Moon crosses the ecliptic moving southward. Because of its inclined orbit, the Moon is usually north or south of the Sun in the sky at the time of new Moon and no eclipse occurs.

5. Open **Favourites > Observing Projects > Solar Eclipses > Eclipse Requirements**.

This view is from the center of a transparent Earth, with the gaze centered and locked upon the star Mebsuta. The green line that passes through the Sun represents the ecliptic plane and the green line that passes through the Moon represents the Moon's orbit. Despite the Moon being new, it is too far from the ecliptic plane to occult any part of the Sun on this date.

6. Measure the angular separation between the centers of the Moon and the Sun.

**Question 1.**     What is the angular separation between the centers of the Sun and the new Moon of June 25, 2006?

**Question 2.**     In which direction is the Moon from the Sun on this date?

7. With the Time Flow Rate set at **3 hours**, click **Play**.

As time advances, the Moon drifts quickly eastward out of the view as it orbits the Earth. The gaze is locked on to a star and so the Sun also appears to drift eastward against the background stars, but much more slowly, as a result of the yearly motion of the Earth in its orbit around the Sun.

8. When the Moon returns to the right side of the view and approaches the Sun, click **Stop** and adjust the hours and minutes of the Time until the Age of Moon as indicated in the HUD is once again New, 0.00 days old.

9. Measure the angular separation between the center of the Sun and the center of the Moon on this date.

**Question 3.**     Has the angular separation between the Sun and the Moon increased or decreased between these two New Moons?

Once again, the Sun and the Moon are too far apart at the time of the new Moon for an eclipse to occur. If a new Moon occurs near to one of the nodes, where the Moon's orbit crosses the ecliptic, the Sun and Moon are aligned closely enough that the Moon can eclipse the Sun as seen from some regions of the Earth.

10. **Centre** the view on to the Sun.
11. Change the Date to **September 22, 2006**, and the Time to **11:46:00 AM**. Use the HUD to verify that the Moon is New, 0.00 days old.

In the view, the new Moon and the Sun are close to the hollow wedge-shaped symbol indicating a node of the Moon's orbit.

Question 4.    Is the node that is visible in this view the ascending or the descending node?

12. Set the Zoom to **10°**.

All of the conditions for a solar eclipse are met in this view.

Question 5.    What are the conditions necessary to produce a solar eclipse?

## B. Eclipse Seasons and the Frequency of Solar Eclipses

As seen from the Earth, the Sun appears to move completely around the ecliptic in one year and this apparent motion brings it close to a node of the Moon's orbit twice every year. The Sun appears to move against the background stars at only about 1° per day, while the Moon moves at about 13° per day in its monthly orbit around the Earth. Consequently, while the Sun moves slowly past a node, it is possible for the relatively fast Moon to move into its new phase at the node and produce an eclipse. On average, a solar eclipse can occur whenever the Sun is within about 15° of either side of one of the nodes of the Moon's orbit. The interval of time over which the Sun is close enough to a node for an eclipse to occur is called an **eclipse season**.

13. Open **Favourites > Observing Projects > Solar Eclipses > Eclipse Season**.

The view is centered on the labeled star Rho Leonis. The descending node of the Moon's orbit is just to the left of this star. The Sun is on the ecliptic in the upper right of the view, about 15° from the node. This marks the beginning of an eclipse season, which will last until the Sun has moved beyond the node by about 15°.

14. With the Time Flow Rate set at **30 days, Step time forward** once and measure the angular separation between the Sun and the node.

Question 6.    Approximately how long, in days, is an average eclipse season?

Question 7.    A synodic month, the duration between repeated phases of the Moon such as full Moon to full Moon or new Moon to new Moon is 29.5 days. (a) Is it possible that no new Moon will occur during an eclipse season? (b) Is it possible for more than one new Moon to occur during an eclipse season? (c) What is the minimum number of solar eclipses that can occur during an eclipse season? (d) What is the maximum number of solar eclipses that can occur during an eclipse season?

The time required between successive passages of the Sun through a specific node is called an eclipse year. If the Moon's orbit were fixed relative to the background stars, an eclipse year would be equivalent to a sidereal year of 365.25 days. Careful observers of the previous sequence may have noticed that, during the interval of the eclipse season, the position of the descending node of the Moon's orbit shifted with respect to the background stars. This suggests that the Moon's orbit is not fixed with respect to the background stars and that an eclipse year is different in length from a sidereal or calendar year. The reason for this drift of the nodes is the slow precession of the Moon's orbit.

15. Open **Favourites > Observing Projects > Solar Eclipses > Eclipse Year.**

The view is centered and locked on the Sun as it is crossing the descending node of the Moon's orbit. The star Zavijava serves as a reference star. North is at the top of the view and west is to the right.

16. Note the Date of this view.
17. Set the Zoom to **90°.**
18. With the Time Flow Rate set at **1 day, Run time forward** to observe the Sun's motion along the ecliptic as it first passes through the ascending node of the Moon's orbit and click **Stop** when it returns to the descending node and note the Date.

Question 8.    How many eclipse seasons are in an eclipse year?

Question 9.    Is an eclipse year longer or shorter than a sidereal year of 365.25 days?

Question 10.    By approximately how many days does an eclipse year differ from a sidereal year?

Question 11.    Is it possible for more than two eclipse seasons to occur in the duration of a calendar year?

Question 12.    What is the minimum number of solar eclipses that occur in a calendar year?

Question 13.    What is the maximum number of solar eclipses that can occur in a calendar year?

## C. Types of Solar Eclipse

Whenever the Sun is within about 15° of a node, a solar eclipse of some kind is inevitable. The type of eclipse that Earth-bound observers will see depends on when the eclipse takes place within the eclipse season. Early and late in the eclipse season, the Sun and Moon are relatively far from the node and therefore appear relatively far from each other in the sky. An eclipse occurring at this time in the eclipse season will be partial.

19. Open **Favourites > Observing Projects > Solar Eclipses > View from Cairo.**

The view is from Cairo, Egypt, and is centered on the Sun at 11:00 AM on October 3, 2005. A label indicates the position of the Moon. The Moon's orbit and the descending node of this orbit are also shown.

20. Set the Time Flow Rate to **3000x** and observe the partial solar eclipse.

When the Sun and Moon are close to a node there will be more overlap of the Moon on the Sun. From some locations on the Earth, the centers of the Sun and Moon will appear to align perfectly and produce a **central eclipse**. There are two types of central eclipse: an annular eclipse, which is also a type of partial eclipse, and a total eclipse. The difference between these two eclipses arises from the fact that both the orbit of the Moon around the Earth and the orbit of the Earth around the Sun are elliptical in shape, which causes the apparent sizes of the Sun and Moon as seen from Earth to vary slightly. When the Moon appears slightly smaller in the sky than the Sun, even if it passes directly in front of the Sun, it will leave a ring, or annulus, of the bright solar disk visible at maximum eclipse to produce an annular eclipse.

21. Open **Favourites > Observing Projects > Solar Eclipses > Cairo from Space.**

The view is looking down on Earth from a position directly over Cairo, Egypt, in order to see the same eclipse you observed from the Earth's surface at Cairo in the last view. In the upper left quadrant of the Earth, the outline of the Moon's shadow is illustrated.

22. Click **Play** and observe the Moon's shadow track across Africa until the Time reaches about **1:20:00 PM** and the complete oval of the Moon's shadow is visible on the surface of the Earth.

23. Notice the darker region near the center of the oval outlining the Moon's shadow, to the left and below the label indicating the location of Cairo on the Earth. **Zoom in** and rest the cursor as accurately as possible over the central, darkest part of the Moon's shadow and select **Go There** from the contextual menu.

24. Use the **Find** pane to **Magnify** the Sun in the view and then use the Time controls to find the time of maximum eclipse.

25. Use the Location Scroller to adjust your viewing location by changing the latitude to align the center of the Sun and the Moon more precisely.

26. Use the HUD to find the Angular sizes of the Sun and of the Moon as seen from Earth on this date.

**Question 14.** What is the angular size of the Moon in the sky?

**Question 15.** What is the angular size of the Sun in the sky?

**Question 16.** Which of the following statements is true of this eclipse?

(a) This is a partial eclipse.

(b) This is a central eclipse.

(c) This is an annular eclipse.

There are times when the elliptical orbit of the Moon brings it closer than average to the Earth. If a central eclipse occurs during this time, the Moon will appear slightly larger in the sky than the Sun and, from certain locations, will be seen to block out the entire disk of the Sun. Observers within this narrow shadow region will see a total solar eclipse. Just as in an annular eclipse, observers on either side of the path of the central eclipse will see only a partial solar eclipse.

There are four distinct contact points in a total eclipse. **First contact** occurs when the Moon first begins to cover the Sun's disk. After first contact, the Moon gradually covers more and more of the Sun's disk during the partial phase of the eclipse. When only the smallest sliver of the Sun's disk remains uncovered, the Moon reveals its topography as the last visible rays of light from the Sun pass through lunar valleys to reach Earth. The result, as seen from the Earth, is a string of beads of sunlight called **Baily's Beads** along the advancing edge of the Moon. When only one such bead remains, the shadow has deepened and the Moon appears encircled by the silvery glow of the solar corona, while the bright solitary bead of photosphere sparkles like a diamond. The effect is aptly called the **diamond ring effect**.

At **second contact**, the Moon completely covers the Sun's disk. Only at this time is it safe to look directly at the Sun without eye protection, and one is encouraged to do so. With the bright photosphere of the Sun completely blocked out by the Moon, the relatively fainter atmospheric layers of the chromosphere and corona of the Sun become visible.

At **third contact**, it is once again important to use proper eye protection as totality ends and the first bead of photosphere is uncovered. This is followed by Baily's Beads and then the final partial phases of the eclipse. At **fourth contact**, the Moon no longer occults any part of the Sun.

27. Open **Favourites > Observing Projects > Solar Eclipses > View from Mauna Kea**.

The view is centered on the Sun as seen from Mauna Kea, Hawaii, on July 11, 1991, just after sunrise. The Moon is above and to the right of the Sun in the view.

28. Use the HUD to find the Angular Size of the Sun and the Moon in the view.

**Question 17.**    As seen from Earth on this date, which appears larger, the Sun or the Moon?

29. Set the Time Flow Rate to **300x** and watch a wide-angle view of this eclipse.
30. Select **File > Revert**.
31. Set the Zoom to **3°** and set the Time Flow Rate to **300x** again to watch the eclipse in more detail.
32. Find the times for each contact point of this solar eclipse.

This sequence, particularly around totality, provides an excellent simulation of a total solar eclipse, including the appearance of bright stars and then fainter stars as the sky darkens, followed by the slow unveiling of the faint corona that can be seen to surround the Sun during totality. It was this type of geometry that allowed astronomers in 1919 to verify the prediction of Einstein's General Theory of Relativity that starlight would be bent by the gravitational field of the Sun.

**Question 18.**    From this location, when do the following events occur? (a) First contact,
(b) Second contact, (c) Third contact, and (d) Fourth contact.

**Question 19.**    What is the duration of totality at this location?

## D. Bonus: Maximizing Totality

The stunning beauty of totality prompts eclipse chasers to try to maximize the time they spend in the shadow of the Moon. Choosing a location close to the centerline of the eclipse track is important to this goal, but other factors also play a role. The closer to a node that an eclipse occurs, the more closely the Sun and Moon will align, increasing the duration of the eclipse. The relative apparent angular sizes of the Sun and the Moon as seen from Earth can also affect the duration of a total solar eclipse. The nearer the Moon is to perigee, the larger it will appear. When the Earth is at aphelion, in July, the Sun will appear relatively smaller than when the Earth is at perihelion, in January. The closer the Moon and Earth are to these ideal conditions, the longer will be the period of totality of the eclipse.

33. Select **File > Revert**. Set the Zoom to **5°** and change the Time Flow Rate to **300x**.
34. Click **Stop** at the time of maximum eclipse at the midpoint between second and third contact.
35. Open the **Find** pane and click the box to the right of the label for the Moon to display its orbit. In addition to the wedge icon indicating the position of the node, the display of the Moon's orbit also shows the point at which the Moon is at perigee, indicated by a short line perpendicular to the orbit.

**Question 20.**    List the factors that contributed to the relatively long duration of the July 11, 1991, total solar eclipse.

In addition to choosing a location on the Earth close to the centerline of the eclipse, choosing a location where the eclipse occurs near midday and near to the Earth's equator will also significantly increase the duration of totality. At midday, the Sun transits the observer's meridian and since the Sun is being eclipsed by the new Moon, the Moon is also on the meridian at midday. The Moon appears slightly larger when it is on the meridian than when it is seen at the time of moonrise or moonset because the rotation of the Earth on its axis has carried the observing location closer to the Moon by a distance of almost the radius of the Earth, if the location is near to the equator.

36. Open **Favourites > Observing Projects > Solar Eclipses > View From Mexico**. Examine the view and the values displayed in the toolbar.

37. **Centre** the view on the Moon which is just visible to the right of the Sun.

38. Select **Show Info** from the contextual menu for the Moon. In the Info pane, expand the layers named **The Moon Info** and **Other Data**.

39. Click the **Rises** time button in The Moon Info layer to change the time to that of Moonrise. Note the apparent Angular size of the Moon at this time. Click the **Sets** button in The Moon Info layer and note the apparent Angular size of the Moon at the time of Moonset. Finally, click the **Transit** button and note the apparent Angular size of the Moon at around the time of the eclipse, when the Moon was close to transiting the meridian.

**Question 21.**     Approximately how much larger does the Moon appear in the sky when it is transiting the meridian compared to its angular size at moonrise or moonset?

The fact that the Moon appears slightly larger when it is transiting the meridian means that some eclipses, called hybrid eclipses, can be annular at some observing locations, where the eclipse occurs in the early morning or late afternoon, but for observers on Earth where the eclipse occurs near midday, the eclipse is total.

40. Select **File > Revert**.

41. Use the Time controls in the toolbar to find the times of each contact point of the eclipse as seen from this location.

**Question 22.**     What is the duration of totality at this location?

Choosing to observe a solar eclipse from the location on the Earth over which the center of the Moon's shadow passes at midday extends the duration of totality for another and more significant reason than the slight increase in angular size of the Moon when it is observed near to the meridian. The rotation of the Earth will carry this observing location more rapidly along the eclipse track in the same direction as the motion of the Moon's shadow and will thus increase significantly the duration of totality. During a total eclipse observed nearer to sunrise or sunset, the Earth's rotation is carrying the observing location nearly directly toward or away from the Moon while the orbital motion of the Moon around the Earth carries the Moon's shadow eastward across the surface of the Earth. Someone observing the same eclipse from a location where the eclipse occurs near to midday is carried in a more direct easterly direction by the rotation of the Earth, and this extends the time of totality since the observer is moving along with the shadow from this location.

42. Select **File > Revert**.

43. Select **Go There** from the contextual menu for the Moon and then use the **Find** pane to **Magnify** the Earth.

This view is centered on Earth as seen from the Moon. Toward the left (west) limb of the Earth, a relatively large semicircle indicates the intersection of the Moon's shadow with the surface of the Earth. Within this region, a small circular outline near the west limb of the Earth shows the size and position of the darkest part of the Moon's shadow, the **umbra**, in which the Moon completely blocks the Sun's disk.

44. Click **Play** and observe the track of the Moon's shadow, particularly the umbra.

45. Select **Edit/Undo Time Step** from the menu to return to the time at which the umbra of the Moon's shadow is near the west limb of the Earth as seen from the Moon. For observers within the umbral shadow at this time, the Sun has just risen.

46. Use the **Options** pane to activate **Surface Guides** under the **Solar System > Planets** layers.

47. Click **Play** and observe the relative speed of the Moon's umbra across the surface of the Earth, paying particular attention to its speed for observers who would be seeing the eclipse near sunrise and sunset, when the umbra is near a limb of the Earth, and for observers who would see the eclipse near midday, when the umbra tracks across the center of the Earth.

**Question 23.** In which direction across the Earth is the Moon's shadow moving?

**Question 24.** In which direction is the Earth rotating?

## E. Challenge: The Speed of the Shadow Track

In this section, you will examine the last solar eclipse over Europe in the twentieth century, which occurred on August 11, 1999. The eclipse started over the Atlantic Ocean. The shadow then moved quickly over the southern tip of England, over northern France, Germany, Austria, and Romania and across the Black Sea before covering a strip of Turkey and continuing over Asia, ending at sunset in the Bay of Bengal on the Indian Ocean. The greatest width of the path of totality was only 112 km and this occurred over the Black Sea. The maximum duration of totality was only 2 minutes, 23 seconds, in Romania.

48. Open **Favourites > Observing Projects > Solar Eclipses > Aug 11 Eclipse Track**.

The observing location is near Bruce Crater on the Moon.

49. Click **Play** and observe the Moon's shadow move across the Earth.

50. Select **File > Revert** from the menu and then **Run time forward** until the small circle outlining the Moon's umbra crosses the center of the image of the Earth and **Stop** time.

51. **Zoom in** and open the contextual menu over the center of the small circle outlining the Moon's umbra and select **Go There**.

52. Use the **Find** pane to **Magnify** the Sun in the view.

53. In the **Find** pane, click the check box to the right side of the entry for the Moon to display the Moon's orbit in the view. **Zoom out** until the node at which this eclipse occurs is visible in the view. Measure the angular distance between the Sun or Moon and the node.

54. Use the HUD to find the Angular size of the Moon at the time of this eclipse.

**Question 25.** If you were to observe this eclipse from a location on Earth where the umbra passes over the location near midday, would you expect totality to be longer or shorter than the view of the July 11, 1991, eclipse from Mexico? Explain your answer using the data available from the HUD and the toolbar.

You can estimate the speed of the eclipse shadow by timing the simulated eclipse at two different sites, one just south of England and the other in the city of Munich, Germany, some 530 miles or 850 km apart.

55. Open **Favourites > Observing Projects > Solar Eclipses > Aug 11 from English Channel.**

56. **Run time forward** and adjust the Time to determine and record the times of second and third contact.

57. Open **Favourites > Observing Projects > Solar Eclipses > View from Munich.**

58. Keeping in mind the fact that Munich is one time zone East of the English Channel location, adjust the Time so that it is simultaneous with second contact at the English Channel location.

59. **Run time forward** and determine the times of second and third contact as seen from Munich.

Question 26.  What is the time of mid-eclipse (calculated from the measurements of times of second and third contacts) for both sites?

Question 27.  Using the two times of central eclipse at these two locations, allowing for the time zone change (subtract 1 hour from your difference), and the distance between the English Channel site and the Munich site of some 530 miles (850 km), what is the speed of the shadow of the Moon as it moves across this area of northern Europe?

## F. Conclusions

In this observing project, you have observed several types of solar eclipses from a variety of locations on the Earth. You have observed the shadow of the Moon as it passed across the Earth, as seen from the Moon and from space. You have used your observations to determine the conditions that are required in order that a solar eclipse will occur. Finally, you have explored the factors that influence the duration of an eclipse and have measured the speed at which the Moon's shadow moves across the Earth.

# Light                                                     12

Most of what we discover about the universe comes from the observation and analysis of the light that we receive from its various components. In this project, you will explore some of the properties of this electromagnetic radiation that we call light and how astronomers measure, use and interpret it.

## A. Magnitude

Observers of the sky many centuries ago developed a system for characterizing the brightness of stars that is still used in a modified form today by modern astronomers. Hipparchus, in the second century B.C., catalogued hundreds of stars and assigned each star a magnitude, a value representing the star's relative brightness. He called the brightest stars in the sky those "of first magnitude," while he called the faintest stars discernible to the human eye those "of sixth magnitude." Modern astronomers still use this system, refining it to reflect the much greater precision with which star brightness can be measured using modern equipment. We can demonstrate this system and introduce the concept of **apparent magnitude** with the following view.

1. Launch *Starry Night*™ and configure the HUD to show ONLY **Name, Object type** and **Apparent Magnitude**.
2. Open **Favourites > Observing Projects > Light > Naked-eye Stars**.

The view shows the southeast horizon and sky over Flagstaff, Arizona, on a summer night, as it might appear to the unaided eye under ideal observing conditions. You might notice that some stars in this view appear brighter than others.

3. Without changing the view, use the HUD to survey the Apparent magnitude of a number of stars.

Question 1.  (a) What is the name of the brightest star in the view? (b) What is its apparent magnitude?

Question 2.  Sample a few of the faintest stars in the view. What is the range of the magnitudes of these faint stars?

The range of brightness of stars visible to the unaided eye was found to be approximately 100. In the middle of the nineteenth century, the magnitude scale was updated and formalized to ensure that a difference of five magnitudes was exactly equal to a 100-fold difference in brightness. Thus, a **difference** of apparent magnitude of 1 represents a **factor** of about 2.5 times. This kind of scale is logarithmic and is useful because a large range of brightness can be represented by simple numbers.

(In fact, the exact figure for this factor is the fifth root of 100, which is 2.512.) Note also that the historical magnitude scheme for star brightness is a reversed scale, in that the **larger** the magnitude, the **fainter** is the star. To demonstrate the basis for this magnitude system, a first magnitude star is

> 2.512 times brighter than a second-magnitude star
>
> $2.512 \times 2.512 \approx 6.31$ times brighter than a third-magnitude star
>
> $2.512 \times 2.512 \times 2.512 \approx 15.85$ times brighter than a fourth-magnitude star
>
> $2.512 \times 2.512 \times 2.512 \times 2.512 \approx 39.82$ times brighter than a fifth-magnitude star
>
> $2.512 \times 2.512 \times 2.512 \times 2.512 \times 2.512 = 100$ times brighter than a sixth-magnitude star

An advantage of the modern definition of magnitude is that the brightness of individual stars can be specified very precisely using fractional magnitudes; for example, a magnitude 2.03 star is slightly fainter than a magnitude 1.97 star and slightly brighter than a magnitude 2.08 star.

You may have noticed that, as described above, magnitude is a relative measurement that compares the brightness of one object against another. In order to assign a precise magnitude to each individual star, as described above, we need to "anchor" the magnitude scale by defining the precise magnitude for one particular star. The modern scale uses the star Vega as the standard reference star with an assigned magnitude of 0.0.

This scheme can be extended to stars fainter than sixth magnitude that are visible with optical aid or to brighter objects such as planets; for example, a magnitude 7 star is 2.512 times fainter than a magnitude 6 star, and a magnitude –1 star is 2.512 times brighter than Vega. (Negative magnitudes are used to express the brightness of objects that are brighter than Vega.)

| | |
|---|---|
| **Question 3.** | How much brighter is a first magnitude star compared to (a) a seventh-magnitude star, (b) an eighth-magnitude star, (c) a ninth-magnitude star, (d) a tenth-magnitude star? |
| **Question 4.** | The full Moon has an apparent magnitude of about –13. What does this mean in terms of brightness of the Moon compared to that of the star Vega? |
| **Question 5.** | (a) Which is brighter, a magnitude 9 star or a magnitude 12 star? (b) Which is fainter, Venus at magnitude –4 or Jupiter at magnitude –1? |

The four stars that form the bowl of the Little Dipper asterism in the constellation Ursa Minor are a convenient sample of reference magnitudes for astronomers.

> 4.  Open **Favourites > Observing Projects > Light > Little Dipper**.

The view shows the Little Dipper with labels indicating the four stars that form its bowl.

> 5.  Use the **K** keyboard shortcut to remove the constellation outlines and labels. Choose **Edit > Select None** from the menu to remove the star labels to see this simulation of magnitudes more clearly. You can use the HUD to find the Apparent magnitude of these four stars.

| | |
|---|---|
| **Question 6.** | In order, from brightest to faintest, list the names and apparent magnitudes of the four stars that form the bowl of the Little Dipper. |

The apparent magnitude of a star refers to the star's brightness as seen from the Earth and is given the symbol $m$. However, we know from common experience that the brightness of a light source also depends on its distance. For example, a car's headlights appear to become brighter as the vehicle approaches. In fact, the brightness of a light source changes in inverse proportion to the square of its distance, a fact that you can verify in the bonus section at the end of this project.

In order to compare the intrinsic brightness of stars and eliminate the dependence of magnitude on distance, astronomers use a measure of brightness called **absolute magnitude**, given the symbol $M$. Absolute magnitude is a measure of the brightness that a star would have if it were to be observed from a standard distance of 10 parsecs, or 32.6 light years; thus, it is also a measure of the star's intrinsic brightness (i.e., its actual light output per second).

A star having an absolute magnitude equal to its apparent magnitude, $M = m$, is therefore 10 parsecs distant from Earth. If a star has an apparent magnitude that is greater than its absolute magnitude (meaning that the star appears fainter in Earth's sky than it would if it were at a distance of 10 parsecs), then the star is further away than 10 parsecs. Conversely, if the star's apparent magnitude is less than its absolute magnitude, then the star is closer to Earth than 10 parsecs.

6. Configure the HUD to include **Absolute magnitude.**

7. Use the HUD to find the Absolute magnitude and the Apparent magnitude of the four stars that form the bowl of the Little Dipper asterism.

**Question 7.** Of the two brightest stars in the bowl of the Little Dipper asterism, Kochab and Pherkad, (a) which appears brighter in our sky (i.e., as seen from Earth)? Explain how you know. (b) Which is intrinsically brighter? Explain how you know.

**Question 8.** Which of the four stars, if any, that form the bowl of the Little Dipper asterism are closer to Earth than 10 parsecs? Explain how you know.

**Question 9.** Which of the four stars that form the bowl of the Little Dipper asterism is intrinsically the brightest? Explain how you know.

A star's distance from Earth can be determined if both its absolute and apparent magnitudes are known. This difference between apparent and absolute magnitude of a star, $m - M$, is called the **distance modulus**, an important tool for determining distances in the universe, as you will learn in a later project. Basically, the greater an object's distance modulus, the farther the object is from Earth.

**Question 10.** (a) Which of the four stars that form the bowl of the Little Dipper asterism is farthest from Earth? (b) Which of the four stars is closest to Earth?

## B. Color

Another interesting property of light is its color. If you look carefully at the stars in the sky, or at the view of the Little Dipper on the screen, you may notice that stars also differ in color as well as in brightness. This is easier to see in long exposure photographs.

8. Open **Favourites > Observing Projects > Light > Star Cluster.**

**Question 11.** How would you describe the range of colors of the stars making up the star cluster in the view?

The introduction of photography in astronomy revealed that the apparent magnitudes of stars captured on film were different from their apparent magnitudes when observed visually. This is because photographic film is more sensitive to blue light whereas the human eye responds preferentially in the yellow-green region of the spectrum. Bluish stars appear brighter and reddish-orange stars appear fainter on film than they appear visually. This discovery led to the concept of the color index of a star. The **color index** of a star is the difference between its apparent magnitude when observed through a standard blue filter, $m_B$, and its apparent magnitude when measured through a standard filter resembling the visual band of the spectrum, $m_V$. This latter magnitude is closely equivalent to that estimated visually with the human eye.

Color index = $m_B - m_V$

This co lor index is also written as $B - V$.

9. Configure the HUD to include **B – V colour.**

A star that has the same magnitude in blue light as in the visual band has a color index of zero. A star that appears brighter in blue light has a lower $m_B$ and will have a color index less than zero. A star that is more yellow or red will appear brighter in the visual color band than in blue light and will therefore have a color index greater than zero.

10.  Open **Favourites > Observing Projects > Light > Orion**.

The view shows the constellation Orion. Labels indicate the four stars Betelgeuse, Rigel, Bellatrix, and Saiph.

11.  Use the HUD to find the color index, B – V colour, of each of the four stars labeled in the view.

> **Question 12.**    (a) According to their color index, which of the four stars that are labeled in the view would you expect to appear the bluest in color? (b) Which of these four stars would you expect to appear the reddest in color?

12.  You can use the *Starry Night™* controls to enhance the colors of stars. Use the **K** shortcut key to remove the constellation outline from the view. Then select **Preferences...** from the **File** (Windows) or **Starry Night** (Mac) menu and choose **Brightness/Contrast** in the dropdown box. Move the Preferences dialog window to the side of the screen so that all four of the labeled stars in the view are visible. While observing these stars in the view, slide the **Star colour** control in the Preferences dialog window all the way to the left (less saturation) and then all the way to the right (more saturation). Return the slide control to your preferred level, or the default level of 0.50, before closing the Preferences window.

Stars resemble an idealized physical object known as a **black body**. For all black bodies, the distribution of the intensity of light across the various colors, or wavelengths, of the electromagnetic spectrum is related to the temperature of the black body. Thus, the overall color perceived by the eye is also related to its temperature.  For example, when heated, a metal or ceramic object begins to glow with a dull red color. Analysis of the intensity of the radiation emitted by this object across the various wavelengths of the electromagnetic spectrum shows the peak intensity in the region of red light. With further heating, the object becomes a more intense white color and the peak of the intensity curve shifts toward the yellow band of the spectrum. Yet further heating results in a bright blue or blue-white color of the object with the peak of the intensity in the blue region of the spectrum. In fact, the wavelength of the peak of an object's spectrum, $\lambda_{max}$, is inversely proportional to its temperature $T$, or $\lambda_{max} \times T$ = Constant. This is known as Wien's law.

Obtaining the full spectrum of a star and comparing this to a standard curve for a black body of a known temperature is a complex and time-consuming process. Measuring a star's apparent magnitude when seen through standard filters to obtain its color index gives astronomers an efficient short cut for determining the temperature of a star. The bluer (i.e., smaller or more negative) a star's color index, the higher is its temperature.

> **Question 13.**    Which of the four labeled stars in the view has the highest temperature?

## C. The Speed of Light

According to Einstein's Theory of Relativity, now established as an accurate representation of our world, nothing can travel faster than light. Thus, it is light that first alerts us to changes in the universe. For example, the first indication we receive that a star has exploded as a supernova is its sudden increase in brightness as the light from the supernova reaches the Earth. So, exactly how fast is light?

The experiences of seeing a flash of lightning and only later hearing its thunder, or seeing someone in the distance clap their hands together but hearing the sound a short time later, tell us that the speed of light is at least much faster than that of sound. The ancient Greeks debated whether light had a finite speed at all or whether it was infinitely fast, such that events were seen instantaneously. The question was not resolved until 1676, when a Danish astronomer, Ole Rømer, obtained a measurement for the speed of light from observations of the eclipses of Jupiter's moon Io.

Rømer noticed that the length of time between eclipses of Io changed as the distance between the Earth and Jupiter changed: When the Earth was farther than average from Jupiter, eclipses of Io occurred later than average, whereas when the distance between the Earth and Jupiter was smaller than average, these eclipses occurred earlier than average. He postulated that this variation in the observed time of these eclipse events was due to the time required for the light signal to travel across the varying distance from Jupiter to the Earth, and he used records of a large number of observations to estimate the speed of light.

You can copy Rømer's idea of using the light signal from an eclipse of Io to measure the speed of light using *Starry Night*™ to observe a single event, the disappearance of Jupiter's inner bright moon Io into the shadow of the planet, from several locations in the solar system.

13. Open **Favourites > Observing Projects > Light > Speed of Light**.

14. Configure the HUD to include **Distance from observer**.

15. Note that the Time panel in the toolbar should display Universal Time, UT. If this is not the case, click the menu icon at the right of the Time panel in the toolbar and select **Display Universal Time**.

16. Click the **FOV** (Field of View) tab and then the **Add...** button in the Other (All Charts) layer and select **Circular...** In the FOV Indicator dialog window, type **10'** for Indicator name and for the Diameter and then click **OK**. Repeat this step to create a second indicator with the name and diameter of **5'**. These fields of view, 10' and 5' will now be available in the Other (All Charts) section of the Current Field of View menu that pops up when you click the **Zoom** panel of the toolbar.

The view shows the solar system from a location in space over 10 AU from the Sun at 12:50:00 UT on January 21, 2015, with the background stars removed. Labels indicate the positions of Io as well as the planets Earth, Mars, Uranus, and Neptune that will serve as your observation locations. The orbits of these planets are also shown to provide perspective in the view.

17. Open the **Find** pane. If necessary, click the magnifying glass icon in the search box and select **Search All** and then clear any contents from the search box in order to show a list of Solar System Items in the Find pane.

18. Beginning with the Earth, for each planet listed in Data Table 1 at the end of this project, click the menu icon for that planet in the Find pane list and select **Go There**. [TIP: Tap the spacebar after selecting this command to speed up the location change.]

19. Set the Zoom to the value indicated in Data Table 1 for the observing location. [TIP: Tap the spacebar after selecting the zoom factor to speed up this change.]

20. In the Find pane, click the menu icon for **Jupiter** and select **Centre**.

21. Adjust the Time in minutes and watch Io carefully until it suddenly decreases in brightness, indicating that it has moved into Jupiter's shadow and has been eclipsed and then adjust the universal time to the nearest second to determine this disappearance time on January 21, 2015. Record the time of this event in Data Table 1. Use the HUD to find Io's Distance from observer and record this in Data Table 1.

22. Go back to step 17 and repeat the previous steps to observe the time at which the light signal of Io's eclipse arrives at the next observing location listed in Data Table 1.

You have observed the light signal of a single event, the eclipse of Io as it moves into Jupiter's shadow on January 21, 2015, from four different locations at varying distances from Io. If light were instantaneous, the time of the eclipse event would be the same at all of the observing locations.

Question 14. Is light instantaneous, or does it travel through space with a finite speed?

You can determine the speed with which this light signal moves through space by comparing its time of arrival at the different locations. Since we do not have an absolute time for the eclipse event, we can use the observation from the Earth as the origin, or zero point, since the Earth was the closest to Io of all of the observing locations, and then measure the extra time the light signal required to reach the more distant locations.

23. First calculate the difference between the Time of Eclipse (UT) at each of the observing locations and the time of the eclipse at Earth and record this difference in Data Table 1 under the column headed dt (hh:mm:ss). For the Earth, this time difference will be 0.

24. Similarly, calculate the difference between Io's Distance from observer at each of the locations and the Distance from observer at Earth and record this in the column headed dd (AU).

25. Now, convert the time difference, dt, to seconds (multiply the number of hours in the time difference by 3600, multiply the number of minutes in the time difference by 60, and add these results to the number of seconds in the time difference and record this in the column headed dt (s)). This column indicates the number of seconds that the light signal of the eclipse requires to travel the extra distance beyond the distance of Earth to reach the observing location.

26. Finally, calculate the value of the speed of the light signal, in AU per second, as measured from each of Mars, Uranus, and Neptune by dividing the difference in the distance by the difference in the time. Record the result for each location in the column headed dd/dt (AU/s) in Data Table 1.

You have made three separate measurements of the speed at which the light signal of Io's eclipse travels through the solar system, in AU per second.

Question 15.    Calculate the average of your measurements of the speed of the light signal to arrive at an estimate of the speed of light in AU per second. Based on your observations, what is the speed of light in AU per second?

27. Convert your answer for the speed of light in the previous question to kilometers per second by multiplying your answer by 149,597,871, the number of kilometers in one AU.

Question 16.    Based on your observations, what is the speed of light in kilometers per second?

Question 17.    The modern accepted value for the speed of light, which is usually given the symbol c, is 299,792,458 meters per second, or, very nearly 299,792 km/s. What is the difference between this and your measured result for the speed of light in km/s?

Question 18.    Rømer's estimate for the speed of light was about 220,000 km/s. What is the difference between Rømer's estimate and the modern accepted value for the speed of light?

Question 19.    By what percentage was Rømer's estimate inaccurate? [HINT: Divide the absolute difference between Rømer's value and the modern accepted value by the modern accepted value and multiply this result by 100.]

Question 20.    By what percentage is your measurement for the speed of light inaccurate?

28. If you wish, you can delete the field of view indicators you added. Click the **FOV** tab and right-click (Windows) or Ctrl-click (Mac) on the indicator you wish to remove from the Other (All charts) section of the FOV pane and select **Delete** from the popup menu.

## D. Bonus: The Inverse Square Law

As light spreads out from a source, it encompasses a growing spherical area and becomes progressively fainter. The area of a sphere is $4\pi r^2$, and so the area of a sphere varies at a rate proportional to the square of its radius, r. Thus, as a quantity of light disperses across larger and larger spherical areas, its brightness decreases in proportion to the increasing area it illuminates. In other words, we expect the apparent brightness of the light to be inversely proportional to the square of the distance from the light source. We can write this mathematically as

Apparent brightness $\propto 1/\text{Distance}^2$                    (1)

To test this logical assumption, you can observe the apparent magnitude of the Sun from the five innermost major planets of the solar system, and then use this observed apparent magnitude to determine the Sun's apparent brightness as seen from each planet.

Before doing this, however, it is more convenient to define the Sun's relative brightness, $F$, as the ratio of its apparent brightness at the planet's distance to its apparent brightness at a reference distance, which we will take as being the Earth's distance (1 AU). The relative brightness of the Sun as seen from a location 1 AU from the Sun is then $F = 1$, so the constant of proportionality in (1) is equal to 1 and

$$\text{Relative brightness} = F = 1/\text{Distance}^2 \tag{2}$$

You can now determine the Sun's relative brightness $F$ at each distance by comparing its apparent magnitude, $m$, with its apparent magnitude as seen from the reference distance, $m_{\text{ref}}$, using the formula

$$F = 2.512^{(m_{\text{ref}} - m)} \tag{3}$$

---

29. Open **Favourites > Observing Projects > Light > Inverse Square Law.**

---

The view shows the Sun in the view as seen from the distance of Mercury.

---

30. Use the HUD to find the Distance from observer and Apparent magnitude of the Sun from this observing location and record these data in Data Table 2 at the end of this project.

---

To confirm the inverse square relationship, the apparent brightness of the Sun must decrease (and therefore the value of its apparent magnitude must increase, i.e., become less negative) as the observing location moves farther from the Sun.

---

31. Under the **Options** menu, change the **Viewing Location** to **the centre of** each of the planets **Venus, Earth, Mars,** and **Jupiter** in turn. At each location, use the **Find** pane to **Centre** the Sun in the view and then use the HUD to find the Distance from observer and Apparent magnitude of the Sun and record these data in Data Table 2.

---

To analyze the data, you will need to convert the observed apparent magnitude of the Sun from each observing location to a scale of relative brightness in which the reference brightness is the apparent brightness of the Sun as seen from the distance of the Earth, 1 AU.

---

32. Substitute into equation (3) the value of the apparent magnitude of the Sun as seen from the distance of Earth for $m_{\text{ref}}$, and substitute the apparent magnitude of the Sun as seen from the distance of each of the other planets in Data Table 2 for $m$ and then use a scientific calculator or spreadsheet application to calculate $F$, the relative brightness of the Sun as seen from each of the planets compared to the Sun's brightness as seen from Earth. Record the result in the Relative Brightness column of Data Table 2.

---

A relative brightness greater than 1 means that the Sun appears brighter than its appearance as seen from the distance of the Earth at 1 AU by a factor equal to its relative brightness. A relative brightness less than one indicates the factor by which the Sun appears dimmer from this distance compared to its brightness at a distance of 1 AU.

**Question 21.** Compared to its brightness when seen from the distance of the Earth at 1 AU, how many times brighter or dimmer does the Sun appear when seen from the distance of (a) Mercury and (b) Jupiter?

**Question 22.** Does the relative brightness of the Sun increase, decrease, or remain unchanged as the distance from the observing location to the Sun increases?

33. In the column headed 1/Distance$^2$ in Data Table 2, calculate the reciprocal of the squared Distance from observer of the Sun for each observing location.

34. Plot the relative brightness of the Sun at each observing location versus the reciprocal of the squared distance from observer of the Sun at that location in Graph Template 1 at the end of this project.

**Question 23.**   From your data, what is the relationship between apparent brightness of a light source and the distance from which it is observed?

## E. Conclusion

In this project, you have explored some of the properties of light and have learned something about how astronomers use the information obtained from light to understand the universe and its various components.

**Data Table 1.** Arrival Time (UT) of Light Signal of the January 21, 2015, Eclipse of Io

| Observing location | Zoom factor | Time of eclipse (UT) | Io's distance from observer (AU) | dt (hh:mm:ss) | dd (AU) | dt (s) | dd/dt (AU/s) |
|---|---|---|---|---|---|---|---|
| Earth | 10' | | | | | | |
| Mars | 10' | | | | | | |
| Uranus | 5' | | | | | | |
| Neptune | 5' | | | | | | |

**Data Table 2.** Brightness of the Sun as from the Five Innermost Planets of the Solar System

| Observing location | Apparent magnitude of the Sun | Distance from observer of the Sun (AU) | Relative brightness | 1/Distance² |
|---|---|---|---|---|
| Mercury | | | | |
| Venus | | | | |
| Earth | | | | |
| Mars | | | | |
| Jupiter | | | | |

**Graph Template 1.** Relative Brightness of the Sun versus 1/Distance²

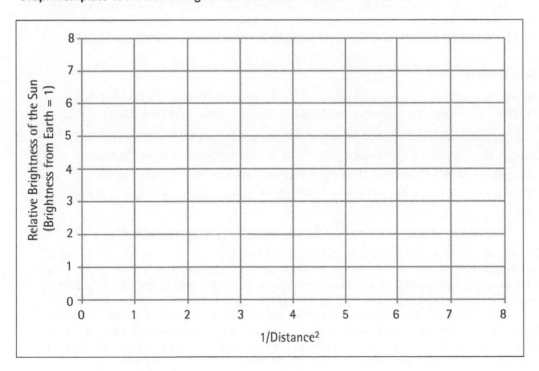

# Grand Tour of the Planets 13

The Earth is one of eight major planets orbiting an average star situated in the spiral arm structure of the Milky Way Galaxy. These planets and other smaller bodies that orbit the Sun were formed from the protoplanetary nebula, a disk of gas and dust that formed from a contracting interstellar cloud. The initial composition of this material was presumably relatively uniform throughout the cloud and yet these planets and their many moons show a remarkable diversity of properties, structure, and chemical makeup. The theoretical study of the formation and development of these objects is a very active field of research. Part of the impetus for this work in recent years has been the discovery by astronomers of planetary systems surrounding other stars and the realization from these observations that most stars in our Galaxy have at least one planet associated with them.

With this diversity of properties in mind, it is instructive to review the planets in our solar system in order to understand both the similarities and differences between them. An equivalent examination of the moons and other minor objects in the solar system would be too extensive for this short survey but a review of their properties in a modern textbook or on the internet would be very rewarding.

We can first look briefly at the orientation of the orbits of these planets in space and look for patterns of behavior such as spin axis alignment within this group of objects. We can then examine in more detail the structure and chemical makeup of the planets, again looking for patterns that might inform us about formation processes involved in their assembly and evolution.

## A. Planetary Orbits

The first step in this survey will be an overview of the different orbital planes and orbital shapes of the planets. These parameters show many similarities but differ in subtle ways from planet to planet.

1. Launch *Starry Night*™ and configure the HUD to include **Distance from observer**.
2. Open **Favourites > Observing Projects > Tour of Planets > Planet Orbit Planes**.
3. **Zoom out** to the widest field of view of **191° x 191°** to show the sky crossed by the ecliptic plane.

This wide-angle view is from the north pole of the Sun at 18:00 UT on November 18, 2015, and is centered on the Earth. You might recognize several of the familiar constellations beyond the Earth in this view. For example, the constellation of Orion can be seen just below and to the left of the Earth. You can now display the orbital planes of each of the planets in turn to compare the alignment of these planes with that of the Earth as represented by the ecliptic. In order to view each of these orbital planes edge-on, it is necessary to move to a date and time when the Sun-Earth line is pointing at one of the positions where the planet's orbit crosses the ecliptic plane. These points are known as **nodes** and are marked on planetary orbits in *Starry Night*™ with small triangular flags.

The date for this initial set-up, November 18, 2015, has been chosen because this condition is approximately satisfied by the orbits of all of the inner terrestrial planets on this date allow you to compare the orbital inclinations directly. (The equivalent average date for the giant planets is January 4, 2016, and can be used when examining the orbits of these planets.)

If desired, you can adjust the date to a specific value for each planet to ensure that the Sun-Earth line is pointing precisely toward a node of its orbit and you are then looking at the orbit edge-on from the Sun. The following table provides a list of such specific dates.

| Planet | Mercury | Venus | Earth | Mars | Jupiter | Saturn | Uranus | Neptune |
|---|---|---|---|---|---|---|---|---|
| Date when Sun-Earth line points to a node | Nov. 11, 2015 | Dec. 9, 2015 | — | Nov. 12, 2015 | Jan. 1, 2016 | Jan. 14, 2016 | Dec. 6, 2015 | Feb. 1, 2016 |

4. Open the **Find** pane and ensure that the **Q** box is empty and that the members of the planetary system are listed. (If this is not so, click on the **Q** and select **Search All**.)

5. You can now display the orbits of each of the terrestrial planets in turn by clicking the checkboxes to the right of each planet's name in turn in the object list.

Question 1. Which of these planets has the greatest orbital inclination?

Question 2. For which of these planets is the orbital plane closest to that of the Earth?

You can now examine the orbits of the Jovian or giant gas planets using the same procedure.

6. Click **Off** all of the orbits for the terrestrial planets.

7. Advance the Date to **January 4, 2016,** to align the Sun-Earth line to the approximate positions of nodes of the orbits of the giant planets.

8. Click **On** the Orbit display checkbox to the right of each giant planet in turn to answer the following questions.

Question 3. List the Jovian planets in order of increasing orbital inclination.

Question 4. In which group of planets, the terrestrial planets or the Jovian planets, are the orbital planes more closely aligned?

Question 5. Which of the following general conclusions can you draw from these observations?

(a) The planets of the solar system move around the Sun in orbits with a wide range of inclinations.

(b) The orbital planes of the planets in the solar system are closely aligned to one another and to the orbital plane of the Earth.

(c) The terrestrial planets orbit in planes that are closely aligned, but this common plane is inclined at a large angle to the orbital planes of the Jovian planets.

You can use the above method to check the orbital planes of two of the largest dwarf planets, Pluto and Eris, to see how different their orbits are from those of the major planets. While this is not a defining factor in the new classification scheme for solar system objects, you will see that in this respect, they differ markedly from the major planets. These two objects, along with Ceres within the asteroid belt and several other small objects orbiting the Sun well beyond Neptune, comprise the present group of dwarf planets.

9. Click **Off** all of the Orbits for the Jovian planets in the Find pane.

10. Set the Date to **January 11, 2016,** to align the Sun-Earth line with one node zzzzzzzzof Pluto's orbit.

11. Expand the **Dwarf Planets** list in the Find pane and click **On** the Orbit checkbox to the right of Pluto to display its orbit edge-on.

**Question 6.** Is the orbit of Pluto close to the ecliptic plane?

12. Click **Off** the Orbit display for Pluto and set the Date to **April 25, 2016**, to align the Sun-Earth line to one node of Eris's orbit.
13. Click **On** the Orbit display for Eris.

**Question 7.** Is the orbit of Eris more or less inclined to the ecliptic plane than that of Pluto?

You can now examine the shapes of the orbits of these planets by viewing them from above the north pole of the Sun.

14. Open **Favourites > Observing Projects > Tour of Planets > Planet Orbits Face-on.**

This view shows the orbit of the Earth from a position 5AU above the surface of the Sun, along the ecliptic polar axis, at 00:00 UT on January 4, 2015, in a field of view of about 62°. From this position, the Earth's orbital plane is perpendicular to the view. The Earth is closest to the Sun on this date, at a position known as **perihelion**. This is indicated by a short line extending outward from the orbit. The Earth will reach a position of **aphelion** in a half-year from this date, when it is furthest from the Sun. You can use measurements of the Sun-Earth distance at these positions to answer the question "Is the Earth's orbit circular?"

15. Use the Angular Separation tool to measure the distance from Earth to Sun on **January 4, 2015**. (This distance is displayed along the Angular Separation line in AU, below the Angular Separation and Position Angle values.)
16. Advance the Date to **July 6, 2015**, when the Earth is at aphelion.
17. Use the Angular Separation tool again to measure the distance from Earth to Sun at this position.

**Question 8.** Does the Earth move in a circle around the Sun? If so, what is its distance from the Sun? If not, what is the ratio of its perihelion distance $R_p$ to its aphelion distance $R_a$?

You can now examine the orbital shapes of the planets from this vantage point above the ecliptic pole.

18. Open the **Find** pane and click **Off** the Orbit checkbox to the right of the Earth and click **On** the Orbits for each terrestrial planet in turn to display these orbits individually and answer the following question.

**Question 9.** Which of the terrestrial planets has the least circular-shaped orbit?

19. **Zoom out** to the maximum field of view of 191°, remove the orbits of all of the terrestrial planets, and display the orbits of each of the Jovian planets in turn to examine the shapes of their orbits and answer the following question.

**Question 10.** Are any of the orbits of the Jovian planets less circular than the orbit of Mercury?

A more thorough examination of the geometry of planetary orbits is included in the bonus section later in this project.

## B. Planet Survey

You can now examine the surfaces and atmospheres of the planets of the solar system beginning with Earth, our home planet.

> 20. Open **Favourites > Observing Projects > Tour of Planets > Earth.**

The view shows the Earth as it would be seen from the North Pole of the Sun on June 21, 2014, with a line showing the plane of its orbit. The spin axis of the Earth is indicated by two poles and the equator by an appropriate line. The prime meridian through Greenwich, England is also shown and will be used to indicate the rotational motion of the Earth. The view is centered on the Americas and shows no cloud cover.

> 21. **Run time forward** at a Time Flow Rate of 1 minute to watch the rotation of our planet.
> 22. **Stop** time flow and **Zoom in** and use the Hand tool to examine more closely the features that appear on this simulated Earth.
> 23. Use **File > Revert** to return to the original view and click **Play** to rotate the Earth to a different position.

In Steps 24–34 below, you can select each planet in turn from the list in Data Table 1 at the end of this project and explore its surface and properties. As you determine the features of each planet, you can use Data Table 1 to record your observations and provide a summary of the relative properties of the planets in the solar system. This table lists rotation, (whether fast, medium or slow, with the Earth's rotation rate taken as medium), rotation direction (whether direct, that is, in the same direction as its orbital motion, or retrograde), whether there is cloud cover on the planet, the tilt of its spin axis (small, medium or large, again with the tilt of Earth's axis considered medium), its measured distance from the Sun and its angular diameter at the observed date and time, for use in calculating its physical diameter. The list of hints below can guide you in the search for relevant features for each particular planet. Each entry in the hints begins with a value for the average time for light to travel from the Sun to the planet, as an indication of the planet's distance from the Sun for comparison with that of other planets.

## Major Planets

<u>Mercury</u> (Sunlight travel time: 3.2 minutes)

*Hints:* Look carefully at its surface features, and compare them particularly to those of the Earth's Moon. (If necessary, use the **Magnify** function on the Moon.)

<u>Venus</u> (Sunlight travel time: 6 minutes)

*Hints:* Look for evidence of volcanic activity, such as lava flows or mountains shaped like volcanic cones.

<u>Earth</u> (Sunlight travel time: 8.3 minutes)

*Hints:* Look carefully at the surface area of the Earth covered by oceans, compared to the solid surface. Do you see evidence of icy polar caps?

<u>Mars</u> (Sunlight travel time: 12.7 minutes)

*Hints:* See if you can identify two different hemispheres on the planet, each with different surface features such as volcanos, valleys or craters. A particularly useful distinguishing feature is the relative density of craters around the planet. How are these two hemispheres oriented (e.g., are they on opposite sides of the planet, or is one northern and the other southern)? Does the appearance of some of the valleys suggest that water might have flowed across this planet in the past? Look also for the two small moons, Phobos and Deimos, which orbit this planet. Are there polar caps on this planet?

<u>Jupiter</u> (Sunlight travel time: 43.3 minutes)

*Hints:* Examine the appearance of the "surface" of this giant gas planet. Does this planet show any evidence of bands of clouds or rotating storm systems? What is the rotation period of this planet in hours or in Earth days? Look for moons orbiting this planet.

**Saturn** (Sunlight travel time: 79.5 minutes (1 hour 19.5 minutes))

*Hints:* Look at the ring system surrounding this planet and for moons. Does this planet show any evidence of bands of clouds or rotating storm systems?

**Uranus** (Sunlight travel time: 160 minutes (2 hours 40 minutes))

*Hints:* Are there clouds above the "surface" of this planet? Do you see evidence for storms within the planet's atmosphere? How does the color of this planet compare to that of Jupiter and Saturn?

**Neptune** (Sunlight travel time: 250 minutes (4 hours 10 minutes))

*Hints:* How does the color of this planet compare with that of the other Jovian planets? Is there evidence of bands of clouds surrounding this planet?

## Dwarf Planets

(Open the Dwarf Planets list in the Find pane.) [NOTE: The surface features shown in *Starry Night*™ of the small object Ceres and of the distant dwarf planets beyond Pluto have never been photographed and are artistic impressions for the purposes of simulation only.]

**Pluto/Charon** (Average sunlight travel time: 329 minutes (5 hours 29 minutes))

*Hints:* Zoom out to about 2 arcseconds to see Pluto's major moon, Charon. How does Pluto's rotation rate compare to Charon's orbital rate? Use 10 minutes as the Time Flow Rate. (Are these motions synchronized?) If you can pick out surface features on Charon, how does Charon's rotation rate compare to its orbital rate? Do Pluto and Charon always turn the same face to each other?

You can use the following procedure to examine each planet in this list in turn and enter your findings into Data Table 1.

24. Open the **Favourites** pane, select **Observing Projects > Tour of Planets** and open the appropriate file for the selected planet.

25. First, note the type of surface shown by the planet, including any specific features mentioned in the hints for this planet, in order to answer the questions at the end of this section.

26. You can examine specific regions or features on the planet in detail by zooming in and by using the Hand tool to move the planet around in the view.

27. Use **File > Revert** to return to the original view of the planet.

28. **Run time forward** with the Time Flow Rate of **1 hour** for Mercury, Venus, and Pluto, and **1 minute** for the other planets. Note the rotation rate of the planet in Column 2 and its direction in Column 3 of Data Table 1. [HINT: The surface of a planet rotating in the same direction as its revolution around the Sun is defined as direct rotation. In this case, the surface will be seen to move from left to right on the screen. The opposite direction is known as retrograde rotation. For comparison, the Earth's rotation is direct.]

29. Click **Stop**.

30. To determine whether this planet has significant cloud cover, open the contextual menu for the planet and click on the **Surface Image/Model**. If the heading **Clouds** appears, click on it to display the planet's cloud cover and complete Column 4 of Data Table 1. Otherwise, use the **Default** option in the **Surface Image/Model** for this planet to make this determination.

31. For the planets closer to the Sun, from Mercury to Mars, use the **M** shortcut key to advance time in 1-month intervals to observe the change, if any, in the spin axis of the planet and complete Column 5 in Data Table 1. For the objects beyond Mars, use the **Y** keyboard shortcut to advance time in 1-year intervals to look for this motion.

32. Select **File > Revert** from the menu to return to the original view.

33. Use the HUD to find the Distance from observer in AU. Record this in Column 6 of Data Table 1.

34. Use the Angular Separation tool to measure the angular radius of the planet in arcseconds. Since we want to determine the physical diameter of the planet, multiply this number by 2 to determine the angular diameter of the planet and note your result in Column 7 of Data Table 1.

You can now use the small-angle formula for the triangle made up of the diameter of the planet and the lines joining each side of the planet to the observer's position at the North Pole of the Sun to calculate the physical diameter of the planet. Figure 1 shows the geometry of this measurement. This small-angle formula uses the unit of radians for angle and we want to determine the planet's diameter in km, but your measurements are in arcseconds and AU, respectively, so the small-angle equation needs to be modified in order to use the measured units.

The angular radius was measured in the above procedure and was multiplied by 2 to determine the value of the angular diameter entered in Data Table 1. We can represent this angular diameter by the symbol θ.

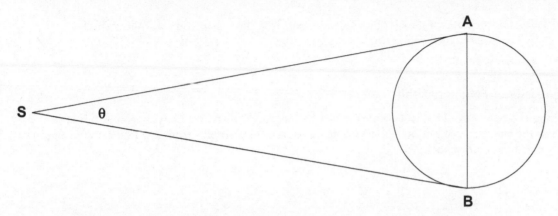

Figure 1. The geometry of the planet's diameter, AB, and the observer on the Sun, S.

In Figure 1, the angular diameter as represented by the angle ASB in radians is equal to θ = AB/SA. θ was measured in arcseconds and SA was measured in AU. Since 1 radian = 57.3 × 60 × 60 = 206,265 arcseconds, and 1 AU = $1.496 \times 10^8$ km, we need to translate these units in order to calculate the distance AB in km from the above measurements in AU and angles in arcseconds.

$$\text{AB (km)} = \theta \text{ (arcseconds)} \times \text{SA (in AU)} \times 1.496 \times 10^8/206,265$$

Thus,

$$\text{AB (km)} = \theta \text{ (arcseconds)} \times \text{SA (in AU)} \times 725.3$$

35. Use this equation and the relevant values in Data Table 1 to calculate the physical diameter of the planet and record this value in Column 8 of Data Table 1.

**Question 11.** Which of the following groups of planets rotates fastest around their axes?
(a) The terrestrial planets
(b) The dwarf planets
(c) The Jovian planets

**Question 12.** Which of the following solar system objects does Mercury most closely resemble?
(a) Venus
(b) Earth
(c) The Moon

**Question 13.** In view of the very high surface temperatures on Venus (733K), is there any evidence of volcanic activity, such as mountains shaped like volcanic cones or lava flows?

**Question 14.** What is odd about the planet Uranus?

**Question 15.** Where is Ceres located in the solar system?

**Question 16.** Why do we see no craters on the surface of Neptune?

Question 17.   Which of the following statements regarding the presence of craters on the surfaces of some of these planets is correct?

(a) There have been many volcanos on these planets.

(b) There have been many impacts of objects on the surfaces of these planets.

(c) There have been many pools of water on these surfaces that have now dried up.

Question 18.   On which planets is there evidence that there is liquid water, or there has been water in the past?

Question 19.   On the basis of the tilt of its rotation axis, is it likely that Mars will show similar seasons to those on Earth?

## C. Bonus: Eccentricity of Planetary Orbits

All objects orbiting the Sun move in ellipses with the Sun at one focus, thereby following Kepler's first law. An ellipse is defined as the shape traced out on a plane when the sum of the distances from any point on the ellipse to two points, known as foci, is constant.

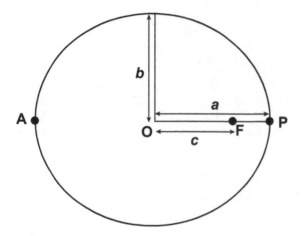

**Figure 2.** Diagram of an ellipse with major axis $2a$, minor axis $2b$ and focus, F at a distance $c$ from the center, O. If F is the Sun, then A is the aphelion position and P is the perihelion position of a planet in this orbit.

Figure 2 represents such an ellipse, with the lengths of the major and minor axes of the ellipse $2a$ and $2b$, respectively, and the distance from center O to one focus equal to $c$. The length of the minor axis of the ellipse is defined by the equation $b^2 = a^2 - c^2$.

The shape of an ellipse is characterized by its **eccentricity**, $e$, defined as the ratio of $c$ to $a$,

$$e = \frac{c}{a}$$

The values of $c$ and $a$ are, however, not easily measured because there is no physical object at O from which to make the measurements. Instead, the value of $e$ is usually calculated from two other more distinctive and easily-measured parameters, the planet's perihelion distance, $FP = (a - c)$, when the planet is closest to the Sun, and its aphelion distance, $FA = (a + c)$, when it is furthest from the Sun. The position of perihelion is marked in *Starry Night*™ by a small line extending radially outward from the orbit, and that of aphelion is directly opposite to perihelion.

The value of the orbital eccentricity can then be obtained from the ratio R of the perihelion to aphelion distances from the Sun:

$$R = \frac{FP}{FA} = \frac{(a - c)}{(a + c)} = \frac{(a - ae)}{(a + ae)} = \frac{(1 - e)}{(1 + e)}$$

Thus,

$$R + Re = 1 - e$$

and, rearranging,

$$e = \frac{(1 - R)}{(1 + R)}$$

Now $R$ can be determined from measurements of the distances from Sun to planet at aphelion and perihelion and the eccentricity of the planet's orbit determined by using this equation.

Eccentricity ranges from 0 to 1 for elliptical orbits. If $e = 0$, then $c = ae = 0$ and the length of the minor axis $b = \sqrt{(a^2 - c^2)} = a$ and the orbit will be circular. However, if $e$ tends toward 1, then $c$ tends toward $a$. Thus, $b$ becomes smaller as $(a^2 - c^2)$ tends toward zero, and the ellipse becomes very narrow.

The following procedure can be used to determine the eccentricity for planetary orbits.

36. Open **Favourites > Observing Projects > Tour of Planets > Planet Orbits Face-on.**

37. Open the **Find** pane and click on the **Selections** box to the left and the **Orbits** box to the right of the name of the selected planet to display its name and its orbit, adjusting the **Zoom** if necessary to ensure that this orbit is fully in view.

38. Adjust the Date and Time if necessary to place the planet at the position of the perihelion marker.

39. Use the Angular Separation tool to measure the distance between the Sun and the planet at perihelion. [TIP: This physical distance is shown along the Angular Separation line, below the angular separation and position angle.]

40. Adjust the Date to place the planet at a position directly opposite to the perihelion marker, at aphelion.

41. Measure the distance between the Sun and the planet at aphelion.

42. Calculate the ratio of perihelion to aphelion distances for the planet and use Equation 1 to determine the eccentricity of the planet's orbit.

43. Repeat this procedure, steps 36–42, for selected planets to answer the following questions.

**Question 20.** What is the eccentricity of the Earth's orbit?

**Question 21.** What is the eccentricity of Mercury's orbit?

Again, it is instructive to look briefly at Pluto to see how different its orbital characteristics are from those of the major planets.

44. In the Find pane, click **Off** all of the Orbits of the major planets and select and display the Orbit of Pluto. You will need to **Zoom out** and move **Increase current elevation** from the Sun to a distance of about 10 AU in order to see Pluto's full orbital path.

45. Use the above procedure to determine the eccentricity of Pluto's orbit. [HINT: Pluto was at perihelion in August of 1989 and will be close to aphelion in August of 2113.]

**Question 22.** Is the orbit of Pluto more elliptical than that of Mercury?

**Question 23.** Using the above times of perihelion and aphelion, what is the orbital period of Pluto?

If desired, you can use this simple technique to produce a full survey of the eccentricity of the orbits for all the major planets.

## D. Conclusions

In this project, you have been able to tour the solar system and examine all the major planets and some of the dwarf planets that orbit the Sun and have been able to form your own database of some important properties of these planets. You have seen that the major planets have a wide diversity of properties but that they share some important characteristics, particularly the planes in which they orbit the Sun and their orbital shapes. In contrast, the dwarf planets move in different orbits.

Many of these planets have attendant moons, and the number of discovered moons continues to grow as we explore our solar system with advanced telescopes and space probes. The moons of these planets are at least as diverse in their properties as are the planets, but the number of these moons and the wide diversity of their properties has precluded the examination of these objects in this project. A review of some of these moons in a textbook or on the internet is worthwhile, if only to recognize this wide diversity of properties. Another particularly interesting topic to read about is the search for water in its liquid and solid forms on these moons, with its implications for the possibility of other life forms in our solar system.

**Data Table 1.** Observations of Solar System Objects

| 1 | 2 | 3 | 4 | 5 | 6 | 7 | 8 |
|---|---|---|---|---|---|---|---|
| Planet/Minor planet | Rotation *Fast-Medium-Slow* | Rotation direction *Direct-Retrograde* | Cloud dover *Yes-No* | Axis tilt *Small-Medium-Large* | Measured distance from observer *AU* | Angular diameter *arcsec* | Calculated physical diameter *km* |
| Mercury | | | | | | | |
| Venus | | | | | | | |
| Earth | | | | | | | |
| Mars | | | | | | | |
| Jupiter | | | | | | | |
| Saturn | | | | | | | |
| Uranus | | | | | | | |
| Neptune | | | | | | | |
| Ceres | — | — | | — | | | |
| Pluto | — | — | | — | | | |
| Haumea | — | — | | — | | | |
| Makemake | — | — | | — | | | |
| Eris | — | — | | — | | | |

# Phases of Venus 14

Galileo's discovery of the variable phases of Venus proved to be a turning point in our understanding of the universe. Prior to Galileo's observations, there were two competing models of the observable universe. The accepted model was **geocentric**, with the Earth at its center. Several philosophers from the Greek era onward had suggested **heliocentric** models, where the **Sun** was assumed to be at the center of the universe. Prior to Galileo, there were no direct observations to allow anyone to differentiate between these two models and most people accepted the geocentric model as the correct view of the world. Galileo's observations of Venus with the newly invented telescope provided decisive support for the heliocentric theory.

The geocentric model had the Moon, the Sun, the planets and all of the stars moving around a fixed Earth. Part of the reluctance of people to accept any model other than this one arose from the fact that they could not sense either the Earth's rotational motion or its orbital motion through space. In this Earth-centered model, the Moon was the closest object to the Earth, and the others in order of increasing distance were Mercury, Venus, the Sun, Mars, Jupiter, Saturn, and finally the "sphere of the stars".

In the simplest geocentric model, each object moved in a constant direction along a circular path at a constant distance from the Earth. However, this model did not duplicate the observations, particularly the occasional **retrograde motion** of planets, where the normal eastward motion of planets in our sky is interrupted by westward motion relative to the background stars. Various complications were added to this early geocentric model in order to reproduce the observed motions more accurately, most notably by Ptolemy around 140 A.D. The most important of these additions was the assumption that each planet moved around a smaller circle called the **epicycle**, the center of which moved along a larger circle, the **deferent**, around the Earth. In order to explain the fact that Mercury and Venus remained relatively close to the Sun in the sky, an additional condition was added that the centers of the epicycles of Mercury and Venus must remain on the line joining Earth to the Sun. This refined model worked very well in predicting planetary motions over short times but became increasingly inaccurate in the centuries following its development.

In the case of Venus, this epicyclic motion would bring the planet alternately closer to the Earth and farther away again, but it did not cause Venus to cross the deferent of the Sun. In this model, therefore, the apparent size of Venus would change as the planet moves around its epicycle due to its changing distance from the Earth, but even at its farthest distance from Earth, Venus would always be closer to the Earth than is the Sun. Thus, we would always see Venus in a crescent phase, or in a "new" phase (entirely dark) when it passes close to the Sun, but we would never see Venus at or near full phase.

In the heliocentric theory, Venus orbits the Sun. Its orbit is smaller than that of the Earth and so we never see Venus stray far from the Sun in the sky. However, it can be anywhere in this orbit as seen from the Earth. If Venus is between the Earth and the Sun, we will see a crescent phase. At this time, it will be closer to us and appear larger. When it is on the opposite side of the Sun from the Earth, we will see it fully sunlit, in its full phase. At this time, it will be more distant and therefore appear smaller. If the heliocentric theory is correct, we should then see a full range of phases from crescent to full and back again as Venus orbits the Sun. Furthermore, the phases should be strongly correlated with the apparent size of the planet—largest at crescent phase and smallest at full phase. It was Galileo's observation of these correlated changes, along with several other crucial measurements, that convinced him that the planets orbited the Sun.

In this project, you can investigate Venus' motion in the sky and see how this motion correlates with its phases and apparent size.

## A. Motion of Venus in Relation to the Sun

1. Launch *Starry Night*™ and configure the HUD to include **Angular size**.
2. Open the **Favourites > Observing Projects > Phases of Venus > Venus' Motion**.

The view is centered on the Sun and shows the sky as seen from the north pole of Earth on November 9, 2010, with daylight and the horizon removed.

3. Click **Play**.

With the gaze locked onto the Sun, you can tell that the Sun moves against the background stars by the way that these stars appear to move continuously behind the fixed Sun. This apparent motion of the stars is an illusion, caused by the fact that we are viewing the Sun from a moving Earth. You get a similar illusion if you stand on the edge of a merry-go-round and fix your eyes on an object at the center—it stays fixed in your vision, while the rest of the world seems to spin past it.

Venus can be seen to move with respect to the Sun, reversing its direction regularly to remain relatively close to the Sun during this motion. Observe particularly the relative speed of this motion as Venus moves from left to right compared to its motion when moving from right to left.

**Question 1.**   Approximately how far does Venus move away from the Sun, in degrees, before turning around and coming back toward the Sun again? For reference, note the total angular width of the screen from one side to the other in the Zoom panel of the toolbar. [HINT: Use the time controls to move Venus to its points of maximum excursion and use the Angular Separation tool to answer this question.]

**Question 2.**   Is the apparent speed of Venus on the screen the same when it is traveling eastwards (from right to left) past the Sun as when it is traveling westward (from left to right)? [NOTE: Make sure that time is running forward when you determine the answer to this question.]

## B. The Ecliptic

You may notice that Venus' motion around the Sun is slightly reminiscent of a figure eight, with a looping path on each side of the Sun. This motion seems to contradict the idea that Venus, as with all planets, orbits the Sun in a single plane.

In fact, the apparent looping motion of Venus is an illusion caused by the tilt of the Earth's equator by 23 ½° relative to its orbital plane. Thus, this orbital plane, known as the ecliptic, is tilted by 23 ½° relative to the celestial equator. Our view from Earth's North Pole is oriented with the top and bottom of our view parallel to the celestial equator and the left and right sides parallel to the Earth's rotation axis. As our view follows the Sun around the ecliptic each year, the ecliptic appears tilted from lower right to upper left when we look toward the Vernal Equinox in March, and from the lower left to upper right six months later, when we look toward the Autumnal Equinox in September. Thus, although the celestial equator and the ecliptic are fixed planes, our changing direction of view causes the ecliptic to appear to sweep through +23 ½° and –23 ½° over the course of a full year. Venus' orbit is almost in the plane of the Earth's orbit and so this orbit will also tilt back and forth along with the ecliptic plane.

4. Press the **F** key on your keyboard to display the ecliptic.

With time progressing forward, you can see that the Sun follows the ecliptic around the sky, and that Venus stays close to the ecliptic (that is, close to the plane of the Earth's orbit) at all times. [NOTE: The apparent curvature of the ecliptic in this view is a consequence of the wide field of view and the projection on to the screen.] The small departures of Venus from the ecliptic are caused by the fact that Venus' orbit is inclined by a small angle of about 3° to the Earth's orbit.

> 5. Open the **Find** pane and click the checkbox to the right of the listing for Venus to display its orbit.
> 6. Click **Stop** and change the Date to **December 9, 2010.**

Venus' orbit is edge-on on this date and intersects the ecliptic at the position of the Sun. Venus is near to the extreme right-hand side of its orbit at this time, a point known as the greatest western elongation. You can see from this fortunate alignment that the angle between Venus' orbital plane and the ecliptic is a few degrees.

> 7. **Centre** the view on Venus and set the Zoom to **15°.**
> 8. Adjust the Date to determine the date of the next greatest western elongation.

**Question 3.** What is the date of the greatest western elongation of Venus after December 9, 2010?

## C. The Phases of Venus

In this section, you will observe the phases of Venus from the North Pole of Earth.

> 9. Open **Favourites > Observing Projects > Phases of Venus > Venus' Phases.**

The view on the screen is similar to that in Part A, except that the view is now locked on Venus on November 5, 2010. With Venus locked at the center of the screen, it becomes easy to zoom in to see the phase of Venus and then to zoom back out again to see Venus' position and motion relative to the Sun.

> 10. Click **Play** and observe the motion of Venus and the Sun.

The view on the screen looks different from that in Part A because the view is locked on Venus. Consequently, the Sun now appears to orbit around Venus. This is an illusion caused by fixing our gaze on a moving planet. The relative orientation of Venus and the Sun remains the same as in Part A, with Venus sometimes to the left and sometimes to the right of the Sun.

> 11. Select **File > Revert.**
> 12. Select **Orbit** from the contextual menu for Venus to display its orbit.

In this part of the project, you will observe Venus at various points in its motion relative to the Sun. At each point you will: (i) record the date, (ii) measure the angular separation between the Sun and Venus, (iii) observe and record the phase of Venus, and (iv) determine the angular size of Venus in the sky.

Note that, on November 5, 2010, Venus is close to the Sun in the sky.

> Sequence 1
> 13. Measure the angular separation between the Sun and Venus and note the Date and the Venus–Sun separation in Data Table 1 at the end of this project.
> 14. **Magnify** Venus and note the phase of the planet for this date in the Data Table.
> 15. Use the HUD to find the Angular size of Venus in the sky and record this value in the Data Table under Apparent Angular Size.
> 16. Set the Zoom to **90°.**

In the steps below, you can watch the phase of Venus change as it moves around the Sun.

17. Ensure that the view is still centered (i.e., locked) on Venus and **Run time forward** to **December 8, 2010**. Repeat the measurements and observations described in Sequence 1 for this date and record your results in Data Table 1.

**Question 4.**   Describe the change in angular separation between Venus and the Sun from November 5, 2010, to December 8, 2010.

**Question 5.**   Describe the change in the phase of Venus between these dates.

**Question 6.**   Has the apparent size of Venus increased, decreased, or stayed the same from November 5, 2010, to December 8, 2010?

18. **Run time forward** to **January 7, 2011**. Repeat the measurements and observations described in Sequence 1 for this date and record your results in the Data Table 1.

Venus is west of the Sun (toward the right on the screen), and should now be at about its greatest angular distance from the Sun. This places Venus near greatest western elongation.

**Question 7.**   What phase does Venus show when it is near greatest western elongation?

**Question 8.**   Has the apparent size of Venus increased, decreased, or stayed the same from December 8, 2010, to January 7, 2011?

19. **Run time forward** to **August 16, 2011**. Repeat the measurements and observations described in Sequence 1 for this date and record your results in Data Table 1.

By August 16, 2011, Venus is close to the Sun again in our sky and moving rapidly toward **conjunction**, the time at which the angular distance between Venus and the Sun is smallest. At this time, Venus is beyond the Sun and at its furthest distance from Earth and hence will appear to be at its smallest. Because Venus is beyond the Sun, this is called a superior conjunction.

**Question 9.**   Describe the change in the phase of Venus between greatest western elongation and conjunction.

**Question 10.**   Has the apparent size of Venus increased, decreased, or stayed the same from greatest western elongation to conjunction?

20. **Run time forward** to **March 30, 2012**. Repeat the measurements and observations described in Sequence 1 for this date and record your results in Data Table 1.

By March 30, 2012, Venus is again near its farthest position from the Sun in the sky, this time to the east of the Sun (toward the left on the screen). Venus is now at **greatest eastern elongation**.

**Question 11.**   Describe the change in the phase of Venus between conjunction and greatest eastern elongation.

**Question 12.**   Has the apparent size of Venus increased, decreased, or stayed the same from conjunction to greatest eastern elongation?

21. **Run time forward** to **June 1, 2012**. Repeat the measurements and observations described in Sequence 1 for this date and record your results in Data Table 1.

By June 1, 2012, Venus is again approaching conjunction with the Sun, this time from the east. Venus will be between the Sun and Earth and the conjunction is called an inferior conjunction.

Question 13. Describe the change in the phase of Venus between greatest eastern elongation and this conjunction.

Question 14. Has the apparent size of Venus increased, decreased, or stayed the same from greatest eastern elongation to this conjunction?

The data in Data Table 1 show you the dependence of angular radius on the Earth-Venus distance and demonstrate the large change in angular size of Venus during this relative motion of Earth and Venus.

The following steps allow you to see the progression in Venus' phase and apparent size in the sky even more clearly than the steps above.

22. Select **File > Revert**.
23. **Magnify** Venus and then click **Play**. Allow time to progress until at least **August 1, 2012**, to show the dramatic changes in the size and phase of Venus during this full cycle.

Question 15. What relationship did you observe between the "fullness" of the phase of Venus (e.g., thin crescent, thick crescent, half full, gibbous, full) and the apparent size of Venus?

Question 16. Do your observations support the geocentric or the heliocentric theory of the universe?

Question 17. Which specific observations support your answer to the previous question?

24. Set the Date to **June 6, 2012**, to see an uncommon occurrence, the transit of Venus across the surface of the Sun. **Zoom out** to see the whole Sun, set the Time Flow Rate to **1 minute**, and **Run time forward** and **backward** to watch the whole event. This event is examined in more detail in a separate project and is related to equivalent events occurring when extra-solar planets pass in front of their parent stars.

## D. Conclusions

With the observations and measurements in this project, you have demonstrated the large variation in the observed angular radius of Venus associated with the changes in the observed phase that was seen by Galileo almost 400 years ago with his primitive but very effective telescope. It was on these measurements that he based his conclusion that Copernicus was correct in believing that the planets orbited the Sun rather than the Earth. You have also seen the simulation of the transit of Venus across the disk of the Sun. Observations of this phenomenon were very important in the measurement of the size of the solar system earlier in the history of astronomy.

**Data Table 1.** Phase and Angular Size of Venus

| Date | Venus–Sun separation ( ° ' " ) | Phase of Venus | Apparent angular size of Venus ( " ) |
|---|---|---|---|
| Nov. 5, 2010 | | | |
| Dec. 8, 2010 | | | |
| Jan. 7, 2011 | | | |
| Aug. 16, 2011 | | | |
| Mar. 30, 2011 | | | |
| Jun. 1, 2011 | | | |

# Planetary Motion: The Retrograde Motion of Mars

# 15

If you could observe an orbiting planet from a stationary position near the Sun, you would see this planet moving relatively uniformly eastward against the background sky. This eastward motion is called **direct** motion.

In fact, we watch a moving planet from a moving Earth. From this viewpoint, the planet appears to follow a complicated path across our sky. Consider Mars, for example. The radius of its orbit is larger than that of the Earth, and thus, it moves more slowly in its orbit than does the Earth. For most of the year we are either on the far side of our orbit from Mars or we are traveling more-or-less toward or away from Mars, and in these cases we see Mars moving "forward" in its orbit, in an eastward direction (i.e., *direct* motion). However, for part of the year, we are on the same side of the Sun as Mars, and overtaking it. Because we are pulling ahead, Mars appears to drop back in a westward direction. This temporary westward motion for planets is known as **retrograde** motion. For the same reason, we see retrograde motion for the other superior planets.

To visualize this, imagine yourself in a fast car driving on the inside of a circular track while a slower car drives on the outside of the track. From most of the track, you will see the slower car moving in the same direction as you against the background. However, when you overtake the slower car, it will appear to be moving in the opposite direction to you and drop back against the background.

You can demonstrate this motion easily with *Starry Night*™ by watching the relative motion of Mars night-by-night against the background stars. You will find that the reversal of apparent motion takes place when the planet is near to **opposition**, on the opposite side of the Earth from the Sun. This is expected from the argument above because it is at opposition when the Earth is overtaking the more distant and slower planet.

The time taken for the Earth-Mars system to move from one opposition to the next is known as the **synodic period** of Mars. This differs from the more fundamental revolutionary period of Mars with respect to the stars, its **sidereal period**. The latter cannot be measured directly from Earth, but its value can be determined from a simple calculation after measurement of the synodic period.

## A. The Motion of Mars as Seen from Earth

1. Launch *Starry Night*™ and configure the HUD to include **Age of Moon, Angular Size, Disk Illumination,** and **Distance from observer.**
2. Open **Favourites > Observing Projects > Planetary Motion > September 2007.**

The view shows the early morning twilight sky from Montreal, Canada, on September 23, 2007. Mars and a reference star, Kappa Aurigae, are labeled. Note that this reference star is almost due south.

3. Click **Play** and observe the motion of Mars in the sky.

If you watch the time display, you will notice that the time of night becomes earlier and earlier. This is because time is flowing in steps of one sidereal day, which is about four minutes short of one solar day. This time interval ensures that the background sky remains fixed as time advances. On September 23, 2007, Mars is just visible in the morning twilight at about 6 AM. As the sidereal days pass, morning twilight deepens into night and by March 23, 2008, the observing time has shifted to about 6 PM with Mars fading into evening twilight.

4. Select **File > Revert** and **Step time forward** to repeat the animation.

The motion of Mars in the sky is initially eastward, but it soon reaches a stationary point where it stops and reverses its direction of motion. Eventually, as evening twilight begins to brighten the sky, Mars reaches a second stationary point where it stops and reverses direction again to resume eastward motion.

Question 1.    What is the name given to the motion that Mars exhibits before the first stationary point and again after the second stationary point?

Question 2.    What is the name given to the motion that Mars exhibits between these two stationary points?

5. Use **File > Revert** to reset the view.
6. **Centre** the view on the reference star, Kappa Aurigae, and set the Zoom to **30°**.
7. Select **Local Path** from the contextual menu for Mars.
8. **Step time forward** or use the **U** key to advance time in steps of one sidereal day. As time advances, a green line traces the path of Mars in the sky.
9. Use the **Step time** buttons or the keyboard shortcuts **U** and **Shift-U** to move time forward and backward in steps of one sidereal day to find the date on which Mars is at each of the two stationary points.

Question 3.    On which dates between September 23, 2007, and March 23, 2008, was Mars at a stationary point?

Question 4.    Between September 23, 2007, and March 23, 2008, for how many days does Mars exhibit retrograde motion?

10. Use the **Step time** controls to move in steps of one sidereal day to **December 23, 2007**, close to the midpoint between the two stationary points and when the Moon is near to Mars in the sky and Mars is near the reference star. Move the cursor over the Moon and find the phase of the Moon from the Age of Moon information in the HUD.

Question 5.    Where is the Sun in the sky at this time, relative to the Earth and Mars? [HINT: Consider the time of day in the view and recall that the reference star Kappa Aurigae is aligned near the south point of the horizon. Also consider the phase of the Moon in the view.]

Question 6.    What would be the configuration of Mars at this time (e.g., conjunction, maximum elongation, opposition, etc.)?

## B. Phase and Angular Size of Mars

In the following simulation, you can observe Mars from the North Pole of Earth with the horizon and daylight removed from the view to give an unobstructed and uninterrupted view of Mars as it moves through one complete synodic period, starting from conjunction with the Sun and progressing through opposition to the next conjunction.

Mars is a superior planet with an orbit larger than that of Earth. Thus, at conjunction this planet is beyond the Sun, whereas at opposition it is much closer to Earth. It will therefore show varying size and brightness over its synodic period. Also, because Mars never passes between the Earth and the Sun, it will not display the full range of phases that are seen for Mercury, Venus, or the Moon.

11. Click the **FOV** side pane tab. In the Other (All Charts) heading of the FOV pane, click **Add... > Circular...** and in the dialog window that opens, set the Indicator name to **1 arcminute** and type **1'** for the Diameter value.

12. Select **Favourites > Observing Projects > Planetary Motion > Mars Phase and Size.**

This view is centered on Mars. Thus, when you advance time in intervals of 1 day, the background stars, the planets, and the Sun move in various ways, while Mars remains stationary. This mode should be maintained throughout this sequence. On October 23, 2006, Mars is at conjunction, appearing just above the Sun in the sky. The synodic period of Mars is the time required for Mars to reach this alignment with the Sun again.

## Sequence 1

13. Record the Date of this observation into Data Table 1 at the end of this project.

14. Use the HUD to find the Distance from observer and Angular size of Mars and record these values in Data Table 1.

15. Set the Zoom to **1 arcminute**.

16. Note the phase of Mars for this date and record it in Data Table 1. [HINT: You can also check Disk illumination in the HUD or Info pane.]

17. **Centre** the view on Mars and set the Zoom to **90°**.

You can now repeat the above measurement sequence twice before Mars reaches its first stationary point, in order to obtain representative values of distance and angular radius of Mars as seen from Earth during this segment of its motion.

18. Use the **M** shortcut key to advance the date four months to **February 23, 2007**. Repeat the measurements and observations described in Sequence 1 above.

19. Advance time another four months to **June 23, 2007**. Repeat the measurements and observations described in Sequence 1.

The next three measurements should be made at stationary points and at opposition.

20. **Run** or **Step time forward** until Mars reaches the first stationary point. Repeat the measurements and observations described in Sequence 1.

21. **Run** or **Step time forward** to **December 23, 2007**. Repeat the measurements and observations described in Sequence 1.

22. **Run** or **Step time forward** until Mars reaches the second stationary point. Repeat the measurements and observations described in Sequence 1.

23. Take two further sets of measurements and observations as described in Sequence 1 at four-month intervals from the second stationary point.

24. Finally, **Run** or **Step time forward** until Mars reaches conjunction again and is near to the Sun in the sky. Repeat the measurements and observations described in Sequence 1 for this date and record your results in Data Table 1.

Question 7.    From your observations, during which part of the synodic period does Mars appear largest as seen from Earth?

Question 8.    During which part of the synodic period is Mars closest to Earth?

Question 9.    Why is the angular size of Mars different at the second conjunction from its angular size at the first conjunction?

Question 10.   What are the phases that Mars shows during a complete synodic period?

Question 11.   What is the measured synodic period, the time required (in days) for Mars to move from the first conjunction to the second conjunction?

## C. Synodic Period of Mars

The synodic period of a planet is the time required for the planet to move from any particular configuration relative to the Sun as seen from the Earth to the next occurrence of the same configuration. This is the period that is measurable from Earth. In the last section, you measured the synodic period of Mars by determining the duration between one conjunction and the next conjunction.

The sidereal period of a planet is the time taken for the planet to orbit the Sun once with respect to the distant stars. It is not possible to measure the sidereal period of another planet directly from Earth. Instead, the sidereal period must be derived from the synodic period by calculation.

The calculation of sidereal period from synodic period is simple. For superior planets such as Mars, the equation relating the sidereal period $P$ to the synodic period $S$ and the orbital period of the Earth $E$ is

$$\frac{1}{P} = \frac{1}{E} - \frac{1}{S}$$

where $P$, $E$, and $S$ must be in the same units.

At this stage, however, let us assume that we know the sidereal period and rearrange the above equation in order to calculate the expected synodic period of Mars. Adding $1/S$ to both sides and subtracting $1/P$ from both sides gives

$$\frac{1}{S} = \frac{1}{E} - \frac{1}{P}$$

Question 12.   The sidereal period of Mars is $P = 687$ days, so, using $E = 365.26$ days, what value does the equation above give for the synodic period of Mars, in days?

Question 13.   How does your measured time for the synodic period of Mars that you obtained in Question 11 compare to this calculated value for the synodic period?

You will note that the calculated value and your measured value are different! This is not experimental error or scientific uncertainty; both numbers are in fact correct values. To explore this discrepancy, begin by measuring the duration of a series of successive synodic periods of Mars beginning with the period starting with the conjunction of October 23, 2006.

25. Select **File > Revert** to return to the conjunction of Mars on October 23, 2006. Change the Time Flow Rate to the measured number of days to the next conjunction that you obtained in Question 11 and click the **Step time forward** button to bring Mars to its next conjunction in 2008.

26. Click the **Step time forward** button once again to advance time by the duration of your measured synodic period for Mars.

Question 14.   Where is Mars in the sky relative to the Sun when you advance time by the measured synodic period to the next "predicted" conjunction in 2011?

27. Determine the duration of the synodic period of Mars from its conjunction in 2008 to its conjunction in 2011. If Mars is at conjunction in the view, then the duration of this synodic period is the same as the previous synodic period. However, if the Sun is west of Mars (to the right of Mars in the view), then this synodic period is longer than the previous one. Count the number of times you must press the **D** keyboard shortcut in order to bring Mars and the Sun into alignment and add this to the number of days in the Time Flow Rate to obtain the duration of this synodic period. On the other hand, if the Sun is east of Mars (to the left of Mars in the view), then this synodic period is shorter than the previous one. Count the number of times you must press the **Shift-D** keyboard shortcut in order to bring Mars and the Sun into alignment and subtract this from the number of days in the Time Flow Rate to obtain the duration of this synodic period.

**Question 15.** What is the measured synodic period of Mars from its conjunction in 2008 to its conjunction in 2011? How does this compare with the duration you measured for the previous synodic period and with the calculated value for the synodic period of Mars?

To understand why the synodic period of Mars varies, it will be helpful to observe the orbits of Earth and Mars from space.

28. Select **Favourites > Observing Projects > Planetary Motion > Orbits.**

In this view, from a location 2.75 AU above the Sun in the direction toward the north ecliptic pole, the stars and other planets of the solar system are hidden while the images of the Earth and Mars have been greatly exaggerated in size. This view is centered on the Sun and shows Mars and Earth and their orbits. On this date, February 12, 1995, Mars is at opposition. From this unique vantage point at the "north ecliptic pole", both orbits look quite circular, but careful observation shows that they are in fact elliptical because the Sun is off-center in each orbit (remember Kepler's first law, which states that the Sun is located at one focus of an elliptical orbit). The perihelion point, the point of the orbit closest to the Sun, is shown for each orbit as a short line directed away from the Sun. You can also see that the orbit of Mars is more elliptical than that of the Earth. The fact that both planets follow elliptical orbits produces the variability in the duration of the synodic period and the discrepancy between the measured synodic period and the accepted value. In fact, this accepted value, which you calculated in Question 12, is an average over long periods and has been determined by careful and complex examination of the orbital paths of these planets.

29. The Time Flow Rate in the toolbar is set to the accepted value for the synodic period of Mars. **Step time forward** by 1 synodic period and observe the actual configuration of Mars and Earth when Mars should be at the next opposition. Continue to **Step time forward** by this time interval or use the **U** keyboard shortcut to observe the positions of Mars and Earth over many subsequent synodic periods of Mars.

**Question 16.** When time advances over many periods corresponding to the accepted duration of the synodic period of Mars, which of the following is true?

(a) Mars is sometimes ahead of Earth and sometimes behind Earth at the predicted times of opposition, but the planets are always near to opposition at the time predicted by the accepted value of the synodic period of Mars.

(b) Mars falls progressively farther behind the Earth after many synodic periods of Mars.

(c) Earth falls progressively behind Mars after many synodic periods of Mars.

An inspection of the orbits of Mars and Earth also shows that some oppositions bring Mars closer to Earth than other oppositions. One such favorable opposition occurred in 2003. At the time of its closest approach, Mars was closer to Earth than it had been for several thousand years.

30. Select **File > Revert** and then **Step time forward** to the predicted opposition in 2003, and use the **D** and **shift-D** keyboard shortcuts to adjust the date closer to the actual opposition when the distance between the Earth and Mars as measured by the Angular Separation tool is a minimum.

**Question 17.**   What was the distance separating the Earth and Mars during the opposition of Mars in 2003?

**Question 18.**   Where was Mars relative to the perihelion point of its orbit during the opposition of 2003?

**Question 19.**   Where was Earth relative to the perihelion point of its orbit during the opposition of 2003?

## D. Variations in Mars–Earth Distance at Opposition

An event such as the close opposition of Mars in 2003 is a rare opportunity to observe Mars from Earth under ideal conditions. Because Mars is at opposition, it is above the horizon throughout the night and its proximity to Earth makes it appear larger.

31. Select **Favourites > Observing Projects > Planetary Motion > Synodic Periods.**

The view is from the North Pole of Earth looking at a magnified view of Mars. Daylight and the horizon have been removed from the view. You will observe ten successive oppositions of Mars beginning with this particular opposition in June, 2001.

32. In Data Table 2, at the end of this project, record the Date of this observation, and use the HUD to obtain the Distance from observer and Angular size of Mars during this opposition.

33. **Step time forward** by one interval.

**Question 20.**   Judging from its phase, is Mars at opposition on this date?

### Sequence 2

34. Move the cursor over Mars to display the HUD and use the **D** and **Shift-D** keyboard shortcuts to adjust the Date until the Distance from observer in the HUD reaches a minimum. This can be assumed to be the position of opposition, although this is not strictly true because of the ellipticity of the orbits of Earth and Mars. (For example, the date of least distance between Earth and Mars that you find for the year 2007 will not necessarily agree with the date of Mars' opposition, but it will be close enough for our purposes here.)

35. Record the Date and the Distance from observer (the Earth-Mars distance) and the Angular size of Mars in Data Table 2.

36. **Step time forward** by one synodic period of Mars.

37. Repeat Sequence 2 to observe a total of 10 successive oppositions encompassing 9 synodic periods.

From these data, you can see that both the distance between Earth and Mars and the angular size of Mars as seen from Earth at successive oppositions vary significantly because of the elliptical orbits of these planets.

38. Use Graph Template 1 at the end of this project to plot a graph of the Earth-Mars Distance for the successive oppositions.

39. Use Graph Template 2 at the end of this project to plot a graph of the Angular Size of Mars for the successive oppositions.

**Question 21.** Which of the oppositions would be the most favorable for observing Mars from Earth?

**Question 22.** From your graph, how is the Earth-Mars distance changing with time (increasing, decreasing, random, periodic, or sinusoidal)?

**Question 23.** If these variations are periodic or sinusoidal, what is the approximate period of the variation; that is, how many synodic periods elapse before the pattern starts to repeat?

**Question 24.** For the 10 oppositions in Data Table 2, what is the average distance between Mars and the Earth at opposition?

**Question 25.** Look at your graph of the Distance from Earth of Mars. Note the least and greatest separation. What is the change in distance between these two extremes? [HINT: Subtract the closest distance from the greatest.]

**Question 26.** Based on the answers to the last two questions, expressed as a percentage, what is the ratio of the change in distance between the two extremes of least and greatest separation to the average Earth-Mars distance at opposition? [HINT: Divide the change in distance by the average distance and then multiply by 100.]

**Question 27.** What is the average angular size of Mars at opposition during this short range of measurements?

**Question 28.** How much larger is the largest angular size of Mars at opposition than its average angular size at opposition? [HINT: Divide largest angular size by average angular size.]

**Question 29.** Occasionally, an email is widely circulated claiming that Mars will appear larger in the sky than the Full Moon (the average angular diameter of the Moon in the sky is about 30 arcminutes). Based on your observations of these 10 oppositions of Mars, one of which includes the closest approach of Mars to the Earth in thousands of years, how credible do you find the claim made in this email?

The adjustments that you needed to make in order to move these planets to their closest approach, after advancing the date by the average synodic period, shows again that the observed synodic period of Mars varies. You can now follow a common scientific procedure that is used when data are variable, and determine an average synodic period from these data. The procedure for determining the correct synodic period for Mars is significantly more complex than this and involves a careful consideration of the orbital paths of Mars and the Earth.

40. Determine the total length of time for the 9 synodic periods encompassed by your observations using the dates of the first and last oppositions from this series and divide this number of days by 9.

**Question 30.** What is the average synodic period for Mars during this 9-cycle sequence?

## E. Challenge: Variation of Synodic Period with Distance from the Sun

In this section, you can investigate how the synodic period of a planet depends on its distance from the Sun and its orbital distance compared to that of the Earth. You can use Kepler's third law and the planet's known distance from the Sun to find its sidereal period. You can then use the sidereal period to find the synodic period.

We know that a planet's sidereal period increases with increasing distance from the Sun, from a short period (88 days) for Mercury, the closest planet to the Sun, to a very long period (248 years) for Pluto, now designated a dwarf planet among several other similar objects.

Kepler's third law gives the specific relationship

$$P^2 = a^3$$

where $P$ is the sidereal period in years and $a$ is the semimajor axis of the planet's orbit in AU.

Recall that the equation for calculating the sidereal period of a superior planet from its synodic period is

$$\frac{1}{P} = \frac{1}{E} - \frac{1}{S}$$

This equation can be rearranged as follows:

$$\frac{1}{S} = \frac{1}{E} - \frac{1}{P} \qquad \text{(Superior planet)}$$

Note: The equivalent equation for inferior planets is

$$\frac{1}{S} = \frac{1}{P} + \frac{1}{E} \qquad \text{(Inferior planet)}$$

In each of these three equations, $S$ (the synodic period), $P$ (the sidereal period), and $E$ (the Earth's period, 1 year, or 365.26 days) must all be in the same units. Here, we will use years.

Data Table 3, at the end of this project, lists the six solar system objects, Mercury, Venus, Mars, Jupiter, Uranus, and Pluto, and six hypothetical planets, A, B, C, D, E and F. The hypothetical planets are included to show how synodic period would depend on distance from the Sun in regions of the solar system where there is no actual planet. Of course, an object such as an asteroid or a spacecraft could orbit the Sun at these distances.

For objects with orbital radii close to that of the Earth, to obtain meaningful sidereal and synodic periods we need to assume that the object is influenced only by the gravitational force of the Sun; that is, the object does not feel any force from the Earth, even if it passes very close to the Earth. In reality, this would not be true: The Earth's gravitational pull perturbs the orbit of any object passing close to it, sending the object into a slightly modified or even greatly modified orbit, depending on the distance of closest approach. This effect happens to asteroids and comets that pass close to any of the planets, particularly Jupiter. The effect has been used deliberately by NASA to save fuel by using a planetary slingshot effect to propel spacecraft to the outer planets. For the purpose of this exercise, however, we ignore this effect and look only at the effect of the Sun on the orbiting object.

The values of $P$, $a$, and $S$ for Mercury, Venus, Mars, Jupiter, and Uranus are filled in for you, along with those for Pluto, in Data Table 3. For the hypothetical planets, the values of $P$ and $S$ need to be calculated from the specified distances from the Sun, using the method described above. For each of the hypothetical planets listed in Data Table 3, complete the steps in Sequence 3, below.

### Sequence 3

41. Use Kepler's third law to calculate the sidereal period, $P$, for the planet and enter the value in the appropriate cell in Data Table 3.

42. Use the relationship between sidereal and synodic period to calculate the synodic period of the planet, $S$, and enter the value in the appropriate space in Data Table 3. Be careful to distinguish between inferior planets and superior planets.

A graph often represents the relationship between two variables with greater clarity than just a list of numbers. Use Graph Template 3 at the end of this project to plot the synodic period, $S$, along the vertical axis against the length of the semimajor axis, $a$, along the horizontal axis of the graph. Notice that the graph uses logarithmic scales on both axes.

**Question 31.** If we were to put a spacecraft into orbit around the Sun at a distance of 0.900 AU and then gradually increase the orbital distance closer and closer to 1 AU (try 0.99, 0.999, 0.9999, 0.99999, ... 0.999999999 AU), what would happen to the synodic period of the spacecraft? Why does this happen?

**Question 32.** Suppose we put the spacecraft into orbit around the Sun at a distance of 1.08 AU and then gradually decrease the orbital distance closer and closer to 1 AU (try, 1.05, 1.01, 1.001, 1.0001, ... 1.000000001 AU), what would happen to the synodic period of the spacecraft?

Question 33.    Based on your answers to the previous two questions, if someone were to ask, "What is the synodic period of an object orbiting the Sun at a distance of exactly 1 AU?" what do you think the answer should be? [The mathematical process involved in obtaining this answer from the reasoning in the previous two questions is called "taking the limit of $S$ as $P$ approaches 1 AU"; that is, we are finding the limiting value of $S$ as $P$ becomes arbitrarily close to 1 AU.)

For the next two questions, look at your graph and think about the value of $S$ shown in Data Table 3 for each planet compared to the value of $P$ (the sidereal period of the planet) and the value of $E$ (the sidereal period of the Earth, equal to 1 year).

Question 34.    What happens to the value of $S$ as the distance from the Sun, $a$, becomes very small? Why does this happen? [HINT: Try 0.1, 0.001, 0.0001, ... 0.00000001.]

Question 35.    What happens to the value of $S$ as the distance from the Sun, $a$, becomes very large? Why does this happen? [HINT: Try 10, 100, 1000, ... 1,000,000,000.]

## F. Conclusions

In this project, you have followed Mars as it orbits the Sun, watching it from a moving platform, the Earth, and have seen it move from direct to retrograde motion as Earth catches up with the slower-moving Mars in its larger orbit. You have measured the change in angular size of Mars that results from this relative motion of Earth and the planet and you have observed the "real" motion of these planets from above the solar system, a position not attainable in real life. This relatively uniform motion around the Sun cannot be seen from the moving Earth.

You then examined the variability in the appearance of Mars during different oppositions, caused by the elliptical orbits of Earth and Mars, and investigated this variability over 10 successive oppositions. You then used these data to determine an average value for this variable synodic period for Mars. Finally, you explored the change in synodic period of a planet or spacecraft as its orbital distance was changed to approach various limits within the solar system. The first exploration moved the circular orbit of the hypothetical planet toward that of the Earth. The second exploration adjusted the object's orbital distance toward zero, when the object would be orbiting very close to the Sun. The third exploration looked at the object orbiting the Sun at very large distances, in the distant realms of the solar system.

**Data Table 1.** Observations of Mars through One Synodic Period

| Configuration | Date | Distance from observer (AU) | Angular size ( " ) | Phase |
|---|---|---|---|---|
| Conjunction | | | | |
| | | | | |
| | | | | |
| Stationary Point | | | | |
| Opposition | | | | |
| Stationary Point | | | | |
| | | | | |
| | | | | |
| Conjunction | | | | |

**Data Table 2.** Angular Size of Mars and Its Distance from Earth at Successive Oppositions

| Date of opposition | Mars–Earth distance (AU) | Angular size of Mars ( " ) |
|---|---|---|
| | | |
| | | |
| | | |
| | | |
| | | |
| | | |
| | | |
| | | |
| | | |
| | | |

**Graph Template 1.** Mars–Earth Distance at Opposition 2001–2020

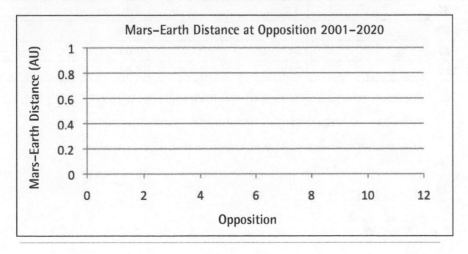

**Graph Template 2.** Angular Size of Mars at Opposition 2001– 2020

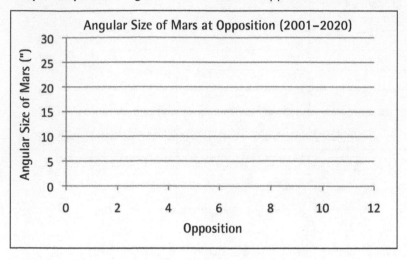

**Data Table 3.** Synodic and Sidereal Periods for a Variety of Real and Hypothetical Planets

| Planet | α (AU) | P (years) | S (years) |
|---|---|---|---|
| **Inferior Planets** | | | |
| Planet A | 0.10 | | |
| Mercury | 0.39 | 0.24 | 0.32 |
| Venus | 0.72 | 0.62 | 1.6 |
| Planet B | 0.900 | | |
| Planet C | 0.930 | | |
| Planet D | 0.99990 | | |
| **Superior Planets** | | | |
| Planet E | 1.0001 | | |
| Planet F | 1.08 | | |
| Mars | 1.52 | 1.9 | 2.1 |
| Jupiter | 5.20 | 12 | 1.09 |
| Uranus | 19.2 | 84 | 1.01 |
| Pluto | 39.5 | 248 | 1.00 |

**Graph Template 3.** Synodic Period versus Length of Semimajor Axis

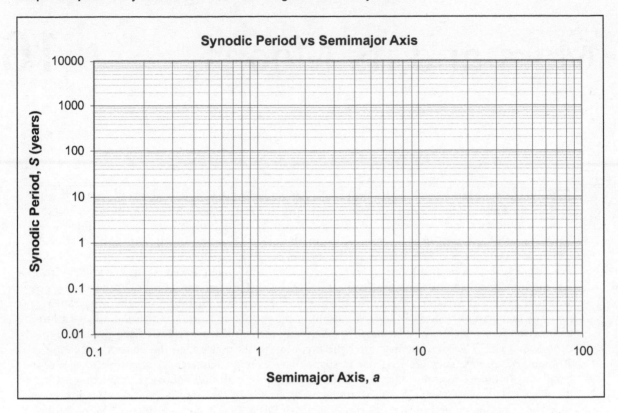

# Mars and Its Moons 16

The planet Mars has fascinated people throughout history. Its reddish color and regular brightening over about a two-year cycle were considered to be significant and auspicious, and this "wandering star" was regarded as a god of war by many civilizations. Later, misinterpreted descriptions of features on its surface led to the belief that Martian inhabitants had constructed canals across its surface. An extensive science fiction literature developed on these themes, and only now, after several sophisticated spacecraft have orbited and landed on Mars' surface and evidence has mounted for the presence of water on or under this surface, has this flurry of speculation given way to a more sober examination of the possibility of elementary life on this neighboring planet.

You can use *Starry Night*™ to look initially at the surface of Mars, and then take a closer look at the two moons, Phobos and Deimos. The American astronomer Asaph Hall discovered these tiny moons in 1877. They were named after the mythical horses that pulled the chariot of Mars, the Roman god of war. They are irregular in shape, have average diameters comparable to that of a small city and move in almost circular orbits at relatively low altitudes above the planet's equator.

Phobos, its name meaning fear, is about twice the size of Deimos. Its period is much shorter than the rotational period of Mars. A consequence of this is that, from the surface of Mars, Phobos will rise in the west and move rapidly across the sky to set in the east several hours later.

Deimos, its name meaning panic, orbits at a much larger distance from the planet than Phobos and hence its orbital period is longer. In fact, Deimos' orbital motion is almost synchronous with the rotation of Mars itself, so Deimos creeps slowly across the planet's sky, taking about three Martian days to go from the eastern horizon to the western.

Historically, it is interesting to note that in 1726, 150 years before the discovery of these satellites of Mars, Jonathan Swift, in his satirical novel, *Gulliver's Travels*, wrote of astronomers in the land of Laputa who had discovered two satellites that revolved around Mars! Their orbital properties were described as follows:

> *They have likewise discovered two lesser stars, or satellites, which revolve about Mars, whereof the innermost is distant from the center of the primary planet exactly three of its diameters, and the outermost five; the former revolves in the space of ten hours, and the latter in twenty-one and a half; so that the squares of their periodical times are very near the same proportion with the cubes of their distance from the center of Mars, which evidently shows them to be governed by the same law of gravitation that influences the other heavenly bodies.*

The references to Kepler's third law of planetary motion and Newton's law of gravitation indicate that Swift, who wrote the book in the latter years of Newton's life but was not a scientist, nevertheless understood this "latest scientific theory" of gravitation. It is difficult to know what to make of his "prediction" of the existence of the moons of Mars, 150 years before their discovery! You will be able to use *Starry Night*™ to compare the actual parameters of the moon's orbits with these predictions.

## A. Mars: Surface Features

In order to observe the planet for a reasonable period of time without interference from the horizon or daylight, we can arrange the viewing location to be at the Earth's North Pole in winter during a period when Mars is relatively close to Earth and at a "stationary point". At this position, Mars appears to stop and reverse its direction of motion against the background stars in our sky.

> 1. Launch *Starry Night*™ and configure the HUD to include **Surface feature**.
> 2. Open **Favourites > Observing Projects > Mars and its Moons > Mars from North Pole**.

You are at the North Pole at midnight on November 5, 2005. You can now examine the surface of Mars briefly and measure its rotation period.

> 3. **Zoom in** to a field of view about **3'** wide.

This view shows Mars with its two tiny moons, and allows you to judge the scale of the moons' orbits compared to the planet's radius. You will measure these parameters later in this project. As you observe the planet, see if you can see features that might have led earlier observers to suggest that they could see canals on the planet.

> 4. Click **Play** to observe these moons move around the planet.

You can now examine some of Mars' surface features.

> 5. Open **Favourites > Observing Projects > Mars and its Moons > Mars Surface Features**.

The rotation axis of Mars at the start of this run is inclined at about 45° to the vertical on the screen. This initial view shows many dark features in the lower half of the planet below a brighter, less featured region.

> 6. **Zoom in** so that the image of Mars nearly fills the screen. **Run time forward** and observe Mars rotate slowly around its axis. **Stop** occasionally and use the HUD to identify some of the features discussed in the following description.

As rotation proceeds, you will discover that Mars has two distinct hemispheres. Around 2 AM, a much darker region with considerable structure appears and leads to another very dark area extending well into the northern hemisphere, an area known as **Syrtis Major Planum**, labeled by a marker. These dark regions are easily visible by 6 AM.

> 7. Location markers similar to that labeling Syrtis Major can be introduced for other features on the surface of Mars. To do this, select **Markers and Outlines...** from the contextual menu for Mars. This opens a dialog window that contains a list of surface features. You can click on the appropriate checkbox to display a label and marker indicating the location of any listed feature on the surface of the planet. Use the dialog window to place a label and marker on the location of the feature named **Valles Marineris**.

Around 1:30 PM, just as Syrtis Major is disappearing, a set of extensive canyons, including Valles Marineris, begins to appear that extend a significant way around the planet. By 5 PM, a line of three large volcanoes appears toward the end of these canyons.

**Question 1.**   What is your estimate of how far this canyon system extends as a fraction of a circumference of Mars?

**Question 2.**   What are the names of these three volcanoes? [HINT: When the cursor is placed over any structure on the planet's surface, the Surface Feature setting on the HUD will identify this structure.]

Near 6:30 PM, a fourth massive volcano, Olympus Mons, has appeared, and by 9 PM it is near the top center of the disk. This volcano has a height about three times that of Mt. Everest and a base that extends over a distance of 600 km.

8. **Zoom in** to a field of view about **10"** wide.

9. Click **Play** and use the HUD to note the different kinds of surface features you see on the surface of Mars.

**Question 3.** What are some of the features that you see on the surface of Mars?

## B. Mars: Rotation Period

In this sequence, you can measure the rotation rate of Mars.

10. Open **Favourites > Observing Projects > Mars and its Moons > Rotation of Mars**.

The view shows a close-up of Mars from the North Pole of Earth. The red line across the face of Mars shows the planet's meridian and pole sticks indicate its axis of rotation. The time has been adjusted so that the meridian line is straight when viewed from Earth.

11. Use the **H** and **T** keyboard shortcuts to advance time in steps of one hour and one minute respectively, and count the number of hours and minutes required for Mars to rotate completely in the view so that the meridian line is again precisely aligned with the poles.

The period you have measured actually represents the synodic rotation period of Mars as measured from a moving platform, the Earth. The required correction to allow for the movement of Earth relative to Mars is small in this case and your value can be compared to the quoted (sidereal) rotation period of this planet.

**Question 4.** What is the rotation period of Mars, in hours and minutes?

**Question 5.** Which of the other terrestrial planets has a rotation period close to that of Mars?

## C. Mars' Moons from Earth

We can observe the moons of Mars from Earth and measure their orbital parameters. From these observations, we can check the "predictions" made by Swift's astronomers in *Gulliver's Travels*.

12. Open **Favourites > Observing Projects > Mars and its Moons > Mars and Orbits of Moons** and set the Time Flow Rate to **3000x** to observe the motions of the moons as they orbit Mars.

The moons move around the planet in the equatorial plane of Mars. The fact that the moons move in ellipses on the screen, rather than following a straight line back and forth across Mars, shows that at this time their orbital planes are inclined away from the Earth.

As time advances, you will see that **Phobos** appears to pass behind Mars. This type of event, where an object is obscured by another object, is known as an **occultation**. Disappearance into an occultation is known as **ingress** while reappearance is known as **egress**.

Phobos will also appear to pass in front of the planet in an event known as a **transit**. During a transit, you will note that Phobos overtakes features on the surface. In fact, its motion is so rapid that, as viewed from the surface, this moon would appear to move in the same direction as the rotation of the planet (i.e., counter to the apparent sky rotation). From this view, you can see how close Phobos is to the planet's surface in its orbit. In contrast, Deimos moves much more slowly in its larger orbit around the planet.

We can now determine the orbital parameters of radius and period for each moon around Mars, assuming that the orbits are closely circular, which is in fact the case.

13. Use the Angular Separation tool to measure the angular radius of Mars in arcseconds, and make a note of this value.

14. Measure and make a note of the orbital radius of Phobos (the angular distance from the center of Mars to either "end" of Phobos' orbit, as seen on the screen) in arcseconds and also the orbital radius of Deimos. (If this angle is more than one minute of arc, multiply the arcminutes by 60 and add this to the number of arcseconds to find the angle in seconds of arc.)

Question 6.    By what factor is the radius of Phobos' orbit greater than Mars' radius?
[HINT: Divide the radius of Phobos' orbit by the radius of Mars.]

Question 7.    By what factor is the radius of Deimos' orbit greater than Mars' radius?
[HINT: Divide the radius of Deimos' orbit by the radius of Mars.]

15. Use a value of 3400 kilometers for the radius of Mars and the ratios you calculated in Questions 6 and 7 to determine the orbital distances of Phobos and Deimos in kilometers.

16. To match the ratios given by Swift, calculate the ratios of these orbital distances to the diameter of Mars (6800 km).

Question 8.    What is the radius, in kilometers, of the orbit of (a) Phobos, and (b) Deimos?

To measure the orbital period of a moon, we need to measure the time taken for the moon to pass completely around the planet, using a reference point for timing this motion. The best reference point for Phobos is the passage of this moon across the edge of Mars' image at the beginning of a transit. (This measurement will be slightly inaccurate because it is carried out from a moving Earth. In practice, the correction for this motion is small and can be ignored.)

17. Select **File > Revert** and **Zoom in** on Mars. Adjust the Time so that Phobos is about to begin to transit the disk of Mars. Now use the **H** and **T** keyboard shortcuts and count the number of hours and minutes required for Phobos to return to this position.

In the case of Deimos, this moon does not cross the planet's limb on this date as seen from the Earth. A convenient reference point is the time when it is passing over the spin axis of the planet.

18. Select **File > Revert** and then click the Surface Guides checkbox in the **Options** pane under the **Solar System > Planets-Moons…** layer to display the polar axis of Mars.

19. Use the Time and Zoom controls to position Deimos over the pole stick at Mars' north pole. You can use the line drawn by the angular separation tool from the center of Mars through this pole to align Deimos accurately. Now, use the **H** and **T** keyboard shortcuts to find the number of hours and minutes required for Deimos to move completely around its orbit and return to this position.

Question 9.     What is the orbital period of Phobos around Mars as seen from Earth?

Question 10.    How does this period compare with the rotation period of Mars?

Question 11.    What is the orbital period of Deimos around Mars as seen from Earth?

Question 12.    How close were the predictions of Mars' orbital distances and periods by Swift's astronomers?

## D. Mars' Moons from the Martian Surface

Because Phobos and Deimos have much shorter orbital periods than our own Moon, it is fascinating to observe their motions as seen from the surface of Mars. Visiting spacecraft to the Martian surface have observed these motions and maybe, one day, space explorers might experience these effects in real life! Until then, we can use *Starry Night*™ to simulate the motions of these moons, as they would be seen from the surface of Mars.

Phobos and Deimos are relatively faint in the Martian sky because of their small sizes. Phobos is several times brighter than is Venus in Earth's sky, while Deimos is about as bright as Venus. Both moons move around Mars in the direction of the planet's rotation, but the orbital period of the inner moon, Phobos, is so short that it moves faster than the Martian surface. Thus, as seen by someone on the surface of Mars, it will appear to move rapidly across the Martian sky from west to east and in fact will cross this sky twice per Martian day. The orbital distance of the outer moon, Deimos, is such that it almost keeps pace with the Martian surface and is seen to move very slowly from east to west across the sky, taking more than five Martian days to complete a full orbit with respect to the planet's surface.

> 20. Open **Favourites > Observing Projects > Mars and its Moons > View from Mars Surface.**

Note that the Time in the toolbar is specified in Universal Time. At this time and location, it is dark on Mars. If you scroll the view around the horizon, you can see the Mars Pathfinder rover *Sojourner* among several rocks that appear toward the NW in this simulation. If you lower your view direction, you will see the spacecraft from which this rover emerged after landing on Mars in July of 1997.

You may recognize several of the constellations in this sky such as **Leo** just above the horizon in the southeast, **Ursa Major** high in the eastern sky, and **Gemini** high in the southern sky.

> 21. Use the **K** keyboard shortcut to display and label the constellations as seen in the Martian sky for comparison with the view from Earth.
> 22. Click **Play** and observe the sky from Mars, paying particular attention to the motions of the moons Phobos and Deimos.

As on Earth, the stars rise in the eastern sky and move toward the west because of the rotation of Mars. Meanwhile, Phobos moves in the opposite direction, from west to east, and soon sets below the same horizon from which the stars are rising. You might notice that the motion of Phobos relative to the background stars is in the same direction (west to east) as that of our own Moon as seen from the surface of the Earth. However, Phobos' orbital motion is so fast that it actually moves from west to east relative to the horizon, whereas our Moon's orbital motion is so slow that the Earth's rotation causes it to drift westward along with the stars, relative to the horizon.

Deimos appears almost to hang in one spot while the stars move past it. This is an illusion created by the rotation of Mars. In fact, it is really Deimos that is moving toward the east past the stars at a rate that almost exactly keeps pace with the rotational motion of Mars. However, its orbit is not quite synchronous with Mars' rotation. If you watch closely, you may see that Deimos moves very slowly toward the west relative to the horizon. It takes just under three days to cross the Martian sky from horizon to horizon, or about 5.5 days to return to the same point in the sky again, relative to the horizon.

At about 18:45:00 UT, just as the landscape begins to brighten before sunrise, Jupiter and the Earth rise almost simultaneously above the horizon. A little over an hour later, the Sun rises into a typical Martian sky. Scattering of sunlight from the very fine dust blown into the atmosphere by frequent windstorms causes the light reddish-brown color. It is well worth re-running this spectacular simulation of a Martian sunrise!

> Question 13.    Besides Jupiter and Earth, are there any other planets visible in the sky just before sunrise? If so, what are they? [HINT: Click on **Labels > Planets-Moons** to label other planetary bodies.]

It is also interesting to look at Earth from Mars as the Sun rises, with the field of view of a telescope, much as future explorers might watch the home planet from their landing site on Mars.

23. Click **Stop** and set the Time in the toolbar to **19:35:00 UT** on **December 31, 2005**.

24. Use the **Find** pane to **Magnify** Earth in the view.

25. Change the Time Flow Rate to **300x** and watch the blue, white and green Earth slowly fade as the sky brightens with sunrise on Mars. Hide **Daylight** to extend this look at Earth from Mars.

**Question 14.**    What is the phase of the Earth as seen from Mars at this time?

**Question 15.**    What is the angular radius of Earth when viewed from Mars at this time?

## E. Bonus: Eclipse of Deimos by Phobos

Because Mars has two moons that both orbit the planet near Mars' equatorial plane, it is possible for an observer on Mars to see the inner moon, Phobos, pass in front of, or eclipse, the outer moon, Deimos. In this section, you will be able to watch a simulation of such an eclipse.

The orbits of Phobos and Deimos are inclined relative to Mars' equator by 1.08 and 1.79 degrees, respectively. An observer close to Mars' equator would then see Phobos' and Deimos' orbits inclined relative to each other by about 0.7 degree and would therefore see the orbits intersect at two points in the sky. This is a similar situation to that which we see from Earth, where the ecliptic and the Moon's orbit intersect at two points. If Deimos were near to one of these intersection points when Phobos passes in front of this point in space, the observer would see an eclipse of Deimos by Phobos.

26. Select **Favourites > Observing Projects > Mars and its Moons > Eclipse-Wide**.

The view is toward the east from the surface of Mars on December 31, 2005, from a location two degrees south of the Martian equator. Phobos and Deimos are visible near the center of the screen, flanked by the Big Dipper on the left and Leo on the right.

27. Click **Play** and watch how the moons move.

As we saw earlier, Phobos moves quickly toward the east (down, in this view), opposite to the apparent motion of the stars while, over the short time represented on the screen, Deimos remains almost stationary above the horizon. At about 15:30 UT, Phobos eclipses Deimos.

28. Select **Favourites > Observing Projects > Mars and its Moons > Eclipse-Telescopic**.

The view shows a telescopic view of Deimos.

29. Change the Time Flow Rate in the toolbar to **30x**.

After a few seconds, Phobos passes rapidly through the area of sky visible on the screen, eclipsing Deimos as it does so.

30. Use **File > Revert** to return to the initial view.

31. **Run time forward**, and click **Stop** when Phobos is near to the upper edge of the screen.

32. Select **Orbit** from the contextual menus of Phobos and Deimos.

33. Change the Time Flow Rate in the toolbar to **1x** and then click **Play** to observe the eclipse again in real time. Continue to watch the view after the eclipse and note the point at which the orbital paths of the two moons intersect. To see the eclipse again, select **Edit > Undo Time Flow** and click the **Play** button.

**Question 16.** How long, in seconds, does this eclipse of Deimos by Phobos last? [TIP: For the beginning of the eclipse, note the time when Phobos first contacts Deimos and for the end of the eclipse, note the time when Deimos is again completely visible in the view.]

### F. Challenge: Mars and Its Moons from Above

You can view the orbits of Mars' moons from above the plane of the ecliptic and watch the moons from a fixed reference point and thus measure their true sidereal periods.

34. Open **Favourites > Observing Projects > Mars and its Moons > Mars and Moons from Space**.

35. Change the Time Flow Rate in the toolbar to **3000x** and observe the moons orbit Mars.

If you look closely, you can see Mars rotating in the same direction as the motion of the two moons. Choose a Martian surface feature that is on the same side of Mars as Deimos, and watch both this feature and Deimos as time passes and notice that the relative orientation of the feature and Deimos remains almost constant, showing that Deimos' orbit is almost synchronous with Mars' rotation.

From this unique view, you can determine the sidereal periods directly by timing the passage of these moons past some reference star.

36. Select **File > Revert**. Select **Orbit** from the contextual menu for Phobos to show the orbital path of this moon. Next, **Centre** Phobos in the view and set the Zoom to **1°**. Locate a star that is on or very near to the orbital path of Phobos (use the Time controls to locate an appropriate star, if necessary). Choose **Select** from the contextual menu for this star to apply a label to it. Now, use the Time controls to determine the sidereal period of Phobos. [TIP: You can use your answers to questions 8 and 10 above as a guide and the **H, T**, and **U** keyboard shortcuts to count the hours, minutes and seconds of this period.]

37. In a similar fashion, find the sidereal period of Deimos.

**Question 17.** What is the sidereal period of Phobos?

**Question 18.** What is the sidereal period of Deimos?

### G. Conclusions

The appearance and rotation of Mars and the revolution of its two small moons have been examined from various novel viewpoints, including the surface of the planet itself. These observations have been used to measure the radii and periods of the orbits of the moons. These values were then compared to the fictitious "predictions" made by Jonathan Swift in his novel, *Gulliver's Travels,* 150 years before the moons were actually discovered! You have also viewed the eclipse of one moon by the other, a phenomenon impossible on Earth because our planet has only one Moon.

# Jupiter and the Galilean Moons

**17**

Jupiter is the largest and most massive of the planets in the solar system and is now known to have many moons. Historically, Galileo noted four moons moving around the planet, a fact that led him to question the conventional wisdom that all objects in the Universe moved around the Earth as required by the geocentric model. These four Galilean moons are of significant size compared to other bodies in the solar system. The inner two moons, Io and Europa, are comparable in size to our Moon while the outer two, Ganymede and Callisto, are roughly the size of Mercury, though of lower density. They are close to spherical in shape and show distinctly different surfaces and structure.

In the present project, you can take a brief introductory look at Jupiter itself and then use *Starry Night*™ to investigate more closely the appearance and motions of Jupiter's Galilean satellites.

## A. Jupiter's Rotation Period

Begin with an observation of Jupiter as it might appear through a telescope from Earth.

> 1. Launch *Starry Night*™ and configure the HUD to include **Name** and **Object type**.
> 2. Open **Favourites > Observing Projects > Jupiter and the Galilean Moons > Jupiter** and click **Play**.

The view is from the North Pole of Earth, with the Earth's horizon and daylight removed from the view. A brief examination of Jupiter shows remarkable structure within the visible "surface" of this fluid planet. Jupiter has no solid surface, and what you are seeing are the tops of clouds above a very deep atmosphere. The obvious turbulence and structure in this atmosphere are caused by differential rotation, where different latitudes of the planet rotate at different rates. (Unfortunately, this differential rotation is not simulated in this view).

You can now use *Starry Night*™ to measure one interesting property of this large and massive planet—its very rapid rotation compared to the smaller and much less massive Earth.

> 3. Open **Favourites > Observing Projects > Jupiter and the Galilean Moons > Rotation**.

The view is again from the North Pole of Earth, but the field of view is slightly larger and the two poles of Jupiter and a meridian line are superimposed on the image of the planet. As you can see, from this location at this time, the meridian is aligned with the pole sticks.

You can use this meridian as a reference line to measure the rotation period of the planet. Since the present simulation does not include the differential rotation, you will measure only the average rotation period for Jupiter.

4. Use the **H** and **T** keyboard shortcuts to count the number of hours and then minutes required for Jupiter's rotation to bring the meridian back into alignment with the pole sticks. Use **Shift-H** and **Shift-T** to reverse time, remembering to subtract from the hours and minutes counts respectively, if you overshoot. The total count of hours and minutes will be the average rotation period of Jupiter.

**Question 1.**     What is the average rotation period of Jupiter?

One effect of this rapid rotation is that Jupiter is not perfectly spherical but takes the shape of an oblate spheroid, slightly flattened at the poles and slightly wider at the equator. This shows that the majority of the Jupiter interior is sufficiently fluid to react to the rapid rotation by forming into this non-spherical shape.

5. Use the Angular Separation tool to measure the angular size of the equatorial and polar radii of Jupiter as seen from Earth on this date. To find the angular size of the equatorial radius, measure from the center of Jupiter to the east or west limb (edge) of the planet parallel to the cloud bands. To measure the angular size of the polar radius of Jupiter, measure from the center of the planet to its north or south limb at the pole.

**Question 2.**     What is the angular size of the equatorial radius of Jupiter as seen from Earth?

**Question 3.**     What is the ratio of the equatorial radius to the polar radius of Jupiter?
[HINT: Divide the equatorial radius by the polar radius. This result should be greater than 1.]

## B. Jupiter's Moons

In the previous views, you may have noticed one or more of Jupiter's moons moving through the view.

6. Open **Favourites > Observing Projects > Jupiter and the Galilean Moons > Galilean Moons.**

The field of view is 15 arcminutes wide (half the diameter of the Full Moon in our sky), and shows Jupiter with the four Galilean satellites near to it. The stars, daylight, and the horizon have been removed from the view.

7. Use the HUD to identify the four Galilean moons in the view.
8. Click **Play** and observe the Galilean moons orbit Jupiter.
9. To assist you in answering the following questions, you can display labels and the orbital paths for each of these moons in turn by opening the **Find** pane and clicking the boxes on either side of the names of the Galilean moons, Io, Europa, Ganymede, and Callisto, listed under Jupiter.

**Question 4.**     Which of the Galilean satellites moves in the smallest orbit and completes its orbit in the shortest time?

**Question 5.**     Which of the Galilean satellites moves in the largest orbit and completes its orbit in the longest time?

At this time and with this geometry, the orbits of all four of the Galilean moons are oriented such that the moons periodically pass in front of Jupiter as seen from Earth, an event known as a **transit**.

10. Select **File > Revert** and then **Zoom in** until Jupiter almost fills the view.
11. Click **Play**.

As Jupiter rotates in the center of the view, you will see Io move toward transit of the planet, followed shortly by its shadow on the cloud-tops. One interesting puzzle about shadows of this kind on Jupiter is that, when they are observed in infrared light, the shaded region appears hotter than the surrounding atmosphere, contrary to expectation. The reason for this is probably that the momentary blocking of sunlight causes clouds in Jupiter's atmosphere to dissipate, allowing infrared detectors to see more deeply into warmer regions of Jupiter's atmosphere. A related effect is the observation that the belts, relatively cloud-free regions around Jupiter that appear dark in visible images, actually appear bright in infrared images. Again, this suggests that optically dark regions are deeper and warmer layers in Jupiter's atmosphere when compared to the cooler cloud tops.

12. Select **Edit > Undo Time Step** and then use the Time controls to make the following observations.

Question 6.    To the nearest minute, when does Io begin its transit across the face of Jupiter during this rotation period?

Question 7.    To the nearest minute, when does Io's shadow begin to cross the planet's face?

Question 8.    Based on your observation of Io's shadow on Jupiter, what do you conclude about the Sun's location? [HINT: Is the Sun directly behind the viewing location on Earth, or is it off to one side?]

In addition to transiting Jupiter, each of these moons also undergoes regular **occultations** at this time as seen from Earth. In an occultation, the moon passes behind the planet.

13. Click **Stop** and change the Time to **2:10:00 AM** on **January 21, 2014**.
14. Use the HUD to identify Europa, the moon just to the right of Jupiter in the view.

Europa can be seen just as it is about to move behind Jupiter.

15. Find the time, to the nearest minute, when Europa is completely occulted by Jupiter during this orbit.

Question 9.    To the nearest minute, at what time is Europa completely occulted by Jupiter in this orbit?

16. Click **Play** and watch carefully as Europa reappears from behind Jupiter and then moves out of the view, paying particular attention to the appearance of this moon over this time.

Question 10.   Describe and explain the appearance of Europa as it emerges from behind Jupiter and then continues in its orbit and moves out of the view.

17. Change the Time and Date to **9:16:00 AM** on **January 28, 2014**.
18. **Zoom out** to a field of view about **2'** wide.
19. Use the HUD to identify Callisto, the moon to the right of Jupiter in the view.
20. **Centre** the view on Callisto and then click **Play** and observe the view until Jupiter moves out of the right side of the view.

Question 11.   Describe your observations and explain the events affecting the appearance of Callisto during this time period.

The four Galilean satellites move around Jupiter in nearly circular orbits in the plane of Jupiter's equator. Jupiter's equatorial plane almost coincides with the ecliptic (the Earth's orbital plane) and from Earth these orbits appear almost edge-on. Indeed, there are times when the geometry of the positions of the Earth and Jupiter are such that two Galilean moons come very close together as seen from Earth, an event known as an **appulse**. When the geometry is particularly favorable, it is even possible to observe one Galilean moon partially occult another.

> 21. Open **Favourites > Observing Projects > Jupiter and the Galilean Moons > Appulse**.

The view is centered on Europa.

> 22. Click **Play** to observe a close-up view of this appulse. When the two moons are closest together in the view, click **Stop** and use the Angular Separation tool to measure the angular distance between the centers of these two moons.

> **Question 12.** What is the angular distance separating Io and Europa at the time of maximum occultation?

There is one more event that you can witness with this simulation, namely the occultation of a star by Jupiter. Observations of the star and its spectrum during such an event, particularly as Jupiter's atmospheric layers occult the star, have been used to determine the chemical make-up and structure of the planet's atmosphere.

> 23. Select **Favourites > Observing Projects > Jupiter and the Galilean Moons > Io**.
> 24. **Run time forward** and watch Jupiter pass in front of the star, TYC1258-377-1 at about the same time as Io and then its shadow traverse the planet. In this view, the gaze is locked onto the star and you see Jupiter moving and rotating, much as you would through a telescope.

In this simulation, the star image appears larger than it would appear in the real sky. A real star would wink out almost instantaneously if the planet had a hard surface. Since Jupiter has a deep fluid atmosphere, successive layers of this atmosphere will diminish the star's light more slowly.

By coincidence, at the beginning of this simulation, Io's orbital motion toward the west almost exactly compensates for Jupiter's orbital motion toward the east so that Io appears to be stationary in our sky. The shadow of Io following the moon across the face of the planet indicates the direction of the Sun. If you continue to watch, Io will gradually start to move eastward as it approaches the western "end" of its orbit as viewed from the Earth.

## C. Close Examination of the Galilean Moons

Before measuring the motions of Jupiter's moons, examine the surface of each moon in detail. The selected observing location in the following simulation is the North Pole of the Earth. From this location, these moons will rotate and thereby show their surfaces. The spin axis of each of the moons is indicated when magnified in the relevant view.

> 25. Open **Favourites > Observing Projects > Jupiter and the Galilean Moons > Surfaces**.
> 26. **Magnify** Io and then click **Play** to examine the whole surface of this very active moon.

The colors on the surface of this moon are indications of sulfur compounds that have been, and are being, deposited by numerous volcanos and geysers all over the moon. As this moon rotates, you will see halos of material around several of the major eruption sites. The source of the heat that generates these outbursts is the continuous tidal disruption of the moon from the influence of Jupiter and the neighboring moons.

> 27. Select **File > Revert** to return to the original view.
> 28. **Magnify** Europa and click **Play** to observe the surface of this moon.

The streaks and cracks that cover the ice surface of Europa are caused by tidal disturbance from Io and other moons as this ice moves over the deep water ocean within this moon's interior.

> 29. Select **File > Revert** and then **Magnify** Ganymede and click **Play**.

Ganymede has a solid core, liquid water in its interior, a covering of dirty ice and a thin atmosphere. Its surface is dark and dotted with lighter craters that appear to show evidence of water ice.

> 30. Select **File > Revert** and then **Magnify** Callisto and click **Play**.

Callisto also contains a liquid water ocean and its icy surface is covered with craters. Look particularly for Valhalla, a huge impact basin with a system of concentric circles that was probably caused by the impact of a large object on Callisto some time in its history.

This short introduction to Jupiter's four large Galilean moons shows how conditions on these very cold worlds are influenced by both tidal disturbance from neighboring moons and by impacts from other objects moving through the solar system.

> **Question 13.** On which of the Galilean moons is there evidence of impacts from external objects?
>
> **Question 14.** On which of the Galilean moons is there evidence of movement or changes on their surfaces?

## D. Synchronous Rotation of Io

One interesting fact about the Galilean moons is the relationship between their rotation periods and their orbital periods. The Earth's Moon has a rotational period that is the same as its orbital period so that from the Earth we see only one face of the Moon, with some minor variations. This synchronous rotation demonstrated by Earth's Moon is caused by the gravitational influence of the Earth on the slightly non-spherical shape of the Moon resulting from gravitational tidal forces. You can observe the rotation periods of the Galilean moons from a viewing location at the center of a transparent Jupiter in order to see whether the Galilean moons demonstrate synchronous rotation.

> 31. Open **Favourites > Observing Projects > Jupiter and the Galilean Moons > Io Rotation**.
> 32. Click **Play** and observe Io move in its orbit.

An interesting event occurs at about 18:45 UT when Io moves into the shadow of Jupiter. Run time back and forward to observe the effect of the shadow of the outer atmosphere of Jupiter crossing the moon before the shadow of the planet darkens the surface.

> 33. Use the **Find** pane to **Magnify** each of the other three Galilean moons.

> **Question 15.** Which of the Galilean moons show synchronous rotation, keeping one face toward the planet at all times?

## E. Conclusions

In this project, you have measured the rotation period of Jupiter and observed and measured the consequence of this rapid rotation upon a largely gaseous body, the oblate shape, with Jupiter having a larger equatorial diameter than its polar diameter. You were then able to see the orbits of the large Galilean moons of this planet and watch transits and occultations of some of these moons. You were able to examine the fundamentally different surfaces of each of these moons and to observe the synchronous rotation of the inner moon, Io, a characteristic shared by all of these large moons of Jupiter.

# Jupiter and Kepler's Third Law

# 18

Several thousand years ago, Greek philosophers followed logic and the principles of scientific investigation to develop models that described the motion of the "wandering stars" in the sky, the so-called planets. These geocentric models were based upon the understandable belief that the Earth was stationary. However, they required many arbitrary assumptions and were able to predict the future motion of the planets with reasonable accuracy only over relatively short periods. Over longer periods, these geocentric models required constant revision and became successively more complex.

In the sixteenth century, Copernicus was able to demonstrate that a model in which the planets orbited the Sun could explain these motions more simply. In this heliocentric model, he was able to show that the apparent complexity of the planetary motions arose from the fact that we were watching these planets from a moving Earth that also orbited the Sun. Copernicus assumed circular orbits for the planets in his model and, while this model was conceptually much simpler and more appealing than the geocentric model, it was no more accurate than the geocentric models of the time in describing the observed planetary motions.

Johannes Kepler built upon Copernicus' ideas. By 1609, using very precise observations of the position of Mars as seen from the Earth, he had developed a simple model that could describe the motion of the planets around the Sun with much better accuracy. In this model, derived from the observations, Kepler found that planetary orbits could be described using only three laws:

1) The orbit of a planet about the Sun is an ellipse with the Sun at one focus.
2) The line joining a planet to the Sun sweeps out equal areas in equal intervals of time.
3) The square of the sidereal period, $P$, of a planet's orbit around the Sun is directly proportional to the cube of its semimajor axis, $a$; that is,

$$P^2 = \text{constant} \times a^3 \qquad (1)$$

where the constant is the same for all planets in the solar system.

For an elliptical orbit, the semimajor axis, $a$, is half the longest diameter of the ellipse; that is, the distance from its center to one end. The sidereal period, $P$, is the length of time that the planet takes to complete one orbit, measured relative to the distant stars. This equation applies to all objects orbiting the Sun, including the Earth. If we measure $P$ in years and $a$ in AU, then for the Earth, $P = 1$ year and $a = 1$ AU and the constant is therefore equal to 1. Thus, for all objects orbiting the Sun, if we use these specific units of years and AU, Equation 1 becomes

$$P^2 = a^3 \qquad (2)$$

Equation 1 is actually true for any object in orbit around any other object, providing that the mass of the orbiting object is much smaller than the mass of the object it is orbiting. The constant of proportionality will depend on the mass of the larger central body in the system and will be different for different units used to describe the length of the semimajor axis and the time of the period. For example, the satellites (moons) of all of the major planets obey Kepler's laws.

In the present project, you will use *Starry Night*™ to investigate the motions of Jupiter's Galilean satellites. You can measure the semimajor axes and periods of each of these four moons and use these measurements to verify Kepler's third law. Then, with a little extra calculation, you can use your measurements to find the mass and mean density of Jupiter.

## A. Motions of the Galilean Satellites of Jupiter

The following procedure will allow you to make measurements of the motions of Jupiter's Galilean moons to verify Kepler's third law for small objects orbiting a more massive body. This will require the measurement of the semimajor axes and orbital periods of these four moons.

> 1. Launch *Starry Night*™.
> 2. Open **Favourites > Observing Projects > Jupiter and Kepler's Third law > Kepler 3**.

The display simulates a telescopic view of Jupiter and the four Galilean moons (indicated with labels) from a viewing location at the North Pole of Earth on February 15, 2015, when Jupiter is close to opposition.

The orbits of the four Galilean moons are almost precisely circular (with eccentricity 0.01 or less), so the length of the semimajor axis is simply the radius of the orbit, or half the diameter. You can therefore measure the length of the semimajor axis, $a$, of any moon's orbit by measuring the length of the line from the center of Jupiter to the moon when this moon is at its greatest angular distance from Jupiter.

To measure the orbital period, $P$, of a particular moon, you can adjust the time to place the moon at a specific and repeatable position with respect to Jupiter and simply count the number of days, hours and minutes that are required to bring the moon back to this position. Specifically, you can use the time of ingress of the moon behind the western edge of Jupiter (the right edge of Jupiter in the view).

Sequence 1 below outlines the steps involved in obtaining these data for a selected moon.

> **Sequence 1**
>
> 3. Select **Orbit** from the contextual menu of one of the Galilean moons.
> 4. Adjust the Zoom so that the moon's orbital path almost fills the view.
> 5. Manipulate the Time flow controls to place the selected moon at one extreme of its orbit.
> 6. Measure the angular distance between the center of Jupiter and the selected moon and record this distance in arcminutes and arcseconds under the column labeled Measured Orbital Radius in Data Table 1 at the end of this project.
> 7. Convert this angle into arcseconds by multiplying the number of arcminutes by 60 and adding the number of arcseconds, and record this number under the column labeled Semimajor Axis, $a$, in Data Table 1.
> 8. Next, adjust the Time to move the moon to a position to the west (right) of Jupiter.
> 9. **Zoom in** until Jupiter almost fills the view and adjust the Time until the moon is at ingress, with half of the moon occulted by the Jupiter's edge.
> 10. **Zoom out** until you can see most of the moon's orbital path.
> 11. Use the keyboard shortcuts **D** and **H**, respectively, to increment first the day and then the hour and count the number of days and then the added number of hours required to move the moon round its orbit and return it close to the western edge of Jupiter. If you overshoot, decrease the day and/or the hour by pressing the **Shift** key as you type the **D** or **H** key, respectively, subtracting from your count of days and hours accordingly. Record the number of elapsed days and hours in the appropriate column of the Measured Period heading in Data Table 1.
> 12. **Zoom in** again and use the **T** key to step and count the extra minutes needed to move the moon to the precise position of ingress, with half of the moon occulted by Jupiter's edge, and note this count in the minutes column of the Measured Period heading in Data Table 1.
> 13. Convert the Measured Period to decimal days. [NOTE: This can be done by dividing the number of minutes in the measured period by 60, adding this fraction to the number of hours, dividing this sum by 24 to convert it to a fraction of a day, and finally adding this fraction to the number of days in the measured period.] Record this number under the column labeled Period, $P$ in Data Table 1.
> 14. Select **File > Revert** and repeat this sequence for the remaining three moons.

Before using your data to verify Kepler's third law, the following questions outline an interesting relationship between the periods of these moons.

**Question 1.** What is the ratio of the orbital period of Europa to that of Io (i.e., how many times does Io orbit Jupiter in one orbital period of Europa)? Is this ratio close to an integer? Which integer?

**Question 2.** What is the ratio of the orbital period of Ganymede to that of Io? Is this ratio close to an integer? Which integer?

**Question 3.** What is the ratio of the orbital period of Ganymede to that of Europa? Is this ratio close to an integer? Which integer?

**Question 4.** From your answers to the above questions, do you see a pattern between the orbital periods of Io, Europa, and Ganymede? Does this indicate that the moons move around Jupiter in a synchronous way?

**Question 5.** Does the orbital period of Callisto follow this pattern?

Equation 1 represents Kepler's third law for objects orbiting a much more massive object. If the orbits are circular, then the semimajor axis, $a$, is equivalent to the orbital radius and $P$ is the orbital period. If we represent the constant in Equation 1 with the letter k, then Kepler's third law becomes

$$P^2 = k \times a^3$$

where the numerical value of k depends on the units that are used for $P$ and $a$. We can rearrange this equation as follows:

$$k = P^2/a^3 \tag{3}$$

Therefore, Kepler's third law can be verified by demonstrating that the value of k is the same for all of the Galilean moons.

15. Using Data Table 1, calculate the value of k for each moon.

If, from your data, k has nearly the same value for all four moons, then you have verified Kepler's law as it is applied to the Galilean moons of Jupiter. For the data used here, the units of k are $(\text{days})^2/(\text{arcseconds})^3$.

**Question 6.** Do the moons of Jupiter obey Kepler's law, according to your data?

**Question 7.** (a) Suppose space scientists wanted to place a spacecraft in orbit around Jupiter to move synchronously with the surface of the planet, to study the Red Spot in detail, for example. If the equatorial rotational period of Jupiter is 0.41 days, what would be the angular radius, $a$, of the required orbit of the spacecraft around Jupiter as measured from Earth? (b) Is this orbit possible (i.e., is this orbital radius greater than the equatorial radius of Jupiter)? [HINT: Measure the angular radius of Jupiter in the view.] (c) If the physical radius of Jupiter at its equator is 71,500 km, calculate the actual orbital radius for this spacecraft in kilometers.

## B. Measuring the Mass of Jupiter

The measurements of the orbital motions of moons around a planet offer the best method for measuring the mass of the planet itself using a version of Kepler's third law derived from Newton's Gravitational Law. Indeed, the measurement of the gravitational influence of one object upon another, such as one component of a binary star system or a galaxy moving close to a second galaxy, is the standard method for determining masses of these objects.

For the special case of an object moving in a circular orbit around an object whose mass is much larger than itself, Kepler's third law becomes

$$R^3 = [GM_J/4\pi^2] \times P^2 \tag{4}$$

where $R$ is the radius of the satellite's circular orbit in meters, $P$ is the satellite's orbital period in seconds, $M_J$ is the mass of the central object (in the present case, Jupiter) in kg, and G is a universal gravitational constant, applicable throughout the universe. Since the Galilean moons are in near-circular orbits and each of the Galilean moons has a mass that is less than 1/1000 of the mass of Jupiter, the required conditions are fulfilled for the application of this equation to the motion of these objects.

Multiplying both sides of Equation 4 by $4\pi^2$ and dividing both sides by $GP^2$, then rearranging, gives

$$M_J = 4\pi^2 \times R^3 / GP^2 \qquad (5)$$

You can derive the mass of Jupiter using Equation 5 and your measurements of the orbital parameters of one or other of the Galilean moons. It is probably best to choose Callisto because Callisto has the largest values of $R$ and $P$, so the uncertainties in measurement are the smallest, relative to $R$ and $P$ themselves. Equation 5 then becomes

$$M_J = 4\pi^2 \times R_C^3 / GP_C^2 \qquad (6)$$

where $R_C$ and $P_C$ are the orbital radius and orbital period of Callisto respectively.

You must first translate the values of $R_C$ into units of meters and $P_C$ into units of seconds. G is the gravitational constant with a value of $6.673 \times 10^{-11}$ N · m$^2$/kg$^2$. The mass of Jupiter, $M_J$, can then be determined, in kilograms.

To determine the radius of Callisto's orbit, $R_C$ in units of meters, you can use the fact that the ratio of this orbital radius to the equatorial radius of Jupiter, $R_J$, is equal to the ratio of measured angular radius of this orbit as measured from Earth, $a_C$ to the measured angular radius of Jupiter, $a_J$. This can be written as

$$R_C/R_J = a_C/a_J \text{ or } R_C = R_J (a_C/a_J) \qquad (7)$$

To use this equation, you need to measure $a_J$.

16. Select **File > Revert** and **Zoom in** until Jupiter almost fills the view.

17. Measure the equatorial angular radius of Jupiter and note this value. You recorded the semimajor axis of Callisto's orbit in arcseconds in Data Table 1. Use your measurement of the angular equatorial radius of Jupiter, $a_J$, and the fact that Jupiter's physical equatorial radius $R_J = 7.15 \times 10^7$ meters to calculate the radius $R_C$ of Callisto's orbit in meters, using Equation 7. This is the value for $R_C$ to use in Equation 6.

18. You recorded the orbital period of Callisto in days in Data Table 1. Multiply this orbital period by $24 \times 60 \times 60$ (= 86,400) to obtain the orbital period of Callisto in seconds, for use as $P_C$ in Equation 6.

19. Use Equation 6 to calculate the mass of Jupiter, in kg.

**Question 8.**　　What is the mass of Jupiter, in kg?

**Question 9.**　　How does this mass compare to the mass of the Earth, which is $5.974 \times 10^{24}$ kg?

## C. Measuring the Mean Density of Jupiter

The above calculations allow you to calculate the average density of this massive body, in kg/m$^3$, and compare this with the density of common materials such as, for example, water, with a density of 1000 kg/m$^3$.

The average density, $\rho$, of a planet is equal to the mass of the planet divided by its volume:

$$\rho = \frac{M}{V} = M / \left[ \frac{4\pi R^3}{3} \right] = \frac{3M}{4\pi R^3} \qquad (8)$$

where $M$ and $R$ are the planet's mass and radius, respectively, and $V$ is the volume of a sphere. Here, we are assuming that Jupiter is close enough in shape to a sphere that we can neglect its rotational flattening.

20. Use Equation 8 to calculate the average density of Jupiter, using your answer to Question 8 as the mass of Jupiter and the value of $7.15 \times 10^7$ meters for the radius of Jupiter.

**Question 10.** What is the density of Jupiter in kg/m$^3$?

**Question 11.** How does your result compare to (a) the density of water (1000 kg/m$^3$), (b) the density of rock (about 2800 kg/m$^3$), and (c) the mean density of the Earth (5500 kg/m$^3$)?

**Question 12.** What does your answer to the last question suggest about the bulk composition of Jupiter?

## D. Conclusions

You used measurements of the motions of Jupiter's moons to verify Kepler's third law of planetary motion and you then carried out a classic experiment to measure the mass of Jupiter from these measurements. These results have allowed you to compare the average density of this massive planet with the density of common materials and speculate on its composition.

**Data Table 1.** Semimajor Axes and Orbital Periods of the Galilean Moons of Jupiter

| Moon | Measured orbital radius | | Semimajor axis, $a$ | Measured period | | | Period, $P$ | k |
|---|---|---|---|---|---|---|---|---|
| | ' | " | " | Days | Hours | Minutes | Days | |
| Io | | | | | | | | |
| Europa | | | | | | | | |
| Ganymede | | | | | | | | |
| Callisto | | | | | | | | |

# Comets 19

Comets are perhaps the most enigmatic of objects in our solar system. Their appearance in the sky has invoked both fear and admiration in many civilizations. The tail of a bright comet can stretch across half the visible sky and be as bright as most stars, if only for a few days. Nevertheless, there is little substance to these ephemeral visitors.

Most of the comets that appear in our sky are regular visitors to the inner solar system. Those with periods shorter than 20 years originate in the Kuiper belt, a flat region of icy objects near the plane of the ecliptic, extending from about 30 AU (just beyond the orbit of Neptune) to 500 AU from the Sun. Those with longer periods, from 20 years to about 30 million years, come from the Oort cloud, a spherical region of icy objects extending from 500 to more than 50,000 AU from the Sun. Whereas Kuiper belt objects move in roughly circular orbits and probably formed where we see them now (except when collisions send fragments plummeting into the inner solar system as comets), the objects in the Oort cloud formed in the region of the Jovian planets and were flung out to great distances by gravitational encounters with the Jovian planets billions of years ago.

The solid part of a typical comet, the comet's **nucleus**, consists of a ball of ice, dust, and rock a few kilometers across. As this insignificant snowball comes close to the Sun, ices in its outer layers evaporate to release atoms, molecules, and dust grains from within the ice into a large cloud surrounding the nucleus. Much of this thin cloud of released material is blown outward from the Sun into a long tail by the action of the solar wind and sunlight. These components produce different parts of the comet's tail. The **gas tail** is composed of the lighter atoms and molecules that are blown directly outward in a radial direction from the Sun by the solar wind and shows fluting and structure in response to variations in this wind and its associated magnetic field. Within a certain distance of the Sun, these atoms and molecules are excited by solar UV radiation and emit light whose spectrum is intrinsic to the specific components. The **dust tail** is composed of the much more massive dust grains that are pushed more gently outward from the comet's orbit, mostly by radiation pressure from sunlight. This component of the comet's tail shows a curved shape with little or no structure and is seen by scattered sunlight except very close to the Sun, where metallic atoms are induced to emit their characteristic emission spectra after excitation by intense solar radiation. In this way, even though a very small amount of matter is involved, a comet can stretch itself across a significant region of our sky and become disproportionately bright during its brief visit to the Sun's vicinity. For example, the tail of Comet Hyakutake (1996) was at least 4 AU in length.

In this project, you will look at several comets and watch in particular the development and alignment of the celebrated and much-studied Halley's comet, named for Edmund Halley in recognition of his prediction of its return in 1758. This prediction was shown to be correct when the comet was 'discovered' on Christmas night of 1758. Regrettably, this observation occurred long after Halley's death! Halley's insight that the appearance of a major comet in 1531, 1607, and 1682 was in fact a returning object and the detailed calculation of its orbit using Newton's newly developed theory of gravitation was a major milestone in the development of a rational explanation for the behavior of objects in the solar system. Halley's comet has been observed on every one of its returns to the vicinity of the Sun on a 76-year cycle since 239 B.C.

The simulations in this project will show the general appearance and behavior of Halley's comet. You will observe the growth, decay, and direction of its tail during the comet's last appearance in

1986, although the detailed and changing structure of this tail under the influence of the variable solar wind is difficult to reproduce in simulation.

You will also be able to use observations of Halley's comet to verify Kepler's second and third laws of planetary motion. The second law, originally stated by Kepler in the form *"As an object orbits the Sun, the line joining planet to Sun will sweep out equal areas in equal times"*, leads to the conclusion that the speed of any object moving under the influence of the Sun will be higher, the closer the object is to the Sun. Halley's comet moves in a long elliptical orbit and as it does so, its distance from the Sun and its orbital speed both change over a wide range. The motion of this spectacular object thus provides a good general test of this law.

## A. Comet Tails

1. Launch *Starry Night*™, and configure the HUD to include **Distance from observer, Name,** and **Object type**.
2. Select **Favourites > Observing Projects > Comets > Halley**.

The view shows the southeast sky from Caracas at 4:00:00 AM on March 7, 1986. Halley's comet can be seen just above the horizon.

3. Change the Time Flow Rate to **300x** and observe Halley's comet until after sunrise.

As time advances, you will see Halley's Comet rise majestically from the horizon, along with the star background. Scattering of sunlight from small dust particles in the comet's tail produces the blue color. We can infer from the color of this scattered light that the typical size of these dust particles is equivalent to the smoke particles from a campfire. As sunrise approaches, the comet's tail slowly fades into the morning twilight.

4. Click **Stop** and set the Time in the toolbar to **6:45:00 AM** on **March 7, 1986**.
5. Hide **Daylight** in order to see the comet more clearly at this time.

Question 1.    In which direction does the tail of Halley's comet point relative to the Sun at this time in March?

6. Select **Favourites > Observing Projects > Comets > Three Comets**.

This view, again from Caracas, shows the sky on January 29, 1986, at 7:30:00 AM. The gaze is centered on the Sun and daylight has been removed so that the stars and Halley's comet are visible in the morning sky.

Question 2.    In which direction does the tail of Halley's comet point relative to the Sun at this time in January?

7. With the Time Flow Rate in the toolbar set to **1 day, Step time forward** and observe the orientation and length of the tail of Halley's comet until it moves out of the view.

Question 3.    In which direction does the tail of Halley's comet point relative to the Sun throughout the time span of the previous step?

It is interesting to observe two further comets that appeared in the sky in the decade or so after the last appearance of Halley's comet and compare their behavior with this comet.

8. Change the Date in the toolbar to **April 21, 1996**.

The view shows the same morning sky from Caracas with daylight removed and the gaze centered on the Sun, but it is now about 10 years later and a different comet appears in the sky.

9. **Step time forward** at 1-day intervals and observe the orientation and length of the tail of this comet.

**Question 4.** Which comet visited the inner solar system in April 1996?

10. Change the Date in the toolbar to **February 25, 1997**.
11. **Zoom out** until the view includes the comet Hale-Bopp.
12. Observe the orientation of the tail of this comet as you **Step time forward** in 1-day intervals until comet Hale-Bopp moves below the horizon.

**Question 5.** Is the orientation of the tail of Halley's comet relative to the Sun a unique trait of this comet?

**Question 6.** Despite a sample of only three comets, what conclusion can you draw from your observations about the direction of a comet's tail relative to the Sun?

## B. Observations of Halley's Comet from Earth

In this section, we return to our examination of Halley's comet. It is possible to watch the movement of this comet against the background stars by stepping time in intervals of sidereal days. This will keep the stars in exactly the same position in your view, night-by-night.

13. Select **Favourites > Observing Projects > Comets > Halley**.
14. With the Time Flow Rate in the toolbar set at **1 sidereal day**, observe the comet as you **Step time forward** to **April 13, 1986**.

In this sequence, it is obvious that the direction of the comet's tail is not controlled by motion of the comet itself because the tail precedes the comet nucleus on this section of its orbit. In fact, the tail is controlled by the direction of sunlight and the prevailing solar wind.

You can watch the majestic sweep of the comet as it moves away from the Sun after this close approach.

15. Use the Hand tool to adjust the gaze direction so that Halley's comet is near the upper left edge of the screen on **April 13, 1986**.
16. Use the **Single step forward** button to advance time until you can no longer see the comet's tail.

**Question 7.** Approximately when does Halley's comet's tail disappear in the view?

You can observe this comet's approach to the Sun and its recession into space again without obscuration by the scattered blue light of the daylight sky.

17. Select **Favourites > Observing Projects > Comets > Daylight Removed**.

The view is of the SE sky from Caracas at 10:00 AM on January 7, 1986, with daylight removed. At this time, the Sun is about 35° above the horizon.

18. **Step time forward** in steps of **1 sidereal day** to **April 8, 1986.**

As time progresses in time steps of 1 sidereal day, the Sun moves eastward toward its sunrise position, accompanied by several planets. Meanwhile, the comet rises as it approaches the Sun and we see the foreshortened tail pointing away from the Sun at the time of the comet's closest approach to the Sun in February.

By the end of March and early April, when the comet has moved to its position of closest approach to Earth, we see a spectacular side-on view of its tail. As we shall see from other viewpoints, this is not the time of maximum intrinsic tail length. This will be when the comet is closest to the energy source that evaporates the ice to produce its tail, the Sun. It is also interesting to note that the tail changes materially day-by-day such that, were you to be watching the comet in real life, you would be viewing a new tail every day! For all its glorious appearance, the amount of material within this tail is miniscule and could probably be packed into a small suitcase. Every atom, molecule or grain of dust is either emitting light or scattering sunlight toward us to produce this great sight.

After this time period, the tail becomes progressively smaller. Apart from the apparent reduction in length caused by foreshortening as we see the tail from an end-on view, there is also a real reduction in the length of the tail as the comet moves away from the Sun. Solar heat falling on the comet's nucleus is reduced as it moves away from the Sun and less of this nucleus is being evaporated to form the tail.

19. Change the Gaze to the SW and hide the **Horizon**.
20. Click **Play** and observe the comet as it moves away from Earth and into space until, by August 1986, it is almost invisible.

After this brief visit to our vicinity, Halley's comet will return again only after about another 75 years. Most of this time will be spent as a cold, icy nucleus invisible from Earth.

21. Select **File > Revert**.
22. Select **Show Info** from the contextual menu for Halley's comet.
23. In the Info pane, expand the **Position in Space** layer. Note the values for Distance from observer and Distance from Sun and watch them as you **Step time forward** in intervals of 1 sidereal day. Use your observations to answer the following questions.

Question 8.    What is the date of closest approach of the comet to the Sun?

Question 9.    How far is the comet from the Sun at closest approach?

Question 10.   What is the date of closest approach of the comet to the Earth (i.e., to the observer)?

Question 11.   How far away is the comet from Earth at its closest approach?

## C. Further Observations of Halley's Comet

The next sequences allow you to observe Halley's comet from novel perspectives.

24. Select **Favourites > Observing Projects > Comets > North Ecliptic Pole**.

The view is from a fixed point in space 2 AU from the Sun in the direction of the north ecliptic pole on January 4, 1986. Labels indicate the positions of the Sun and inner planets as well as Halley's comet. The view also displays the orbital paths of Earth and the comet. Note the short line perpendicular to the orbital path of the comet to the right of the Sun. This marks the perihelion point of the comet's orbit. As the simulation begins, Halley's comet lies beyond the Earth's orbital distance from the Sun. From this fixed viewpoint in space, the objects in the solar system move, while the background stars remain stationary, as time advances.

25. With the Time Flow Rate in the toolbar set to **6 hours**, click **Play** and watch the comet progress through the inner planetary system.

26. Select **File > Revert** and then **Centre** Halley's comet in the view. Click **Play** to see the animation again, but this time tracking the comet in the view.

27. Select **File > Revert** and then **Magnify** Halley's comet. **Play** the animation at this zoom level. Observe the comet's tail as it grows and shrinks again under the varying influence of the Sun's heat as the comet traverses the inner solar system.

**Question 12.** Does Halley's comet orbit the Sun in the same direction as the planets or in the opposite direction?

**Question 13.** Near what point of the comet's orbit does its tail appear longest?

**Question 14.** On what date does the comet appear to cross the Earth's orbit on its way into the inner solar system?

**Question 15.** On what date does the comet appear to cross the Earth's orbit as it leaves the inner solar system?

**Question 16.** In which part of the comet's orbit does it come closest to the Earth, incoming or outgoing?

**Question 17.** To which planet does the comet pass closest during this orbit?

28. Use the Time controls to find the date of closest approach of the comet to the planet identified in Question 17.

29. Use the Angular Separation tool to find the distance of closest approach of the comet to the planet identified in Question 17.

30. Change the Time Flow Rate to **1 day** and **Step Time Forward** until the comet is closest to the mark that indicates the perihelion point of the comet's orbit.

**Question 18.** (a) On which date does Halley's comet come closest to the planet identified in Question 17? (b) How close does the comet get to this planet? [TIP: The Angular Separation tool displays the physical distance between two objects in the view as well as their angular separation.] (c) How many days does it take for Halley's comet to reach perihelion after its closest approach to this planet?

**Question 19.** Describe how you would expect Halley's comet to appear in the sky of the planet identified in Question 17 on the date of closest approach to this planet compared to its appearance from Earth at the time of the comet's closest approach to our planet? In your answer, explain what factor or factors led you to your conclusion.

31. To check your answer to the last question, set the Date in the toolbar to the date at which Halley's comet makes its closest approach to the planet identified in Question 17. Open the contextual menu for the planet and select **Go There**. Use the Hand tool or cursor keys to look around the sky until you find the comet. [NOTE: The **Go There** command puts you at an elevation above the surface of the planet, but the comet's appearance will not be significantly different from its appearance from the surface.]

32. Use the Angular Separation tool to measure the angular size of the comet's tail.

33. Select **File > Revert** and set the Date in the toolbar to the date of the closest approach of the comet to Earth. Then select **Go There** from the contextual menu for the Earth. Use the Hand tool to look around the view until you find the comet in the sky.

34. Use the Angular Separation tool to measure the angular size of the comet's tail.

**Question 20.** What is the angular size (to the nearest degree) of the comet's tail as seen from the planet identified in Question 17 at the time of the comet's closest approach to this planet?

**Question 21.** What is the angular size (to the nearest degree) of the comet's tail as seen from the Earth at the time of the comet's closest approach to our planet?

In the next sequence, you can watch the passage of Halley's comet through the inner solar system from a different perspective, looking edge-on across the plane of the Earth's orbit.

35. Select **Favourites > Observing Projects > Comets > Crossing Ecliptic**.

This view is along the ecliptic plane with the Earth's orbit (green) edge-on. The orbits of Mercury (red), Venus (gray), and Mars (tan) are shown along with the orbit of Halley's Comet in blue.

36. **Run time forward.**
37. Select **Edit > Undo Time Flow** and use the Time controls to review parts of the animation.

**Question 22.** On what date does the comet pass northward through the ecliptic plane in its 1985/6 apparition?

**Question 23.** On what date does the comet pass southward through the ecliptic plane in its 1985/6 apparition?

**Question 24.** How does the inclination of the orbit of Halley's comet to the ecliptic compare with that of the planets Mercury, Venus, and Mars?

## D. Comet Orbits

In this section, you will explore some of the orbital characteristics of a sample of comets.

38. Select **Favourites > Observing Projects > Comets > Orbits**.

The view is centered on the Sun from a fixed point in space about 71 AU from the Sun. The orbital paths of the planets of the solar system and the orbital paths of the three comets you observed previously in this project are shown in the view.

39. Use the Location Scroller and Hand tool to look at the orbital paths of these comets from different perspectives.
40. Click the **Play** button and run time back and forward to watch the motions of these three comets as they approach and recede from the inner solar system.
41. Open the **Find** pane and expand the **Comets** layer. Click the checkbox to the right of the names of a number of comets in the list to display their orbital paths around the Sun. If you widen the Find pane you will notice that the semimajor axis is given for each comet's orbit. Select comets with a wide range of orbital sizes and orientations.

**Question 25.** From your observations, how do the orbital paths of comets differ from those of the planets?

### E. Bonus: Kepler's Roller Coaster (A Ride on Halley's Comet)

In this section, you will use the orbit of Halley's comet to explore Kepler's second and third laws of planetary motion.

42. Select **Favourites > Observing Projects > Comets > Riding Halley's.**

You are viewing the solar system from the surface of Halley's comet with the gaze centered on the Sun and the horizon removed from the view. It is September 1947. The current distance of the comet from the Sun is displayed in the upper right corner of the view.

43. Note that the Time Flow Rate in the toolbar is set to **10 days**.

44. Click **Play** and observe your motion and distance from the Sun (as shown in the upper right corner of the view) as you approach, pass through, and recede from the inner solar system, riding Halley's comet in its orbit around the Sun.

45. To observe this journey against a fixed background, select **File > Revert** and choose a star near to the Sun, such as Theta Aquilae, the first bright star to the upper right of the Sun in the view. **Centre** this star and click **Play** to experience the slingshot-like effect produced by the high eccentricity of this comet's orbit.

**Question 26.**  Describe the rate at which Halley's comet moves throughout its orbit?

**Question 27.**  Which of Kepler's laws describes this motion?

46. Select **File > Revert** and use the Time controls to find the point at which Halley's comet is at aphelion, when its distance from the Sun, as shown in the upper right corner of the view, reaches a maximum and note this distance.

47. **Run time forward** and stop time advance when you (and Halley's comet!) are near to the Sun.

48. Use the Time controls to find the date on which the Distance to the Sun reaches a minimum, showing that you have reached perihelion, the closest point in the orbit to the Sun and make a note of this distance.

The sum of the aphelion and perihelion distances you measured is equal to the length of the long axis of Halley's elliptical orbit and one-half of this sum is equal to the semimajor axis, $a$, of this orbit. With this information, we can test Kepler's Third Law of planetary motion, which relates the length of the semimajor axis, $a$, to the period, $P$, of the orbit by the equation:

$$a^3 = P^2 \tag{1}$$

where $a$ is expressed in AU and $P$ in years. Taking the square root of both sides of Equation 1 gives

$$P = a^{3/2} \tag{2}$$

You can use Equation 2 to determine the period that Kepler's third law predicts for Halley's comet from your measurement of its semimajor axis and then test Kepler's third law by using this period to predict the next dates at which Halley's comet will return to perihelion.

49. Use equation (2) to find the period, in years, of Halley's comet that is predicted by Kepler's third law. Ignoring the decimal fraction of the result for the moment, add the number of years to the Year of the Date currently in the toolbar.

50. Type the value of the Year for the predicted return of Halley's comet to perihelion into the appropriate field of the Date display in the toolbar.

51. Multiply the fractional number of years that you calculated for the period of Halley's comet by 365.25 to find the number of days that you will need to advance time to get to the perihelion point of the orbit, as predicted by Kepler's third law. Use the **Step time forward** and **backward** buttons with a Time Flow Rate of **1 day** to test whether the prediction of the next date of perihelion for Halley's comet was correct.

**Question 28.**    What is the period of Halley's comet in years?

**Question 29.**    What date did Kepler's Law predict for the next perihelion of Halley's comet?

**Question 30.**    When did the next perihelion actually occur?

**Question 31.**    How does the date predicted for the next perihelion of Halley's comet by Kepler's Third Law compare with the actual date of the next perihelion of this comet?

## F. Challenge: The Speed of Halley's Comet and Kepler's Second Law

In this section, you can measure the speed of Halley's comet at two points in its orbit. You can make these observations from the center of the Sun. The two points at which you will measure the speed of the comet are when it is near to perihelion and near to aphelion. Thus, you will measure the comet's speed when it is moving fastest and slowest, respectively. Another important reason for choosing these points in the comet's orbit is that it is moving at right angles to the line of sight at these points. Thus, you can measure the comet's velocity by observing its angular change in position in the sky without needing to account for projection effects. You can thus use these observations and measurements to verify Kepler's second law of planetary motion.

52. Select **Favourites > Observing Projects > Comets > Speed at Perihelion**.

The view shows Halley's comet and its orbital path as seen from the center of the Sun in February 1986 when the comet is near perihelion. The mark on the orbital path of Halley's comet, just to the right of the comet in the view, is the perihelion point of its orbit.

53. Open the contextual menu for Halley's comet and select **Add FOV Indicator**. In the sub-menu that appears, select **Circular...** from the upper group of options under the heading To This Chart. In the FOV Indicator dialog window, set the Diameter to **0.001"** (be sure to type the double quote symbol for arcseconds). Set the Positioning option to **RA/Dec**. Then click **OK** to place this indicator at the current position of Halley's comet.

54. **Step time forward** by one step of **2 seconds**. During these two seconds, the comet passes perihelion. Measure the angular separation between the center of the comet and the indicator showing its position two seconds previously. Record the result under Angular motion of comet in interval, θ in Data Table 1 at the end of this project.

55. Use the HUD to find the Distance from observer near perihelion and record this in Data Table 1. Since you, the observer, are at the center of the Sun, this distance is equal to the comet's distance from the center of the Sun when it is at this point in its orbit.

Now you can make measurements to determine the comet's speed when it is near to aphelion.

56. Select **Favourites > Observing Projects > Comets > Speed at Aphelion**.

The view shows Halley's comet as seen from the center of the Sun in February 1948 when Halley's comet was near aphelion.

57. Open the contextual menu for Halley's comet and select **Add FOV Indicator**. In the sub-menu that appears, select **Circular...** from the upper group of options under the heading To This Chart. In the FOV Indicator dialog window, set the Diameter to **0.001"** (be sure to type the double quote symbol for arcseconds). Set the Positioning option to **RA/Dec** and then click **OK**.

58. With the Time Flow Rate at **1 hour, Step time forward** once and note the direction in which Halley's comet moves in this interval of time from its previous position as marked by the FOV indicator.

59. Measure the angular separation from the indicator to Halley's comet. Record this value in Data Table 1 in the column labeled Angular motion of comet in interval, θ in the row labeled Aphelion.

60. Use the HUD to find the Distance from observer of Halley's comet on this date and record this distance in Data Table 1.

You can now translate these angular movements into actual comet speeds in more familiar units such as kilometers per second. You can use the small-angle formula since the angles subtended by the motion of the comet in the selected time intervals are very small. For example, assuming that the distance moved by the comet at aphelion is $D$ km and the distance to the Sun is $r$, then the angle subtended by the comet's motion, if measured in radians is

$$\theta = \frac{D}{r}$$

or  $D = \theta \times r$

This equation has to be transformed if θ is measured in arcseconds and $r$ is in AU in order to calculate $D$ in km. 1 radian = 206,265 arcseconds and 1AU = $1.496 \times 10^8$ km and thus, the equation is then $D$ (km) = θ (arcseconds) $\times r$ (AU) $\times 1.496 \times 10^8/2.06265 \times 10^5$, which becomes

$$D = 725.3 \times \theta \times r \tag{3}$$

where θ is the angular motion of the comet in the interval, in arcseconds (column 3 of Data Table 1), and $r$ is the distance of the comet from the Sun in AU (column 4 of Data Table 1).

61. For the perihelion and aphelion points of the comet's orbit, use Equation 3 to determine the distance that the comet moved during the time interval, in kilometers, and record this in Data Table 1 (column 5). Now you can find the speed of the comet at these two points in its orbit in units of kilometers per second by dividing this distance by the number of seconds in the Time Interval over which the motion was measured (column 2 of the data table) and enter these values in column 6.

Question 32.    What is the speed, in kilometers per second, of Halley's comet at (a) perihelion, and (b) aphelion?

Question 33.    How much faster does Halley's comet move at perihelion compared to its speed at aphelion?

Question 34.    How much faster does Halley's comet move when it is at perihelion compared to the average speed of the Earth in its orbit (29.79 km/s)?

In terms of everyday speeds, you can translate these values from km/s to km/hour by multiplying by the number of seconds in an hour, namely 3600. (To translate these speeds to mph, divide the speeds in km/hour by 1.6.) You can see that, on its close approach to the Sun, this celestial visitor is traveling very fast indeed and could inflict great damage on any planet in its path!

As you have seen, Halley's comet moves through a wide range of distances from the Sun as it traverses its orbit. Thus, we can use these measurements, taken at the extremes of the comet's motion, to verify Kepler's second law over this range of distances.

Kepler defined this law in the following terms: *"A line joining a planet and the Sun sweeps out equal areas in equal intervals of time."* Figure 1 shows a diagrammatic representation of the elliptical orbit of Halley's comet with the Sun at S, one focus of the ellipse. The two comet positions $P_1$ and $P_2$ are close to perihelion, with a certain time interval between them. The other two positions $A_1$ and $A_2$ are close to aphelion and are separated by the same time interval as the two perihelion positions. In practice, if this time interval is 1 second, the angles $P_1SP_2$ and $A_1SA_2$ would be very small and the triangles formed by these positions at the Sun would be very thin. If the distances $P_1P_2$ and $A_1A_2$ are measured in kilometers, then the distances $P_1P_2$ and $A_1A_2$ would represent the speeds of the comet at these positions in km/s.

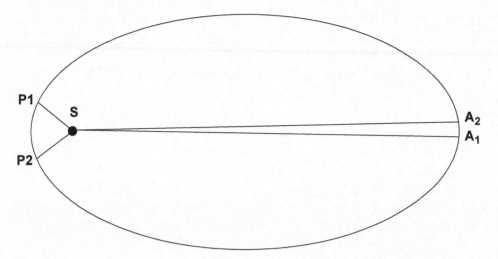

**Figure 1.** Diagrammatic representation of the elliptical orbit of Halley's comet.

Thus, in Figure 1, the area of triangles $P_1SP_2$ and $A_1SA_2$ will be equal. The angles subtended by $P_1P_2$ and $A_1A_2$ at the Sun are very small if the time interval is 1 second and the lines $P_1P_2$ and $A_1A_2$ can be considered to be straight. The area of a triangle is equal to one-half of the product of the base and the height of the triangle. Assuming the bases of these triangles to be $P_1P_2$ and $A_1A_2$, respectively, their areas will be ½ $P_1P_2 \times SP_1$ and ½ $A_1A_2 \times SA_1$. In 1 second, $P_1P_2$ is just the velocity $v_p$ at perihelion and $A_1A_2$ is the velocity $v_a$ at aphelion, while the distances between Sun and the comet at these positions are $r_p$ and $r_a$, respectively. Kepler's second law for these two positions in Halley's comet orbit can then be represented by

$$\text{½ } v_p\, r_p = \text{½ } v_a r_a$$

or

$$v_p/v_a = r_a/r_p$$

To verify Kepler's law, one needs simply to take the ratios of the distances at aphelion and perihelion and demonstrate that this ratio is the inverse of the ratio of the respective speeds obtained in the above procedure.

62. Calculate the ratio of the aphelion and perihelion distances and compare this ratio with the inverse of the ratio of the speeds, determined in Question 33.

**Question 35.** Do your measurements of Halley's speeds at aphelion and perihelion verify the correctness of Kepler's second law?

## G. Conclusions

You have explored the motion and changing appearance of Halley's comet on its last apparition in our sky in 1985 and 1986. You have watched this motion from several locations, some not accessible in real life. You made observations from these unique locations that allowed you to determine the speeds of Halley's comet at the extremes of its orbit and to verify that the comet obeys Kepler's laws of planetary motion.

**Data Table 1.** Speed and Distance from the Sun of Halley's Comet at Perihelion and at Aphelion

| Column 1 | Column 2 | Column 3 | Column 4 | Column 5 | Column 6 |
|---|---|---|---|---|---|
| Position of Halley's comet in its orbit | Time interval (s) | Angular motion of comet in interval, $\theta$ (") | Comet's distance from Sun, $r$ (AU) | Distance comet has moved in time interval (km) | Comet speed (km/s) |
| Perihelion | 2 | | | | |
| Aphelion | 3600 | | | | |

# Parallax 20

Parallax is the apparent shift in the position of a relatively nearby object against a more distant background caused by a change in an observer's position. Measurement of this shift provides a valuable method for measuring distance. In astronomy, this method of distance measurement for relatively close objects gives us a foundation on which our knowledge of the size of the universe is built. The measurement of distance is crucial to the determination of many other parameters of importance in astrophysics. For example, the luminosity of a star, its total energy output, can only be determined from the measured intensity of the light that reaches us if we know the distance of the star from the Earth.

A simple experiment demonstrates the parallax effect. Close your right eye and note the position of your outstretched hand against a distant background when observed along the line of sight of your left eye. Now close your left eye and open the right. The difference in the line of sight between your two eyes causes your hand to appear to "jump" to the left against the background. The closer an object, the more pronounced the effect. You can verify this by repeating the experiment with your hand held closer to your face.

The parallax effect also depends on the distance between the two viewing points; that is, the length of the observational baseline. In the experiment above, the baseline is the distance between your two eyes (specifically, the pupil-to-pupil distance). If you try to repeat the experiment by observing an object much further away, for example a tree trunk or signpost about 30 meters away, and compare its position against an even more distant background when viewed through each eye independently, it is unlikely that you will notice any parallax. However, if you note the position of the tree trunk or signpost against the background from one spot and then move several meters to the right or left, the parallax effect becomes obvious once more.

The form of parallax described above is called **trigonometric parallax**. When it is applied to astronomical objects, the distance to the object of interest is generally much greater than the observational baseline. The angle, $\theta$, in radians, through which an object at a distance $d$ shifts against a much more distant background, when observed from two different locations a known distance $X$ apart and measured in the same units as $d$, is then given by the small-angle formula:

$$\theta = X/d \tag{1}$$

As you can see from Equation 1, the parallax angle of an object, $\theta$, is directly proportional to the length of the observational baseline, $X$, and inversely proportional to the distance to the object, $d$. Two interesting and very useful consequences of this result are:

a.  For an object at a given distance, increasing the length of the observational baseline produces a larger parallax angle, thus increasing the accuracy of the measurement of the distance to this object.

b.  For a given observational baseline, the more distant an object, the smaller is its parallax angle; thus, for a given baseline (e.g., the diameter of the Earth), the minimum measurable angle of parallax determines the maximum measurable distance to an object.

Parallax angles in astronomy are usually very small and are expressed in arcseconds, whereas the formula above assumes that the angle is expressed in radians. For convenience therefore, astronomers usually rewrite Equation 1 to include a factor to convert radians to arcseconds. A full circle is 360°, or 360 × 60 × 60 arcseconds. In radians, a full circle is equal to $2\pi$ radians. Thus, 1 radian = 360 × 60 × 60 arcseconds / $2\pi$ = 206,265 arcseconds.

If we measure the parallax angle of an object in arcseconds, we can rearrange Equation 1 to determine the distance to the object as

$$d = 206,265 \, X/\theta \tag{2}$$

where $\theta$ must be in arcseconds, and the distance, $d$, will be in the same units as the observational baseline, $X$.

## A. Parallax of the Moon

In this section, you can observe and measure the parallax shift of the Moon by using two observing sites on opposite sides of the Earth.

1. Launch *Starry Night*™ and configure the HUD to include **Distance from observer, Rises**, and **Sets**.
2. Open **Favourites > Observing Projects > Parallax > Moon from 90W**.

The date is November 9, 2004, and the viewing location is on the equator of Earth at longitude 90° W. The local time is 3:08:06 AM. The gaze is fixed on a point on the celestial sphere. The field of view is 5° wide, with north at the top and east to the left. Within this field, a waning crescent Moon is visible against the background of the celestial sphere.

3. Open **Favourites > Observing Projects > Parallax > Moon from 90E**.

This view shows the same region of sky as the previous view but the viewing location has been moved to the opposite side of the Earth, on the equator at longitude 90° E. The date and time have been specifically chosen so that the Moon is near to the celestial equator and is transiting the meridian as seen from the prime meridian on Earth at longitude 0°, half-way between the two observing locations. The Universal Date and Time at the prime meridian are displayed in the top right corner of the view.

4. Use the **Favourites** pane to flip back and forth between the two views: **Moon from 90E** and **Moon from 90W**.

You can see that while the positions of the stars remain static between the two views, the Moon appears to move through a significant angle in the sky when viewed from these diametrically opposite locations on the Earth.

**Question 1.** When you flip the view from the location at longitude 90° E to the view from the location at 90° W, in which compass direction (east or west) does the Moon appear to move? [HINT: North is at the top and east is to the left.]

**Question 2.** As seen from longitude 90° E, is the Moon rising or setting? [HINT: The horizon is hidden in the view. Check the Rises and Sets times for the Moon in the HUD.]

**Question 3.** At this same instant of time, if you were standing on the equator of the Earth at the prime meridian, longitude 0°, (a) what would by your local time? (b) At which specific point in the sky would you see the Moon?

One specific star, TYC281-1009-1, can be seen to the right of the Moon from both viewing locations. This star is labeled and will serve as our reference star for measuring the parallax shift of the Moon.

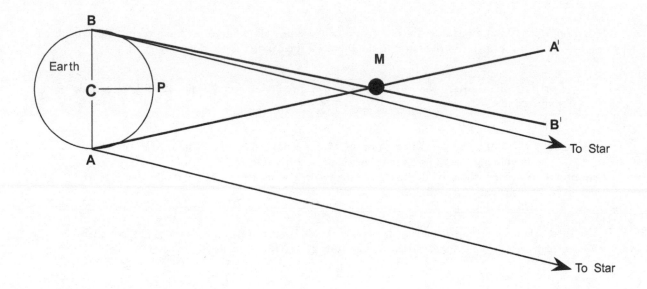

**Figure 1.** Parallax Geometry

Figure 1 illustrates the geometry of the parallax effect that you will measure and use to calculate the distance to the Moon. Points A, P, and B are all on the Earth's equator, and the Moon is on (or very close to) the celestial equator; thus, A, P, B, and M all lie in the same plane. The Moon is just rising as seen from A, on the meridian as seen from P, and just setting as seen from B.

The reference star, TYC281-1009-1, is assumed to be at infinity compared to the finite distance to the Moon. Parallel lines of sight converge at infinity, so the two lines labeled "To Star" representing the lines of sight from the viewing locations to the reference star are parallel to each other.

The lines of sight from the viewing locations to the much closer Moon are not parallel but form the angle AMB, which is equal to the angle subtended by the Earth's diameter as seen from the Moon. (The size of this angle is exaggerated in the figure for clarity.) Angle AMB is also equal to the parallax shift of the Moon as seen by an observer who moves from B to A. This equivalence can be seen by imagining that the reference star is at the point B' that is coincident with the center of the Moon when viewed from position B. If you move from B to A, the star does not appear to move because it is infinitely far away, but the Moon does appear to move because of parallax. In this ideal case, the angle between the star and the Moon's apparent position when seen from A will be the parallax angle. The sight-lines to the imaginary reference star at B' from the viewing locations A and B are parallel and line AM crosses these parallel lines. In this situation, the opposite angles, AMB and A'MB' are equal. Thus, in this ideal situation, the angle subtended by the Earth's diameter, angle AMB, is equal to the angle between the star and the Moon when seen from A.

A star cannot be seen if it is behind the Moon, so our chosen reference star, TYC281-1009-1, is at a small angle to the west of the imaginary reference star in the preceding paragraph so that it can be seen from both positions A and B. This small offset is constant, so it can be removed by subtraction in the following method.

> 5. Measure the angular separation between the center of the Moon and the labeled reference star TYC281-1009-1 in each of the two views and calculate the difference between these angles by subtracting the measured angular separation between the center of the Moon and the reference star as observed from longitude 90° E from the measurement obtained from the viewing location at longitude 90° W.

The difference between these two measurements that you calculated in the previous step is the observed parallax shift of the Moon produced by moving from 90° W to 90° E on the Earth at this time on this date. This angular measurement corresponds to Θ in Equation 2 and is equivalent to the angle AMB in Figure 1.

The observational baseline between points A and B in Figure 1 that produced this parallax shift is the distance between the viewing locations, X in Equation 2, and is equal to the diameter of the Earth, 12,756 km. Finally, the distance from the center of the Earth to the center of the Moon, which corresponds to d in Equation 2, is the distance between point C and point M in Figure 1.

**Question 4.**    What angle does the observational baseline (AB in Figure 1) make with the line from the center of the Earth to the center of the Moon (CM in Figure 1)?

6. Convert the parallax shift of the Moon that you measured to arcseconds. [1° = 3600 arcseconds and 1′ = 60 arcseconds.]

**Question 5.**    What is the parallax shift of the Moon produced by observing it from these two viewing locations on this date, in arcseconds?

**Question 6.**    Using Equation 2 and the parallax shift you measured, calculate the distance to the Moon, in kilometers.

7. Use the HUD to find the Distance from observer to the Moon and compare the given value with your calculation of the distance to the Moon from its parallax shift.

**Question 7.**    How does your calculation for the distance to the Moon compare to that given in the HUD?

## B. Geocentric Parallax

Parallax from a baseline limited to the diameter of the Earth is called **geocentric parallax**. The strict definition of geocentric parallax is the angular shift in position of an object when observed from a location on the surface of the Earth in a tangential direction to the Earth's surface when compared to the equivalent, hypothetical, observation made from the center of the Earth. The baseline would then be the radius of the Earth. This is equivalent to the parallax shift that would be seen by making an observation of the position of the Moon against the celestial sphere from either location A or B in Figure 1, compared with an observation from a point at the center of the Earth, point C in the figure. As you can see from the figure, this would be exactly one-half of the parallax shift that you measured along the baseline of the diameter of the Earth.

**Question 8.**    What is the geocentric parallax, in arcseconds, of the Moon on the date observed in the previous sequences?

Stated another way, the geocentric parallax of an object is equal to the angular radius of the Earth as seen from the distance of that object. You can demonstrate this equivalence with the following simulation.

8. Select the view **Moon from 90W** and change the viewing location to **Huxley crater** on **the surface of The Moon**. Then use the **Find** pane to **Magnify** the Earth in the view.
9. Measure the angular radius of the Earth in this view.

**Question 9.**    (a) What is the measured angular radius, in arcseconds, of the Earth as seen from the Moon at this point in time? (b) How well does your measurement of the radius of the Earth agree with your answer to the previous question?

**Question 10.**    Assume that you are using equipment for measuring parallax that can detect angular displacements as small as one-half of an arcsecond (0.5″) and that the observational baseline you will use is equal to the diameter of the Earth (12,756 km). (a) What is the distance, in kilometers, to the furthest object for which you could measure a parallax shift? (b) What is this distance expressed in AU? [HINT: 1 AU = $1.496 \times 10^8$ km.] (c) What is the furthest planet in the solar system for which you could measure parallax, using this Earth baseline? [HINT: Pluto is no longer considered a planet.]

## C. Geocentric Parallax of Vesta

Distances in the solar system beyond that of the Moon are more usefully expressed in astronomical units (AU) than in kilometers. To find the distance to an object in the solar system in AU by measuring its parallax shift in arcseconds, you will also need to express the baseline distance, $X$ in Equation 2, in terms of AU. If this baseline is the Earth's diameter, then it needs to be converted from kilometers to AU. Since 1 AU = $1.496 \times 10^8$ km and the diameter of the Earth is 12,756 km, this conversion factor is

$$12{,}756/1.496 \times 10^8 = 8.527 \times 10^{-5}$$

Combining this with the factor 206,265 for converting radians to arcseconds into a single constant simplifies Equation 2 to

$$d \, (AU) = 17.59/\theta \, (\text{arcseconds}) \tag{3}$$

where $\theta$ is the observed parallax shift with the diameter of the Earth as baseline.

You can use the method of trigonometric parallax to measure the distance to the asteroid, Vesta. *Starry Night*™ provides a convenient, reliable and accurate method for measuring this parallax by displaying a Field of View circle of appropriate size on the sky surrounding Vesta from one location. This circle will remain in the same position when the observing location is changed. The change in Vesta's apparent position can be measured accurately by referring to this circle of known radius.

> 10. Select **Favourites > Observing Projects > Parallax > Vesta from 121W.**

The current view is from the equator of Earth at longitude 121° 17.46' W. The view is centered on the star TYC291-188-1. Vesta is visible in the upper right of the view. The local time at this location is 5:28:57 AM daylight time on October 28, 2006.

> 11. Select **Favourites > Observing Projects > Parallax > Vesta from 59E.**

At this location, also on the equator but separated from the previous location by 180° of longitude, the local time is 5:28:57 PM daylight time on October 28, 2006. This time and date have been chosen so that Vesta is transiting the meridian at a longitude half way between the longitudes of the two views.

**Question 11.** What is the distance between the two viewing locations? [HINT: Draw a diagram of a cross-section of the Earth at the equator similar to Figure 1 and put on the two observing positions to help you to answer this question.]

**Question 12.** At what longitude would you need to be to see Vesta transit the meridian at this time on this date? [HINT: Look at Figure 1.]

**Question 13.** Where is Vesta relative to the celestial equator in these views? [TIP: Select **View > Celestial Guides > Equator** from the menu to help answer this question.]

> 12. Use the **Favourites** pane to flip back and forth between the views **Vesta from 121W** and **Vesta from 59E.**

**Question 14.** Which of the objects in the view show a parallax shift as you move from one viewing location to the other?

**Question 15.** Do any of the stars in the view shift their relative position as you move from one viewing location to the other? Why do you think this is so?

You can now measure this shift between the views from the two different locations, using a convenient Field of View circle centered on the position of Vesta when viewed from one location.

13. Select the view **Vesta from 59E**.

14. **Centre** the view on Vesta.

15. **Zoom in** to a field of view about **12"** wide.

16. Select **Add FOV Indicator** from the contextual menu for Vesta. In the sub-menu that appears, choose the **Circular...** option from the group of options under the label To All Charts.

17. In the dialog window that opens, set the Indicator name to **East**, choose **RA/Dec** for the Positioning option in order to keep the FOV circle fixed on the sky when the apparent position of Vesta changes and set the Diameter to **0.003** degrees. This angle is equal to 0.003 × 60 × 60 arcseconds = 10.8", and so the radius of this circular FOV is 5.4". Click **OK** to display this circle around Vesta.

18. Use the Angular Separation tool to check that the radius of this circle is 5.4".

You now need to change observing location to move to the opposite side of the Earth.

19. Use the **Favourites** pane to select the view **Vesta from 121W**.

20. **Centre** Vesta in the view and then **Zoom in** to see Vesta and the FOV circle in the view.

21. You will see that the FOV circle that was centered on Vesta's position from the first location is now offset from Vesta. The radius of this circle is 5.4". Thus, you can measure the parallax movement of Vesta from the first location to the second by simply measuring the angular distance between Vesta and the nearest point on the FOV circle. The radius of the circle was chosen so that this angle would be sufficiently small that the enhanced precision of the Angular Separation tool would come into operation, providing measurements with a precision as high as 0.01". **Zoom in** as close as possible to keep both Vesta and an arc of the FOV circle visible in the view. Measure the angular distance between the center of Vesta and the nearest point on the FOV circle and add this value to 5.4" to calculate the change in position of Vesta due to parallax when the viewing location changes to the opposite side of the Earth.

22. Substitute the measurement from the previous step of the parallax shift of Vesta into Equation 3 to calculate the distance from the Earth to Vesta in AU.

23. Use the HUD to find the Distance from observer of Vesta.

Question 16.    (a) What is the parallax shift of Vesta from the above measurements? (b) What is the geocentric parallax of Vesta?

Question 17.    What distance, in AU, did you calculate for Vesta based on your measurements of its parallax?

Question 18.    How does your result compare with the value for the distance to Vesta given in *Starry Night*™?

24. To remove the FOV circle from the view, click the **FOV** tab to open this pane and expand the **Other (All charts)** layer to locate the marker named East that you added. Click the color bar to the right of the marker's name and then click **Delete Indicator** in the pop up dialog window.

## D. Bonus: Parallax of Other Solar System Objects

It is possible to apply the same method of parallax measurement to other objects in the solar system. For each of the objects listed in Data Table 1, which is at the end of this project, follow the instruction sequence below to measure the parallax shift of the object and determine its distance. The objects chosen are moons of the giant planets. You can identify the planets to which they are associated by referring to your textbook or other reference books.

25. Expand the **Observing Projects > Parallax** folder in the **Favourites** pane and select the specific view indicated in Data Table 1 for the chosen object.

26. Open the contextual menu for the object and select **Add FOV Indicator**. In the submenu choose **Circular...** from the group headed To This Chart.

27. Set the Positioning option for the indicator to **RA/Dec** in order that the FOV circle remains fixed on the sky.

28. Set the Diameter of the indicator to the value of the Suggested FOV circle diameter appropriate to the chosen object, as listed in Data Table 1. (The "double-quotes" key on the keyboard should be used to indicate the diameter in arcseconds.) The relevant value for the radius, $R$, of this reference circle in arcseconds is shown in the data table. Click **OK** to display this circle around the object.

You can now change your observing location to the opposite side of the Earth by adding 180° to the longitude of the present observing location.

29. Select **Options > Viewing Location...** and click the **Latitude/Longitude** tab. Add 180° to the Longitude and replace the number preceding the degrees symbol with this new value. Click the **Go To Location** button and press the spacebar to move to this new location quickly.

30. Open the **Find** pane and type the name of the chosen object in the search box followed by the Enter key.

31. **Zoom in** to a field of view that includes the object of interest and an arc of the FOV indicator in the view. [TIP: If you zoom in too close, the FOV circle will disappear. In that case, zoom out to a slightly larger field of view.]

32. Measure the angular distance between the center of the object and the nearest point on the FOV circle and enter this value in Data Table 1, in the Measured angle to circle, $\Delta$ column. Add this value to the FOV radius, $R$ of the indicator, and enter the sum in the Parallax shift, $R + \Delta$ column of Data Table 1.

33. Use Equation 3 to calculate the distance from the Earth to the object in AU and enter this value in the Calculated distance column of the data table.

34. Use the HUD to find the actual distance of this object under Distance from observer and enter this value in Data Table 1 under Actual distance.

35. Repeat the sequence of steps beginning at instruction 25 for each of the views listed in Data Table 1.

**Question 19.** What distance did you calculate from the parallax shift of (a) Europa, (b) Iapetus, (c) Miranda, and (d) Nereid?

From these measured values and from those for the Moon and Vesta, you can see that excellent accuracy can be obtained with this method when used in this simulation. In real life, very careful observations are needed in order to achieve high precision and this method of distance measurement has been superseded by other, much more precise methods utilizing space techniques, since spacecraft have visited all of these distant objects.

## E. Conclusion

In this project, you have measured the parallax of different objects in the solar system to determine their distances from the Earth. You have repeated classical experiments that established the size of the planetary system and laid the foundation for the distance scale of our universe.

**Data Table 1.** Parallax and Distance from Earth of Several Solar System Bodies

| View | Suggested FOV circle diameter | FOV radius, $R$ | Measured angle to circle, $\Delta$ (") | Parallax shift, $R + \Delta$ (") | Calculated distance (AU) | Actual distance, from HUD (AU) |
|---|---|---|---|---|---|---|
| Europa | 5" | 2.5" | | | | |
| Iapetus | 3" | 1.5" | | | | |
| Miranda | 1" | 0.5" | | | | |
| Nereid | 0.5" | 0.25" | | | | |

# Proper Motion of Stars 21

Stars are not fixed in the sky. They move relative to one another, but this motion is very slow compared to that of the Moon and planets. Thus, stars appear to remain fixed in position over the period of a person's lifetime, but over thousands of years, the shapes of the familiar constellations would change noticeably because of the relative motions of nearby stars. We can detect the relative movement of stars only by comparing very precise measurements made over many years, most often with photographic or modern imaging technology. In recent years, space telescopes have provided very precise measurements of positions and motions of hundreds of thousands of stars in our near neighborhood and have provided valuable information on the movement of these stars within the Milky Way Galaxy.

In general, a star has a velocity in three-dimensional space known as its **space velocity**. The component of this velocity along the line of sight to the observer is known as the star's **radial velocity**. The component perpendicular to the line of sight is known as its **tangential velocity**. Each of these velocities is expressed in units of linear speed such as km/s. The apparent change in position of a star in the sky is known as its **proper motion** and is measured in units of angle as a function of time, such as arcseconds per year. This parameter is measured by comparing the position of a star with that of more distant objects in the background on a sequence of photographs or images. Tangential velocity of a star can be determined from proper motion provided that the distance to the star is known. Radial velocity is determined from the Doppler shift of the star's spectrum. A combination of these velocities provides the star's true velocity in space, its space velocity.

Sir Edmund Halley discovered proper motion in 1718. Halley, for whom Halley's Comet is named, compared his measured positions of stars to those measured by the ancient Greek astronomers Ptolemy and Hipparchus 1500 to 2000 years earlier and realized that the stars Sirius, Aldebaran, and Arcturus had moved slightly relative to the other stars.

The discovery and measurement of proper motion of other stars became far easier after the invention of photography and its application to astronomy in the late nineteenth century. With this technique, it became possible to compare directly the positions of many stars on two photographs taken several years apart.

In 1916, the American astronomer E. E. Barnard discovered the star with the highest known proper motion, a faint star in the constellation Ophiuchus. This star is now known as Barnard's star and is situated 5.94 LY from Earth at the present time. It is a small star, having a mass and a diameter of about 1/6 of that of the Sun and an apparent magnitude in our sky of +9.5, too faint to see with the unaided eye. It is traveling toward the solar system and will pass within 3.8 LY of the Sun somewhere around 10,000 AD. For comparison, the nearest known stars to the Sun at the present time are those in the Alpha Centauri triple system, at a distance of about 4.3 LY.

In this project, you can investigate the proper motions of Barnard's star and other stars.

## A. The Time-Scale of Proper Motion

Proper motion is the angular change in direction of a star in the sky per year and this change is very slow for most stars. For a star to show proper motion, at least a part of its physical motion through space must be across our line of sight. It is possible to obtain some idea of proper motion by watching the change in the pattern of stars in familiar constellations over a significant time interval in simulation.

1. Launch *Starry Night*™ and configure the HUD to include **Name** and **Distance from observer**.
2. Open **Favourites > Observing Projects > Proper Motion > Changing Constellations**.

The view is of the winter constellations. Your observing location is at the position of Earth in space, but this location does not move with the Earth and so is unaffected by Earth's rotation or precession.

3. With the Time Flow Rate set at **1 year**, observe the constellations as you **Run time forward** for about one thousand years.

Question 1.    As time flows at this rate, do you see the sky change?

4. Watch the view carefully and click the **Now** button in the toolbar to move back to the present time quickly.

Question 2.    (a) Did the constellations appear to change in the last step? (b) What does this suggest about proper motion?

5. Observe the constellations and click the **AD** field in the Date display panel in the toolbar to change it to **BC**. This moves you back in time approximately 4000 years. Click this field again repeatedly to toggle back and forth across four thousand years of time.
6. Use the hand tool and Gaze buttons to observe all of the constellations in the sky, repeating the process of toggling back and forth from **AD** to **BC** in time for each region observed.

Question 3.    Did every constellation stick figure pattern change over this time span of over 4000 years? In which constellations were the changes most noticeable?

This very slow motion of stars can be observed at highly accelerated speed by changing the Time Flow Rate to 200 years.

7. Open **Favourites > Observing Projects > Proper Motion > Changing Constellations-02**.
8. Use the Hand tool or Gaze buttons to choose a region of the sky to observe.
9. **Run time forward**.
10. To repeat this time-lapse view of different constellations, stop time advance, select **File > Revert**, change the Gaze direction and click **Run time forward**.

Question 4.    Is proper motion a common property of stars?
Question 5.    (a) If all stars in a constellation were moving directly toward or away from you in the simulation, would these motions affect the shape of the constellation? Explain. (b) Is this type of radial motion of a star the same as proper motion? Explain.
Question 6.    A star appears to remain fixed over thousands of years of observation. From this positional information alone, can you say for certain that this star is stationary in space?

## B. Proper Motion of Barnard's Star

The star with the highest known proper motion is Barnard's star.

11. Select **Favourites > Observing Projects > Proper Motion > Motion of Barnard's star.**

This view is from the North Pole of Earth in the year 497 AD and is centered on a reference star TYC421-2053-1 with a field of view of about 6° wide.

12. With the Time Flow Rate at **1 year, Run time forward.**

Because the view is locked on to the reference star TYC421-2053-1, this star and most of its neighbors appear to remain fixed as time advances. However, you will observe three things:

(a) Barnard's star moves very rapidly across the sky, demonstrating a very high proper motion as it passes almost directly through the position of the reference star sometime in 1107 AD.

(b) Even in this small region of the sky spanning a few degrees in width, several other faint stars show noticeable movement with respect to their neighbors over a long time period.

(c) The whole sky appears to rotate slowly because of the precession of the Earth's spin axis.

13. Select **File > Revert,** and then click **Run time forward** to see the animation again and watch these three features of star motion in this region of the sky.

14. Select **Favourites > Observing Projects > Proper Motion > Barnard's star.**

This magnified view shows the position of Barnard's star in the year 1107 AD, the point in time when Barnard's star appears to be very close to the reference star TYC421-2053-1, as seen from Earth.

15. **Step time forward** one step of **10 years.**

16. Measure the angular separation, in arcminutes and arcseconds, between Barnard's star and the reference star TYC421-2053-1. Record this measurement in Data Table 1 at the end of this project.

17. Repeat the previous two steps until Barnard's star moves out of the view. Convert your measurements to arcseconds by multiplying the number of arcminutes by 60 and adding the product to the number of arcseconds in the measurement.

18. Plot your observations of the proper motion of Barnard's star on Graph Template 1, at the end of this project.

19. Attempt to draw a straight line through your data points.

**Question 7.**  Which of the following best describes the line connecting the data points?
(a) Straight horizontal line
(b) Straight line sloping up over time
(c) Straight line sloping down over time
(d) Sinusoidal line (i.e., a wavy line that goes alternately up and down over time)

Note that the graph plots angular motion against time. The slope of the line through your data points, the ratio of its rise along the vertical axis over its run along the horizontal axis, is its angular motion in arcseconds divided by the time in years and is therefore the star's proper motion in arcseconds per year.

20. Calculate the slope of the line through the data points on the graph.

Question 8.     What is the proper motion of Barnard's star? [HINT: The slope of the line in the graph.]

Question 9.     Does Barnard's star appear to move uniformly through our sky over time, or does its rate of motion change with time?

Question 10.    Toward which direction does Barnard's star move?

21. **Step time backward** until Barnard's star comes back into the view. Use the HUD to find the Distance from observer of Barnard's star, in light years.

To determine the true speed of a star across our line of sight in AU/year, we need to use the small-angle formula. In one year, the small angle $\theta$ through which we see a star move in the sky, perpendicular to the line of sight, when it is at distance $R$ and moves through a distance of $d$ is $\theta = d/R$, with $d$ and $R$ measured in the same units, giving $\theta$ in radians. Rearranging this equation, $d = \theta \times R$. The measured quantities need to be converted in order to provide the speed of the star in AU/year. The measured proper motion, $\mu$, is measured in arcseconds per year and, since 1 radian = $57.3 \times 60 \times 60 = 206,265$ arcseconds, $\theta = \mu/206,265$. The distance to the star, $R$, is in light years, and 1 light year = 63,240 AU. Thus, rewriting the above equation to obtain $d$ in AU/year with $R$ in light years and $\mu$ in arcseconds per year:

$$d = \theta \times R = \frac{63240}{206265} \mu \times R = 0.31\mu R$$

Question 11.    What is the speed of Barnard's star across our line of sight in this simulation, expressed in AU/yr? [HINT: Use the above small-angle formula.]

As discussed earlier, proper motion of a star is a measure of the component of its angular motion across our line of sight. Any motion directly toward or away from us will not show up as proper motion.

Question 12.    If we assume that this calculated speed is the actual speed through space of Barnard's star, how long would it take for this star to cover a distance equivalent to that between Neptune and the Sun, about 30.1 AU?

A complete description of the proper motion of Barnard's star requires that we also specify a direction for this motion in the sky. The direction of this proper motion is measured with respect to north and is expressed as Position Angle (PA), the angle in degrees from north, measured in an eastward direction. For example, proper motion directly toward the east would have a PA = 90°, while a motion toward the southwest would be expressed as proper motion with a PA = 225°.

22. Select **File > Revert** from the menu so that Barnard's star and the reference star TYC421-2053-1 are close together in the sky in the year 1107 AD.

23. **Step time forward** by one ten-year interval. Use the Angular Separation tool to connect the reference star TYC 421-2053-1 to Barnard's star. The position angle of Barnard's star will be displayed below the angular separation between these stars. [TIP: Select **Deselect Barnard's star** from the contextual menu of this star to make the reading of the position angle display easier.]

Question 13.    What was the position angle of the proper motion of Barnard's star in the year 1117 AD?

## C. Proper Motion of Star Clusters

It is interesting to look briefly at the motions of stars in two different clusters as they move as a group through space.

24. Select **Favourites > Observing Projects > Proper Motion > Hyades.**

This view is of the open cluster, the Hyades, from a position in space about 1 AU away from the Sun in November 2010 with a field of view of about 21°. Observing from this position rather than from the surface of the Earth avoids the apparent movement of the sky caused by the rotation of the Earth around an axis tilted at an angle to its orbital plane and by the revolution of the Earth around the Sun.

25. Click **Play** and observe the stars of this cluster move with respect to both the field of view and the background stars over many centuries.

You can see that the cluster stars all follow similar paths across the sky at about the same angular speed. Note that one bright star, which at the present epoch appears to be a member of the cluster, moves away rapidly from the rest of the stars, identifying it as a non-member.

26. **Stop** time advance to allow you to answer the following questions.

Question 14. What is the name of the bright star that is seen in this view, but which is not a member of the Hyades cluster?

Question 15. What is the distance of this star compared to the stars within the cluster?

*Starry Night*™ can display the proper motions of stars as vectors showing both direction and relative magnitude of the angular change of the position of the stars with time.

27. Select **File > Revert**.
28. Open the **Options** pane, expand the **Stars** layer and open the **Stars** list and click the checkbox to turn on the **Proper Motion Vectors** option.
29. You can reduce the confusion in this view and show only the stars within the cluster by restricting the range of star distances. Click the **Limit by Distance** option under the Stars heading in the Options pane. This restricts the view so that only stars between 100 and 200 light years from Earth are shown. You can confirm these distance limits by selecting **Options > Stars > Star Magnitude and Distance Limits...** from the menu.

Again, you can see that the stars of the cluster all show similar vectors for proper motion. If you examine these vectors in detail, however, you will see that the cluster stars appear to be converging on a common point like the points shown in Figure 1 below. This is the effect of perspective, in much the same way that a flock of geese flying overhead will appear to be flying toward a point in the distance, or where railway tracks that are obviously parallel to one another appear to converge to a point in the distance.

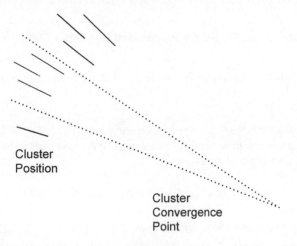

Cluster
Position

Cluster
Convergence
Point

**Figure 1.** Apparent convergence of cluster member stars

You can quantify this convergence effect by using the Angular Separation tool as an alignment tool to measure the position angles of the motions of several representative stars for the cluster.

30. For a few selected stars from each side of the cluster, use the Angular Separation tool to draw a line from the star toward the lower-left edge of the view, aligning it carefully along the proper motion vector associated with the selected star and make a note of the position angle of this line.

**Question 16.**    What is the approximate range of position angles for proper motions of stars across the Hyades cluster?

The geometry of this effect has been used by astronomers to develop a method for estimating distances to close clusters. A relationship can be derived between the distance to each star in the cluster, the proper motion of the star, and the angle between the star and the convergent point of the cluster. The distance to the cluster's center of mass can then be found from the distances to the stars in it. This method augments and supports other methods of distance measurements to stars in the Sun's near neighborhood.

You can compare the proper motion of this cluster with another nearby open cluster, the Pleiades. This cluster is further away than is the Hyades, so the upper limit on distance has been set to 450 light years for this cluster.

31. Select **Favourites > Observing Projects > Proper Motion > Pleiades.**

32. Again, to restrict the view to stars within this cluster, select **Options > Stars > Star Magnitude and Distance Limits...** and check that the distance range is 300 to 450 ly. Click the **Limit stars by distance** checkbox and then click **OK.**

33. You can now use the **Options** pane to display **Proper Motion Vectors** of the stars in this cluster.

Note that this cluster is moving in a different direction to that of the Hyades in our sky and that the average proper motion vectors are different in this more distant cluster.

**Question 17.**    How does the average proper motion of stars in the Pleiades compare to the average proper motion of Hyades stars?

## D. The Proper Motion of Other Stars

The proper motion of other stars is so much smaller than that of Barnard's star that we will need a much longer time step in order to see this motion clearly on the screen. We can watch sky motions over the full time span available in *Starry Night*™. If we observe these motions from Earth, the precession of the spin axis causes the whole sky to appear to rotate and this motion of the sky partially masks the effect of proper motion. We can remove this rotation by positioning ourselves at a fixed position in space at a point on the Earth's orbit.

34. Select **Favourites > Observing Projects > Proper Motion > Other Stars.**

The view is of the stars in a region of sky about 23° wide and 16° high near the constellation Hercules in the year 99998 BC.

35. Click **Play** and when *Starry Night*™ reaches its limiting date, select **Edit > Undo Time Flow** from the menu. Repeat this step several times at different Zoom levels and watch the proper motion of the stars over nearly 200,000 years of time.

**Question 18.**    Do all of the stars move in the same direction or do different stars move in different directions?

**Question 19.**    Do all of the stars move with the same speed?

**Question 20.**    In the time interval 1 AD to 2001 AD, which star moves with the highest proper motion in the simulation?

## E. Relationship between Proper Motion and Distance

Suppose you are standing near to a street, looking directly north at the sky. A jetliner that is traveling at about 600 km/hr toward the west comes into your field of view. Without shifting your gaze from the north, you watch as the jet slowly crosses your line of sight. In the meantime, a car moving at about 50 km/hr comes down the street, also traveling west. You will note that the jet is still visible long after the car disappears from your field of view. This is a parallax effect. The car travels much more slowly than the jet but it is much closer to you and does not need to travel very far in order to travel completely across your field of vision. As you gaze north you might be able to perceive distances along the road of about a half block to the east and the west. At the distance of the jet, however, your field of vision spans many kilometers.

In this section, you will explore the statistical relationship between observed proper motion of a star and its distance from the Earth, using a small sample of stars within a particular field of view in one region of the sky.

36. Select **File > Revert**.

37. **Run time forward** and choose a star that shows high proper motion. **Stop** time flow and use the HUD to identify the chosen star and record its Name and Distance from observer under the sub-heading High Proper Motion Stars in Data Table 2 at the end of this project. Then click **Play** to resume time flow and repeat this step until you have compiled a list of five stars that show relatively high proper motion.

38. Select **File > Revert**. Then **Run time forward** and choose a star that shows almost no proper motion. Use the HUD to record the Name and Distance from observer for this star into Data Table 2 under the sub-heading Low Proper Motion Stars. Repeat this step until you have compiled a list of five stars that show almost no proper motion.

**Question 21.**   From your survey, what approximate relationship is there between proper motions of stars in the solar neighborhood and their distances from Earth?

**Question 22.**   Does the observation of the proper motions of the Hyades and the Pleiades clusters agree with this conclusion?

**Question 23.**   What causes this relationship?

## F. Conclusions

In this project, you observed and measured the proper motion of our Sun's fastest-moving neighbor, Barnard's star, as it moves through our sky. You then examined the common motions of stars in clusters and observed the apparent convergence of the stars in the Hyades open cluster, the result of perspective as these stars move parallel to each other, away from our position in space. You have also been able to catch a glimpse of the complex motions of a small sample of stars near to our Sun as they move in space over many centuries.

**Data Table 1.** Proper Motion of Barnard's Star

| Time interval (years) | Angular motion | | Angular motion (") |
|---|---|---|---|
| | ' | " | |
| 10 | | | |
| 20 | | | |
| 30 | | | |
| 40 | | | |
| 50 | | | |
| 60 | | | |

**Graph Template 1.** Template for Plotting the Proper Motion of Barnard's Star

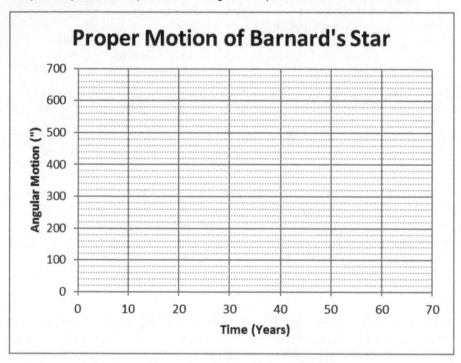

**Data Table 2.** Distances to Stars Showing High and Low Proper Motion

| Star name | Distance to star (ly) |
|---|---|
| **High proper motion stars** | |
| | |
| | |
| | |
| | |
| | |
| **Low proper motion stars** | |
| | |
| | |
| | |
| | |
| | |

# The Hertzsprung–Russell Diagram

# 22

We learn about stars by analyzing the light and other forms of radiation emitted by them into space. This radiation originates at the surface or atmosphere of each star and comes to us across vast distances. The interior of the star, where most of the star's mass resides and where all its energy is generated, is hidden from our view.

Analysis of this starlight reveals that most stars, at least in their outer layers, are composed primarily of the simplest element, hydrogen, with a relatively small fraction of helium and a much smaller fraction of heavier elements. Astronomers refer to elements heavier than hydrogen and helium as "metals." It is only this very small metal abundance that varies significantly from one star to another.

Given this great similarity in their observed composition, it is perhaps surprising that stars can take on such a wide variety of forms, from large to small, bright to faint, and hot to cool. This variety of forms suggests that the overall characteristics of a star depend more on its interior structure than on the composition of its surface layers. Also, the fact that stars radiate copious amounts of energy means that they must change with time and "evolve" from one form into another.

To understand these forms and how they might be related to each other, astronomers more than a century ago began to classify stars into categories. The desire to explain why stars fall into these categories then prompted scholars to construct theoretical models of stars using the laws of physics and known properties of matter. The most important test of these models is that they must match the observed properties of actual stars. Present-day theoretical models have been developed to the point where they can predict the structure and evolution of stars from birth to death with reasonable accuracy.

Several easily measured stellar parameters are used in the classification of stars. Stellar brightness at certain well-defined colors has been measured using the techniques of photometry, initially using visual observations and then photographic imagery, and finally photoelectric measurements. A star's brightness is related to its energy output and is expressed in a logarithmic scale of *magnitudes*. If the measurement is made from Earth then the star's brightness is represented by its apparent magnitude, given the symbol $m$, often with a subscript denoting the color at which the measurement is taken (e.g., $m_B$ is the apparent magnitude measured in the blue region of the spectrum).

In this logarithmic scale, magnitude values increase as brightness decreases. This method of assigning brightness to a star has its origins in ancient history. Stars were assigned a "magnitude" by early Greek astronomers, the brightest being of "first magnitude," the faintest of "sixth magnitude." Astronomers still use a modern version of this inverted logarithmic scale even though it is inconvenient when compared to discussing actual brightness on a linear scale. In this inverted logarithmic scale, a magnitude increase of 1.0, for example from magnitude 1.0 to magnitude 2.0, represents a brightness *decrease* by a factor of 2.512. Thus, a change from first magnitude (bright) to sixth magnitude (faint) is 5 magnitudes difference, which translates to a factor of $2.512 \times 2.512 \times 2.512 \times 2.512 \times 2.512 = 100$ to match approximately the ratio of the brightness of first- to sixth-magnitude stars as defined by the early Greek observers.

If stars emit radiation approximately as a black body, an assumption that is reasonable for most stars, then photometry at different wavelengths can be used to define **stellar surface temperature**, another important parameter for classifying stars.

Spectroscopy, the detailed examination of the spectra of stars, also provided a convenient classification method in early studies. Stars with different sets of absorption lines in their spectra were assigned different letters. When it was discovered that the different types of absorption-line spectra were related to stellar surface temperature, these letters were placed in a sequence, O, B, A, F, G, K, and M, relating to decreasing temperature. (A useful key for remembering this important sequence comes from the initials of the words in the sentence "Oh, Be A Fine Girl, Kiss Me!")

The measurement of distances to stars, for a long time a difficult task, has made it possible to estimate the absolute brightness of stars by adjusting the apparent brightness for distance via the inverse square law. This has led to a parallel scale of absolute magnitudes, designated by the capital letter "$M$", again with a suffix appropriate to the color at which this brightness measure is defined. For example, $M_V$ represents absolute visual magnitude. Absolute magnitude is defined as the magnitude that a star would have if it were at a standard distance of 10 parsecs, or 32.6 light-years, from Earth and therefore represents a measure of star output that is independent of distance from the observer.

These absolute brightness values at certain colors could then be combined by using the overall shape of the black body spectrum of the star derived from the temperature to provide an estimate of the total energy output of the star, its **luminosity**, $L$. This measure of total energy output of the star is usually represented in terms of the luminosity of the Sun.

There is a relationship between a star's luminosity, $L$, temperature, $T$, and size represented by its radius, $R$. A black body at a temperature $T$ is known to emit a certain amount of energy per unit area per second, $E$, that is related to its temperature by $E = \sigma T^4$, where $\sigma$ is a constant. If we assume that a star emits light like a black body, a star of radius $R$ with a surface area of $A = 4\pi R^2$ will emit a total amount of energy per second represented by its luminosity $L = E \times A$, or $L = 4\pi R^2 \sigma T^4$.

Early in the last century, two astronomers, Ejnar Hertzsprung in Denmark and Henry Norris Russell in the United States, began to experiment with ways to represent stars collectively in terms of these observed and derived parameters. They independently hit on a graphical method that has become the keystone, not only of classification of stars, but also of the study of the evolution of stars with time.

The **Hertzsprung-Russell diagram**, or H-R diagram as it is often called, is a scatter diagram of the luminosity of stars plotted as a function of their surface temperatures. In view of the wide range of these parameters for stars, the luminosity and temperature are usually plotted with non-linear scales. Luminosity is plotted logarithmically along the vertical axis, while the horizontal axis shows either temperature plotted logarithmically, or the spectral letter classifications O, B, A, F, G, K, and M. Other versions of the H-R diagram may denote absolute magnitude of the stars against their spectral classification. All H-R diagrams plot temperature in an inverse direction, with high temperatures on the left and low temperatures on the right.

When plotted in this fashion, the majority of stars are concentrated in a diagonal sweep across the diagram from high-temperature/high-luminosity to low-temperature/low-luminosity (i.e., from upper left to lower right). This region is known as the **main sequence**. It is where theoretical models predict that stars will congregate when they are "burning" hydrogen in nuclear reactions in their interiors. The lower edge of the main sequence, known as the Zero Age Main Sequence (ZAMS), designates the line where stars of different mass first begin to burn hydrogen in their cores. This line is thus the locus of points for stars that have reached the time in their lifetimes when pressure generated by the heat of nuclear burning in their cores is sufficient to balance the gravitational force that has been shrinking and condensing the pre-main-sequence stars.

Few stars are found below the ZAMS and those that are form a class of very hot stars that nevertheless have very low luminosity because they are extremely small in size. These *white dwarf* stars represent old and highly evolved stars that have shed their outer layers to reveal very small but extremely hot and dense inner cores. White dwarfs no longer generate energy but are merely emitting light as they cool.

Stars with high luminosities but relatively low temperatures occupy a wide region above the main sequence. Theoretical prediction indicates that the majority of these stars have consumed all the hydrogen in their cores and have expanded and cooled as a result of internal readjustment but are still burning helium and other elements. These stars are the *red giants*.

There are stars with enormous outputs of energy represented by very high luminosities that cannot be very old because they are burning their fuel at a prodigious rate. These are the *supergiants*, and they can be hot or cool, hence blue or red in color.

A final stellar parameter that is difficult to measure but that is vital to theoretical modeling is **mass**. Stellar mass represents the amount of fuel that is available for nuclear burning. It is found that the cores of stars with higher initial mass are hotter, which leads to more vigorous nuclear fusion and consequently higher energy output or luminosity. The energy output of a higher-mass star is so great that, despite the larger amount of fuel, it uses up its fuel in a shorter time than does a lower-mass star. Because of this effect, we find a relationship between the mass of a main-sequence star and both its luminosity and its lifetime. The larger the mass of a star, the greater is its energy output and the shorter is its lifetime. This in turn leads to the conclusion that the more massive stars at the high-temperature/high-luminosity end of the main sequence are young and will evolve rapidly away from this position.

Two further concepts concerning the H-R diagram are interesting. The first concerns regions on this diagram where no stars appear. There are two reasons why this can be so. First, conditions may never be suitable for the production of stars with these luminosities and temperatures. Second, a star can possess these values of luminosity and temperature but the transition through this region in its evolution is so rapid that the probability of finding a star in this position is small. Theoretical modeling of stellar evolution can predict a star's path across the H-R diagram (and thus delineate the regions of the H-R diagram that will not be occupied by stars) and the speed at which it follows this path. The observed number of stars in the different regions of the H-R diagram will therefore provide an important test of the stellar evolutionary theories.

The second concept concerns the classification of stars in a cluster of stars. A cluster forms from a single interstellar cloud, or even from just part of a single interstellar cloud, so we can be reasonably sure of three conditions. First, an interstellar cloud has a relatively uniform composition, so the stars in the cluster form with the same chemical make-up. Second, we can assume that all of these stars formed at about the same time and therefore have the same age. Third, the differences in observed star properties are then caused by differences in the initial mass that came together to form each star. This makes the study of clusters important for the verification of evolutionary models. The massive and highly luminous stars at the top end of the main sequence evolve more rapidly, and so leave the main sequence sooner. This means that such stars will be absent for an old cluster. Indeed, the position of the upper end of the remaining main sequence on the H-R diagram of a cluster, the so-called **turn-off point**, is a good indication of the age of the cluster.

## A. Classification of Stars on an H-R Diagram

Data Table 1, at the end of this project, contains a list of many bright stars in our sky, with a wide range of properties. You will use *Starry Night*™ to observe these stars and plot them on an H-R diagram. Although you cannot measure all the various necessary parameters of these stars, astronomers already have accomplished these measurements over many years and the relevant information is in the *Starry Night*™ database.

1. Launch *Starry Night*™ and configure the HUD to show **Absolute magnitude, Name**, and **Temperature**. Note that the absolute magnitude indicated in the HUD is the star's absolute visual magnitude, $M_V$.

2. Open **Favourites > Observing Projects > HR Diagram > Local Neighborhood Stars**.

3. Open the **Find** pane, click the icon in the search box and select **Star** from the menu.

4. For each star listed in Data Table 1, type the name of the star into the search box exactly as it is written in the data table and then press Enter. The view pans to center the chosen star in the view. [TIP: Press the spacebar after the Enter key to move rapidly to the new view.]

5. Point the cursor at the labeled star and copy the values of the star's Absolute magnitude and Temperature from the HUD into Data Table 1.

Template 1, at the end of this project, is an H-R Diagram template that you can use to plot the absolute magnitude of each star against its temperature. (You can print out extra copies of this template. Navigate to the folder **Program Files/Starry Night College 6/Sky Data/Extras**, where you will find this figure in several formats.) The template includes indications of the regions where different types of stars are found, including supergiants, giants, main-sequence stars, and white dwarfs. Within the main sequence region, a solid line shows the approximate center of the main sequence band. The temperature scale along the bottom increases logarithmically toward the left. Across the top of the diagram, the spectral classifications are shown. The absolute visual magnitude, a linear scale, is on the left vertical axis. The luminosity scale on the right is logarithmic and indicates a star's luminosity compared to that of the Sun, the luminosity of which is unity by definition on this scale. Diagonal lines in the background of the graph show a logarithmic grid of stellar radii, normalized to the Sun's radius. These lines represent the relationship between the radius of the star, its luminosity and its temperature described above.

6. Note that each of the stars in Data Table 1 has been assigned an ID number. To plot a star on Template 1, write its ID number inside a small circle indicating its position on the graph. Plot the absolute magnitude of each star in Data Table 1 vertically against the temperature horizontally. Note that the absolute magnitude scale is inverted, increasing downward and the temperature scale is reversed and non-linear. Data Table 1 includes the parameters of a few representative white dwarf stars, which are not included in the *Starry Night*™ database.

7. From the star's position on the graph, determine whether it is a white dwarf, main-sequence, giant, or supergiant star and record this in the column labeled "Type of Star" in Data Table 1.

| | |
|---|---|
| **Question 1.** | Are there regions on your H-R diagram that appear to be devoid of stars? If so, where are they (e.g., high-temperature/high-luminosity, low-temperature/high-luminosity, etc.)? |
| **Question 2.** | Are these regions also devoid of stars in more extensive H-R diagrams displayed in your textbook or other astronomy texts? |
| **Question 3.** | Based on the three white dwarf stars, what is the luminosity of a typical white dwarf star in terms of the Sun's luminosity? |
| **Question 4.** | What are the radii of the three white dwarf stars? [HINT: Use the diagonal "R" reference lines.] |
| **Question 5.** | To which spectral classifications might a white dwarf star belong? |
| **Question 6.** | In which classification group—white dwarf, main sequence, giant, or supergiant—is the star Betelgeuse? |
| **Question 7.** | To which spectral class does the star Betelgeuse belong? |
| **Question 8.** | (a) Which is the most luminous star on the list? (b) To which spectral class does it belong? (c) To which group (i.e., white dwarf, main sequence, giant, supergiant) does it belong? (d) Approximately how much more luminous is this star than the Sun? (e) How does this star's radius compare to that of the Sun? (f) What is the ratio of the surface temperature of this star to that of the Sun, 5800 K? |
| **Question 9.** | (a) Which star in the list has the lowest surface temperature? (b) To which spectral class does it belong? (c) To which group (white dwarf, main sequence, giant, or supergiant) does it belong? |
| **Question 10.** | (a) Which star on the list has the highest surface temperature? (b) To which spectral class does it belong? (c) To which group does this star belong? |
| **Question 11.** | What is the approximate range of radii of stars in the main sequence compared with the size of the Sun? |
| **Question 12.** | (a) Could a main-sequence star with the radius of the Sun achieve the luminosity of Deneb? (b) For a star to have the same luminosity as Deneb and still be on the main sequence, what would its radius and temperature have to be? |
| **Question 13.** | (a) Of the stars on the list, which is the closest in size and luminosity to the Sun? (b) Do you think that the Sun is much hotter or cooler than this star? Why? |
| **Question 14.** | (a) What is the approximate maximum surface temperature that a star the size of the Sun could have and still be on the main sequence? (b) What is the approximate minimum temperature that a star the size of the Sun could have and still be on the main sequence? |
| **Question 15.** | Approximately how much larger would the radius of a star with the same surface temperature as the Sun (5800 K) have to be before it could be classed as (a) a giant star, and (b) a supergiant star? |
| **Question 16.** | Approximately how much hotter would a star the size of the Sun need to be in order to reach the same luminosity as (a) a giant star, and (b) a supergiant star? |

## B. The H-R Diagram of Clusters and Stellar Age and Evolution

*Starry Night*™ provides the facility to display the H-R diagram of the brightest stars in any region of the sky. You can use this to display the stars in the region that you have just examined. This display will include a wider range of stars than the limited set of selected stars that you plotted on your H-R diagram.

8. Select **File > Revert** from the menu to return to the original view.
9. Open the **Status** pane and expand the **Hertzsprung-Russell** layer to reveal a small H-R diagram of the stars in the view.
10. You can explore the characteristics of an individual selected star by moving the cursor over it in the main view, whereon a red dot will denote the star's position on the H-R diagram.

One further facility in *Starry Night*™ allows you to restrict the range of distance of the stars displayed on the H-R Diagram.

11. Expand the **H-R Options** layer in the Status pane and click on the **Distance cut-off** feature. Adjust the distance range sliders to display only the close stars (within about 100 light-years of the Sun) in the view and in the H-R diagram. Note what kind of stars remain in the nearby space around the Sun.

**Question 17.** Where on the H-R diagram are the majority of the stars that are close to the Sun?

The study of clusters of stars has been very important in the development of stellar evolution models. There are two distinct types of star cluster. The **open**, or galactic, star cluster contains relatively few stars, and these are randomly arranged and widely spaced apart. The stars in open clusters are often surrounded by the remnants of dust and gas from which they were formed. In contrast, the **globular** cluster is made up of a large number of closely spaced stars, symmetrically distributed around a common center. There is no evidence of dust or gas within globular clusters. The locations of these types of clusters within a galaxy are also different. Open clusters are found within the spiral arms of a galaxy, while globular clusters are uniformly distributed in the region surrounding the center of the galaxy. Open clusters are found to be young, while globular clusters have significantly greater ages, in some cases comparable to that of the Universe.

Unfortunately, data for individual stars in the older globular clusters are not included within the H-R data set in *Starry Night*™. Thus, a direct comparison cannot be made between the H-R diagrams of open and globular clusters using this program. Nevertheless, it is instructive to examine several examples of open clusters whose individual stars are represented in the H-R diagram data set in *Starry Night*™.

Data Table 2, at the end of this project, lists selected clusters along with their distances from the Sun. These clusters are the Pleiades and the Hyades, relatively rich clusters that are easily visible in the night sky in the constellation of Taurus, and the clusters in Coma Berenices and Ursa Major, which have far fewer stars but still represent stars that were formed together.

12. Open **Favourites > Observing Projects > HR Diagram > Pleiades** to display a restricted region of the sky around this open cluster.
13. Open the **Status** pane and expand both the **Hertzsprung-Russell** and **H-R Options** layers. Note the distribution of all the stars in the view on the H-R diagram. Now turn on the **Distance cut-off** feature in the H-R Options panel to limit the display of stars in both the view and H-R diagram to member stars of the cluster.

Note that the majority of the stars in the Pleiades are still on or close to the main sequence on the H-R diagram. The parameter of interest in determining the age of the cluster is the turn-off point, the maximum absolute visual magnitude, $M_V$, for main-sequence members of the cluster. Figure 1 below shows the approximate dependence of $M_V$ as a function of the age of the cluster in years.

14. Record the maximum $M_V$ of the main-sequence stars in the cluster in Data Table 2. Use this value with the graph in Figure 1 to estimate the age of this cluster and record this value in the table. (Note that the age in this figure is given in millions of years and is on a logarithmic scale.) Also note the distribution of stars on the H-R diagram, particularly whether there are giant or red supergiant stars within this cluster.

15. Open the views for the other star clusters listed in Data Table 2 from the **Favourites > Observing Projects > H-R Diagram** folder and repeat steps 13 and 14 above.

You can see that the main sequence of stars in these open clusters differs depending on the age of the cluster. [NOTE: The equivalent H-R diagram for a globular cluster would show a much-shortened main sequence with no blue supergiant stars and many more stars in the red giant and red supergiant phases of evolution.]

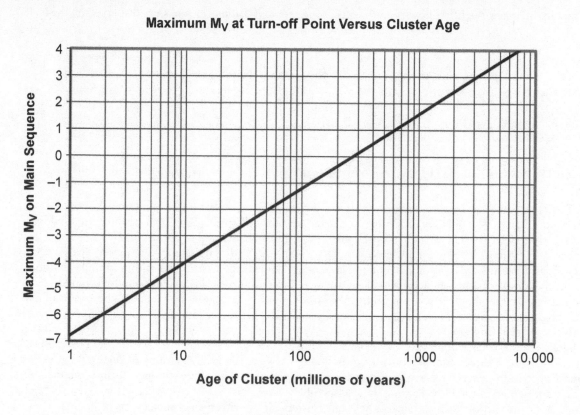

**Maximum $M_V$ at Turn-off Point Versus Cluster Age**

Figure 1. Dependence of the maximum main-sequence $M_V$ on age of a cluster.

Question 18.   From their respective H-R diagrams, how would you rank the four clusters in Data Table 2 from youngest to oldest?

Question 19.   How does the turn-off point help to establish the age of the cluster?

## C. Masses of Main–Sequence Stars

Mass is an important physical parameter of a star but it is difficult to measure directly. In fact, the mass of a star can be measured directly only if the star is a member of a binary system in which the star's gravitational influence on its companion star can be observed. This can be done only for a select few nearby stars where the properties of the binary system can be measured. Thus, the Mass-Luminosity relation for main-sequence stars, verified for a few stars by direct measurement, is very important in providing estimates of mass for a much wider range of stars.

The theoretical basis for this relationship comes from the idea that the more massive the star, the more intensely the nuclear fusion reactions "burn" the hydrogen in its interior, producing a higher energy output from the star (i.e., a higher luminosity). Densities and temperatures of hydrogen in the interiors of stars with masses lower than about 0.1 solar masses will never be sufficient to trigger nuclear reactions, and such stars will merely emit energy that has been generated by the contraction of the gas by gravity. Because of the absence of nuclear reactions, these objects are not true stars, and they are usually called **brown dwarfs**. Above a higher mass limit of about 80 to 100 solar masses, stars become extremely unstable, with the nuclear furnace burning so vigorously that stars rapidly reach an explosive and destructive stage.

The mass-luminosity relationship for main-sequence stars can be represented approximately by a power law, in which luminosity is proportional to mass to a high power. When luminosity and mass are expressed in terms of the luminosity and mass of the Sun, this approximation is given by the formula

$$L = M^{3.6}$$

> **Question 20.** Using the formula above, how much more luminous than the Sun would a star that had a mass 10 times greater than the Sun be?

## D. Variable Stars

Many stars are found to vary in brightness periodically with a wide range of oscillation periods. Some of these stars vary in brightness with precise regularity, while others are much less regular. This variation in brightness is accompanied by coincidental changes in temperature and size. When plotted on the H-R diagram, these stars are found to occupy positions that are related to their period. For example, a range of stars with regular periods of between 1 and 100 days are known as Cepheid variables. They occupy an almost vertical band above the main sequence known as the **instability strip**, extending across a range of luminosities through the yellow giant and supergiant regions.

An important relationship has been established between the period of a Cepheid variable and its luminosity. Thus, merely recognizing that a star is a Cepheid variable and measuring its period establishes its intrinsic brightness. When combined with a measurement of its apparent brightness, this information can be used to provide a measure of its distance from the Sun. Cepheid variables are sufficiently bright that they can be identified in nearby galaxies, and so this method of distance measurement is one crucial rung in the so-called distance ladder, allowing astronomers to determine distances over vast ranges and to estimate the overall scale of the Universe.

Other stars with much longer and somewhat variable periods, the long-period variables, LPV, occupy a region on the cooler side of the H-R diagram, again extending over a wide range of luminosities.

16. Open **Favourites > Observing Projects > H-R Diagram > Variable Stars.**

The view shows a 180-degree field of the night sky. Labels point to a sample of nine different variable stars.

17. Open the **Status** pane and expand both the **Hertzsprung-Russell** and **H-R Options** layers. Point the cursor at each labeled variable star in the view. Confirm that the Name of the star is shown in the HUD and note the red highlighted point which indicates the position of the star on the H-R diagram.

> **Question 21.** Which of the labeled stars in the view has (a) the highest luminosity, and (b) the least luminosity?
>
> **Question 22.** Through which regions (e.g., white dwarf, main sequence, giants, or supergiants) of the H-R diagram does the instability strip represented by the variable stars in the view extend?
>
> **Question 23.** To which of the spectral classes (e.g., O, B, A, F, G, K, M) do the variable stars in the view mostly belong? [HINT: Choose **Spectral class** under **Labels** in the **H-R Options** layer of the Status pane.]

## E. Challenge: Average Density of Stars

The value of the mass-luminosity relationship discussed previously is that it provides a means of estimating the mass of a star from its observable luminosity. Raising both sides of the formula given for the mass-luminosity relationship above to the power 1/3.6 gives: $L^{1/3.6} = M$.

18. Configure the HUD to include **Luminosity** and **Radius**.

19. Use the **Find** pane to find and center each of the main sequence stars listed in Data Table 3 at the end of this project. Then use the HUD to obtain the Luminosity and Radius of these stars and record these values in the table.

20. Use the form of the mass-luminosity relation given above to calculate the mass, in solar masses, of each star in the list and record this value in Data Table 3.

The average density, $\rho_S$, of a star is the ratio of its mass, $M_S$, to its volume, $V_S$, given by $4\pi R_S{}^3/3$, where $R_S$ is the radius of the star. Therefore,

$$\rho_S = \frac{M_S}{4\pi R_S^3/3} = \frac{3M_S}{4\pi R_S^3} \tag{1}$$

Since the values you have for the mass, $M_S$, and the radius, $R_S$, of these stars are given in terms of the solar mass, $M_{Sun}$, and solar radius, $R_{Sun}$, respectively, you will need to do some conversions to obtain a value for the average density of these stars in terms of kg/m³. To make these conversions, you need to multiply the value of the mass of the star in terms of solar masses by the mass of the Sun and, similarly, you need to multiply the radius of the star in terms of solar radii, by the radius of the Sun. Therefore,

$$\rho_S = \frac{3M_S M_{Sun}}{4\pi (R_S R_{Sun})^3} = \left[\frac{M_S}{R_S^3}\right]\left[\frac{3M_{Sun}}{4\pi R_{Sun}^3}\right] \tag{2}$$

The term in the right-hand pair of brackets in the above equation is simply the average density of the Sun, $\rho_{Sun}$. Therefore,

$$\rho_S = \left[\frac{M_S}{R_S^3}\right]\rho_{Sun} \tag{3}$$

Using values of $1.99 \times 10^{30}$ kg for its mass, and $6.96 \times 10^8$ meters for its radius, the average density of the Sun is $\rho_{Sun} = 1410$ kg/m³. Therefore, the average density in kg/m³ of a star whose mass, $M_S$, and radius, $R_S$, are given in terms of the solar mass and radius is

$$\rho_S = 1410 \frac{M_S}{R_S^3} \text{ kg/m}^3 \tag{4}$$

21. Use Equation 4 and the values for Radius and Mass for each star in Data Table 3 and calculate the average density of each of these stars. Since the density of water is 1000 kg/m³, divide your result by 1000 and record the result in the table in order to get a sense of what this density value means by comparing it with the density of water.

Question 24.  Which of the stars in Data Table 3 have average densities greater than water?

Question 25.  (a) Which star from the list in Data Table 3 has the lowest average density?
(b) Which star from the list in Data Table 3 has the highest average density?
(c) What is the ratio of highest to lowest average density in this selection of stars?

As you can see from Data Table 3, there is a significant range of average density among main sequence stars. Of course, the density of a star varies enormously over its volume, from extremely low density at the outer reaches of the star's atmosphere to extremely high density in its central core.

It is interesting to calculate the density of a white dwarf star. White dwarfs are the burned out cores of low-mass stars and consist of highly condensed degenerate matter. While main-sequence stars show a relationship between mass and luminosity, white dwarf stars show a relationship between mass and radius, with the stellar radius of the star decreasing as the mass increases.

**Question 26.** The white dwarf 40 Eridani B has a radius of 0.014 solar radii and a mass of 0.43 times that of the Sun. (a) What is the average density of this star, in $kg/m^3$? (b) How much greater is this than the density of water? (c) The volume of a teaspoon is about 5 cubic centimeters. What is the mass of a teaspoon of matter from 40 Eridani B?

## F. Conclusions

In this project, you have emulated professional astronomers in plotting an H-R diagram for a selected set of typical stars, but without having to measure spectra, star brightness or star distances, as an astronomer would. However, you have the satisfaction that you have been able to use the best available data set in the world for this type of investigation, the *Hipparcos* database incorporated into *Starry Night*™. You have also examined the H-R diagrams of selected open clusters of stars and obtained approximate ages for these clusters from the point of turn-off on the main sequence of these stars. You explored the relationship between the mass and luminosity for main-sequence stars. You were able to investigate the properties of a sample of variable stars from their positions on the H-R diagram. Finally, you have had the opportunity to calculate the average densities of a set of main-sequence stars, comparing these densities to that of water and you have determined the (very high) density of the degenerate matter that forms a white dwarf star.

Data Table 1. Absolute Magnitude and Temperature of Selected Stars

| ID # | Star | Absolute visual magnitude, $M_V$ | Temperature (K) | Type of star |
|---|---|---|---|---|
| 1 | Vega | | | |
| 2 | Aldebaran | | | |
| 3 | Capella | | | |
| 4 | Procyon | | | |
| 5 | Betelgeuse | | | |
| 6 | Bellatrix | | | |
| 7 | Merope | | | |
| 8 | Fomalhaut | | | |
| 9 | Beta Pictoris | | | |
| 10 | Alpha2 Centauri | | | |
| 11 | Theta Lyrae | | | |
| 12 | Spica | | | |
| 13 | Deneb | | | |
| 14 | Canopus | | | |
| 15 | Phecda | | | |
| 16 | Pollux | | | |
| 17 | Antares | | | |
| 18 | Nunki | | | |
| 19 | Acrux | | | |
| 20 | Sirius B | +11.5 | 26,000 | White Dwarf |
| 21 | 40 Eridani B | +11.0 | 15,000 | White Dwarf |
| 39 | Procyon B | +13.0 | 8,200 | White Dwarf |

Data Table 2. Age of Open Clusters by $M_V$ of Brightest Member on Main Sequence

| Name of cluster | Distance from Sun | Maximum $M_V$ of main-sequence stars | Age of cluster |
|---|---|---|---|
| Pleiades | 390 ly | | |
| Hyades | 150 ly | | |
| Coma Berenices | 280 ly | | |
| Ursa Major | 71 ly | | |

Data Table 3. Luminosity, Mass, Radius, and Average Density of Several Main-Sequence Stars

| Star | Luminosity (Sun = 1) | Radius, $R_S$ (Sun = 1) | Mass, $M_S$ (Sun = 1) | Average density, $\rho_S$ (kg/m$^3$) | Average density (Water = 1) |
|---|---|---|---|---|---|
| Low temperature | | | | | |
| Alpha2 Centauri | | | | | |
| Mu Cassiopeiae | | | | | |
| Medium temperature | | | | | |
| Procyon | | | | | |
| Fomalhaut | | | | | |
| Altair | | | | | |
| Beta Pictoris | | | | | |
| High temperature | | | | | |
| Bellatrix | | | | | |
| Spica | | | | | |

# Hertzsprung – Russell Diagram Template

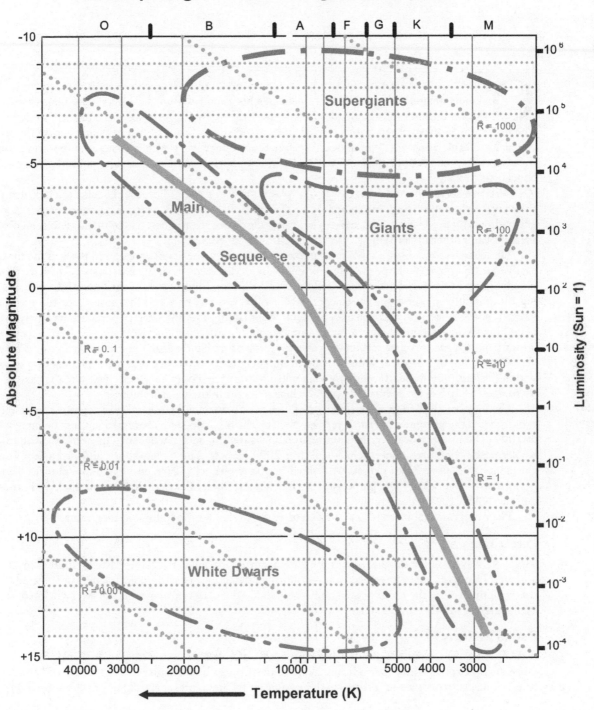

# Discovering Extra-Solar Planets: The Transit Method

# 23

One of the most exciting discoveries in astronomy in the last two decades is the detection of planets around stars in the Sun's near neighborhood within the Milky Way Galaxy. This work continues the age-old desire to answer the question, "Are we alone in the Universe?" The main aim of these observations is to identify planets with Earth-like dimensions within the so-called "habitable zone" or "Goldilocks" region around their parent stars, where temperatures on their surfaces could support liquid water. It is on such planets that life as we know it on Earth could conceivably exist.

Direct observation of distant extra-solar planets is very difficult because the reflected light from their surface is extremely faint compared to the light of their parent stars. As a consequence, several indirect methods have been developed, using ingenious techniques. These methods often complement each other in verifying planets detected by other techniques.

These measurements are difficult to make; consequently, the results are biased toward the most easily detected planets—large planets orbiting at small distances from the parent star. They are also mostly limited to a very local region within several thousand light-years of the Sun. Notwithstanding the difficulty of these measurements, recent observations, particularly those from the French CoRoT space telescope and the more recent Sun-orbiting NASA Kepler space observatory, are beginning to detect significant numbers of objects with planet-like characteristics. Indeed, extrapolation from the most recent results indicates that it is probable that almost every star in our Milky Way Galaxy has at least one planet! Furthermore, there is now evidence that many planets may exist within the habitable zone. Recent approaches using space telescopes have demonstrated the capability to detect Earth-sized planets, despite the bias inherent in the measurements.

The number of planets discovered and subsequently verified by several telescopes is increasing rapidly, with the present number of verified planets (those cataloged by several agencies) being close to 1000. The number of unverified but reliably measured planets, particularly from the CoRot and Kepler space telescopes, has reached well over 2000 planets. These planets are of four basic types: gas giants, hot super-Earth planets with short-period orbits, ice giants, and Earth-like planets. Two of the major catalogs of these planets are the Extra-Solar Planet Encyclopaedia maintained in France and the NASA Exoplanet Archive.

The observational methods can be described briefly under the following categories.

## Direct Imaging

At visible wavelengths, the glare from the parent star overwhelms the faint scattered light from a planet. However, there have been a few confirmed detections of extra-solar planets at infrared wavelengths, where the thermal emission from relatively hot, giant planets is not overwhelmed by the glare from the parent star.

## Radial Velocity

A star-planet system rotates about a common center of mass. Thus, the small planet forces the more massive star to move periodically in space in its own much smaller orbit. The use of high-resolution spectroscopy to measure small periodic shifts in narrow spectral lines in the spectrum of candidate stars was instrumental in the early discovery of several extra-solar planets. This method has been the most productive in confirming the existence of these planets.

## Astrometry

The gravitational influence of the planet on its parent star will produce small periodic positional changes of the star when compared to nearby stars. This is a difficult technique to apply in practice but future space observations are planned to exploit this relatively direct method.

## Microlensing

The gravitational field of a star can act as a lens, magnifying the light from distant stars. If the foreground star has planets, these planets can produce detectable changes in this magnification. A few planets that exist at large distances from their parent stars have been detected in this way.

## Pulsar Timing

Pulsars are very compact remnants of the implosion that occurs during supernova explosions of stars. They produce regular pulses at many wavelengths with extremely precise periods as they rotate rapidly. Small changes in the timing of these pulses caused by the gravitational perturbation of a planet can be used to infer the existence of such objects around these remnant stars.

## Transit Method

If an orbiting planet passes in front of, or "transits", the disk of a parent star, the observed brightness of the star will appear to drop by a small amount. The probability of this happening will depend on the planet's orbital motion carrying the planet in front of the star and will be very low for any specific star. Nevertheless, if the geometry is correct, an observed dimming of the brightness of this star at regular intervals would serve to verify the presence of a planet. The level of this dimming will depend on several factors, particularly the relative sizes of planet and star. The decrease will be very small, making the measurement of this effect very difficult, particularly from ground-based observatories, where variations in our atmosphere produce fluctuations in the measured stellar intensity. The use of space platforms to avoid these effects, particularly the French CoRoT and the more recent NASA Kepler spacecraft, has been very successful in detecting several thousand planetary candidates, and active work continues to verify these observations of planets using several different techniques.

## A. The Transit Method and the Transit of Venus

Of all of these sophisticated methods for detecting extra-solar planets, the transit method using space telescopes has been the most successful. The capabilities of the CoRoT and Kepler instruments are approximately equivalent, being able to detect a diminution of as little as 30 parts per million in star intensity when observing a star of magnitude $m_v = +12$ in a 6.5-hour observing period.

Each telescope examined a large number of stars in a wide field of view. For example, the Kepler telescope field of view contained over 500,000 stars and the telescope has monitored the brightness of some 150,000 stars continuously to very high precision since its launch in March, 2009. Unfortunately, the failure of one part of the guiding system in May 2013 prematurely terminated observations. Similarly, CoRoT covered several wide fields of view, but recent computer failure on board this spacecraft has also led to the termination of a successful observing campaign.

The observations consist of the search for periodic decreases in the intensity of any of the monitored stars. If these decreases were produced by the transit of a planet, then an important feature of these decreases would be that they would be periodic and of equal depth and of the same duration. The depth of this diminution of starlight provides a measure of the size of the planet relative to its parent star while the time period between these decreases in overall observed brightness can be used to determine the size of the planet's orbit and the planet's mass. Furthermore, from the characteristics of the parent star and the size of the planet's orbit, an estimate can be made of the expected temperature on the surface of the planet. This latter parameter is vital in determining whether life as we know it could survive on the planet.

You can explore the methodology of the transit method of detecting extra-solar planets around other stars by simulating the similar effect of Venus transiting our Sun when viewed from Earth. Measurements of this transit can be used to estimate whether the CoRoT and Kepler space telescopes would be able to detect this transit if this type of event were to be viewed from a distant star.

Historically, the transit of Venus was a very important event for astronomers. Several centuries ago, the accurate timing of the onset and ending of the transit provided an accurate method for determining the overall size of the planetary system. Modern methods of astronomy have provided far more accurate measurements of the dimensions of the solar system but the relative rarity of these transits and the chance to observe Venus as a small black disk moving across the Sun's disk makes this a worthwhile observation. Even though Venus's orbital period is a fraction of a year, transits are rare. This results from the fact that we are observing these events from a moving platform, the Earth, which is orbiting the Sun on a slightly different plane from that of the orbit of Venus. Thus, the times when the Earth and Venus are correctly aligned as they follow their respective orbits are uncommon. At the present time in history, two transits about 8 years apart are followed by a period of 121.5 years, after which two more transits occur within 8 years, and, finally, a period of 105.5 years completes the cycle of 243 years.

Two transits of Venus occurred recently, the first in June 2004, the second in June 2012. The present simulation will show the latter event from Anchorage, Alaska, USA, where Venus reached the middle of its transit at just after 4:00 PM. You can observe the geometry of the passage of Venus's silhouette across the Sun's disk, calculate the depth of the diminution in solar brightness caused by this transit and determine whether a space telescope with the capabilities of CoRoT or Kepler would be able to detect this diminution if an equivalent planet to Venus were to pass in front of a solar-type star within their respective fields of view.

1. Launch *Starry Night*™ and configure the HUD to show **Name, Angular size,** and **Luminosity**.

2. Open **Favourites > Observing Projects > Planetary Transit > Venus Transit**.

This daylight view is of the Sun in a field of view of about 2 degrees at 12:45 PM on June 5, 2012, from Anchorage, Alaska. The view is centered on Venus, just to the east of the Sun, as would be seen by a camera installed on a telescope tracking the planet.

3. Click **Play** to advance time at the selected Time Flow Rate of **3000x** and observe the transit of Venus across the face of the Sun. Note that the transit ends just before sunset, when the horizon obscures the view.

4. Select **File > Revert** to return to the pre-transit view at 12:45 PM.

You can now determine the times of transit, known as **contacts**. These are shown in Figure 1 and are referred to as 1st, 2nd, 3rd, and 4th contacts. [NOTE: In practice, Venus is much smaller relative to the Sun than is shown in the diagram.] As can be seen from Figure 1, the times between 1st and 2nd contact and between 3rd and 4th contact can provide a measure of the size of the planet when orbital parameters have been determined by other means. While this is not important in the case of Venus since we have more modern methods to determine its diameter, this kind of measurement will prove very useful in the case of observations of extra-solar planets.

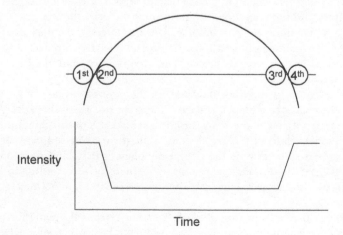

**Figure 1.** The position of Venus at each of the four contacts and an idealized graph of the small change in the overall intensity of the Sun as Venus passes in front of it.

5. Select **View > Hide Daylight** from the menu and then **Zoom in** to a field of view of about 5 arcminutes to make the measurements of these contact times easier. [HINT: It might be helpful to brighten the image of Venus by selecting **Options > Solar System > Planets-Moons...** and, in the **Surface** panel, click **On** the **Show Dark Side** option and move the brightness slider to the right to adjust the Venus brightness to a suitable value.]

6. Use the Time controls to find the time to the nearest minute when Venus appears to touch the solar disk and note the time of 1st contact.

7. Adjust time in minutes and hours to find the times to the nearest minute of the 2nd, 3rd, and 4th contacts.

**Question 1.** What are the times of the four contacts for this June 2012 transit of Venus?

## B. Determination of the Light Decrease During Transit

The transit method of observing extra-solar planets makes use of the fact that the passage of the planet across the disk of its parent star temporarily reduces the brightness of the star as seen from the Earth, as shown in the lower portion of Figure 1. The area blocked out by the planet can then be calculated from the relative diminution in brightness of the star; that is, the ratio of the decrease in brightness of the star during the transit (the amount of light blocked out by the planet) to the brightness of the star before or after the transit (without the planet in front of it). In this project, you will calculate the equivalent ratio for the transit of Venus in front of the Sun when observed from the Earth. Figure 2 shows the approximate geometry of the Venus transit when seen from Earth. Unfortunately, *Starry Night*™ does not provide a measure of the brightness of the Sun under these conditions, so the present method will determine directly the area of the Sun's disk that is obscured during the Venus transit.

In the case of observing the transit of Venus from Earth, the distance between the observer on the Earth and the planet is relatively small. Consequently, the diameter, $d$, of the surface area of the Sun that is blocked out by Venus is larger than the diameter, $d_v$, of the cross-sectional area of Venus as seen from Earth. However, when viewing an extra-solar planetary transit in front of a very distant star, the light reaching the observer is essentially parallel and the area of the star's disk covered by the planet will be equal to that of the planet's profile.

The relative diminution in brightness calculated in this way assumes that the Sun is of uniform brightness across its disk. In practice, the Sun is brighter at the center of its disk because of the effect of limb darkening, and this will change the shape of the intensity profile in Figure 1, rounding off the corners of the profile. This effect can be allowed for in the analysis of extra-solar planetary transits.

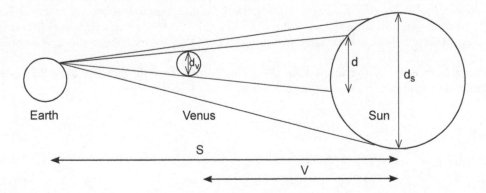

**Figure 2.** Geometry of the transit of Venus as observed from Earth.

## Calculations

If the diameter of the area of the Sun that is obscured by Venus is $d$, its area is $\pi d^2/4$. With a diameter of the Sun equal to $d_s$, its cross-sectional area is $\pi d_s^2/4$. The ratio of these areas is

$$R = \left( \frac{\frac{1}{4}\pi d^2}{\frac{1}{4}\pi d_s^2} \right) = \left( \frac{d}{d_s} \right)^2 \tag{1}$$

*Starry Night*™ can be used to measure the angular size, or diameter, of objects such as Venus and the Sun in the sky. Thus, we need to relate the cross-sectional areas of these objects to these angular diameters.

With $d_s$ as the diameter of the Sun and $S$ as its distance from the Earth, and using the small-angle relationship, the angular diameter of the Sun will be, in radians,

$$\alpha_s = \frac{d_s}{S} \tag{2}$$

In this equation, $d_s$ and $S$ must be expressed in the same units. Similarly, the obscured area of the Sun's surface has a diameter of $d$ and its angular diameter will be

$$\alpha_d = \frac{d}{S} \tag{3}$$

This derivation assumes that the distance from the Sun's surface to its center is small compared to the Earth-Sun distance. As can be seen from Figure 2, the angular diameter, $\alpha_d$, that Venus blocks out on the Sun's surface is equal to the angular diameter, $\alpha_v$, of Venus itself when viewed from Earth:

$$\alpha_v = \alpha_d \tag{4}$$

Using (2), (3), and (4),

$$d = \alpha_d S = \alpha_v S \tag{5}$$

and

$$d_s = \alpha_s S \tag{6}$$

After substituting (5) and (6) into (1), the relative diminution in the Sun's brightness during a transit is represented by the ratio

$$R = \left(\frac{d}{d_s}\right)^2 = \left(\frac{\alpha_v}{\alpha_s}\right)^2 \tag{7}$$

It is useful to consider what happens to these relationships if the distance of the observer from the Sun were to be increased and to extrapolate this to the observation of an equivalent transit of an extra-solar planet in front of its parent star when observed from a very large distance, such as the situation with the CoRot or Kepler space telescopes.

If the distance from Venus to the Sun is $V$, as shown in Figure 2, then the distance from the Earth to Venus is $S - V$, and the angular diameter of Venus as seen from the Earth can be written as

$$\alpha_v = \frac{d_v}{(S - V)} \tag{8}$$

where $d_v$ is the true physical diameter of Venus.

Then, substituting (2) and (8) into (7),

$$R = \left(\frac{\alpha_v}{\alpha_s}\right)^2 = \left(\frac{d_v S}{(S - V)d_s}\right)^2 \tag{9}$$

or

$$R = \left(\frac{d_v}{d_s}\right)^2 \cdot \left(\frac{S}{(S - V)}\right)^2 \tag{10}$$

In this equation, the factor $\dfrac{S}{(S-V)}$ can be written as $\dfrac{1}{\left(1-\dfrac{V}{S}\right)}$. If the observer were to move away from the Sun, S would increase and therefore $\dfrac{V}{S}$ would decrease, eventually tending toward 0, leading at large distances to a ratio of the decrease in intensity divided by the original intensity of the Sun of

$$R = \left(\frac{d_{\mathrm{v}}}{d_{\mathrm{s}}}\right)^2$$

(10)

In other words, at large distances, the depth of the diminution in brightness during a transit will reflect the actual diameter, $d_{\mathrm{v}}$, of the planet. The observation of the depth of the decrease of intensity in transits of extra-solar planets from large distances will thus provide direct measurement of the sizes of these planets relative to their parent stars.

## Measurement of the Venus Transit

8. Select **File > Revert** to return to the pre-transit position.
9. Select **View > Hide Daylight** from the menu and then set the Zoom to **1°**.
10. Set the Time to about **4 PM** to place Venus at about mid-transit.
11. Use the HUD to find the Angular size of Venus and note this value as $\alpha_{\mathrm{v}}$.
12. Use the HUD to find the Angular size of the Sun and note this value as $\alpha_{\mathrm{s}}$.
13. Convert $\alpha_{\mathrm{s}}$ to arcseconds (1 arcminute = 60 arcseconds).
14. Calculate the ratio $R = (\alpha_{\mathrm{v}}/\alpha_{\mathrm{s}})^2$. [NOTE: These values of angular size must be in the same units.]
15. To compare this decrease in intensity with the quoted sensitivities of the CoRoT and Kepler space telescopes of about 30 parts per million, multiply $R$ by $10^6$ to assign an intensity value of 1 million to the Sun, thereby representing this ratio in parts per million.

**Question 2.** What is the decrease in sunlight caused by the obscuration of light during the transit of Venus, in parts per million?

**Question 3.** Would the space telescopes be able to detect the passage of Venus across the face of the Sun if measured from an orbit around the Earth?

## C. Distant View of the Sun During Venus Transit

It is instructive to use this transit of Venus to simulate the observation of equivalent transits of extra-solar planets by space telescopes. To do this, we can examine the solar system from a large distance away from the Sun, in the direction of Venus from the Sun on the date and time of the Venus transit investigated above. The star HIP 83297 was in almost this direction, at a distance of about 1970 light-years from the Sun. This is close to the distance limit of the CoRot and Kepler telescopes.

16. Open **Favourites > Observing Projects > Planetary Transit > View from HIP83297**.

The view from this star, covering a field of view 90° wide, shows the Sun within a group of stars, somewhat away from the plane of the Milky Way, as seen from a distance of about 1970 light-years. For comparison, the fields of view of the space telescopes contained several hundred thousand stars, of which a proportion was selected as suitable candidates for examination during the lifetimes of the telescopes.

You can zoom in on this field of view and verify that the Sun and Venus are centered within the view.

To use *Starry Night*™ to measure the angular diameters of Venus and the Sun and thereby determine the expected relative diminution in brightness of the Sun during this transit, the observing position will need to be moved about 100,000 times closer to the Sun, to a distance of about 1000 AU. While very close to the Sun compared to stellar separations, this position is still significantly further away from Venus and the Sun than was the Earth in the transit observation from Anchorage, Alaska. From this position in space, the relative diminution in light during a transit will be essentially the same as that seen from much larger distances. The following set-up places the observer at the above position. This step is equivalent to using a powerful telescope from space to view the Sun and the transits of Venus.

17. Open **Favourites > Observing Projects > Planetary Transit > Distant Transit.**

In this field of view 4 arc seconds wide, the Sun, seen from a distance of 980.5AU in the direction of HIP83297, almost fills the view. Venus is near the center of the Sun's disk at 8:30 UT on June 7, 2012. You can now determine the effect of the planet transit on the overall intensity of light from the Sun by using the above analysis.

18. Use the Angular size display of the HUD to find the angular diameter of the Sun, $\alpha_s$ and the angular diameter of Venus, $\alpha_v$ and then use Equation 7 to calculate the value of $R$, the relative diminution of light caused by the transit. Multiply this value by $10^6$ to express this value in parts per million of the Sun's intensity.

**Question 4.**   What is the diminution of the Sun's light caused by the transit, in parts per million?

**Question 5.**   Would the space telescopes detect this diminution?

From this vantage point, the Earth is also within the field of view.

19. Advance time by 12 hours to bring the Earth close to the center of the Sun's disk. Use the HUD to find the angular diameter of the Earth and the Sun and use these values to calculate the equivalent value of $R$ for the Earth's transit.

20. Note also that the Earth's Moon transits the Sun! Use the HUD to find the angular diameter of the Moon and use this value to find $R$, the ratio of diminution of brightness of the Sun that its transit produces.

**Question 6.**   What is the diminution of the Sun's light caused by the Earth's transit, in parts per million?

**Question 7.**   Would the space telescopes detect this diminution?

**Question 8.**   What is the diminution of the Sun's light caused by the Moon's transit, in parts per million?

**Question 9.**   Would the space telescopes detect this diminution?

In this simulation of observations from a fixed and distant location, transits should repeat at fixed intervals. Since we know the period of Venus around the Sun, we can verify that transits occur at these intervals.

21. Select **File > Revert** to return Venus to its position close to the center of its transit.

22. Venus's orbital period is 224.7 days, which is 7 months, 10 days, 17 hours. Advance the Date and then the Time to verify that Venus transits the Sun again after this time interval.

23. You can also check that transits of the Earth repeat as expected. Select **File > Revert** to return to the initial time and date for Venus transit and advance time by 12 hours to place the Earth at the center of its transit.

24. The period of the Earth, 1 year, is in fact 365.25 days or 1 year and 6 hours. Advance the Date by 1 year and then 6 hours to verify the expected repetitive transit pattern into 2013. (Note that we use a calendar in which an extra day is added to every leap year and so the date will need to be adjusted back by one day every 4 years to see the continued pattern through further years.)

## D. Distribution of Stars with Accompanying Planets

After exploring the transit method for the discovery of planets associated with other stars, you can use *Starry Night*™ to examine the distribution of stars in our local neighborhood that have planets orbiting them. As an example of the exploration of the properties of these extra-solar planetary systems, you can investigate briefly the luminosities of several selected stars with accompanying planets and consider the implications of these luminosities on conditions on the planet's surface.

25. Click **Home** to obtain a view of your home sky.
26. Hide **Daylight** and the **Horizon** from the view.
27. Expand the **Stars** layer in the Options pane, then expand the **Stars** item and check the **Mark stars with extrasolar planets** option. Each of these stars will be shown with a blue marker.
28. Use the Hand tool to move around the sky to examine the distribution of these stars in our local neighborhood.
29. In turn, **Find** and **Centre** each of the following stars in the view: (i) 47 Ursae Majoris (three known planets); (ii) 51 Pegasi (one known planet); (iii) 70 Virginis (one known planet); (iv) Rho Coronae Borealis (one known planet). [TIP: Open the **Find** pane, enter the star's name in the search box and then press Enter and the spacebar to center the star in the view.] For each star, use the HUD to find its Luminosity.

Question 10.  Which of the four stars that you observed in the previous instruction step are more luminous than the Sun?

Question 11.  Which of the four stars that you observed in the previous instruction step are less luminous than the Sun?

Question 12.  How might the differences in luminosity of these stars have affected temperatures in the nebula from which each star's planets formed?

## E. Conclusions

You have observed simulations of the June 2012 transit of Venus across the face of the Sun from both an Earth-based site and a location in space. In doing so, you have measured the area of the Sun's face obscured by the planet relative to the total cross-sectional area of the Sun. This blockage results in an intensity drop of light from the Sun and it is this diminution of light that is measured in experiments that have been very successful in searching for and identifying extra-solar planets orbiting remote stars. You have also examined briefly the distribution of stars in our near neighborhood that have been shown to have planets in orbits around them.

# The Distance Ladder 24

It has been only relatively recently that astronomers have begun to appreciate the immense size of our Universe. As recently as 1920, the astronomer Harlow Shapley argued in a celebrated debate with Heber Curtis of Lick Observatory that the Milky Way encompassed the entire Universe. Prior to this debate, Shapley had used the distribution of globular clusters in the sky to deduce the position of the Sun within the Milky Way and to provide a better insight into the size of this galaxy. However, he also concluded erroneously that "spiral nebulae" were within the Milky Way and argued this point forcefully in the debate. It was only three years later that Edwin Hubble, working at Mount Wilson Observatory, found very strong evidence to prove Shapley wrong. Hubble discovered that one of these "spiral nebulae", the Andromeda Nebula, was in fact a completely separate galaxy, far removed from our own Milky Way. This initial discovery was soon followed by the identification of many other galaxies, or "separate worlds", to use Curtis's phrase. Since Hubble's discovery, astronomers have found evidence that the Universe contains billions of other galaxies and have developed techniques for estimating their distances. In this way, astronomers have systematically probed the limits of the observable Universe, discovering objects at distances so vast that it has taken billions of years for their light to reach us. Our understanding of the size and evolution of the universe has been profoundly altered by these discoveries.

Astronomers use various methods to measure distances in the cosmos. Each of these methods is useful over a particular range. Fortunately, these ranges overlap to some extent, allowing astronomers to calibrate farther-reaching techniques against more reliable closer-range methods. In this way, a so-called distance ladder has been assembled, each rung of the ladder representing a technique that extends the range of measurable distances in the Universe.

In this project, you will "climb" the distance ladder. You will be able to ascend each "rung" by making observations that use or simulate the distance measuring technique appropriate to that "rung".

## A. Parsecs and Light-years

The parsec is a unit of distance based on the first rung of the distance ladder, the parallax effect. As discussed in a previous project, parallax is the apparent shift in position of a relatively nearby object against a more distant background, caused by a change in an observer's position. An object at a distance of one parsec shows a *par*allax shift of one arc*sec*ond when the observer's position changes by a distance of 1 AU. With the parsec defined in this way, the formula for calculating the distance in parsecs, $d$, of an object that shows a parallax shift of $p$ arcseconds when the observer's position changes by 1 AU is

$$d = \frac{1}{p} \tag{1}$$

Seen from another perspective, a parsec is equivalent to the distance from which the average radius of the Earth's orbit, 1 AU, would span an angular size of one arcsecond.

1. Launch *Starry Night*™ and configure the HUD to include **Absolute Magnitude, Apparent Magnitude, Distance from Observer**, and **Name**.
2. Open **Favourites > Observing Projects > Distance Ladder > Parsec**.

The view is from a location in space 3.26 ly above the Sun in a direction toward the north ecliptic pole so that the Sun is centered and the plane of the Earth's orbit is face-on. Note that the field of view is only 4″ wide and the size of the Earth has been exaggerated.

3. Use the Angular Separation tool to measure the angular separation between the Sun and the Earth.

**Question 1.** What is the physical distance in AU between the Sun and the Earth in the view? [TIP: The Angular Separation tool tells you the physical distance between the two objects in addition to the angle separating them.]

**Question 2.** What is the angular separation between the Sun and the Earth in the view?

**Question 3.** Using Equation 1, what is the distance of the viewing location from the Sun in parsecs?

Another unit used for measuring vast astronomical distances is the light-year, the distance that light, moving with a speed of almost $3 \times 10^8$ m/s, travels in one year. One parsec is equal to 3.26 light-years, so the parsec is in fact a larger unit of distance than the light-year.

**Question 4.** What would be the observed parallax angle of a star 1 light-year away from Earth?

With this introduction to the units appropriate to the vast distances that you will measure in the following sections of this project, you are now ready to climb the first rung of the distance ladder.

## B. Stellar Parallax

The largest observational baseline available to earthbound astronomers for measuring parallax is 2 AU, the diameter of the Earth's orbit. To achieve this baseline, the astronomer measures the parallax shift of a relatively nearby star against a background of more distant stars on two occasions separated by an interval of six months. During those six months, the Earth carries the observer to the opposite side of its orbit, a total distance of 2 AU, the mean diameter of the Earth's orbit, from the position of the first observation. Because parallax is directly proportional to the length of the observational baseline, the measured shift of the star in arcseconds is twice the shift that would be seen in observations made from positions 1 AU apart. The measured shift must then be divided by a factor of 2 and used as the parallax angle, $p$, in Equation 1 in order to determine the distance to the star in parsecs.

Despite this larger baseline used in stellar parallax observations, even the nearest stars have parallax angles of less than one arcsecond. Stellar parallax is thus a very subtle and difficult parameter to measure. It was not until 1838 that Wilhelm Friederich Bessel made the first successful measurement of stellar parallax. In recent years, astronomers have been able to use modern ground-based telescopes to measure parallax angles of 0.01 arcseconds. The most recent and major advance in this important field of astrometry has been the satellite *Hipparcos*, whose name is an acronym for High Precision Parallax Collecting Satellite. This Earth-orbiting satellite revolutionized our knowledge of star distances and positions by measuring the parallaxes of over 100,000 stars to an accuracy of 0.001 arcseconds in the early 1990s, despite being placed in a wrong orbit. Star positions and properties derived from this space mission are included in the *Hipparcos* database and its companion the Tycho database and these databases have been incorporated into *Starry Night*™, hence the HIP and TYC prefixes associated with stars in this program.

Thus, parallax measurements using these techniques have been able to determine distances of objects to about 1000 pc, or 3300 light-years, from the Sun.

**Question 5.** Assuming that a parallax angle of 0.01 arcseconds is the minimum that can be reliably measured using telescopes on the Earth, what is the maximum distance (in parsecs) that can be determined from parallax observations?

**Question 6.**   If *Hipparcos* measured a parallax angle of a particular star to be 0.004 arcseconds, what is the distance of this star from the Earth? [HINT: Use Equation 1.]

The next sequence of instructions presents the method for determining stellar parallax.

> 4.  Select **Favourites > Observing Projects > Distance Ladder > Stellar Parallax**.

The viewing location is a position in space about 2200 AU above the North Pole of the Earth. The gaze is centered on the very distant star TYC9007-5631-1. Also shown in this view are the stars Alpha2 Centauri and its companion, Rigil Kentaurus.

> 5.  Measure the angular separation between Alpha2 Centauri and the reference star TYC9007-5664-1. Note this angular distance.
>
> 6.  Note that the Time Flow Rate is set at **1 half-year**. Click the **Step time forward** button once to advance time by this interval, 182.625 days, to July 5, when the Earth is at aphelion. Measure the angular separation between Alpha2 Centauri and the reference star TYC9007-5664-1 again.

**Question 7.**   What is the difference between the two angular separation measurements?

**Question 8.**   How long is the baseline used in this measurement of the parallax shift of this star?

**Question 9.**   From the measured parallax shift, what is the distance to Alpha2 Centauri in parsecs and in light-years? [HINT: Remember that the definition of parallax is based on a baseline of 1 AU.]

**Question 10.**   How does your result compare with the value for Distance from observer given in the HUD for Alpha2 Centauri? How do you account for the discrepancy?

The next sequence of steps demonstrates a technique for using *Starry Night*™ to measure stellar parallax with greater accuracy. To make these subtle measurements, you will view the change in the position of a star from a location attached to the Earth as you orbit the Sun over a period of a year. The chosen viewing location is 2238 AU above the North Pole of the Earth. At this elevation, *Starry Night*™ disables the display of the proper motions of stars that otherwise complicates the measurement of their parallax. By placing the viewing location at an elevation above the North Pole, the observing location moves through a duplicate orbit to that of the Earth with a radius of 1 AU but displaced 2238 AU toward the North Celestial Pole in space. The observed effect is just as if you were viewing the parallax effect from the Earth.

As the Earth carries the observing location around an orbit of radius 1 AU, a star will appear to move due to parallax. The shape of each star's motion will be different. Depending on the star's position relative to the ecliptic (the plane of the Earth's orbit), some stars will appear to move in a circular motion while others will describe ellipses of varying eccentricity, and still others will move back and forth in nearly a straight line.

For each of the stars listed in Data Table 1 at the end of this project, follow the steps in Sequence 1 to measure its parallax.

> **Sequence 1**
>
> 7.  Open the **Favourites** pane and select the view that matches the name of the star in Data Table 1 from the **Observing Projects > Distance Ladder** folder, beginning with **Alpha2 Centauri**.
>
> 8.  Use the Zoom buttons in the toolbar to **Zoom in** to a field of view close to or at the limit of **<1" × <1"** (In several cases, the star may move out of the view at this limit and you will have to expand the field of view to a few arcseconds.) As you zoom in, watch the field of view indicator change in the compass display in the right upper corner of the view window, as it indicates the direction of the star in the sky. Also, as you decrease the field of view and get close to maximum zoom, you will see the star drift away from the center of the view. This is because the gaze direction is centered and locked onto a position with specific coordinates of right ascension and declination on the celestial sphere that is near to, but not at the star's location.

9. With the Time Flow Rate set at **3 days**, **Run time forward** and watch the motion of the star over a year or so of time. Note the direction of the star's motion (clockwise, CW, or counter clockwise, CCW) and the approximate shape of the motion (circle, wide ellipse, thin ellipse, straight line) in the appropriate cells of Data Table 1.

10. Click **Stop** when the star is near one end of its apparent motion. Then **Step time forward** or **backward** to position the star as close as possible to one end of the longest axis of its motion.

11. Select **Add FOV Indicator** from the contextual menu for the star. This will bring up a sub-menu with two groups of options. Select the **Circular...** option from the upper group (beneath the heading named To This Chart). Type the value **0.001"** in the Diameter box of the FOV Indicator dialog window, (remember to type the double-quote key for arcseconds when defining this FOV), and select the **RA/Dec** option from the drop-box labeled Positioning. Click the **OK** button to close the dialog window. The current position of the star will now be marked with a cross.

12. Use the **M** keyboard shortcut to advance time by six months.

13. Measure the angular separation between the apparent position of the star on this date and the cross indicating its apparent position six months ago. Divide this measurement by 2 and enter the result, in arcseconds, into Data Table 1 under the column headed Measured Parallax ("). If the star's parallax is not very large, you may find it helpful to add FOV markers to the view about 1 month or less apart to trace the path of the apparent motion of the star and thus get a better idea of the orientation of the long axis of its motion. Then use the Time controls to move the star to one end of its parallax path and measure the distance to the opposite end of the marked path.

14. Use the value you found for Measured Parallax in the previous step for the value of $p$ in the formula $d = 1/p$ to determine the distance to the star in parsecs. Multiply this result by 3.26 to convert this distance to light-years. Record these results in the appropriate cells of Data Table 1.

15. Copy the Distance from observer given in the HUD into Data Table 1 under the column Given Distance. [NOTE: *Starry Night*™ rounds off these values to the nearest light-year. More exact values for the nearby stars Alpha2 Centauri, Procyon, and Vega are already listed in the table.]

16. Return to the beginning of Sequence 1 and select another star from the list in Data Table 1.

You will note that the closest of these stars, Alpha2 Centauri, is in the southern part of the sky and moves significantly over a year because of parallax.

> **Question 11.** What is the shape and direction of the motion of Alpha2 Centauri in the view?
>
> **Question 12.** How long does it take for the star to complete this pattern of motion?

It is interesting to compare the distance from the observer of this closest star to the offset distance from the North Pole of Earth at which these measurements have been made, to determine if this large offset from the Earth is likely to make a significant difference to the observation of parallax for this close star.

> **Question 13.** Convert the distance to Alpha2 Centauri into AU (1 light-year = 63,240 AU). Expressed as a percentage, what is the ratio between the elevation of the viewing location above the surface of the Earth and the distance to Alpha2 Centauri?
>
> **Question 14.** Comment on the difficulty in measuring the parallax of T Monocerotis. Can you see any reason why you could measure no parallax motion for this star?

You will notice that Data Table 1 includes a column labeled Ecliptic Latitude. This column of given data indicates the latitude of the star with respect to the ecliptic plane, with positive ecliptic latitude indicating that a star is north of the ecliptic plane and a negative ecliptic latitude indicating that a star is south of the ecliptic plane.

> **Question 15.** What relationship, if any, do you see between the rotational direction of the parallactic motion of stars and their ecliptic latitude?

Question 16.     What relationship, if any, do you see between the shape of the parallax path and the ecliptic latitude of the star?

Question 17.     If a relatively nearby star were to be precisely at the North Ecliptic Pole, which of the following choices would best describe its parallactic path?
(a) A straight line back and forth
(b) A perfect circle
(c) An ellipse with the shape of that of the Earth's orbit

## C. Spectroscopic Parallax

The next rung of the cosmic distance ladder is the technique of spectroscopic parallax. Despite its name, this method for determining astronomical distances does not use the measurement of parallax angles. Rather, spectroscopic parallax relies on the concept of standard candles, objects whose luminosity or absolute brightness is known. If we know the absolute brightness of a particular star and compare this to its apparent brightness as seen from the Earth, we can determine the star's distance from Earth using the inverse square law. The method of spectroscopic parallax thus depends on astronomers identifying "standard candles" and determining their absolute brightness.

One such method uses the classification of the spectrum of a star to place it on the Hertzsprung-Russell (H-R) diagram. The H-R diagram shows the absolute magnitude of a star as a function of its surface temperature. If the star's spectrum can be classified and its temperature and type (for example, main sequence, giant or supergiant) established, then it can be placed on the H-R diagram and its absolute magnitude determined. This absolute magnitude is defined as the magnitude or brightness that this star would have if it were at a standard distance of 10 pc, or 32.6 light-years, from the Sun and is directly related to the star's luminosity or total energy output. With this knowledge of the star's magnitude at a distance of 10 pc and a measurement of its apparent brightness, its distance can be determined using the inverse square law. This powerful method of distance measurement can provide estimates of stellar distance for stars as far as millions of light-years away. Unfortunately, the precision of this method is limited to about 10% at these large distances because of the uncertainty in determining absolute magnitude and luminosity class from the spectrum of the star.

17. Open the **Favourites** pane and select the appropriately named view of the selected star from **Observing Projects > Distance Ladder** for the stars listed in Data Table 2 at the end of this project.

18. Use the HUD to find the Apparent magnitude and Absolute magnitude of the star and record these values in the appropriate columns of Data Table 2.

A direct relationship can be derived between the difference in a star's apparent and absolute magnitudes and its distance in parsecs, using the inverse square law and the definition of the magnitude scale for stars.

The total energy emitted by a star, known as its luminosity, $L$, in watts, spreads out into space and the energy per unit area at a distance $d$ meters is the measured brightness of the star, $b$, in watts per square meter. At this distance, this total energy is spread uniformly over the surface of a sphere whose area is $4\pi d^2$. Thus, the brightness is

$$b = \frac{L}{4\pi d^2}$$

This is known as the inverse square law governing the change of radiation intensity as a function of distance away from the source.

Two stars of brightness $b_1$ and $b_2$, at distances $d_1$ and $d_2$, respectively, whose luminosities, or total energy output, are $L_1$ and $L_2$ and related by

$$\frac{b_1}{b_2} = \frac{L_1}{L_2} \left[ \frac{d_2}{d_1} \right]^2$$

This ratio will hold in any units of distance, whether in meters or parsecs.

The difference between the magnitudes of two stars is a measure of the ratio of their brightnesses, such that a difference of $m_2 - m_1 = 1$ magnitude corresponds to a ratio of $b_1/b_2 = 2.512$. This odd value is chosen so that a 5-magnitude difference is exactly 100 [i.e., $(2.512)^5 = 100$]. Furthermore, the magnitude scale is inverted, such that the larger the magnitude, the smaller the ratio. Brighter stars have lower magnitudes!

Thus, the equation relating two stars of magnitude $m_1$ and $m_2$, whose brightnesses are $b_1$ and $b_2$, respectively, is

$$m_2 - m_1 = 2.5 \times \log\left[\frac{b_1}{b_2}\right]$$

We can now use this relationship and the inverse square law to relate the brightness, $b$, of a star when measured from a distance, $d$, from which it has magnitude, $m$, to the brightness, $B$, of the same star when measured from the distance of 10 pc, corresponding to the absolute magnitude, $M$. The luminosity, $L$, of the star does not depend on distance, so $L_1 = L_2$. Then, from the inverse square law, the ratio of the brightnesses $b$ and $B$ is

$$\frac{b}{B} = \left[\frac{10}{d}\right]^2$$

In magnitudes, this can be represented as

$$m - M = 2.5 \times \log\left[\frac{B}{b}\right]$$

$$= 2.5 \times \log\left[\frac{d}{10}\right]^2$$

$$= 2 \times 2.5 \times \log\left[\frac{d}{10}\right]$$

Recognizing that the logarithm of a ratio is the difference of the logarithms of the components of the ratio, this equation becomes

$$m - M = 5\,[\log d - \log 10]$$

Thus, since $\log 10 = 1$,

$$m - M = 5\log d - 5 \tag{2}$$

Thus, $d$, in parsecs, can be derived from knowledge of $m$ and $M$. This difference, $m - M$, between a star's apparent magnitude as seen from Earth, $m$, and its absolute magnitude, $M$, is called the **distance modulus** of the star.

The apparent magnitude of the star is measured through observation. By rearranging the distance modulus formula, the distance to the star (in parsecs) can be calculated as follows:

$$d = 10^{\left[\frac{m-M+5}{5}\right]} \tag{3}$$

19. Use the formula in Equation 3 above to calculate the distances to the stars listed in Data Table 2. Take care with the sign of the magnitude values. Compare your results with those you obtained in Data Table 1 for those stars that are in both tables.

**Question 18.** Did you encounter any difficulty determining the distance to T Monocerotis using spectroscopic parallax?

**Question 19.** Which method of determining stellar distances has the greater range, stellar parallax, or spectroscopic parallax?

The two methods for determining the distance to a star can be used to verify each other. For example, we can calculate the absolute magnitude of Regulus from the inverse-square law using its apparent magnitude and the distance, $d$, in parsecs, to Regulus as determined by stellar parallax. To do so, simply rearrange Equation 2 to solve for $M$ as shown in Equation 4, below:

$$M = m + 5 \log (d) - 5 \tag{4}$$

**Question 20.** (a) Using the value for the distance in parsecs for Regulus in Data Table 1 and the apparent magnitude of Regulus in Data Table 2, calculate Regulus' absolute magnitude using Equation 4. (b) How does your result compare to the absolute magnitude of Regulus as determined from its spectral characteristics?

**Question 21.** Using the distance (in parsecs) from Data Table 2, calculate the stellar parallax for the following stars: (a) Delta Cephei, and (b) T Monocerotis.

**Question 22.** How does the predicted stellar parallax of Delta Cephei compare to the parallax that you measured?

**Question 23.** (a) Would the *Hipparcos* satellite be able to measure the stellar parallax of T Monocerotis? (b) How do you think the distance to T Monocerotis that is given in *Starry Night*™ was determined?

## D. Population I Cepheid Variables

Cepheid variable stars are stars that have evolved away from the main sequence and occupy the so-called instability strip on the H-R diagram. Cepheids vary regularly in brightness in a specific and identifiable pattern. They received their name from the prototype for this class of stars, δ (delta) Cephei.

There are two features of Cepheid variable stars that make them extremely useful for measuring distances in the Universe. First of all, the period over which the brightness of a Cepheid varies is related directly to its average intrinsic luminosity, or absolute magnitude. This relationship is called the period-luminosity relation. Secondly, Cepheids are intrinsically very bright, with luminosities ranging up to at least 10,000 times the luminosity of the Sun. Consequently, they can be seen from distances of millions of parsecs and their apparent magnitudes measured. Using the equations above, the measured apparent magnitudes can be combined with the absolute magnitudes determined from the period-luminosity relation to provide distances over a much larger range than the previous methods, thereby extending the range of the distance ladder significantly.

Data Table 3 at the end of this project contains a sample of Cepheid variable stars and includes data on each star's period of variability. For each star in this list, follow the steps below.

20. Open the **Favourites** pane and select the appropriately named view from the **Observing Projects > Distance Ladder** folder.
21. Copy the value for the star's Absolute magnitude from the HUD into Data Table 3.
22. Plot the data in Data Table 3 onto the graph in Graph Template 1 at the end of this project.

**Question 24.** What type of relationship does your graph suggest between the period of variability and the absolute magnitude of Cepheid variable stars?

23. Draw a best-fit straight line through your data points.

If the data plotted in Graph Template 1 shows a reasonable relationship between these parameters, then you should be able to find the distance to another Cepheid variable simply by observing the period of its variability. With a measurement of this period, you can find its absolute magnitude and by comparing this absolute magnitude to its apparent magnitude, you can determine its distance using the inverse-square law. This technique is similar to spectroscopic parallax but depends on the period-luminosity relationship rather than the star's spectral characteristics and the H-R diagram for determining its absolute magnitude. Moreover, the distance you determine for a Cepheid variable from this period-luminosity relationship should agree with its distance as determined by other methods, particularly the method of stellar parallax. You have already determined the distance for Delta Cephei, the star for which all the other stars in the class of Cepheid variables are named, by measuring its stellar parallax and calculating its spectroscopic parallax. Follow the next steps to determine the distance to this star from the period-luminosity relationship.

24. The period of the Cepheid variable star Delta Cephei is 5.37 days.

25. Locate the point for a period of 5.37 days on the horizontal axis of Graph Template 1. Draw a vertical line through this point and mark where it intersects the best-fit line that you drew through the data points. Read the corresponding absolute magnitude for this star from the vertical axis of the graph. Use this absolute magnitude value and the apparent magnitude of Delta Cephei ($m = 4.06$) in Equation 3 above to determine its distance.

**Question 25.**    (a) What is the absolute magnitude of Delta Cephei based on the period-luminosity graph? (b) Does this agree with the absolute magnitude of this star in Data Table 2, as determined from its spectroscopic parallax?

**Question 26.**    (a) What is the distance to Delta Cephei based on its period of variability? (b) How does this compare with the distance you obtained for this star by measuring its parallactic shift?

The astronomer Henrietta Leavitt used observations of a much larger sample of Cepheid variables when she established this period-luminosity relationship in 1912. Since her pioneering work, two different types of Cepheid variable stars have been identified: Population I and Population II Cepheids. Each shows a specific period-luminosity relationship. Thus, in addition to identifying a star as a Cepheid, astronomers must also determine in which population the star belongs before a definitive luminosity can be assigned to it.

Another class of variable stars, the population II RR Lyrae stars, also show a period-luminosity relationship. RR Lyrae stars are generally not intrinsically as luminous as Population I Cepheid variables, and have a very narrow but well-defined range of luminosities. While they do not provide as great a range of distance measurement as Cepheids, these stars are much more common and have therefore been important in the verification of other rungs in the cosmic distance ladder. Also, in 1920, Harlow Shapley used the period-luminosity relationship of RR Lyrae stars in globular clusters to determine the distances to these star groups in our Milky Way Galaxy. From the distances and distribution of these globular clusters, he was able to deduce the size and extent of the Milky Way Galaxy.

As mentioned above, the other reason that Cepheid variables are so important in the distance ladder is that they are intrinsically highly luminous stars, visible at vast distances from Earth. Cepheid variable stars can even be resolved in other galaxies. In 1923, Edwin Hubble used the 100-inch telescope at Mount Wilson to observe Cepheid variables in what was then called the Andromeda nebula, an object considered to be in our own Galaxy. From the period-luminosity relationship, Hubble determined that this "nebula" was in fact an independent star system approximately two million light-years distant from the Sun. Since Hubble's time, Population I Cepheid variables have extended the distance ladder to a range of up to 30 Megaparsecs (Mpc), which is equivalent to almost 100 million light-years. Thus, Cepheid variable stars provide a crucial foundation for the next rung in the distance ladder.

## E. The Hubble Law

There are several other distance determination methods that astronomers use that overlap and otherwise corroborate those we have examined so far in this project. These include the use of naturally occurring masers in space, the Tully-Fisher relation and the use of Type Ia supernovae as standard candles.

Notwithstanding these intermediate methods for distance measurement to neighboring galaxies, it is the Cepheid variable method that provides the direct link of distances to galaxies and the link to the final rung in the distance ladder: the Hubble law.

A few years after uncovering the true nature and distance to the Andromeda Galaxy, Edwin Hubble discovered a relationship between the distance to a galaxy and the speed at which it appears to be receding, as measured by the redshift of the lines in its spectrum. This relationship, called the Hubble law, has allowed astronomers to estimate distances to the limits of the observable Universe. Furthermore, this relationship has profoundly altered our knowledge of the evolution of the Universe.

A significant feature of Hubble's results is that, apart from a few nearby galaxies such as the Andromeda Galaxy and members of the Local Group, which appear to be gravitationally bound together, most other galaxies in the universe appear to be receding from each other. Cosmologists, supported by Einstein's General Theory of Relativity, have been able to conclude that this redshift is a consequence of the expansion of space itself. By extrapolating this expansion into the past, cosmologists have suggested that the universe was born about 14 billion years ago from the explosion of an infinitesimal point of infinite density. Supporting evidence for this Big Bang cosmology has come from the study of the residual radiation from this explosion, the cosmic microwave background radiation.

The Hubble Law states that the distance to a galaxy, $d$, is proportional to its velocity of recession, $v$, and is simply expressed in the formula

$$d = \frac{v}{H_0} \tag{5}$$

where $H_0$ is a constant called the Hubble constant and is expressed in units of kilometers per second per megaparsec.

Before we can use Equation 5 to find the distance, $d$, to a galaxy, we need to know $H_0$, and we also need a method to find the recession velocity, $v$. The determination of the Hubble constant has been an on-going process, with early measurements from different techniques providing widely varying values. Recent work has now determined its value with reasonable accuracy to be 70 km/s/Mpc.

The value of $v$ in Equation 5 for any distant galaxy can be found from the galaxy's redshift. This redshift occurs because space is expanding while the light is traveling from the galaxy to the Earth, and the wavelength of the light increases to match the expansion. Consequently, a spectral line that has a wavelength $\lambda_0$ when the light leaves the galaxy will have a longer wavelength, $\lambda$, when the light arrives at the Earth. The redshift, $z$, is defined to be the change in wavelength divided by the wavelength:

$$z = \frac{\lambda - \lambda_0}{\lambda_0} = \frac{\Delta\lambda}{\lambda_0} \tag{6}$$

The **cosmological redshift** (or **expansion redshift**) is not a Doppler shift, but for small recession velocities, it can be approximated by the Doppler shift formula,

$$z = \frac{v}{c} \tag{7}$$

where $c$ is equal to the speed of light.

> **Question 27.** The galaxy cluster Abell 478 has a redshift of $z = 0.0881$. Using Equation 7, what is the recession velocity of this galaxy cluster? [HINT: $c = 2.9979 \times 10^5$ km/s.]
>
> **Question 28.** What is the distance to Abell 478 (a) in megaparsecs (Mpc), and (b) in light-years? [HINT: Use Equation 5 and $H_0 = 70$ km/s/Mpc.]

Astronomers continue to use other rungs of the distance ladder, particularly Type Ia supernovae and the Tully-Fisher relation, to calibrate this important cosmological constant.

## F. Climbing the Distance Ladder

Now that we have reached this final rung of the distance ladder, it is perhaps instructive to see how far our distance measuring techniques have taken us.

> 26. Select **Favourites > Observing Projects > Distance Ladder > Parallax to Hubble Law**.

The view shows the Sun and the planets.

> **Question 29.** Which rung of the distance ladder is appropriate for determining distances in the solar system?

> 27. **Increase current elevation** to about **32 ly from Sun**. Use the Location Scroller to look around the view. This is equivalent to moving around on the surface of a sphere with a radius of 32 ly, centered on the Sun. Notice that, as the Location Scroller changes your viewing location on this sphere, different stars appear to move by different amounts in the view. You can use the HUD to determine the Distance from observer of these stars. You will note that those stars closest to the observer appear to move the most as you move around the sphere.

**Question 30.** What distance determination techniques would be suitable for the majority of objects in this view?

28. **Increase current elevation** to about **3200 ly from Sun**. Use the Location Scroller to look around the view.

The local neighborhood of stars around the Sun and the surrounding disk of the Milky Way are visible in the view.

**Question 31.** Which distance determination technique is most suitable for objects that are at the distance of the Sun from this viewing location?

29. **Increase current elevation** to about **0.326 Mly from Sun** (0.326 million light-years). Use the Location Scroller to look around the view.

The Milky Way Galaxy and the nearby Andromeda Galaxy are labeled in the view. All of the other points of light in the view are other galaxies. Some of these galaxies, such as the Andromeda Galaxy, are near enough to the Earth that astronomers can use the very luminous Cepheid variables and the period-luminosity relation to determine the distances to these galaxies. Beyond the reach of Cepheid variables, other, even more luminous, standard candles such as Type Ia supernovae extend our distance measuring capability to even more distant galaxies, out to about 3.2 billion light-years.

30. **Increase current elevation** to about **326 Mly from Sun** and look around the view with the Location Scroller.

At this distance, you are seeing the large-scale structure of our universe, with walls of galaxies surrounding huge voids of space that contain few galaxies. Other corroborative distance measuring techniques can be used at this range but we are now firmly within the realm of the Hubble law.

31. **Increase current elevation** to about **1800 Mly from Sun** (1.8 billion light-years) and look around the view with the location scroller.

At this distance from the Sun, the database of galaxies in *Starry Night*™ has reached its limit. The boundary you see in the view is artificial. The empty space surrounding the cube of galaxies in the view is itself filled with billions of other galaxies out to the limits of our observation at about 12 billion light-years from the Earth. You will note the galaxy labeled NGC 2484 near the boundary of the *Starry Night*™ database limit. This galaxy is receding from us and has a measured redshift, $z$, of 0.042836.

**Question 32.** Using the formula $v = z \times c$, where $z$ is the redshift and $c$ is the speed of light, what is the recessional velocity, $v$, of NGC 2484? [HINT: $c = 2.9979 \times 10^5$ km/s.]

**Question 33.** Assuming a value for the Hubble constant, $H_0$, of 70 km/s/Mpc, what is the distance to this galaxy from the Sun (a) in megaparsecs (Mpc), and (b) in light-years?

## G. Conclusions

In this project, you have had the opportunity to review the techniques that astronomers employ to measure distances to objects in the cosmos and you have employed the basic principles of these techniques in software simulations. Finally, you learned about the distance ladder and how its various rungs not only extend the range of measurable distances but also verify and calibrate other rungs where they overlap in applicable ranges.

Data Table 1. Parallax and Distance of a Sample of Nearby Stars

| Star | Ecliptic latitude (°) | Direction of star's motion (CW or CCW) | Shape of star's motion | Measured parallax (") | Measured distance (pc) | Measured distance (ly) | Given distance (ly) |
|---|---|---|---|---|---|---|---|
| Alpha2 Centauri | −42.6 | | | | | | 4.365 |
| T Monocerotis | −16.2 | | | | | | |
| Procyon | −16.0 | | | | | | 11.4 |
| Alpha Sextantis | −11.0 | | | | | | |
| Regulus | +0.5 | | | | | | |
| Capella | +23.0 | | | | | | |
| Delta Cephei | +59.5 | | | | | | |
| Vega | +62.0 | | | | | | 25.3 |
| Polaris | +66.5 | | | | | | |

Data Table 2. Spectroscopic Parallax and Distance of a Sample of Nearby Stars

| Star | Apparent magnitude, $m$ | Absolute magnitude, $M$ | Calculated distance (pc) | Given distance (ly) | Given distance (pc) |
|---|---|---|---|---|---|
| T Monocerotis | | | | | |
| Alpha Sextantis | | | | | |
| Regulus | | | | | |
| Delta Cephei | | | | | |
| Polaris | | | | | |
| Zeta Geminorum | | | | | |

Data Table 3. Period and Absolute Magnitudes of a Sample of Cepheid Variable Stars

| Star | Period (days) | Absolute magnitude |
|---|---|---|
| Zeta Geminorum | 10.15 | |
| TT Aquilae | 13.75 | |
| Eta Aquilae | 7.18 | |
| T Vulpeculae | 4.44 | |
| DT Cygni | 2.50 | |

**Graph Template 1.** Absolute Magnitude Versus Period for a Sample of Cepheid Variables

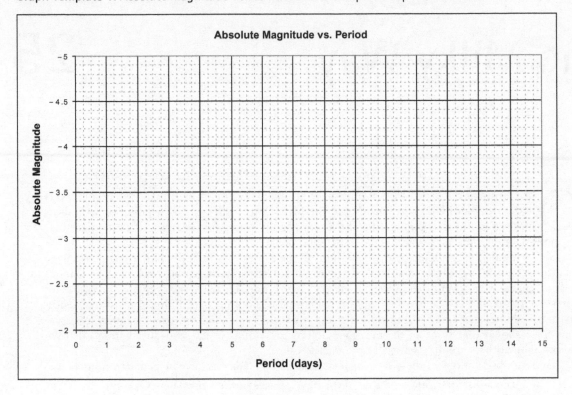

# The Milky Way           25

One feature of the night sky that must have attracted the attention of the very first observers is the ribbon of light that encircles it, the Milky Way. Sadly, the light pollution of today's modern world robs many of us of the opportunity to see this beautiful if subtle light that originates from within our home Galaxy in the cosmos.

Galileo made the first telescopic observations of the Milky Way in 1609. His telescope resolved the diffuse band of light into countless individual stars. Later telescopic observers, such as Charles Messier, began to discover other objects in the sky that appeared fuzzy in the eyepiece and could not be resolved into stars. Little was known of these mysterious objects except that some were eventually resolved into clusters of stars, while the rest remained nebulous. In the past century, observations have shown that some of the nebulous objects are clouds of gas and dust within our own Galaxy, while others are themselves distant galaxies.

Modern observations of these star clusters, nebulae and galaxies have helped astronomers to:

1) Establish accurate estimates of the physical size of the Milky Way Galaxy
2) Develop an understanding of its physical and dynamic structure
3) Determine that our Milky Way Galaxy is but one of billions of such galaxies in the Universe
4) Construct theories about the origin and structure of the Universe, based on the observed filamentary distribution and relative motion of the billions of galaxies within it

In this project, you will use *Starry Night™* to make observations of the Milky Way and some of these nebulous telescopic objects.

## A. The Milky Way and the Broad Structure of the Galaxy

The term "Milky Way" refers specifically to the diffuse ribbon of luminosity that sweeps majestically across our night sky. This is the edge-on view of our Galaxy as seen from Earth.

1. Launch *Starry Night™* and open the **Favourites > Observing Projects > Milky Way > Cornwall**.

The view is of the southern sky from Cornwall, Ontario, Canada. The time is midnight on the date of the June solstice. The Teapot and Fish Hook asterisms are visible near the southern horizon and the band of the Milky Way sweeps diagonally upward to the left.

2. Select **Options > Stars > Milky Way...** from the menu and, in the dialog window that pops up, use the slide control to adjust the Brightness of the Milky Way to its maximum and click on **OK**.

Were you to go outside at the time and place of this simulation and look south at the Teapot asterism, you would see the Milky Way appearing to rise like steam from the teapot's spout, then sweep upward across the sky toward the Summer Triangle near the zenith and finally arc back down through the "W" of Cassiopeia in the northeast before reaching the horizon again.

3. Use the Hand tool to drag the sky in a manner that allows you to follow the path of the Milky Way as described in the previous paragraph.

You can see that the Milky Way forms a band of varying width across the sky from horizon to horizon.

4. Hide the **Horizon** and use the Hand tool to drag the view and follow the complete path of the Milky Way around the sky.

**Question 1.**    Does the Milky Way appear as a continuous band as it encircles the sky or are there apparent breaks in this structure?

5. Select **View > Constellations > Astronomical.**
6. Use the Hand tool to drag the view and again follow the complete path of the Milky Way around the sky. As you do so, observe the size and brightness of the Milky Way in order to answer the following questions.

**Question 2.**    Toward which constellations does the Milky Way appear broadest?

**Question 3.**    In the direction of which constellations does the Milky Way appear narrowest?

Speculate on your observations. The fact that the Milky Way encircles the sky as seen from Earth suggests that the solar system is somewhere inside the Milky Way Galaxy. If this were not the case, then the Milky Way would appear discontinuous and confined to a particular direction in the sky. The fact that the Milky Way appears as a relatively narrow band suggests that the Milky Way Galaxy has a flat structure. We know from observations of other galaxies that such a flat, disk-like structure is characteristic of spiral and barred spiral galaxies.

Consequently, we can deduce that the Milky Way Galaxy is a type of spiral galaxy. If it were elliptical or irregular, stars would be dispersed across the sky instead of being concentrated in such a narrow band. If this deduction is correct, then the Milky Way Galaxy must also have a central bulge. As seen from our position on Earth inside the Galaxy, this bulge would likely reveal itself as a broader region in the Milky Way.

**Question 4.**    Using the logic of the previous paragraph and your answer to Question 2, toward which constellation(s) must an observer on Earth look to see the center of the Milky Way Galaxy?

**Question 5.**    Toward which constellation would an observer on Earth need to look in order to look directly out of the Galaxy, away from the center along the plane of its disk?

7. Select **File > Revert,** use the **K** keyboard shortcut to remove the asterism outlines and labels and again adjust the brightness of the Milky Way to its maximum by selecting **Options > Stars > Milky Way...** from the menu.
8. Change the Time Flow Rate to **300×** and use the Hand tool to follow the position of the Milky Way along the horizon as time advances. Daylight has been hidden to allow you to observe the variable angle that the Milky Way makes with the horizon as time progresses.

The reason for the variable angle and rising point of the Milky Way is that the plane of the Galaxy is inclined to the equatorial plane of Earth.

9. Select **Favourites > Observing Projects > Milky Way > Galactic Plane.**

In this view of the Milky Way, the stars have been hidden and lines representing three significant planes are superimposed on the sky. The red line is the Celestial Equator, the projection of the plane of Earth's equator onto the celestial sphere. The green line is the ecliptic, the plane of Earth's orbit around the Sun. The blue line is the Galactic equator, the plane of the disk of the Milky Way Galaxy. The angles between these various planes can be obtained by measuring the angles in the sky between the poles of these planes.

> 10. Change the Gaze to the **Z**enith and set the Zoom to **180°**.

Three points are marked in the sky: the North Celestial Pole, the North Ecliptic Pole, and the North Galactic Pole.

> 11. You can determine the inclination angle of the Earth's rotation axis to the plane of the Galaxy by using the Angular Separation tool to measure the angle between the North Celestial Pole and the North Galactic Pole.
>
> 12. You can estimate the angle at which the ecliptic plane is inclined to the galactic plane by measuring the angular separation from the North Galactic Pole to the North Ecliptic Pole.

**Question 6.** What is the approximate angular separation between the North Celestial Pole and the North Galactic Pole?

**Question 7.** At approximately what angle does the galactic plane intersect the celestial equator?

**Question 8.** What is the approximate angular separation between the North Ecliptic Pole and the North Galactic Pole?

**Question 9.** At approximately what angle does the ecliptic intersect the galactic plane?

## B. Details of the Structure of the Milky Way

You probably noticed some interesting dark encroachments into the band of the Milky Way during the observations you made in the previous section.

> 13. Select **Favourites > Observing Projects > Milky Way > Great Rift**.

In this view from Cornwall, Canada, toward the south at midnight on June 21, the Milky Way stretches diagonally across the sky. Beginning at the star Deneb in Cygnus and extending to the star nu Ophiuchi (ν Oph) in the lower right, the Milky Way is split by a dark intrusion known as the Great Rift. The northern part of this structure is known as the Cygnus Rift, or the Northern Coalsack, for a reason that you will discover shortly.

The Great Rift is representative of a broad class of objects within the Galaxy called **dark nebulae**. Dark nebulae reveal themselves by obscuring the light of a radiant background such as the rich star fields of the Milky Way. As you can see, the Great Rift creates the illusion that the Milky Way splits into two branches.

Dark nebulae range in size from relatively small, almost spherical, Bok globules to immense clouds of gas and dust such as the Great Rift. Modern estimates suggest that the mass of the gas and dust contained in the Great Rift is equivalent to one million Suns! You can use two bright stars whose positions are at either end of the rift, Deneb and nu Ophiuchi, to obtain an estimate of angular extent of this dark nebula in our sky.

> 14. Measure the angular separation between Deneb and nu Ophiuchi (ν Oph).

**Question 10.** What is the approximate angular extent of the Great Rift in our sky?

For observers in the southern hemisphere, an equally impressive dark nebula is the Coalsack. Like its northern namesake, the Coalsack is easily seen and appreciated with the naked eye.

15. Open **Favourites > Observing Projects > Milky Way > Coalsack**.

The Coalsack, named for its darkness and its shape, is visible below the Southern Cross asterism.

16. To identify the Southern Cross asterism, Select **View > Constellations > Asterisms** and **View > Constellations > Labels** from the main menu. Use the **K** keyboard shortcut to toggle the constellation and label display off again.

17. To get a better view of the Coalsack, set the Zoom to **10°**.

18. Use the Angular Separation tool to estimate the approximate radius in degrees of this dark nebula.

Question 11.    What is the approximate radius of the area of sky that is obscured by the Coalsack dark nebula and what is the approximate area of this region of sky, in square degrees? [HINT: The area of a circle of radius $R$ is $\pi R^2$.]

Question 12.    By way of comparison, the full Moon, as seen from Earth has an angular radius of about 15' (0.25°). How much larger in area in the sky is the Coalsack than the full Moon? [HINT: Divide the area of the Coalsack by the area of the full Moon.]

Dark nebulae represent visible evidence for the existence of interstellar matter in the Galaxy. Roughly half of this interstellar matter is in the form of immense, gravitationally bound structures known as **giant molecular clouds**. On average, these vast clouds contain a mass of more than 10,000 Suns. Most of this mass is in the form of hydrogen and helium gas, plus a small fraction of heavier elements and dust. The dust consists of tiny, solid particles of graphite or silicates.

Despite the low density of this extremely rarified interstellar medium, its pervasiveness within the vast dimensions of the Galaxy has led astronomers to estimate that the matter of the interstellar medium amounts to approximately 10% of the total mass of the Milky Way Galaxy.

## C. HI and HII Regions

The dark nebulae in the Galaxy are often called **HI regions** (pronounced "H one"), HI being the symbol used to describe un-ionized hydrogen. These nebulae are cool (with a temperature of about 100 K) and the hydrogen they contain is therefore neutral rather than ionized. Astronomers have learned that dark nebulae are often the birthplaces of stars. If some of these newborn stars are hot and massive O and B stars, their ultraviolet light ionizes the hydrogen in the part of the HI region surrounding them to form an **HII region** (pronounced "H two"), this symbol describing ionized hydrogen. Because of the energy absorbed from the ultraviolet light, HII regions are hot, typically about 10,000 K. Subsequent recombination of the electrons and ions causes HII regions to emit light at visible wavelengths, predominantly in the strong Balmer-$\alpha$ spectral line in the red region of the spectrum. Because of this emission, HII regions are also called **emission nebulae**.

The HI regions surrounding HII regions often appear as silhouettes. They can also become visible by reflecting the light of nearby hot, young stars. Since the dust grains within these cold HI clouds preferentially scatter light of shorter wavelength, these **reflection nebulae** shine with a blue color.

19. Open **Favourites > Observing Projects > Milky Way > M8, M20, and M21**.

There are two different HII regions, M8 and M20, within this 5° field of view, in addition to the open cluster of stars designated M21.

20. **Magnify** M8 (the Lagoon Nebula) in the view and then select **Show Info** from the contextual menu for this object. In the Info pane, expand the Description layer and read about this HII region.

21. Set the Zoom to **10°** and then **Magnify** M20 (the Trifid Nebula).

You will notice that both of these objects contain rich open clusters of newborn stars.

22. Set the Zoom to **5°** and then **Magnify** M21. Select **Show Info** from the contextual menu for this object and read the Description in the Info pane.

Question 13.    Approximately how old is the star cluster that forms M21?

Question 14.    Approximately how many stars are readily visible in M21 when viewed through a small telescope?

23. Select **Favourites > Observing Projects > Milky Way > M42**.

M42, the Great Orion Nebula, is a region of very young stars within a giant molecular cloud whose total mass is estimated to be approximately 500,000 times that of the Sun. M42 lies on the edge of its parent giant molecular cloud, at about 1600 light-years from Earth. This molecular cloud in turn is but one of a vast system of such clouds found in this part of the Galaxy. Near the central portion of M42 lies the Trapezium, named for the four brightest components of the system of recently formed and very hot O and B type stars that are providing the radiation that lights up the surrounding nebulae. There are several prolific stellar nurseries near M42 in the parent molecular cloud, within which many new clusters of stars are forming at the present time.

24. In this magnified view of M42, use the HUD to identify the Trapezium and **Magnify** the view of this group of stars.

25. Select **File > Revert**.

26. Open the **FOV** pane and select the **30 Arcminutes** field indicator from the Other (All Charts) layer. Use the field of view indicator to estimate the angular diameter of M42. Then turn this feature off again by clicking the checkbox for this indicator in the FOV pane.

Question 15.    What is the approximate average angular diameter of M42?

Question 16.    At its distance of 1600 light-years from Earth, what is the approximate physical diameter of M42 in light-years? [HINT: You need to use the small angle formula, $\theta = d/R$, where $\theta$ is the angular diameter of M42 in radians, $R$ is the distance to the object, and $d$ is the physical diameter of the object in the same units as $R$. To convert into radians the approximate angular diameter of M42, $\alpha$, that you obtained in arc-minutes, remember that 1 radian = $57.3° = 57.3 \times 60 = 3438$ arcminutes. Therefore, $d = \theta \times R = (\alpha/3438) \times R$.]

HII regions make splendid targets for small and large telescopes alike, forming large, bright canvases against which the marvellously complex morphology of the surrounding, colder dark HI clouds is silhouetted. When viewed (and particularly when photographed) through a telescope, the combination of newborn stars, dark nebulae, reflection nebulae and HII regions make the stellar nurseries of the Galaxy provocatively beautiful.

## D. Evolution of HII Regions

Stellar winds from newborn stars at the core of an HII region create shock waves that can trigger new regions of star formation within the surrounding dark nebula.

27. Select **File > Revert**.

In the magnified image of M42, you can see such a shock wave, which appears as a slightly brighter edge in the boundary between the blue reflection nebula and red HII region in the lower left part of the image.

The lifetime of a typical HI region is only several million years because its gas and dust are concentrated over time into new stars within HII regions by gravity and by the pressure within shock waves. The remnant gas in an HII region is hot and is not gravitationally bound and so expands outwards. Eventually, very little gas or dust remains, leaving only a cluster of newborn stars in its wake.

> 28. Select **Favourites > Observing Projects > Milky Way > M16**.

M16, popularly called the Eagle Nebula because of the shape of the dark nebula silhouetted against it, is an HII region approximately 7000 light-years from Earth in a direction toward the inner part of the Galaxy. The members of the embedded cluster of stars are estimated to be less than one million years old.

> 29. Open the **Info** pane and read the Description of this HII region.
> 30. Open the **Sky Guide** pane and click on the **Guided Tours** hyperlink. Then navigate through the following links: **Night Sky Tours > The voyage of the Hubble Space Telescope > Nebulae > The Eagle nebula**. Read the information on this object.

In this Hubble image, protostars can be seen as they emerge from their enveloping cocoons of gas and dust.

**Question 17.**    If you were shown an image of a dark nebula surrounding an HII region, (a) where would you expect to see the effects of a shock wave, (b) how would you recognize this shock wave, (c) where would you expect to see new stars in this region, and (d) what would be the predominant color of these stars?

## E. Open Clusters

**Open clusters** are the progeny of HI regions. On the whole, the member stars of an open cluster are gravitationally bound to one another. Over time, however, some members of the cluster, perhaps nudged by the gravity of other stars in the cluster, escape the gravitational hold of their siblings. This reduces the overall mass of the cluster as a whole, thereby decreasing its gravitational hold on the members that remain. Thus, an open cluster gradually "evaporates" over a time of several million to several billion years, as its member stars disperse through the Galaxy. Virtually all of the stars in the disk of the Galaxy were once members of such "families" of stars.

Several open clusters are visible to the naked eye and have been known since antiquity. These include the Pleiades (the Seven Sisters) and the Hyades, both in Taurus, and Praesepe (the Beehive) in Cancer.

> 31. Select **Favourites > Observing Projects > Milky Way > M45**.

In this telescopic view of the Pleiades, the brighter members of the cluster gleam brilliantly, their light reflected in residual strands of the gas and dust from which they were born. As with all reflection nebulae, the scattered light from the interstellar dust is predominantly blue.

> 32. Select **Favourites > Observing Projects > Milky Way > Open Clusters**.

Three open clusters, all in the constellation Auriga, are visible in this field of view: M36, M37, and M38. All three clusters are approximately the same distance from the Earth, about 4000 light-years. This fact suggests that they might all have been born within the same HI region.

> 33. Use the contextual menu and select **Magnify** and **Show Info** for each of these objects to see a close-up image of these star clusters and read their Description in the Info pane.

**Question 18.**    What is the estimated age of the open star cluster M36?

## F. Globular Clusters

The Galaxy contains another type of star cluster, the **globular cluster**, which gets its name from its strongly condensed, distinctly globular shape. Unlike open clusters, which are concentrated in the spiral arms of the Galaxy's disk, globular clusters are distributed in a vast and roughly spherical halo around the Galaxy's central bulge.

Globular clusters are much older and much richer than their open counterparts, containing tens of thousands to millions of member stars. The spectra of the stars in globular clusters show them to be metal-poor (to an astronomer, any element heavier than helium is a metal!), their chemical composition being not far removed from the abundance of elements produced in the Big Bang. In contrast, the stars of open clusters, and virtually all of the other stars in the galactic disk, have metal-rich spectra. This relative absence of heavy elements in stars of globular clusters is a sign that these stars are old and were formed from material with lower heavy-element content. The stars of open clusters have been made more recently from material in which heavy element content has been enhanced by nuclear fusion within the interiors of supernova stars. Another feature of globular clusters is the virtual absence of dust and gas within the cluster, in distinct contrast to open clusters—another sign of old age for these well-organized star clusters.

From their age and distribution, globular clusters are thought to have formed from the central condensation of matter in the protogalaxy that became the Milky Way. Globular clusters are spectacular sights when seen through a telescope.

34. Select **Favourites > Observing Projects > Milky Way > Omega Centauri**.

The view shows a telescopic image of the finest globular star cluster in the sky, Omega Centauri, catalogued as NGC 5139. This cluster of over one million stars is approximately 16,000 light-years from Earth in the direction of the constellation Centaurus. As you can see, globular clusters are aptly named.

35. Open the **Info** pane and read the Description of Omega Centauri. Also note the Angular size of this object in the sky, as given in the Other Data layer of the Info pane.

Question 19. Using the angular size of this object as provided in the Info pane as its angular diameter, what is the approximate angular radius of the globular cluster Omega Centauri?

Question 20. Given that the distance to this object is 16,000 light-years, what is the physical radius of Omega Centauri in light-years? [HINT: Use the small-angle formula.]

Question 21. If we assume that Omega Centauri is spherical and that it contains 1 million stars, what is the average density of the cluster in units of stars per cubic light-year? [HINT: The volume of a sphere of radius $R$ is $4\pi R^3/3$.]

## G. Planetary Nebulae and Supernova Remnants

After stars are born in the stellar nurseries of HI regions, their subsequent lifetime on the main sequence, as well as their destinies once the fuel in their cores is exhausted, depends on their initial mass.

Low-mass stars, those whose initial masses on the main sequence were less than eight solar masses, die by gently ejecting their outer layers into the interstellar medium to produce the so-called **planetary nebulae**. The ejection is caused by bursts of nuclear energy in shells of matter near the boundary of the star's core.

The material of these ejected shells consists of hydrogen and helium, as well as atoms of heavier elements such as carbon and oxygen that were produced in various phases of the star's evolution after it left the main sequence. Radiation from the hot but dying parent star excites atoms in the shell of gas and these atoms then re-radiate energy at characteristic wavelengths to produce the light of the planetary nebula.

The ejection of the outer part of the star leaves behind the very hot central core, which is now the central "star" of the planetary nebula. By this time, all nuclear burning within the core has ceased, and it remains behind as a small, but very hot, white dwarf star. The whole visible structure of a planetary nebula lasts about 50,000 years. The concentric shells of gas within the nebula gradually become fainter as they disperse into the interstellar medium.

36. Select **Favourites > Observing Projects > Milky Way > M57**.

37. Open the **Info** pane and expand the Description layer to learn more about M57.

The white dwarf star, the core of the star that produced the planetary nebula, is visible in this view of the Ring Nebula, M57, at the center of the doughnut shaped shell of ejected gas.

> **Question 22.** According to astronomers' estimates, how long ago did the central star of the Ring Nebula blow off this shell of gas? [HINT: Check the description in the Info pane associated with this object.]

For high-mass stars, whose mass when on the main sequence exceeded eight solar masses, death arrives in a much more spectacular fashion. These stellar heavyweights end their lives in gigantic thermonuclear conflagrations. In these supernovae, the star's core collapses to become a neutron star or a black hole, while the rest of the star is ejected outward violently, scattering debris into the interstellar medium.

As this debris blasts into the dust and gas of the interstellar medium at supersonic speeds, it excites the surrounding gas and causes it to glow. The visual manifestation of this collision is called a **supernova remnant**. In contrast to the gentler ejections that produce the small planetary nebulae around dying stars of lower mass, supernova explosions are so large and violent that the debris hurled into space continues to disperse at very high speeds for tens of thousands of years. Consequently, many supernova remnants cover fairly large areas of the sky.

38. Select **Favourites > Observing Projects > Milky Way > Crab Nebula**.

39. Measure the approximate angular radius of this object.

M1, the Crab Nebula, is the remnant of a supernova, the light from which arrived at Earth on July 4, 1054 AD. We know this because Chinese astronomers of the time recorded this explosion as a "guest star" that remained visible in the daytime for a period of more than 20 days before fading into the blue sky of daylight.

> **Question 23.** What is the angular radius of M1?
>
> **Question 24.** Given that the distance to M1, the Crab Nebula, is 6500 light-years, what is its physical radius in light-years?
>
> **Question 25.** Given the present size of this nebula and its known age, what will have been its average expansion rate, in kilometers per second? [HINT: One light-year is equal to about $9.46 \times 10^{12}$ kilometers, and one year contains about $3.17 \times 10^7$ seconds. The nebula's age is the difference between when it was discovered as an exploding star and the present date, about 2014 AD.]

## H. Distribution of Objects in the Milky Way Galaxy

It is instructive to examine the distribution within the Milky Way Galaxy of the various types of objects that were surveyed in the previous sections of this project.

40. Select **Favourites > Observing Projects > Milky Way > Galactic Object Distribution**.

The view is the same as that of Section A. The southern sky is shown from Cornwall, Canada, at midnight on June 21. However, the horizon, stars, planets, moons, asteroids, and comets have all been removed from the display, leaving only the Milky Way and a line representing the galactic equator.

First, you can examine the location of open clusters in our Galaxy.

41. Open the **Options** pane and expand the layer labelled **Deep Space** and then the **NGC-IC Database** layer.

42. In the NGC-IC Database, click the **Open Cluster** checkbox to display the positions of many of the open clusters in the Milky Way.

43. Use the Gaze controls to survey the sky, noting the distribution of open star clusters in the Milky Way.

> **Question 26.** Relative to the galactic equator, where are most of the open clusters in the Galaxy found?

44. In the **Options** pane, turn off the display of **Open Clusters** in the NGC-IC Database layer and select the **Globular Cluster** checkbox instead.

45. Survey the distribution of this sample of globular star clusters in the Milky Way Galaxy.

46. Select **View > Constellations > Boundaries** and **View > Constellations > Labels** from the main menu and repeat your survey of the sky, noting in which constellation or constellations these globular clusters occur most frequently and least frequently.

> **Question 27.** Are globular clusters found in the same distribution as open clusters?
>
> **Question 28.** Toward which constellation or constellations do most of the globular clusters appear?

In 1920, Harlow Shapley published the results of his observations of variable RR Lyrae stars in 93 globular clusters. RR Lyrae stars show systematic variations in brightness whose period of variation has been found to be directly related to their luminosity. This period-luminosity relationship allows astronomers to determine the absolute magnitude of these stars. Comparing the absolute magnitude of the stars determined from this relationship with their apparent magnitudes as seen from Earth, the distances of these stars from Earth can be determined.

Knowing their positions in the sky as well as their distances, Shapley was able to analyze the three-dimensional distribution of globular clusters. He noted that the clusters were distributed in approximately a spherical halo centered over a point lying in the direction of the constellation Sagittarius. Shapley assumed that this distribution was centered on the central gravitational mass of the Galaxy and concluded that the center of the Milky Way Galaxy was approximately 20 kiloparsecs from the Sun in the direction of Sagittarius. Shapley actually overestimated this distance by a factor of about two because he failed to account for the effect of **interstellar extinction,** in which intervening galactic dust artificially reduces an object's apparent brightness and consequently inflates the estimate of its derived distance. Modern observations suggest that the radius of the Galaxy's disk is about 25 kiloparsecs and that the Sun is approximately 8 kiloparsecs from the center.

> **Question 29.** Using the modern observations, what is the approximate diameter of the disk of the Milky Way in light-years?
>
> **Question 30.** How far from the center of the Galaxy is the solar system in light-years?

## I. The Location and Orientation of the Solar System in the Galaxy

47. Select **Favourites > Observing Projects > Milky Way > Overall Structure**.

The view shows a simulated image of the Milky Way Galaxy, with the position of the Sun in the center of the view as this galaxy might appear from a position in space 110,000 light-years from the Sun. The grouping of bright stars around the Sun includes the familiar stars that form the constellations as seen from Earth.

48. Use the Location Scroller to drag the view upward until the line of sight is along the plane of the disk of the Milky Way (i.e., the Milky Way appears edge-on). If necessary, move the image left or right to spin the image of the Galaxy so that the group of stars representing the Sun's local neighborhood is in a direct line with the center of the Milky Way.

49. Hold down the **Decrease current elevation** button until the distance from the Sun indicated in the Viewing Location panel in the toolbar is about **0.2 ly**. Carefully examine the pattern of stars near the Sun and look for a constellation or asterism that lies in the direction of the center of the Milky Way Galaxy. [HINT: Look for the Fish Hook asterism to the right of the Sun and the Teapot asterism below the image of the Sun.]

50. Select **View > Constellations > Labels** and **View > Constellations > Boundaries** from the main menu.

**Question 31.**    Toward which constellations in the Earth's sky is the center of the Milky Way?

51. Select **File > Revert**.

52. Again, use the Location Scroller to drag the view so that the plane of the galaxy is seen edge-on. Then spin the Galaxy so that the center of the Milky Way lies directly between the viewing location and the knot of stars representing the Sun's local neighborhood of stars.

53. Hold down the **Decrease current elevation** button until the distance from the Sun as indicated in the Viewing Location panel in the toolbar is about **0.2 ly**. Carefully examine the pattern of stars near the Sun and look for a constellation or asterism that lies in the direction of the outer reaches of the Milky Way Galaxy. [HINT: Look for the belt of Orion in the lower left quadrant of the view.]

54. Select **View > Constellations > Labels** and **View > Constellations > Boundaries** from the menu.

**Question 32.**    Toward which constellation or constellations do you need to look if you want to look at the outer reaches of the Milky Way that lie opposite its center, as seen from Earth?

We can use *Starry Night*™ to gain another perspective on the orientation of the plane of the Milky Way relative to the ecliptic that we explored previously.

55. Select **File > Revert** and then use the Location Scroller to adjust the view so that the disk of the Milky Way is seen edge-on and is horizontal across the view, with the Sun and its neighboring stars between your location and the center of the Milky Way.

56. Hold down the **Decrease current elevation** button to zoom in on this view until the distance to the Sun displayed in the Viewing Location panel is about **2 AU**. In this view, several planets are visible, and the Earth's orbit is shown. Use the Location Scroller again to adjust the view slightly so that the ellipse representing the Earth's orbit closes to become approximately a straight line.

**Question 33.**    What is the approximate angle between the ecliptic plane and the galactic plane?

57. Select **File > Revert** and take a few minutes to observe the Milky Way from various points of view. Use the Location Scroller to view the Galaxy face on and examine this simulated image for evidence of dark clouds of gas and dust interspersed among the spiral arms. Note that gas clouds outline the spiral arms and that few individual stars appear within the arms in this view. Note also the position of the Sun and local neighborhood of stars within the Galaxy.

Your observations in the last few steps have revealed that the disk of the Galaxy is quite flat. Modern observations indicate that the disk of the Galaxy is only approximately 0.6 kpc (2000 light-years) thick and the central bulge has a diameter of approximately 2 kpc (6500 light-years).

## J. The Evolution and Spiral Structure of the Galaxy

The disk shape of the Galaxy suggests that the immense cosmic nebula from which the Milky Way formed had some overall rotational component prior to condensing under its own gravity. As the protogalaxy that evolved into the Milky Way condensed out of the foam of the Big Bang, its overall rotation speed increased in order to conserve angular momentum. The increased rotational speed caused material to flatten into a plane perpendicular to the rotation axis of the overall mass.

All of the stars and matter of the Galaxy rotate around its central gravitational mass. The Sun and its system of planets revolve about the center of the Galaxy with a speed of about 220 km/s and complete one orbit in about 220 million years.

Question 34. Current estimates suggest that the Sun is approximately 5 billion years old. In that time, how many orbits of the Galaxy has it completed?

Question 35. Using a figure of 200,000 years as the age of the human species, through what angle around the center of the Galaxy has the Sun carried us since the dawn of humanity?

Modern radio observations and Doppler studies of the Milky Way Galaxy in the 21-cm radio emission line of neutral hydrogen show that all of the stars, dust, and gas in the Galaxy move around its center in the same general direction and with roughly the same speed throughout most of the Galaxy's disk. This is different from the motion of the planets around the Sun, where Kepler's laws are obeyed and objects move more slowly, the further away they are from the central axis. This finding suggests that the Galaxy possesses a vast spherical halo around its center that contains significant mass, the true nature of which is unknown at the present time but which is referred to as **dark matter**. There is growing evidence for the presence of this enigmatic material elsewhere in our Universe, especially in large clusters of galaxies.

Finally, you can take a brief look at the heart of the Galaxy at a wavelength that penetrates the dust and gas that shrouds the galactic center, from the Chandra X-ray telescope in space. The present evidence suggests that our Galaxy contains a supermassive black hole at its center and that our Galaxy is not alone in having this kind of type of object at its core. The X rays are presumed to arise from very hot material condensed into very high densities as it falls into the black hole.

58. Open the **Sky Guide** pane and go to the home page (click the button with the house icon). Then navigate the links: **Guided Tours > Night Sky Tours > The voyage of the Chandra Telescope > Milky Way Galaxy > X-ray mosaic of galactic centre** and read the description of the Chandra X-ray image of the center of the Milky Way that appears in the view.

## K. Conclusions

In this project, you have examined the Milky Way Galaxy as it appears from Earth and from space. In addition, you have observed many different classes of objects found in our Galaxy and have learned about the evolution of these various objects with time.

# Galaxy Classification   26

I n this project, you will classify galaxies according to an accepted scheme devised by Edwin Hubble, for whom the highly successful Hubble Space Telescope is named.

Hubble separated galaxies into four groups according to their general appearance:

1) Spirals, which have the designation S

2) Barred spirals, designated SB

3) Ellipticals, denoted by E

4) Irregular galaxies, which have the designation Irr

Hubble further subdivided galaxies within these groups based on particular details in their shapes and summarized his classification scheme by drawing the various forms of galaxies on a tuning-fork diagram, as in Figure 1 below.

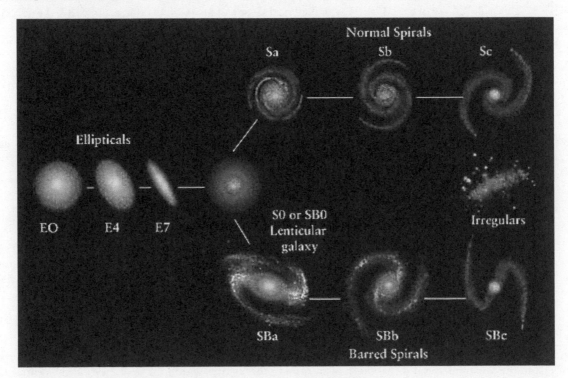

Figure 1. The Hubble Tuning Fork Diagram of Galaxy Classification

In this diagram, the elliptical galaxies are arranged in sub-classes from E0 to E7 along the handle, and the spiral and barred spiral galaxies are arranged into a, b, and c subclasses along the two tines of the tuning fork. At the junction of the handle and the tines, Hubble placed galaxies that had some features of elliptical galaxies and some features of spiral galaxies. He called these lenticular galaxies and subdivided them based on whether they showed evidence of a central bar. As the tuning fork diagram suggests, Hubble originally theorized that elliptical galaxies evolve into spiral galaxies. However, the irregular galaxies, of which Hubble recognized two subgroups, did not fit this evolutionary theory. Although Hubble's theory of galactic evolution was wrong, his classification scheme has remained a useful tool.

## A. Elliptical Galaxies

Elliptical galaxies are so-named because of their shape. Although they are all elliptical in shape, the ellipse can vary from essentially circular to very flat. Hubble classified them in terms of their apparent flattening, from E0 to E7, in which E0 galaxies are nearly circular in appearance and E7 galaxies show the most flattening.

> 1.  Launch *Starry Night*™ and open **Favourites > Observing Projects > Galaxy Classification > M89**.

The view shows a telescopic view of the galaxy M89 in the constellation Virgo. As you can see, M89 appears to be nearly circular.

> **Question 1.**     What Hubble classification would you assign to the galaxy M89?

> 2.  Open **Favourites > Observing Projects > Galaxy Classification > M110**.

This view shows a telescopic view of the galaxy M110, a companion galaxy to the Andromeda Galaxy, which in turn is a neighboring galaxy of the Milky Way in the Local Group of galaxies. In contrast to M89, the galaxy M110 appears more elongated and flattened.

> **Question 2.**     What Hubble classification would you assign to the galaxy M110?

> 3.  Set the Zoom to **5°**.

Now the view, still centered on M110, shows the Andromeda Galaxy and another of its companion galaxies, M32.

> **Question 3.**     Which of these elliptical galaxies, M32 or M110, shows the most flattening?
> **Question 4.**     What Hubble classification would you assign to the galaxy M32?

The appearance of an elliptical galaxy in this classification scheme does not necessarily describe the true three-dimensional nature of the galaxy. An E0 galaxy might be spherically symmetric or it might be a flattened disk seen face-on from our view. A cigar-shaped galaxy seen end-on might also appear to be spherical and be classified as an E0 galaxy.

## B. Spiral Galaxies

The distinctive feature of spiral galaxies is a relatively flat disk of stars encircling a central bulge. The term spiral comes from the apparent spiral distribution of stars and other matter within the disk, beyond the central bulge of these galaxies. The Andromeda Galaxy, the large galaxy in the view, is a spiral galaxy.

As mentioned in the previous section, the telescopic appearance of an elliptical galaxy observed from Earth does not necessarily reflect the actual form of the galaxy but depends on the perspective of the observer. This is different from the classification of spiral galaxies, where the appearance of the spiral arms indicates the viewing direction on the galaxy from our point of view. We see examples of all directions of alignment of spiral galaxies to our line of sight, so we can be fairly certain that we know the true three-dimensional shapes of these galaxies.

4. Open the **Find** pane. Click the **Q** icon in the search box and select **Messier Objects** from the popup menu.

5. Type **M81** in the search box. Click the icon next to the name of this galaxy when it appears in the found object list and select **Magnify**. Then use the same technique to **Magnify** the galaxy **M104**.

Barred spirals are distinguished from other spiral galaxies by the appearance of a straight bar across the central bulge. In these galaxies, the spiral arms in the disk start at the ends of this bar and not at the edge of the central bulge.

6. Open the **Find** pane and type **M74** into the search box. Click the menu icon next to the name of this galaxy when it appears in the found object list and select **Magnify**.

7. Click the **Q** icon in the search box of the Find pane and select **Search All**. Then, type **NGC 1365** into the search box and press Enter to observe this galaxy.

**Question 5.**    Which of these two galaxies, M74 and NGC 1365, would qualify as a barred spiral?

Both normal spiral and barred spiral galaxies are sub-classified into three main categories: Sa, Sb, or Sc and SBa, SBb, or SBc, respectively. These sub-classifications are made according to the following criteria:

(a) Sa and SBa galaxies have fat central bulges and tightly wound spiral arms.

(b) Sb and SBb galaxies have moderate central bulges and moderately wound spiral arms.

(c) Sc and SBc galaxies have small central bulges and loosely wound spiral arms.

The galaxies M81 and M74 that you observed in steps 5 and 6 are examples of Sa and Sc galaxies, respectively. The Andromeda Galaxy that you observed at the beginning of this section, with a central core intermediate in size between that of M81 and M74 and its reasonably well-defined spiral arms, is an example of an Sb galaxy.

Another feature of spiral galaxies that contrasts with elliptical galaxies is that spiral galaxies contain lots of gas and dust and many of their stars appear to be relatively young. Differences between Sa, Sb, and Sc galaxies may be related to the amount of dust and gas within their spiral arms. This dust and gas component is important in the production of new stars within galaxies. The approximate percentage of the mass of these galaxies in the form of dust and gas is 4% for Sa galaxies, 8% for Sb galaxies, and 25% for Sc galaxies.

The dust and gas within the spiral galaxies make their appearance much more dramatic than that of elliptical galaxies. In the spiral galaxies, blue and violet light from young, hot stars illuminates the dust and gas clouds. These stars have been formed fairly recently in the galaxy's history and outline the spiral arms, making them very distinctive. In contrast, the lack of dust and gas in elliptical galaxies shows that star formation ceased in these galaxies long ago. Elliptical galaxies are composed of old, red stars and show no evidence of spiral structure. Nevertheless, elliptical galaxies come in the widest range of sizes and masses, from the largest known galaxies to very small aggregates of old stars. Often, the gravity from the mass of one or two giant elliptical galaxies will dominate the motions of an entire group or cluster of galaxies.

Lenticular galaxies resemble elliptical galaxies in lacking gas and dust and in showing no spiral structure, but they appear to have a definite central bulge. Hubble denoted these as S0 for normal lenticular galaxies and SB0 galaxies if they showed a bar.

8. Use the Find pane to **Magnify** the galaxy **M86** to see an example of a lenticular galaxy.

**Question 6.**    Is there evidence of gas and dust or a spiral structure in the galaxy M86?

**Question 7.**    Is there an identifiable central bar in the galaxy M86?

**Question 8.**    What Hubble classification would you assign to the galaxy M86?

## C. Irregular Galaxies

The irregular galaxies did not fit into Hubble's tuning fork. Nevertheless, Hubble defined two types: 1) Irr I galaxies, which look like undeveloped spiral galaxies and contain many young stars and lots of dust and gas, and 2) Irr II galaxies, which are distorted and show no particular symmetry. They appear to have been formed by collisions with other galaxies or disturbed by violent activity within their interiors.

These galaxies differ not only in appearance but also in composition. Irregular galaxies contain many young stars as well as dust and gas, which makes them similar to spiral and barred spiral galaxies but distinctly different from elliptical galaxies, which contain older stars and no dust or gas.

The Magellanic clouds, companion galaxies of our Milky Way, are examples of Irregular galaxies.

9. Open **Favourites > Observing Projects > Galaxy Classification > Magellanic Clouds**.

The view shows the Large Magellanic Cloud (LMC) and the Small Magellanic Cloud (SMC) as they might be seen by an observer in the southern hemisphere of Earth.

10. Select **Magnify** from the contextual menu of one of these galaxies to observe it more closely. Then select **File > Revert** and **Magnify** the other galaxy using its contextual menu.

**Question 9.** Is there any evidence of spiral structure or a central bulge in either the LMC or SMC?

**Question 10.** Is there evidence of gas and dust and star-forming regions in the Magellanic Clouds?

## D. Challenge: Classify Galaxies

In this section, you will have the opportunity to use what you have learned about the Hubble classification of galaxies to classify a number of galaxies.

11. Open **Favourites > Observing Projects > Galaxy Classification > Virgo – Coma Berenices**.

The view shows a region of sky near the border between the constellations of Virgo and Coma Berenices. This region of the sky contains the Virgo cluster of galaxies, which is about 50 to 60 million light-years from Earth. Many members of this galaxy cluster are visible from Earth through smaller backyard telescopes. The labels in the view indicate a number of these galaxies that are best observed in March and April.

12. For each labeled galaxy in the view, select **Magnify** from its contextual menu to observe it more closely. Assign a Hubble classification to the galaxy and record this in Data Table 1 at the end of this project. Then select **File > Revert** and repeat this step.

13. Open **Favourites > Observing Projects > Galaxy Classification > Canes Venatici**.

This view shows a number of galaxies in the region of sky near the constellations Canes Venatici and Ursa Major. All of the galaxies labeled in the view were catalogued by Charles Messier in the eighteenth century. The labels show the common names for these galaxies (except for M109). The Messier numbers for these galaxies are shown in parentheses in Data Table 1.

14. For each labeled galaxy in the view, select **Magnify** from its contextual menu to observe it more closely. Assign a Hubble classification to the galaxy and record this in Data Table 1. Then select **File > Revert** and repeat this step.

**Question 11.** What is peculiar about the two galaxies, the Whirlpool galaxy (M51) and M106?

## E. Conclusions

In this chapter, you learned about the classification scheme for galaxies that Edwin Hubble developed in 1926. You have observed examples of the different types of these galaxies and then classified a number of these galaxies yourself from images provided in *Starry Night™*.

Data Table 1. Classification of Galaxies

| Galaxy | Hubble classification |
|---|---|
| M58 | |
| M59 | |
| M60 | |
| M84 | |
| M87 | |
| M88 | |
| M90 | |
| M91 | |
| M98 | |
| M99 | |
| M100 | |
| M 106 | |
| M109 | |
| Bode's Galaxy (M81) | |
| Cat's Eye Galaxy (M94) | |
| Cigar Galaxy (M82) | |
| Pinwheel Galaxy (M33) | |
| Spindle Galaxy (M102) | |
| Sunflower Galaxy (M63) | |
| Whirlpool Galaxy (M51) | |

# The Local Neighborhood of Galaxies

# 27

M any centuries ago, Greek astronomers debated the question of the position of the Earth within the Universe, and concluded that the Earth was at its center. This was the majority opinion until significant advances in the sixteenth and seventeenth centuries led to a rationalization of the solar system in which the Sun replaced the Earth as the dominant object and the Sun was then considered to occupy a central position in the Universe. Further observations revealed the true nature of the Milky Way as a galaxy of stars in which the Sun was a member, and the study of clusters of stars within this galaxy led to the realization that the Sun was not at the center of this galaxy. Furthermore, observational evidence in the early part of the twentieth century began to show that the Milky Way was not the only large structure of its kind and that the Universe was populated by many billions of such structures distributed over vast expanses of space. More recent work has shown that these distant galaxies are assembled into clusters and superclusters of galaxies that form great walls surrounding relatively empty regions or voids in space.

Thus, our increasing base of knowledge has slowly downgraded the status of the Earth from the central object of the Universe to an average planet in orbit around a rather ordinary star, accompanying many other stars in a galaxy of stars among billions of such galaxies.

In this project, you will use *Starry Night*™ to explore the Milky Way and its neighboring galaxies, known as the Local Group. You will then explore a nearby rich cluster of galaxies containing many more galaxies than the Local Group. *Starry Night*™ contains a database of the three-dimensional positions of 28,000 galaxies within a distance of about 350 million light-years from the Milky Way, known as the Tully Database. Even though this is an enormous distance, this region is a relatively small part of the observable Universe that extends to a distance of about 12 billion light-years and contains billions of galaxies.

## A. Zone of Avoidance

As you learned in the project on the Milky Way, our Galaxy contains large quantities of dust and gas. This material obscures our view of certain regions of the sky from the Earth.

1. Launch *Starry Night*™ and configure the HUD to include **Distance from observer, Galaxy thickness, Galaxy diameter, Galaxy group ID,** and **Name**.
2. Open **Favourites > Observing Projects > Local Group > Zone of Avoidance**.

In this view, you are moving around the Milky Way at a distance of 132,000 light-years from Earth. This allows you to see the magnificent spiral structure of our Galaxy's arms outlined by gas and dust clouds that are illuminated by bright stars, along with many individual stars dotted along these arms. The arms connect to a rather small central bulge. The Sun is located in a bright group of stars within a rather indistinct spiral arm of this galaxy.

You can see that many bright points surround the Milky Way Galaxy. Almost all of these are individual galaxies at large distances from your observing position.

3. **Stop** time flow and use the HUD to identify a number of these galaxies, noting their distances from your observing location.

4. Use the Location Scroller to view the Milky Way edge-on, with the Sun directly between the observing location and the center of the Milky Way. [NOTE: The slight curvature of the galaxy is a result of the wide angle of the view.]

From this perspective, the line of sight is similar to our view from Earth when looking toward the center of the Galaxy. There is a region surrounding the Milky Way where there appear to be no galaxies. This is the **zone of avoidance**, where gas and dust in the Milky Way plane have obscured the distant Universe from our view on Earth, limiting our knowledge of the distribution of galaxies in these directions. Thus, there might be, and almost certainly are, galaxies there but we cannot see them from Earth. You can explore the extent of this zone by rolling the Galaxy on its axis.

5. Position the Location Scroller at one end of the edge-on Galaxy and move it along the plane of the Galaxy's disk to rotate the galaxy completely around its axis like a wheel, in order to observe the extent of the Zone of Avoidance across the sky.

**Question 1.**   Does the Zone of Avoidance extend all around the sky?

**Question 2.**   (a) With respect to the center of the Galaxy as seen from Earth, in which direction is the Zone of Avoidance widest? (b) In which direction is this zone the narrowest? [HINT: Rotate the plane of the Milky Way Galaxy slightly to note the position of the Sun.]

## B. The Milky Way and its Closest Neighbors

In this section, you will use *Starry Night*™ to investigate several of the galaxies that are companions to the Milky Way.

6. Open **Favourites > Observing Projects > Local Group > Neighbors.**

This view, from a point in space over 300,000 light-years from the Sun, is centered on the Milky Way and shows three of its companion galaxies indicated with labels: the Large Magellanic Cloud (LMC), the Small Magellanic Cloud (SMC), and Sagittarius.

7. Point the cursor at the Milky Way and each of its companion galaxies in turn and record the Galaxy thickness and Galaxy diameter shown in the HUD into Data Table 1 at the end of this project.

8. Use the Angular Separation tool to find the Distance separating the Milky Way from each of the three selected companion galaxies and record this in Data Table 1. [TIP: This distance is shown in blue below the Angular Separation display.]

**Question 3.**   Expressed as a percentage, what is the ratio of the thickness of each galaxy to its diameter?

**Question 4.**   From their appearances, what broad Hubble classification—spiral, elliptical, or irregular—would you apply to the Milky Way and each of the three companion galaxies in the view?

**Question 5.**   How much larger is the diameter of the Milky Way than the diameter of (a) the Small Magellanic Cloud, (b) the Large Magellanic Cloud, and (c) Sagittarius? [HINT: Divide the diameter of the Milky Way by the diameter of each galaxy.]

Question 6.    (a) Which of the indicated galaxies in the view is the closest companion galaxy to the Milky Way? (b) What is the distance separating this galaxy from the Milky Way?

Question 7.    What is the distance separating the two Magellanic Clouds?

## C. The Distribution of Galaxies Near the Milky Way

A further characteristic of galaxies is their distribution in space. These massive collections of stars and other matter also seem to congregate together in clusters. The number of galaxies in a cluster can vary widely. Those with few members are known as **poor clusters** and are often termed groups, while those with many hundreds and thousands of galaxies are known as **rich clusters**. Furthermore, their distribution around some center of concentration leads to a second classification. Those clusters with a distinct spherical appearance are called **regular** clusters whereas those whose galaxies appear to be scattered randomly over a large region of space are called **irregular** clusters.

The properties of these massive conglomerates of galaxies are not yet fully understood. For example, gravitational effects have been observed in galaxies and clusters of galaxies that appear to require far more mass than is provided by the obvious visible matter, resulting in the postulation of the existence of **dark matter**. Some experiments have been mounted to observe this new component of matter directly here on Earth but these searches have been unsuccessful to date.

Our Milky Way Galaxy is a member of a poor cluster known as the Local Group. This group contains at least 40 other galaxies and extends out to a distance of approximately 10 million light-years from the Milky Way. Faint new members of this Local Group are still being discovered as astronomers develop improved observing techniques. Many members may never be discovered because they lie within the Zone of Avoidance, obscured by the gas and dust of the Milky Way.

The two largest subgroups within the Local Group are Group 223, of which the Milky Way is the dominant member, and Group 222, dominated by the Andromeda Galaxy.

9. Select **Favourites > Observing Projects > Local Group > Group 223**.

The view is centered on the Milky Way from about 2 million light-years away. Member galaxies of Group 223, which includes the Milky Way, are highlighted in yellow. The Magellanic Clouds and Sagittarius are also members of Group 223 and are indicated with labels. The view is restricted to the closest galaxies. The images of thousands of background galaxies have been removed from this view for convenience.

10. Select **Options > Deep Space > Tully 3D Database...** set the **Visibility range** slide control in the dialog window all the way to the right to see the background galaxies in the view. Then click the **Cancel** button.

11. Use the Location Scroller to look around the view. Note that the HUD displays the Galaxy group ID of 223 for the highlighted galaxies.

12. Select the Angular Separation tool and survey the distance separating the Milky Way from each of the other galaxies of Group 223.

13. Use the **Centre** command from the object contextual menu of a sample of some of the member galaxies of Group 223 and then **zoom in** until an image of the galaxy appears. Use the Location Scroller to examine the galaxy and determine its Hubble classification. Use the HUD to obtain the dimensions of this galaxy. Then select **File > Revert** and repeat this step for another highlighted galaxy.

Question 8.    Which is the largest member of the subgroup of galaxies called Group 223?

Question 9.    To which Hubble class do most of the galaxies in this group belong?

Question 10.    (a) Which galaxy in Group 223 is furthest from the Milky Way? (b) What is the distance that separates this galaxy from the Milky Way?

14. Select **File > Revert**.

15. Select **Options > Deep Space > Tully 3D Database...** from the menu. Click the checkboxes for **Entire dataset** and **Highlighted filaments/groups** and then click the **OK** button.

*Starry Night*™ shows a box that outlines the extent of Group 223 against lines that show the extent of the Tully database. Recall that the background galaxies in the Tully database are not shown in this view.

16. Use the Location Scroller to observe this group from various perspectives. Adjust the viewpoint so that the box bounding Group 223 is seen face-on. Use the Angular Separation tool to measure the angular distance between the two opposite sides of the long axis of the box. Zoom in or out as necessary to facilitate this measurement. Round off the measurement to the nearest degree and record the result in Data Table 2 at the end of this project. Do the same for the width of the bounding box around Group 223. Then adjust the view with the Location Scroller so that the bounding box is edge on and measure its angular height in a similar fashion.

17. Using a value of 2 million light-years as the distance of your viewing location from the Milky Way, you can determine the physical dimensions, in light-years, of the extent of this group of galaxies dominated by the Milky Way. Multiply your angular measurement in degrees by 2 million light-years and divide by the number of degrees in one radian, which is 57.3°. The resulting calculation reduces to:

Physical distance (ly) = Angular distance (°) × 34,904

**Question 11.** What is the approximate volume of space occupied by Group 223? [HINT: The volume of a rectangular box is simply the product of the lengths of each of its sides.]

The dimensions of even our tiny region of the Universe are staggering. Light, traveling at the fastest possible speed in our Universe, takes tens of thousands of years to reach us, even from our nearest neighbor galaxies. And yet, these galaxies are close compared with the distant field of galaxies in the Tully database, which extends as far as 350 MLY from Earth. Our own subgroup of galaxies is certainly in our backyard compared with the most distant galaxies recently imaged by the Hubble Space Telescope and by several large new telescopes in Hawaii and South America. These modern instruments have produced images from light that left these much more distant galaxies up to12 billion years ago and has only recently reached Earth!

## D. The Andromeda Subgroup of Galaxies

While the Milky Way dominates Group 223, the Andromeda Galaxy dominates the other major subgroup of galaxies in the Local Group. This galaxy is about 2 million light-years from Earth and yet it is visible to the unaided eye from Earth under dark-sky conditions.

18. Select **File > Revert**.

The Andromeda Galaxy is at approximately the 2 o'clock position from the Milky Way in the view.

19. Identify the Andromeda Galaxy with the HUD and note the dimensions of this galaxy.

**Question 12.** Is the Andromeda Galaxy larger or smaller than the Milky Way?

20. Use the contextual menu to **Centre** the view on the Andromeda Galaxy.
21. The distance of the viewing location from the Andromeda Galaxy is shown in the upper-right corner of the view. Use the **Decrease current elevation** button to set this distance to somewhere between 500,000 light-years (**0.5 Mly**) and 600,000 light-years (**0.6 Mly**) and use the Location Scroller to examine this galaxy and its close neighbors.

**Question 13.** What is the Hubble classification of the Andromeda Galaxy?

**Question 14.** Earlier, you saw that the Milky Way has near neighbors, Sagittarius and the Magellanic Clouds. Does the Andromeda Galaxy also have close companions? If so, identify them using the HUD.

22. Select **Highlight "222" Group** from the contextual menu for the Andromeda Galaxy.

Now, the subgroup dominated by the Andromeda Galaxy is highlighted in yellow.

23. **Increase current elevation** until the distance to the Andromeda Galaxy as shown in the upper right corner of the view is about **10 Mly**.
24. Select **Options > Deep Space > Tully 3D Database...** and click the checkboxes labeled **Entire dataset** and **Highlighted filaments/groups**. Then click the **OK** button.
25. Use the Location Scroller to examine this subgroup of galaxies.
26. Use the contextual menu of the Milky Way and select **Centre "223" Group** in order to compare these two subgroups of the Local Group.

**Question 15.** Which is the richer subgroup of galaxies in the Local Group, Group 222 dominated by the Andromeda Galaxy or Group 223 dominated by the Milky Way?

**Question 16.** Which is the larger of the subgroups in the Local Group, Group 222 or Group 223?

## E. The Local Group within the Universe

After this brief look at a few of the Local Group of galaxies, you can conclude this exploration by exploring where this cluster of galaxies fits into the larger scale of things.

27. Select **Favourites > Observing Projects > Local Group > Local Group of Galaxies**.

The view is centered on the Milky Way from a distance of about 10 million light-years and shows the Local Group, consisting of subgroups 222 and 223 highlighted in yellow.

28. Select **Options > Deep Space > Tully 3D Database...** from the menu.
29. Drag the Tully 3D Database Options dialog window to the upper left corner of the screen and watch the view as you gradually move the **Visibility range** slide control in the dialog box toward the right until it is about at the midpoint of the scale. Click the **OK** button to exit the dialog.
30. Use the Location Scroller to look around the view, now populated with more distant clusters of galaxies.

**Question 17.** Would you describe the Local Group as a rich or a poor cluster?

**Question 18.** Would you describe the Local Group as a regular or irregular cluster?

31. Select **File > Revert** and again adjust the brightness of the galaxies in the Tully 3D database by selecting **Options > Deep Space > Tully 3D Database...** from the menu and adjusting the **Visibility range** slide control to about the middle of its range.
32. Gradually **Increase current elevation** to between **50 Mly** and **70 Mly** from the Sun. You will notice that a rich cluster of galaxies appears in the upper left of the view. This is the Virgo cluster of galaxies. To highlight its member galaxies, open the **Find** pane and type **The Eyes**, the name of one of the member galaxies of the Virgo cluster, in the search box and press the Enter key.
33. Select **Highlight "GA Virgo Cluster" Filament** from the contextual menu for The Eyes.

**Question 19.**    Does this cluster appear richer or poorer than the Local Group?

34.  Select **Favourites > Observing Projects > Local Group > Virgo Cluster.**

The view is from a location within the Virgo cluster of galaxies and the gaze is centered on the galaxy labeled "The Eyes."

35.  Use the Location Scroller to look around the view from within this rich cluster of galaxies. Use the Angular Separation tool to find the distances separating some of these galaxies.
36.  Set the Zoom to **90°.**
37.  Use the Location Scroller to adjust the view so that the Milky Way, labeled, is visible in the view.
38.  Use the Angular Separation tool to find the distance between The Eyes and the Milky Way, making sure that the HUD indicates that you are pointing at the Milky Way before noting the measurement.

**Question 20.**    How long does it take light from the stars in the galaxy called The Eyes to reach the Earth?

39.  **Increase current elevation** gradually, pausing occasionally to look around the view with the Location Scroller. You may also wish to change the Time Flow Rate to **3000×** and watch as *Starry Night*™ presents an animated and changing view of this part of the Universe.

As the elevation increases and the observing location moves farther from the Virgo cluster of galaxies, you will find that collections of galaxies tend to be formed into rather thin wall-like structures. These walls surround vast voids in which few if any galaxies are found. Clusters of galaxies are found within these walls and the whole structure of deep space seems to resemble that of a collection of soap bubbles. The more concentrated clusters and superclusters are found at the interstices of these bubbles. You will have the opportunity to explore this larger scale structure of the Universe in another project.

## F. Conclusions

You have explored the relationships between our Galaxy and its near neighbors in the Local Group of galaxies and measured the scale of this space. You have also classified some members of this loose cluster of galaxies. You have been able to observe a rich cluster of galaxies relatively near to the Milky Way and you have been able to place yourself within the large-scale structure of the Universe in a way that two-dimensional pictures could never do, allowing you to glimpse the bubble-like features that lace our local extragalactic neighborhood.

Data Table 1. Physical Data for the Milky Way and Its Nearby Companion Galaxies

| Galaxy | Diameter (ly) | Thickness (ly) | Distance from Milky Way (ly) |
|---|---|---|---|
| Milky Way | | | |
| Small Magellanic Cloud | | | |
| Large Magellanic Cloud | | | |
| Sagittarius | | | |

Data Table 2. Dimensions of Group 223

| Measurement | Angular distance (°) | Physical distance (ly) |
|---|---|---|
| Length of bounding box | | |
| Width of bounding box | | |
| Thickness of bounding box | | |

# Large-Scale Structure of the Universe

# 28

Our own Milky Way Galaxy is a gravitationally bound structure consisting of a huge, flattened disk made up of about 200 billion stars and large quantities of dust and gas in spiral arms that surround a central bulge. Our increasingly precise and penetrating observations of the Universe over the past century have revealed that the Milky Way is but one of many billions of such collections of matter, many of them part of immense clusters and superclusters of galaxies. The last few decades in particular have led us to the realization that even galaxies outside these huge galaxy clusters are not randomly distributed in space but occur within huge walls surrounding vast voids that contain few, if any, galaxies. Thus the present view of the large-scale structure of the Universe is one that resembles a collection of soap bubbles. Clusters and superclusters of galaxies appear to occupy the lines where the walls of the bubbles (or voids) meet, the largest of them being where two or more lines meet. Furthermore, at least one of these superclusters, dubbed the Great Attractor, appears to exert sufficient gravitational influence on galaxies including our own Milky Way that they are moving collectively toward this region of space. The big puzzle in the present study of galaxies and their environment is that the mass of the total visible matter in these structures seems to be completely inadequate to explain the observed gravitational effects. These observations have led to the search for so-called **dark matter** that is assumed to pervade galaxies and clusters of galaxies.

In this project, you will use *Starry Night™* to venture among these vast structures, stopping at important way stations to examine the detailed and interrelated collections of galaxies that make up our corner of the Universe.

## A. The Milky Way and the Local Wall

You can start your observations with the Milky Way and move slowly outward to visualize its position within the Local Group, a poor cluster of more than 40 galaxies.

1. Launch *Starry Night™*.
2. Open **Favourites > Observing Projects > Large-Scale Structure > Milky Way** and click **Play**.

As time changes, you are moving around the Milky Way at a distance of about 128,000 LY from the Sun. Almost all of the bright points in the view are distant galaxies, far beyond the Milky Way. Before speeding off into deep space, it is instructive to examine the Universe from this "local" position. You will note in particular that, when you are looking at the Milky Way edge-on, there is a significant region on our sky that appears to be devoid of galaxies. This happens because matter within the Milky Way absorbs the light of distant galaxies. It is helpful to look at the effect that this **Zone of Avoidance** has on our view.

3. Click **Stop** and use the Location Scroller to move your view of the Milky Way so that it appears edge-on.

You will note the apparent absence of galaxies around the plane of the Milky Way. This lack of galaxies is not real but shows our ignorance of this region of the sky because of absorption of light by material in our own galactic environment. You should keep this limitation in mind as you explore farther into space.

4. Use the Location Scroller to roll the Milky Way around its axis like a wheel to demonstrate that the Zone of Avoidance extends completely around our position, as expected. Also note that this Zone of Avoidance is larger in extent when the view is toward the center of the Galaxy when compared to the view out of the Galaxy.

As you move your viewpoint, you may notice that local galaxies such as the Large and Small Magellanic Clouds and the giant Andromeda Galaxy move relatively rapidly across the view.

Question 1.   What is this effect called, where closer galaxies appear to shift their positions against the more distant background galaxies as your point of view changes?

You can take a brief look at this group of neighboring galaxies.

5. Select **File > Revert** and use the Location Scroller to place the Milky Way edge-on again, with its plane horizontal across the view and the Sun between the observing location and the center of the Milky Way.
6. To reduce the confusion from distant galaxies, select **Options > Deep Space > Tully 3D Database...** and in the dialog box, move the slider on the **Visibility range** scale so that the left edge of the slider button aligns with the Near tick mark.
7. [Optional] You may want to adjust the **Brightness** control slightly toward the More setting.
8. Click the **Labels** check box in the Tully 3D Database dialog box to turn this option on.
9. Click the **OK** button to exit the Tully 3D Database Options dialog.
10. **Increase current elevation** to about **4 Mly** from the Sun.

As you move away from the Sun, you will see the Milky Way and its near neighbor galaxies recede into the distance as the other sub-cluster of galaxies around the giant Andromeda Galaxy comes into view at about this distance, in the bottom-left corner of the view.

11. **Increase current elevation** further to about **8 Mly** from the Sun.

A few of the outlying galaxies of our Local Group come into the view.

12. Gradually **Increase current elevation** to about **40 Mly** from the Sun.
13. Select **Labels > Tully 3D Database** to turn off the labels.
14. Use the Location Scroller in a top-left to bottom-right motion to rotate around the position of the Milky Way in the center of the view, to see how the Local Group of galaxies fits into a narrow wall of galaxies. You can use the Location Scroller to move this wall to an edge-on position and then roll it along like a wheel to explore its relationship with other structures in this region of space.

As you can see, the Milky Way resides within a wall that separates two voids, as shown by the lack of local galaxies in the regions adjacent to the wall.

15. Select **Highlight "GA Coma-Sculptor Cloud" Filament** from the contextual menu of the Milky Way to highlight this wall of galaxies.

16. Select **Options > Deep Space > Tully 3D Database...** and click the checkboxes at the top of the dialog window labeled **Entire dataset** and **Highlighted filaments/groups**. Then click **OK** to close the dialog window.

17. **Increase current elevation** to about **150 Mly** from the Sun and use the Location Scroller to look around the view again.

*Starry Night*™ displays a cube representing the extent of the entire Tully Database of 28,000 galaxies. Within this cube is a box representing the boundaries of the highlighted GA Coma-Sculptor Cloud. The GA designation indicates that this wall is part of the Great Attractor supercluster.

18. Select **View > Constellations > Labels**. Click **Play** to watch an animation of changing viewpoints of this wall of galaxies. **Stop** the animation and use the Location Scroller to adjust the view so that you are looking along the long axis of this wall, first from one end and then from the other, to see how it got its name.

**Question 2.** Toward which constellations does the long axis of this wall of galaxies point?

19. Select **Favourites > Observing Projects > Large Scale Structure > Local Wall**.

20. Use the Angular Separation tool to obtain an estimate of the thickness of this wall of galaxies. To do so, measure the angular distance from the midpoint of the wall facing the label for the constellation Norma at the level of the Milky Way, through the Milky Way to the midpoint of the side of the wall that is facing the label for the constellations Musca and Crux. Record this value, to the nearest degree, as the angular size of the thickness of this wall in Data Table 1 at the end of this project.

21. Be sure that the view is centered on the Milky Way and use the Location Scroller to view this wall of galaxies face-on so that the Milky Way is positioned just above the label for the constellation Canis Major. Use the Angular Separation tool to estimate to the nearest degree the angular length and width of this wall of galaxies and record the results in Data Table 1.

**Question 3.** What are the approximate angular dimensions of this structure?

22. To determine the size of the dimensions of this wall in millions of light years, first convert your angular size measurements in degrees to angular size in radians. To do this, divide the angular size in degrees by 57.3, the number of degrees in one radian. Enter the results in the column labeled Angular Size (Radians) in Data Table 1.

23. To obtain values for the physical dimensions of this wall, use the small-angle formula: size = angular size (in radians) × distance. Multiply each of the angular sizes in radians by the distance of the observing location from the Sun, which is shown in the Viewing Location pane of the toolbar.

**Question 4.** What are the approximate dimensions of this wall of galaxies in millions of light years (Mly)?

**Question 5.** What is the approximate volume of this wall of galaxies in cubic light years? [HINT: Volume = length × width × thickness.]

It is perhaps somewhat humbling to recognize that each bright point in this image is a galaxy in its own right, each one containing many thousands or maybe billions of stars, and that you are looking (in simulation, admittedly) at the Universe on a truly vast scale.

24. Select the view named **Favourites > Observing Projects > Large Scale Structure > Local Wall and Virgo.**

In this view, you will see a tight cluster of galaxies called the Virgo cluster, above the box outlining the Local Wall.

25. Again, you can use the Location Scroller (or click **Play** to animate changing viewpoints) to see the relationship between the wall containing the Milky Way and this cluster, in the corner of a void.

26. Click **Stop** and select **Centre** from the contextual menu for one of the galaxies in the Virgo cluster. Then set the Zoom to **30°**. Open the object contextual menu over a highlighted galaxy near the center of the cluster and select **Centre**.

27. Use the Location Scroller to position any side of the box surrounding the cluster face-on in the view. Then use the Angular Separation tool to measure the physical distance separating a galaxy at one end of the cluster from a galaxy at the opposite end of the cluster to obtain an estimate of the physical diameter of this cluster of galaxies.

**Question 6.** What is the approximate diameter of this cluster of galaxies in millions of light years (Mly)?

**Question 7.** What is the approximate volume of this cluster in cubic light years? [HINT: Volume of a sphere = $(4\pi/3) \times (D/2)^3$, where $D$ is the diameter of the sphere.]

**Question 8.** How does the volume occupied by the Virgo cluster compare to the volume occupied by the Coma-Sculptor wall that contains the Milky Way?

**Question 9.** How does the number of galaxies contained in the Virgo cluster compare to the number in the Coma-Sculptor wall that contains the Milky Way?

28. To see the whole of a giant wall of galaxies that includes the Virgo cluster and the Coma-Sculptor cloud that contains the Milky Way, select **Favourites > Observing Projects > Large-Scale Structure > Supergalactic Equatorial.**

The view is zoomed in on the Milky Way from a distance of about 80 Mly from the Sun.

29. **Zoom out** to a field of view about **130°** wide to see the highlighted galaxies that form this gigantic wall.

30. Use the Location Scroller to rotate the sky again to demonstrate that this is a relatively flat wall by finding the direction from which this structure is edge-on to your viewpoint and note that it lies along the line drawn on the screen representing the extragalactic equator. This wall is used to define an "Equatorial Plane" for reference when discussing this region of extragalactic space.

31. **Increase current elevation** to about **300 Mly** from the Sun. Change the Time Flow Rate to **3000×** and observe the linear structures within this wall of galaxies as it rotates in your view.

32. **Stop** time and position the cursor over any one of the galaxies in the dense cloud of galaxies near the center of this wall and open the object's contextual menu. The checked Highlight item in the menu will identify the cluster of galaxies to which this galaxy belongs.

**Question 10.** Which cluster is near the center of the Supergalactic Equatorial wall of galaxies?

## B. Superclusters of Galaxies

As you saw at the end of the last section, large superclusters of galaxies lie at the ends of walls of galaxies. You can examine one of these superclusters in more detail with the following procedure.

33. Select **Favourites > Observing Projects > Large-Scale Structure > Virgo Cluster.**

The view is centered on the Milky Way from a location about 100 Mly from the Sun. At this position, you can easily see the wall that you explored above. The Virgo cluster is highlighted in the upper right of the view. This rich cluster of galaxies contains about 3000 member galaxies.

34. Use the Angular Separation tool to measure the distance from the Milky Way to M87, the labeled galaxy at the heart of the Virgo cluster. The distance between these objects is displayed beneath the angular separation measurement.

**Question 11.**    How far is the Virgo cluster from the Earth?

35. Select **Options > Deep Space > Tully 3D Database...** and slide the **Visibility range** control all the way to the left (Near); then click **OK**.
36. Select **Centre** from the contextual menu for M87 in the Virgo cluster.
37. **Decrease current elevation** to about **70 Mly** from the Sun.
38. Use the Location Scroller to look all around the Virgo cluster, noting the position of M87 within it.

**Question 12.**    What is the position of M87 within the Virgo cluster?

39. Select **Go There** from the contextual menu for M87.
40. Use the Location Scroller to look at this galaxy from different viewpoints.

**Question 13.**    What is the Hubble classification of M87?

This galaxy is very bright at radio wavelengths and is also known by its radio source name of Virgo A. The galaxy contains a prominent jet emanating from a bright star-like core. It is obvious that some very energetic processes are going on in this core to produce this energy and the jet.

41. Click the **Home** button in the toolbar.
42. Open the **Options** pane and expand the **Deep Space** layer. Click the boxes to the left of the entries to remove the checkmarks from all of the options in this layer except for **Chandra Images**.
43. Open the **Find** pane. Click the magnifying glass icon in the search box and select **Chandra images** from the menu. Then type **M87** in the search box.
44. Click the menu icon for M87 in the list and select **Magnify**. If *Starry Night*™ informs you that this object is not currently visible, click the **Best Time** button and then click the menu icon for M87 in the Find pane and select **Magnify** once more. The view shows an X-ray image of this galaxy obtained by the Chandra X-ray Observatory.
45. To view the equivalent optical image of this very active galaxy, open the **Options** pane and click the Messier Objects option. Then reduce the brightness of the Chandra image from this composite image by moving the slide control (at the right of the Chandra heading) toward the left to see the optical image of the elliptical galaxy.

You can also look briefly at the enigmatic jet of material emanating from the core of this galaxy. *Starry Night*™ has a Hubble Space Telescope image of this jet, somewhat offset from M87 to avoid confusion.

46. In the **Options** pane, click the checkbox for **Hubble Images** in the **Deep Space** layer to turn this option on. Then open the **Find** pane and click the magnifying glass icon in the search box and select **Hubble Images**. Click the menu icon for M87 in the found items list and select **Magnify** to see a high-resolution image of the jet.

Obviously, at least some giant elliptical galaxies have gigantic powerhouses at their cores, probably associated with supermassive black holes.

## C. The Great Attractor

The galaxies in a large volume in the vicinity of the Milky Way appear to be moving toward a region of the sky filled with a relatively high density of galaxies that make up a complex structure. Because of this coordinated motion, the region toward which these galaxies appear to be moving has been called the Great Attractor. We can travel out to a distance from which we can view this as an entity, examine its structure and position, and measure its distance from the Milky Way.

47. Open **Favourites > Observing Projects > Large-Scale Structure > Great Attractor**.

The view is centered on the Milky Way from a position about 300 Mly from the Sun. The highlighted galaxies comprise the Great Attractor, a huge pinwheel structure almost filling the view, with a giant supercluster at its center. Many thousands of galaxies make up this structure, and the attractive force that this structure exerts on the surrounding galaxies shows that there is a high concentration of mass there.

48. Use the Location Scroller to see the three-dimensional structure of the Great Attractor and locate its approximate center.
49. You will notice the large, rich cluster near the center of the Great Attractor. Open the contextual menu over this cluster. The checked Highlight option indicates the name of this collection of galaxies.

**Question 14.**    Which cluster lies at the center of the Great Attractor?

In rotating the Great Attractor around in the sky, you will note that it has a long, linear feature. You can measure the linear extent of this overall structure.

50. **Increase current elevation** to about **700 Mly** from the Sun and use the Location Scroller to rotate the view so that the longest axis of the Great Attractor stretches across the screen. Then use the Angular Separation tool to measure the distance between two highlighted galaxies at either end of this axis.

**Question 15.**    What is the approximate length of the linear structure of the Great Attractor?

Note that there is an almost continuous line of galaxies from end to end along this linear structure.

## D. The Great Wall and Other Colossal Walls

In this section, you will explore several other huge wall-like structures of galaxies in the region of the Universe surrounding our position in the Milky Way. From distances that take you to the limit of the present Tully Collection of galaxies, you can observe these structures and discover the bubble-like voids separating these vast walls of galaxies.

51. Open **Favourites > Observing Projects > Large-Scale Structure > Great Wall**.

The view is from about 500 Mly from the Sun and the structure called the Great Wall is highlighted.

52. Use the Location Scroller to examine this vast structure from various points of view. Adjust the view so that you are looking at this structure edge-on. Again, this wall is thin and relatively flat and extends over a huge distance.

This vast collection of galaxies is arranged on a surface surrounding a huge volume almost devoid of galaxies.

53. Select **Favourites > Observing Projects > Large-Scale Structure > Great Wall and Great Attractor**.

The view shows both of the structures you examined in the previous sequences: the Great Wall and the Great Attractor.

54. Change the Time Flow Rate to **3000×** to animate the view. Occasionally **Stop** time and use the Location Scroller to alter the perspective and then click **Play**.

Note that the region between these two vast structures contains relatively few galaxies. Observing the Universe from this perspective, you get the sensation of moving through bubbles of space with thin walls of galaxies separating large voids.

Random processes cannot have formed this type of structure and such structures provide an important clue to the evolution of our Universe following its origins in the Big Bang. There are other equally impressive structures stretching across this corner of the Universe that have become apparent as astronomers have determined distances to galaxies and placed them in this three-dimensional mesh.

55. Open **Favourites > Observing Projects > Large-Scale Structure > Southern Wall**.

The view shows another huge curtain of galaxies, somewhat closer to the Milky Way and smaller than the Great Wall and on the opposite side of the sky from our viewpoint.

56. Use the Location Scroller and/or the animation controls to examine this structure from different points of view.
57. Open **Favourites > Observing Projects > Large-Scale Structure > Two Walls**.

The view highlights both the Southern Wall and the Great Wall. In addition to the Milky Way, two other galaxies are labeled in the view: ESO 605-16 in the Southern Wall and MCG 3-31-2 in the Great Wall.

58. Use the Angular Separation tool to find the distance between these two labeled galaxies and between these two galaxies and the Milky Way.

**Question 16.**   What is the approximate distance between the Great Wall and the Southern Wall?

**Question 17.**   What is the approximate distance between the Milky Way and the Great Wall, and between the Milky Way and the Southern Wall?

**Question 18.**   From your measurement of the position of the Milky Way with respect to these two walls of galaxies, do you feel that it is correct to say that the Earth and the Milky Way are at the center of the Universe? Discuss your reasoning. (For example, you might like to discuss how the Tully Database may have been obtained.)

## E. Voids

In this section, you will explore one of the regions of the nearby Universe that has a relatively sparse number of galaxies surrounded by walls of richer clusters.

59. Open the **Favourites** pane and under **Observing Projects > Large-Scale Structure**, select the following views in turn: **South Pole Void – front, South Pole Void – back.**

The two rich lanes of galaxies you observed in the last step surround a region that has relatively few galaxies within its volume.

60. Select **Favourites > Observing Projects > Large-Scale Structure of Universe > South Pole Void – all.**
61. Use the Location Scroller to examine this void from different viewpoints.
62. **Increase current elevation** to about **900 Mly** from the Sun and change the Time Flow Rate to **3000×** in order to get a sense of the structure of this void from various viewpoints as the animation progresses.

The Tully Collection of galaxies extends out to about 600 MLY and *Starry Night*™ provides you with the opportunity to examine the type and position of the full 28,000 galaxies in three-dimensional space. This remarkable data set is nevertheless limited and conclusions about more distant realms are more speculative, even though astronomers have a wide range of information about objects beyond this limit.

**Question 19.**   Extrapolating from what we can see within 600 Mly, what do you think the Universe beyond the Tully Database is like?

## F. Conclusions

In this wide-ranging project, you have explored the large-scale structure of our Universe in a way that is impossible in real life, using some of the best data in the world to travel vicariously though the soap-bubble features of the realm of the distant galaxies. You can investigate individual galaxies and collections and their characteristics and spacing at will by following the guidelines and methods outlined in this project.

Data Table 1. Dimensions of the GA Coma-Sculptor Cloud

| Dimension | Angular size (°) | Angular size (radians) | Linear size (Mly) |
|-----------|------------------|------------------------|-------------------|
| Thickness |                  |                        |                   |
| Length    |                  |                        |                   |
| Width     |                  |                        |                   |